lonely planet

I10645385

Discover

...tents

France

Throughout this book, we use these icons to highlight special recommendations:

 The Best...
Lists for everything from bars to wildlife – to make sure you don't miss out

 Don't Miss
A must-see – don't go home until you've been there

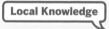 Local experts reveal their top picks and secret highlights

 Detour
Special places a little off the beaten track

 If you like...
Lesser-known alternatives to world-famous attractions

These icons help you quickly identify reviews in the text and on the map:

 Sights

 Eating

 Drinking

 Sleeping

 Information

This edition written and researched by

Oliver Berry

Alexis Averbuck, Stuart Butler, Kerry Christiani,
Steve Fallon, Emilie Filou, Catherine Le Nevez,
Tom Masters, Daniel Robinson, Miles Roddis,
John A Vlahides, Nicola Williams

Paris & Around p51

Normandy & Brittany p107

Champagne & Northern France p149

Loire Valley & Central France p181

Lyon & the French Alps p221

Bordeaux & French Basque Country p255

Provence & the French Riviera p289

Contents

Contents

On the Road

In Focus

Survival Guide

This Is France

Snooty, sexy, superior, chic, infuriating, arrogant, officious, inspired, France never fails to stir up passionate opinion. Even if you've never set foot on French soil, it's a place that already seems immediately familiar: every time you've gazed at an Impressionist painting, watched a new-wave film or sipped on a glass of sparkling Champagne, you've been letting a little bit of Gallic flair seep into your soul.

From world-class wines to rich culture and even richer food, France is all about enjoying the finer things in life.

This is, after all, the country that invented the very idea of *joie de vivre*. Whether it's soaking up the atmosphere of a Breton street market, indulging in some après ski on the slopes around Chamonix, or savouring a long, lazy lunch under Provençal skies, one thing's for sure: the French certainly know how to live life to the full.

This is also a place with more history and heritage per square inch than practically anywhere else in Europe.

With a turbulent past spanning Roman rule to Revolution, France is awash with historical sights: prehistoric monuments, crumbling castles, grand châteaux, medieval churches and hilltop villages, each with its own fascinating tale to tell.

And though France is certainly a nation in touch with its history, it is far from stuck in the past.

For centuries, the French have been breaking rules and setting trends for the rest of the world to follow, and it's a habit that's hard to break. From cutting-edge fashion to ground-breaking architecture, France remains one of the world's great cultural icons. It's at the same time seductive and aloof, old fashioned and forward looking, enthralling and exasperating in equal measures, but always characterised by a certain *je ne sais quoi*.

> **❝ the French certainly know how to live life to the full ❞**

Gardens, Château de Versailles (p105)

PHOTOGRAPHER: DENNIS JOHNSON

25 Top Experiences

1. Parisian Bistros
2. Eiffel Tower
3. Mont St-Michel
4. Loire Châteaux
5. Champagne Tasting
6. Outdoor Sports, Chamonix
7. Ste-Chapelle & Chartres Cathedral
8. D-Day Beaches
9. Three Corniches
10. Carcassonne
11. Dune du Pilat
12. Pont du Gard
13. Markets, Provence
14. Villages, Vézelay
15. Wine Route, Alsace
16. Centre Pompidou-Metz
17. Carnac Megaliths
18. Bouchons, Lyon
19. Monet's Garden, Giverny
20. Fontenay Abbey
21. Grotte de Lascaux
22. Bayeux Tapestry
23. Chantier Médiéval de Guédelon
24. Gorges du Verdon
25. Winetasting, Bordeaux

25 France's Top Experiences

Parisian Bistros

The latest buzzword in the capital is *néo-bistro* (new bistro), a small, casual address serving outstanding cuisine under the tutelage of a talented (and often 'name') chef. Take Christian Constant's Les Cocottes (p92), a stone's throw from the Eiffel Tower or Jadis (p90), hidden on an unknown street in the middle-of-nowhere 15e. Tables are jammed as tight as ever, dishes of the day are still chalked on the blackboard and cuisine is just as simple except for one new ingredient – a creative twist. Le Comptoir du Relais (p90)

HELEN CATHCART/ALAMY

Eiffel Tower

Seven million people visit annually but few disagree that each visit is unique. From an evening ascent amid twinkling lights to lunch at 58 Tour Eiffel (p92) in the company of staggering city views, there are 101 ways to 'do' it. Pedal beneath it, skip the lift and hike up, buy a crêpe from a stand here or a key ring from the street, snap yourself in front of it, visit it at night or – our favourite – try to time your visit for the odd special occasion when all 324m of the tower glows a different colour.

FRANCE'S TOP 25 EXPERIENCES

Mont St-Michel

The dramatic play of tides on this abbey–island in Normandy is magical and mysterious. Said by Celtic mythology to be a sea tomb to which souls of the dead were sent, Mont St-Michel (p129) is rich in legend and history, keenly felt as you make your way barefoot across rippled sand to the stunning architectural ensemble. Walk around it alone or, better still, hook up with a guide for a dramatic day hike across the bay.

The Best...
Châteaux

VERSAILLES
France's grandest, busiest and most glorious château, just a quick skip from Paris. (p104)

FONTAINEBLEAU
It's not quite as grand as Versailles, but this Renaissance residence is still a wonder. (p96)

CHAMBORD
François I's modest country retreat features a staircase rumoured to have been designed by Leonardo da Vinci. (p197)

CHENONCEAU
This château is the work of several aristocratic ladies, hence its nickname: the Château des Dames (Ladies' Chateau). (p202)

CHEVERNY
Impossibly elegant and still owned by its founding family. (p196)

The Best...
Medieval Villages

SARLAT-LA-CANÉDA
Golden and gorgeous, the Dordogne's gem boasts some of France's most-beautiful medieval architecture. (p213)

CARCASSONNE
Be bewitched by the witch's-hat turrets of this Languedoc beauty. (p324)

ST-ÉMILION
Combine wine tasting with medieval enchantment in this Unesco-listed village. (p271)

ST-PAUL DE VENCE
Art history sits alongside historic architecture in this hilltop village on the French Riviera. (p334)

DINAN
Wander the cobbled streets and sturdy ramparts of one of Brittany's oldest villages. (p144)

DIANA MAYFIELD

4 Loire Valley Châteaux

If it's aristocratic pomp and architectural splendour you're after, head for this regal valley west of Paris. Flowing for over 1000km into the Atlantic Ocean, the Loire is one of France's last *fleuves sauvages* (wild rivers) and its banks are riddled with beautiful châteaux. If you're seeking the perfect fairy-tale castle, head for moat-ringed Azay-le-Rideau (p204), Villandry and its gardens (p200), and less-visited Beauregard (p200). Château de Chambord (p197)

NEIL SETCHFIELD

5 Champagne Tasting

You simply can't visit this corner of France and not sample some bubbly. Several of the region's world-famous Champagne brands are based in Reims (p160) and Épernay (p164), and offer guided tours of their cellars, followed by a tasting session. Further afield you'll find lots of small-scale *vignerons* (winegrowers) dotted across the countryside, where you can pick up a few bottles of vintage bubbly to take home.

Champagne vineyards

Adrenalin Kick, Chamonix

Every minute of the five hours it takes to make Vallée Blanche's (p247) more than 20km off-piste descent, from the spike of the Aiguille du Midi to mountaineering mecca Chamonix, will pump more adrenalin in your body than anything you've ever done. Craving more? Hurl yourself down Europe's longest black run, La Sarenne, at Alpe d'Huez (p249).

Ste-Chapelle & Chartres

This is a top experience reserved strictly for sunny days and those who like looking at the world through rose-coloured glass. Be stunned and inspired by the sublime stained glass in Paris' Ste-Chapelle (p65), one of Christendom's most beautiful places of worship. Then head out of town to Chartres, where you can't get bluer than the awesome stained-glass windows of Cathédrale Notre Dame de Chartres (p105). Leave with the true blue of so-called Chartres blue firmly imprinted in your mind. Jamb figures of the Royal Portal, Notre Dame de Chartres (p105)

D-Day Beaches

The broad stretches of sand and breeze-blown bluffs are quiet now, but early on 6 June 1944 the beaches of northern Normandy (p124) were a cacophony of gunfire and explosions, the bodies of Allied soldiers lying in the sand as their comrades-in-arms charged inland. Just up the hill from Omaha Beach, long rows of symmetrical gravestones at the Normandy American Cemetery & Memorial bear solemn, silent testimony to the price paid for France's liberation from Nazi tyranny. Omaha Beach (p126)

The Best...
Cathedrals

CATHÉDRALE DE NOTRE DAME, PARIS
The cathedral to end all cathedrals; sadly, no hunchbacks in sight when we visited. (p80)

CATHÉDRALE NOTRE DAME, CHARTRES
If stained glass is your thing, you won't find any finer than in the luminous windows of Chartres cathedral. (p105)

CATHÉDRALE NOTRE DAME, STRASBOURG
Climb the spire for a bird's-eye view of Strasbourg. (p167)

CATHÉDRALE ST-ÉTIENNE, METZ
This lacy beauty is famous for its intricate spire. (p174)

CATHÉDRALE NOTRE DAME, AMIENS
Marvel at the largest Gothic cathedral in France. (p176)

The Three Corniches

It is impossible to drive this dramatic trio of coastal roads (p340), each one higher and more hairpin bend–riddled than the next, without conjuring up cinematic images of Grace Kelly, Hitchcock, the glitz of Monaco high life and scandalous royals – all to the standing ovation of big view after big view of sweeping blue sea fringing Europe's most mythical coastline. To make a perfect day out of it, before leaving Nice, shop for a picnic at the morning market on cours Saleya (p330).

The Best...
Nature Parks

PARC NATIONAL DES PYRÉNÉES
These remote mountains harbour some of France's most endangered wildlife. (p287)

PARC NATIONAL DES ÉCRINS
Miles of high-altitude trails make this a hiker's paradise. (p250)

PARC NATIONAL DE LA VANOISE
France's oldest national park is as close as you'll get to untouched wilderness. (p250)

PARC NATUREL RÉGIONAL DE CAMARGUE
These wonderful wetlands are famous for their horses and flamingos. (p314)

PARC NATIONAL DES CALANQUES
Clifftop paths wind through France's newest national park, due for inauguration in June 2011. (p317)

Carcassonne at Dusk

10

That first glimpse of La Cité's sturdy, stone, witch's-hat turrets above Carcassonne (p324) in the Languedoc is enough to make your hair stand on end. To properly savour this fairy-tale walled city, linger at dusk after the crowds have left, when the old town belongs to its 100 or so inhabitants and the few visitors staying at the handful of lovely hotels within its ramparts. Don't forget to look back when you leave to view the old city, beautifully illuminated, glowing in the warm night. La Cité, Carcassonne (p324)

Dune du Pilat

11

The Dune du Pilat (p275) is a 'mountain' that just has to be climbed. Not only is the coastal panorama from the top of Europe's largest sand dune a stunner – it takes in the Banc d'Arguin bird reserve and Cap Ferret across the bay – but also the nearby beaches have some of the Atlantic Coast's best surf. Cycle here from Arcachon and top off the heady trip with a dozen oysters, shucked before your very eyes and accompanied by *crepinettes* (local sausages). Sandboarding, Dune du Pilat (p275)

SALLY DILLON

Pont du Gard

This Unesco World Heritage Site (p323) near Nîmes in southern France is gargantuan: 35 arches straddle the Roman aqueduct's 275m-long upper tier, containing a watercourse that was designed to carry 20,000 cu metres of water per day. View it from afloat a canoe on the River Gard or pay extra to jig across its top tier. Oh, and don't forget your swimming gear for a spot of post-Pont, daredevil dives and high jumps from the rocks nearby – a plunge that will entice the most reluctant of young historians.

Provençal Markets

Shopping at a bustling morning market is a quintessential French pastime. Even the tiniest Provençal villages have their own chaotic markets (see p339), featuring stalls laden with local goodies: fragrant herbs, fresh olives, handmade charcuterie and pungent cheeses. The best known are held in Carpentras, Narbonne, Vaison-la-Romaine and Aix-en-Provence, but there are lots more to discover – just follow your nose. Aix-en-Provence (p310)

Hilltop Villages

Impossibly perched on a rocky peak above the Mediterranean, gloriously lost in back country, fortified or château-topped... southern France's portfolio of *villages perchés* is vast, impressive and calls for go-slow touring – on foot, by bicycle or car. There are hundreds to choose from, but one of our enduring favourites is the holy village of Vézelay (p216), which rises picturesquely from a rocky outcrop in rural Burgundy, surrounded by fields of vines and sunflowers. St-Cirq-Lapopie (p216)

The Best...
Boutique Sleeps

HIDDEN HOTEL
Packed with Parisian style, and tucked away just off the Champs-Élysées. (p84)

L'OUSTAU DE BAUMANIÈRE
Sleep and dine in serious style at this legendary Provençal address. (p320)

COUR DES LOGES
Four period townhouses in old Lyon; one superb boutique hotel. (p241)

L'HÔTEL PARTICULIER
Top spot in Arles, housed inside an 18th-century private mansion. (p315)

HÔTEL ERMITAGE
Retro styling and a knock-out location overlooking St-Tropez. (p339)

LA COLOMBE D'OR
Indulge in this former hang-out of Chagall, Matisse and Picasso. (p334)

The Best...
Foodie Cities

PARIS
Bursting with buzzy bars, iconic bistros, historic cafés and Michelin-starred marvels. (p64)

LYON
Famous for its pig-centric cuisine, and often touted as France's top foodie town. (p234)

MARSEILLE
Tuck into authentic *bouillabaisse* (fish stew) in Marseille's atmospheric old port. (p310)

STRASBOURG
Savour sauerkraut, sausages and lots of beer in an Alsatian *winstub* (wine room). (p167)

15

Alsatian Wine Route

It is one of France's most popular drives – and for good reason. Motoring in this far northeast corner of France takes you through a kaleido-scope of lush green vines, perched castles and gentle mist-covered mountains. The only pit stops en route are half-timbered villages and roadside wine cellars, where fruity Alsace vintages can be swirled, tasted and bought. To be truly wooed, drive the Route des Vins d'Alsace (p173) in autumn, when vines are heavy with grapes waiting to be harvested and colours are at their vibrant best. Left: Kaysersberg (p173)

LEFT: DAVID TOMLINSON; RIGHT: HOLGER LEUE

Centre Pompidou-Metz

16

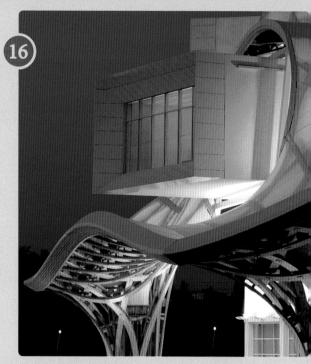

Bright white by day, all aglow after dark, this new star of the northern France art scene is on the tip of everyone's tongue. A provincial cousin to the well-known Centre Pompidou in Paris, this modern art museum (p174) was designed by Shigeru Ban and Jean de Gastines, a world-class, Japanese–French duo of architects and is as much architectural gem as exhibition powerhouse – easily on a par with Bilbao's Guggenheim and London's Tate.

Carnac Megaliths

17

Pedalling past open fields dotted with the world's greatest concentration of mysterious megaliths (p143) gives a poignant reminder of Brittany's ancient human inhabitation. No one knows for sure what inspired these gigantic menhirs, dolmens, cromlechs, tumuli and cairns to be built – a sun god? Some phallic fertility cult?

JOHN ELK III

Lyonnais Bouchons

The red-and-white checked tablecloths, closely packed tables and decades-old bistro decor could be anywhere in France. It's the local cuisine that makes *bouchons* in Lyon (p242) so unique, plus the quaint culinary customs, like totting up the bill on the paper tablecloth, or serving wine in a glass bottle wrapped with an elastic band to stop drips, or the 'shut weekends' opening hours. Various piggy parts drive Lyonnais cuisine but, have faith, this French city is said to be the gastronomic capital of France. Dine and decide.

The Best...
Famous Beaches

PLAGE DE L'ÉCLUSE
Old-fashioned bathing tents bring an air of the belle époque to this exclusive Breton beach, in Dinard. (p136)

PROMENADE DES ANGLAIS
Join the sun-worshippers on Nice's pebbly beach. (p326)

BLVD DE LA CROISETTE
Private beaches full of rich and famous guests characterise Cannes' cinematic seafront. (p335)

PLAGE DE PAMPELONNE
Pout like Bardot in the classic Riviera resort at St-Tropez. (p338)

GRANDE PLAGE & PLAGE MIRIMAR
Biarritz's beaches have been in vogue since the Second Empire. (p280)

Monet's Garden at Giverny

Claude Monet purchased this idyllic Norman country house (p120) in 1883, and spent the next thirty-odd years redesigning its gardens and grounds: adding trees, greenhouses, ornamental ponds and – most famously of all – a supremely graceful Japanese bridge. Don't be surprised if it looks rather familiar. Giverny's grounds provided the inspiration for some of Monet's most-famous (and priceless) works, most notably his iconic *Nymphéas* (Water Lily) series.

CHRISTOPHER WOOD

The Best...
Viewpoints

EIFFEL TOWER
The metal asparagus needs no introduction – it's just a must. (p88)

BASILIQUE DU SACRÉ COEUR
This Montmartre landmark gives a different perspective on the capital. (p62)

MONT VENTOUX
Panoramic Provençal views (but you'll need to wrap up warm). (p317)

AIGUILLE DU MIDI
Gaze across peaks and glaciers all the way to Mont Blanc. (p246)

FOURVIÈRE
The essential viewpoint for admiring Lyon's architecture. (p238)

PIC DU MIDI
You'll never forget the Pyrenean panorama from this former observatory. (p287)

Abbaye de Fontenay

20

Though the majority of France's great abbeys were torn down during the Revolution, a few have survived the centuries relatively intact. The fascinating Fontenay Abbey (p212) is tucked away in the heart of the Burgundy countryside, and is one of Europe's best-preserved Cistercian monasteries. Wandering the tranquil grounds it's possible to visit the monks' barrel-vaulted dorm, the monastery refectory, the abbey church and even an early smelting forge.

BETHUNE CARMICHAEL

Grotte de Lascaux

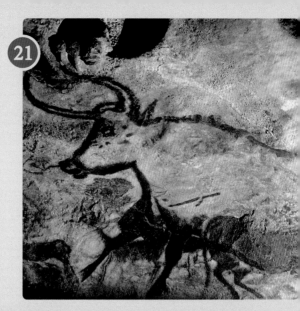

21

Europe's oldest prehistoric paintings are hidden deep in the limestone caves of the Vézère Valley. None are more breathtaking than those inside the Grotte de Lascaux (p217), which is decorated with the most sophisticated cave art ever discovered, including a mural of a bull measuring over 5.5m. The original cave is closed to avoid damage to the paintings, but key sections have been re-created in another cave nearby.

22

Bayeux Tapestry

Stretching for an astonishing 68.3m, this monumental piece of embroidery (p123) is one of France's most-treasured historical artefacts. Recounting William the Conqueror's invasion of England in 1066, the tapestry is thought to have been commissioned as a commemorative work by William's half-brother, Bishop Odo of Bayeux.

Chantier Médiéval de Guédelon

Ever wondered how medieval castles were built? Well, now's your chance to find out. For the last two decades a dedicated band of French artisans have been building this replica medieval castle (p213) using only tools and techniques that were available during the Middle Ages – so no concrete, steel or diggers, and certainly no power tools. It's a massive undertaking – the project's already been going for 14 years, and is still more than a decade from completion.

The Best...
Island Escapes

ÎLE DE LA CITÉ
This little island in the heart of Paris is a refuge from the modern metropolis. (p65)

BELLE ÎLE
Brittany's largest island is as beautiful as its name suggests. (p139)

ÎLES DE LÉRINS
These tiny islands provide the perfect getaway from Cannes' summer bustle. (p335)

ÎLES D'HYÈRES
A trio of Mediterranean islands fringed by sand, coast paths and crystal-clear sea. (p346)

ÎLE D'OUESSANT
Explore shipwrecks on this wild, windswept island 32km off the Breton coastline. (p139)

Gorges du Verdon

In a country blessed with countless natural beauty spots, the Gorges du Verdon (p317) still manage to raise a gasp. This enormous canyon system – the longest in Europe – snakes for 25km through the Provençal countryside, and in places the sheer cliff walls tower 700m overhead. By far the best way to explore is with a paddle – there are lots of local companies that hire out equipment and arrange guided canoe and kayak trips.

The Best...
Shopping

PARIS
From flea markets to haute couture, Paris' shops have it all. (p97)

CHAMPAGNE
Épernay and Reims are stocked with champagne cellars where you can pick up bottles of bubbly direct from the source. (p160)

NICE
Don't miss the Riviera's largest outdoor market, on the cours Saleya. (p331)

QUIMPER
Buy colourful *faïence* (earthenware) in Brittany's half-timbered capital. (p141)

BORDEAUX
Tour the vineyards, and take home some top vintages. (p267)

STRASBOURG
Pick up handmade chocolates, sweets and gingerbread in this stately northern city. (p171)

25

Winetasting in Bordeaux

What could be more French than sampling the fruits of the vine? And where better to do it than the illustrious vineyards of Bordeaux (p264)? There are over 8500 wine producers around the Bordeaux region, but it's the big names that get the tastebuds going – Petrus, Pomerol, Château Lafite, Cheval Blanc and Mouton Rothschild, to name a few. The best way to visit the vineyards is on an organised minibus tour, which will allow you to tipple to your heart's content without needing to draw straws for a designated driver.

France's Top Itineraries

Paris to Rouen
Capital Trips

5 DAYS

Five days should be just enough time to delve into the delights of the City of Lights and add on a few days' sightseeing beyond the capital, including visits to Versailles, Monet's gardens at Giverny and the elegant city of Rouen.

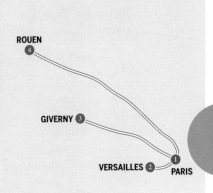

ROUEN ④

GIVERNY ③

VERSAILLES ② **PARIS** ①

① Paris (p64)

Every French adventure simply has to begin in Paris. With a couple of days you should be able to squeeze in the **Eiffel Tower**, **Notre Dame** and the **Louvre**, plus a **river cruise** along the Seine and a stroll around **Montmartre**. Base yourself on the Left Bank to be near the main sights.

AROUND PARIS

🚇 Paris' underground is the best way to explore the capital.

② Versailles (p104)

Day three takes you to Louis XIV's country retreat at **Versailles**. Connoisseurs claim this is the grandest château of them all, and it's hard to disagree. Guided tours take in the château's main rooms, including the **royal apartments** and the incredible **Hall of Mirrors**. Leave time for a leisurely wander among the fountains and gardens.

PARIS ➡ VERSAILLES

🚍 **30 minutes** From Pont de Sèvres in the 15e.
🚆 **30 minutes** From Paris' Left Bank stations on the RER Line C5

Statues outside Musée d'Orsay (p85)
PHOTOGRAPHER: LOU JONES

③ Giverny (p120)

On day four, catch the train from Paris to **Claude Monet's house and gardens** in Giverny. It's where the artist painted some of his most famous canvases. Whatever you do, don't miss the photo opp on the **Japanese bridge**. At the nearby **Musée des Impressionismes**, the work of American impressionists takes centre stage.

PARIS ➡ GIVERNY

🚆 **50 minutes** From Paris St-Lazare, followed by a quick shuttle bus trip. 🚗 **One hour** Along A13 and N13; follow signs to Vernon.

④ Rouen (p118)

On the last day, say goodbye to Paris for good, and head north to Normandy's elegant capital, Rouen. This attractive city is a delight to explore on foot, with a charming old centre full of wonky half-timbered houses, and a historic clocktower spanning one of the main shopping streets. Make time for the **fine arts museum** and a meal at Michelin-starred **Gill**.

PARIS ➡ ROUEN

🚆 **1¼ hours** From Paris St-Lazare. 🚗 **90 minutes** Mainly along the A13 motorway.

33

5 DAYS

Paris to Tours
Architectural Elegance

France is synonymous with fabulous châteaux, and they don't get much more fabulous than in the Loire Valley. This trip from Paris follows the course of the Loire River via the elegant cities of Orléans and Tours.

PARIS

ORLÉANS ①

BLOIS ② ③ CHAMBORD

AMBOISE

TOURS ⑤ ④

① Orléans (p192)

From Paris, catch a zippy TGV to Orleáns, a well-to-do city that's renowned for its connections with Joan of Arc. Apart from the Maid of Orléans, it's a great place for some shopping and dining, and also boasts one of France's top provincial **arts museums**.

PARIS ➲ ORLÉANS

🚆 **Just over one hour** From Paris Gare d'Austerlitz. 🚗 **90 minutes** Along the A6 and A10 motorways.

② Blois (p195)

A quick train trip from Orléans brings you to Blois, once the seat of power for the French monarchy. The town's **château** showcases four different periods from French architecture, and its lavish main hall featured in Luc Besson's 1999 biopic of Joan of Arc.

ORLÉANS ➲ BLOIS

🚆 **40 minutes** From Orléans to Blois. 🚗 **45 minutes** Along the A10 motorway.

③ Chambord (p197)

Devote day three to the Loire's most magnificent **castle**, Chambord. It was built by François I as a country retreat, but he hardly ever stayed there. A famous double-helix staircase spirals up to the rooftop, which gives wonderful views over the château's landscaped park. If time allows, squeeze in a detour to **Cheverny**: both are included in organised minibus trips from Blois.

BLOIS ➲ CHAMBORD

🚗 **20 minutes** Along the D33. 🚆 **40 minutes** From Blois.

④ Amboise (p202)

From Blois, head west to Amboise, where you can visit another impressive **royal château**, as well as Leonardo da Vinci's retirement home, **Clos Lucé**. Life-size prototypes of da Vinci's inventions are dotted around Clos Lucé's house and grounds.

BLOIS ➲ AMBOISE

🚆 **20 minutes.** 🚗 **30 minutes** Along the N152.

⑤ Tours (p198)

The final day takes you via the lovely **Château de Chenonceau** en route to Tours, the Loire's main city. The twin-towered Gothic **cathedral** dominates the skyline, but you can also visit several fascinating museums including the **Musée du Compagnonnage**, devoted to the work of France's top craftspeople.

AMBOISE ➲ TOURS

🚆 **35 minutes.** 🚗 **30 minutes** Along the D751 or N152.

Château de Chenonceau (p202)
PHOTOGRAPHER: CHRISTOPHER WOOD

10 DAYS

Paris to Avignon
Unesco Treasures

This trip takes in France's biggest, finest, oldest and loveliest; every stop is a Unesco World Heritage Site, making the trip a must for culture vultures and history buffs. From otherworldly abbeys to iconic cathedrals and Roman ruins, this adventure has it all.

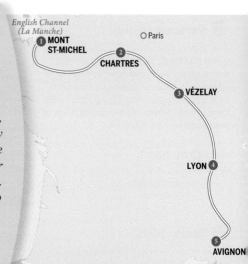

English Channel
(La Manche)

○ Paris

1 MONT ST-MICHEL

2 CHARTRES

3 VÉZELAY

LYON 4

5 AVIGNON

① Mont St-Michel (p129)

Start the trip with a visit to France's iconic island abbey, the Mont St-Michel. It's best seen at dawn and dusk, or after dark when it's lit up like a Roman candle. If you have time, it's worth taking a guided walk across the sands to see the abbey from an entirely new perspective.

PARIS ○ MONT ST-MICHEL

🚗 **Three hours** Along the N13 and A84. 🚆 **3½ hours** TGV from Paris to Rennes, then a regional train to Pontorson and Bus 6 to Mont St-Michel.

② Chartres (p105)

Gothic monuments don't get much grander than **Chartres Cathedral**. The church's stained glass is famous for its intense blue tones – visit on a sunny day, when the light really has to be seen to be believed. Spend a couple of days exploring the châteaux of **Versailles** and **Fontainebleu**, which are both within easy reach of Chartres.

MONT ST-MICHEL ○ CHARTRES

🚗 **Three hours** Along the A81 and A11 motorways. 🚆 **Three hours** From Pontorson, with changes at Rennes and Le Mans.

③ Vézelay (p216)

Burgundy has two wonderful World Heritage Sites. First up is the fabulous hilltop basilica of Vézelay, rescued from near-collapse by the great 19th-century French architect Viollet-le-Duc. Just a short drive away is the Cistercian abbey of **Fontenay**. Though the monks are long gone, the abbey still makes a delightful place for quiet contemplation. Both sites are around an hour's drive from **Dijon**.

CHARTRES ○ DIJON

🚗 **3½ hours** Along the A19, A6 and A38. 🚆 **Three hours** From Chartres to Paris St-Lazare, then from Paris Montparnasse to Dijon.

④ Lyon (p234)

Lyon's architectural heritage encompasses everything from Roman ruins to Renaissance townhouses, and most of the city has been designated a World Heritage Site. The monuments and museums are a major draw, while the city's culinary reputation ensures its *bouchons* (bistros) are kept busy round the clock.

DIJON ○ LYON

🚗 **2¼ hours** Along the A31 and A6. 🚆 **Two hours**.

⑤ Avignon (p316)

The beautiful walled city of Avignon has two Unesco-listed monuments: an impressive **papal palace** and an amazing **medieval bridge**. Further afield, Provence is littered with monuments left over from the days of Gallo-Roman occupation. Admire the engineering of the **Pont du Gard**, the world's largest and best-preserved Roman aqueduct, then put yourself in a gladiator's shoes in the imposing amphitheatres of **Orange** and **Arles**. All can be easily reached by rail or road from Avignon.

LYON ○ AVIGNON

🚗 **2¼ hours** Along the A7. 🚆 **One hour** Via the TGV.

Pont du Gard (p323)

10 DAYS

Nice to Biarritz
Coast to Coast

This tour begins on the big blue Mediterranean before crossing the Pyrenees to the Atlantic Coast. En route you'll encounter ritzy cities, quaint villages and lofty mountains – not to mention a wealth of unforgettable views.

English Channel
(La Manche)

GERMANY

SWITZERLAND

Atlantic Ocean

ITALY

NICE
CANNES ❶

BIARRITZ ❷
❻ PYRENEES ❺ ❹ ❸ MARSEILLE
CARCASSONNE

SPAIN

MEDITERRANEAN
SEA

① Nice (p325)

Start the trip in the Côte d'Azur's classic beach town, Nice. Kick back along the **Promenade des Anglais**, shop at the **Cours Saleya markets** and explore the backstreets of **Vieux Nice**. With an extra day, you could visit the city's **art museums**, admire the views from the **Colline du Château**, or head along the coast to moneyed **Monaco**.

PARIS ➔ NICE

✈ **Two hours** From Paris. 🚆 **Just under six hours** From Paris Gare de Lyon via the TGV.

② Cannes (p335)

After Nice, head west to star-spangled **Cannes**. Spot famous faces along **blvd de la Croisette**, cruise out to the idyllic **Îles de Lérins**, then spin along the Mediterranean coastline for a day in chi-chi **St-Tropez**.

NICE ➔ CANNES

🚆 **30 minutes**. 🚗 **45 minutes** Along the coastal N98.

③ Marseille (p302)

Rough-and-ready Marseille encapsulates the fiery spirit of the French south. Sample **bouillabaisse** by the harbour, climb to the **basilica** and cruise to the island fortress of the **Château d'If**. An optional detour might also take in **Aix-en-Provence**, where Cézanne painted his most famous canvases.

CANNES ➔ MARSEILLE

🚗 **Two hours** Along the A8 motorway, longer along the coastal N98. 🚆 **Two hours**.

Looking out to Château d'If from Basilique Notre Dame de la Garde (p303), Marseille

PHOTOGRAPHER: DAVID TOMLINSON

④ Carcassonne (p324)

A three-hour spin along the Mediterranean takes you to Carcassonne, one of the Languedoc's most beautiful medieval towns. Nearby **Narbonne** boasts a wonderful street market where you can stock up on local produce and soak up the southern atmosphere.

MARSEILLE ➔ CARCASSONNE

🚗 **3½ hours** Along the coastal N98. 🚆 **Three hours**.

⑤ The Pyrenees (p287)

West of Carcassonne, the snowcapped peaks of the Pyrenees zig-zag along the Franco–Spanish border. Less visited than the Alps, these wild mountains offer fantastic walking and wildlife-spotting. Admire the mountain panorama from the top of the **Pic du Midi**, tackle the trails around **Cauterets** or visit the holy city of **Lourdes**.

CARCASSONNE ➔ PYRENEES

🚗 You'll need your own wheels to explore the Pyrenees.

⑥ Biarritz (p279)

Switch the saw-tooth peaks of the Pyrenees for the glitzy beaches of Biarritz. With its belle époque architecture and gorgeous bays, this coastal city is ideal for further forays into the **French Basque Country**: the ancient pilgrims' village of **St-Jean Pied de Port** and the riverside town of **Bayonne** are literally on your doorstep.

THE PYRENEES ➔ BIARRITZ

🚆 **1¾ hours** From Pau or **2¾ hours** From Lourdes. 🚗 **2½ hours** From Cauterets to the coast.

Paris to Paris
The Grand Tour

This is the big one: a whistle-stop circular adventure around France, taking in as many must-see sights as possible. It's doable in two weeks if you pack things in, but we've suggested optional side-trips for each area if your timetable allows a bit more flexibility.

1 Paris (p64)

Kick off with at least two days in the French capital, ticking off as many sights, museums and restaurants as you can. Add in another couple of days for day trips to either the châteaux of **Versailles** and **Fontaine-bleu** or the champagne capital of **Reims**.

AROUND PARIS
🚇 Paris' underground is the best way to explore the capital.

2 Lyon (p221)

From Paris, it's a speedy TGV trip to the lovely city of Lyon. Spend a day exploring the city's sights, monuments and museums, followed by an evening meal in a typical Lyonnais *bouchon*. Ideally, you should allow some time to explore the French Alps – especially **Chamonix** and **Annecy** – but if you're pushed for time, skip the mountains and head directly to the French Riviera.

PARIS ⟶ LYON
🚇 **Two hours** From Paris Gare de Lyon via the TGV.
🚌 **About five hours** Along the A6 motorway.

3 French Riviera (p325)

You could soak up weeks lounging along the Côte d'Azur, but for this trip we've allowed two days: one for the lively city of **Nice**, and another for the playground principality of **Monaco**. En route you'll have the chance to experience France's most memorable drive along the famous clifftop **corniches**.

LYON ⟶ NICE
🚇 **Four to five hours** On the TGV. ✈ **Less than one hour**

4 Bordeaux (p266)

Mark the start of week two with a cross-country flight to the capital of French winemaking, **Bordeaux**. It's a beautiful city in its own right, but for most people it's Bordeaux's viticultural heritage that's the main draw. Tailored minibus trips are ideal if you're short on time: try to choose one that includes visits to the vineyards of the **Médoc** and the hilltop village of **St-Émilion**

NICE ⟶ BORDEAUX
✈ **Two hours** 🚇 **Eight hours** Via direct TGV, longer if changes are required.

Chamonix (p245)
PHOTOGRAPHER: JOHN ELK III

7 Normandy (p118)

From the Loire, travel north via the abbey of **Mont St-Michel** en route to Bayeux, which makes an ideal base for tracing the story of two landmark invasions. William the Conqueror's raid on England in 1066 is dramatically recounted in the **Bayeux Tapestry**, while **Normandy's beaches** will be forever linked with the historic events of 6 June 1944 – known to the French as Jour-J, and to the rest of the world as D-Day. From Bayeux, it's a short hop back to journey's end in **Paris**.

TOURS ◯ BAYEUX
🚗 3¼ hours 🚆 5 hours Change at Caen.

5 The Dordogne (p213)

Meander inland through the rolling countryside of the **Dordogne** en route to one of France's loveliest medieval towns, **Sarlat-la-Canéda**. Devote at least a day to visiting the amazing artworks of the **Grotte de Lascaux** and the other caves of the **Vézère Valley**.

BORDEAUX ◯ SARLAT-LA-CANÉDA
🚆 2¾ hours 🚗 2¼ hours Along regional roads.

6 The Loire Valley (p192)

From Bordeaux, it's on to the Loire Valley and its ostentatious **châteaux**. Base yourself in the smart city of **Tours**, and visit da Vinci's house in **Amboise**, the delicate palace of **Chenonceau** and François I's lavish hunting lodge, **Chambord**.

SARLAT-LA-CANÉDA ◯ TOURS
🚗 Four hours 🚆 Six hours Usually with changes at Souillac and Limoges.

France Month by Month

 ## January

With New Year festivities finished, it's time to play snow bunnies in the Alps. Crowds thin out once school's back, but this is still a busy month. On the Mediterranean coast, mild winters cast a wonderful serenity over an area that's mad busy the rest of the year.

 ### Vive le ski!

Grab your skis or board and hit the slopes. Resorts in the Alps, Pyrenees and Jura open in mid- to late December, but January is the start of the ski season in earnest. Whether a vast purpose-built station or a lost Alpine village, France has a resort to match every mood and moment.

 ### Hunting Black Diamonds

No culinary product is more aromatic or decadent than black truffles (p365). Snout them out in the Dordogne (southeastern France) and Provence (southwestern France) – the truffle-hunting season runs from late December to March but January is the prime month.

 ## February

Crisp cold weather in the mountains translates as the ski season in top gear. Alpine resorts are mobbed by families during the February school holidays; don't turn up without a reservation.

 ### Nice Carnival

While northern France shivers, Nice makes the most of its mild Mediterranean climate with France's largest street carnival (www.nicecarnaval.com), As well as the usual parade and costume shenanigans, merrymakers pelt each other with blooms during Carnaval de Nice's legendary flower battles.

Top Events

- ### Festival d'Avignon, July
- ### Fête du Citron, February
- ### Fête des Lumières, December
- ### Fêtes d'Arvor, August
- ### Cannes Film Festival, May

Left: Sculpture for Fête du Citron
PHOTOGRAPHER: DAVID TOMLINSON

Citrus Celebrations

It's no surprise that Menton on the French Riviera was once Europe's biggest lemon producer, given its exotic Fête du Citron (www.feteducitron.com). These days it ships in lemons from Spain to sculpt into gargantuan carnival characters.

March

The tail end of the ski season stays busy thanks to ongoing school holidays and milder temperatures. Down south, the first buds of spring herald the start of the bullfighting season and, depending on the year, *Pâques* (Easter).

 ### Féria Pascale

No fest sets passions in France's hot south blazing more than this, held each Easter in Arles to open the bullfighting season (www.feriaarles.com, in French).

April

Dedicated ski fiends can carve glaciers in the highest French ski resorts until mid-April. Otherwise, it's off with the ski boots and on with the hiking gear.

 ### Counting Sheep

During the centuries-old Fête de la Transhumance in late April or May, shepherds all over France walk their flocks up to lush green summer pastures; St-Rémy de Provence's is among the best known.

May

As the first melons ripen in Provence and outdoor markets burst forth with newfound colour, there is no lovelier month to travel.

 ### May Day

May 1 is a national holiday that incites a real summer buzz with its *muguets* (lilies of the valley) sold at roadside stalls and given to friends as good-luck charms. In Arles, Camargue cowboys show off their bull-herding and equestrian skills at the Fête des Gardians.

 ### Pèlerinage des Gitans

Roma from all over Europe flock to the Camargue on 24 and 25 May and again in October (nearest Sunday to 22 October) for a flamboyant fiesta of street music, dancing and dipping their toes in the sea (www.gitans.fr, in French).

 ### Starring at Cannes

In mid-May film stars and celebrities walk the red carpet at Cannes, the biggest of Europe's cinema extravaganzas (www.festival-cannes.com).

 ### Monaco Grand Prix

How fitting that the most glamorous race of the Formula One season rips around the streets of one of the world's most glam countries (www.formula1monaco.com).

June

With the onset of midsummer France's festival pace quickens and the first bathers are tempted into the sea.

 ### Fête de la Musique

Orchestras, crooners, buskers and bands fill streets and squares with music during France's vibrant nationwide celebration of music on 21 June (www.fetedelamusique.culture.fr, in French).

July

If lavender's your French love, this is the month to catch it in flower in Provence.

Nice Jazz Festival

Jive between Roman ruins to jazz cats at this soulful music fest in Nice (www.nicejazzfest.fr).

 # August

It's that mad summer month when the French join everyone else on holiday. Paris, Lyon and other big cities empty; traffic jams test the patience of a saint; and temperatures soar.

Proud to be Breton

The Fêtes d'Arvor is a passionate celebration of Breton culture. Think street parades, concerts and dozens of authentic *festoù-noz* (night festivals) spilling across the half-timbered, cobbled Vannes (www.fetes-arvor.org, in French).

Celts Unite!

Celtic culture is the focus of the Festival Interceltique de Lorient (www.festival-interceltique.com), when hundreds of thousands of Celts from Brittany and abroad flock to Lorient.

September

As sun-plump grapes hang heavy on darkened vines and that August madness drops off, a tranquillity falls across autumnal France. It's the start of the *vendange* (grape harvest).

The Rutting Season

Nothing beats getting up at dawn to watch mating stags, boar and red deer at play. Observatory towers are hidden in woods around Château de Chambord (p185), but when a valley like the Loire is so full of Renaissance hunting pads, who cares which one?

School's out for the summer, and the country teems with tourists and traffic.

Tour de France

The world's most prestigious cycling race ends on av des Champs-Élysées in Paris on the third or fourth Sunday of July, but you can catch it for two weeks before all over France – the route changes each year but the French Alps are a hot spot (www.letour.fr).

Bastille Day

The storming of the Bastille, 14 July 1789, is celebrated countrywide, with firework displays, balls, processions and parades.

Festival d'Avignon

Rouse your inner thespian with Avignon's legendary performing-arts festivals (p318; www.festival-avignon.com). Street acts in its fringe fest are as inspired as those on official stages.

Braderie de Lille

The mountains of empty mussel shells engulfing the streets after three days of munching have to be seen to be believed. Then there's the real reason for visiting Lille the first weekend in September – its colossal flea market is Europe's largest.

 # November

It's nippy now, especially in northern France, and many sights switch to shorter, winter opening hours. Lots of restaurants close two nights a week, making dining out on Monday a challenge in some towns.

 Beaujolais Nouveau

At precisely the stroke of the midnight on the third Thursday in November the first bottles of cherry-red Beaujolais *nouveau* wine are cracked open – and what a party it can be in Beaujolais, Lyon and other places nearby!

 # December

Days are short and it is cold everywhere bar the south of France. But there are Christmas school holidays and festive celebrations to bolster sun-deprived souls, not to mention some season-opening winter skiing in the highest-altitude Alpine resorts from mid-December.

 Alsatian Christmas Markets

Meandering between fairy-light-bedecked craft stalls, mug of *vin chaud* (warm mulled wine) in gloved hand, at Alsace's traditional pre-Christmas markets, exudes cinematic romance.

 Fête des Lumières

France's biggest and best light show, on 8 December, transforms the streets and squares of Lyon into an open stage (www.lumieres.lyon.fr).

Far left: Tour de France **Left:** Lavender fields, Provence (see p43)

PHOTOGRAPHERS: (FAR LEFT) ANGUS OBORN: (LEFT) BETHUNE CARMICHAEL

What's New

For this new edition of Discover France, our authors hunted down the fresh, the revamped, the transformed, the hot and the happening. Here are some of our favourites. For up-to-the-minute recommendations, see lonelyplanet.com/france.

1 JADIS, L'AGRUME & DERRIERE, PARIS
This hot trio is among a flurry of top-drawer, casually understated dining spaces to recently woo the capital. Even big-name chefs like Christian Constant and William Ledeuil are at it (p86).

2 CENTRE POMPIDOU-METZ
The space-age curves of Metz' gleaming white modern-art museum, sudden architectural star of the provincial north, is as much a show-stopper as its Parisian big brother (see the boxed text, p174).

3 L'AVENTURE MICHELIN, CLERMONT-FERRAND
Now this is apt: the French tyre company that does so much more than rings of rubber finally tells its tale at this museum – travel has always been a big theme (www.laventuremichelin.com; 32 rue du Clos Four; adult/child €8/5, audioguide €2; ⏱10am-6pm Tue-Sun).

4 RUE LE BEC, LYON
Lyon's most creative chef proves he's still on top with his latest ground-breaking venture – a wholly affordable, market-style dining space on the Confluence aka rejuvenated industrial wasteland (p242).

5 BRIVE-VALLÉE DE LA DORDOGNE AIRPORT
France's latest regional airport to open with budget flights between the Dordogne, Paris and London (www.aeroport-brive-vallee-dordogne.com).

6 JEAN NOUVEL IN SARLAT-LA-CANEDA
Architect of Paris' Arab World Institute and Musée du Quai Branly is at it again, this time with a panoramic lift inside a village-church-turned-market in the Dordogne (p213).

7 GORGE FLOATING
Squeeze into a wetsuit, strap a buoyancy bag to your back and float between rocks on green water – this is *the* new big thrill of Provence's Gorges du Verdon (p317).

8 FRENCH RIVIERA GLAMOUR
Hôtel Ermitage is the latest hip hotel to swing onto the scene in St-Tropez. It's hot, it's edgy, it's a 1950s-design must-stay that the celebs love (p339).

9 CITÉ INTERNATIONALE DE LA DENTELLE ET DE LA MODE, CALAIS
Victorian-era machinery clatters and clanks in Calais to turn thread into lace at this port city's newest museum – lace is what made Calais a big name in textiles (International Centre of Lace & Fashion; ☎03 21 00 42 30; www.cite-dentelle.fr; 135 quai du Commerce; adult €5; ⏱10am-5pm or 6pm except Tue).

10 CANAL ST-MARTIN, PARIS
The shaded towpaths of this tranquil canal in Paris' eastern suburbs have undergone a real urban renaissance – enter one of the capital's hippest areas to drink, dine, stroll and picnic (p81).

Get Inspired

Books

○ A Year in the Merde (Stephen Clarke) Expat Brit sounds off on dog poo, bureaucracy and more.

○ Another Long Day on the Piste (Will Randall) Comic tales of a French ski resort.

○ More France Please, We're British (Helena Frith Powell) English author on her experiences of life in rural France.

○ Charlotte Gray (Sebastian Faulks) Tale of a female undercover agent in occupied France.

○ Everybody Was So Young (Amanda Vaill) Life on the French Riviera in the roaring twenties.

Films

○ Les Quatre Cents Coups (1960) New-wave classic loosely based on Truffaut's childhood.

○ Cyrano de Bergerac (1990) Glossy version of the classic French fable, starring Gérard Depardieu.

○ Nikita (1990) Luc Besson's sexy spy thriller.

○ La Môme (La Vie en Rose; 2007) Biopic of French singer Édith Piaf.

○ Bienvenue Chez Les Ch'tis (2008) Comedy satirising France's north–south divide.

♫ Music

○ Eternelle (Édith Piaf; 2002) Excellent intro to the sparrow chanteuse.

○ Histoire de Melody Nelson (Serge Gainsbourg; 1971) The classic album by the classic French crooner.

○ L'Absente (Yann Tiersen; 2001) Raw, emotional music from a multitalented Breton musician.

○ Gibraltar and **Dante** (Abd al Malik; 2006 & 2008) Top albums by Franco-Congolese rapper and slam-poet.

○ Made in Medina (Rachid Taha; 2000) Cross-cultural sounds from Franco-Algerian DJ and singer.

Websites

○ French Word a Day (http://french-word-a-day.typepad.com) Learn French in daily steps.

○ Météo France (www.meteo.fr) The latest weather forecasts.

○ SNCF (www.sncf.com) France's national railways.

○ Mappy (www.mappy.fr) Calculate road routes, travel times and toll costs.

○ France 24 (www.france24.com/en) Round-the-clock news.

 Short on time?

This list will give you an instant insight into the country.

Read *A Year in Provence* (Peter Mayle) made *everyone* want to up sticks and move to rural France.

Watch *Amélie* (2001) is a feel-good and very French film about a quirky café worker who sets out to make her Montmartre neighbourhood a happier place.

Listen *Moon Safari* (1998) offers Gallic electronica from French duo AIR ('Amour, Imagination, Rêve').

Log on www.franceguide.com is the main website for the French government tourist office.

Basilique du Sacré Coeur (p63)

Need to Know

Currency
Euro (€)

Language
French

ATMs
At airports, most train stations and every other city street corner.

Credit Cards
Visa and MasterCard widely accepted.

Visas
Generally not required for stays of up to 90 days (or for EU nationals); some nationalities need a Schengen visa.

Mobile Phones
European and Australian phones work.

Wi-Fi
Free in many hotels, train stations and airports.

Internet Access
Most towns have at least one internet café. €2-6 per hour.

Driving
Steering wheels on the left, drive on the right. Be aware of the 'priority to the right' rule.

Tipping
At least 10% for good service. *Service compris* means service is included.

When to Go

Brittany & Normandy •
GO Apr–Sep

• Paris
GO May & Jun

•French Alps
GO late Dec–early Apr (skiing) or Jun & Jul (hiking)

French Riviera •
GO Apr–Jun, Sep & Oct

Corsica •
GO Apr–Jun, Sep & Oct

Warm to hot summers, mild winters
Warm to hot summers, cold winters
Mild year-round
Mild summers, cold winters
Mountain climate

High Season
(Jul & Aug)
o Queues at big sights and on the road, especially August
o Christmas, New Year and Easter equally busy
o Late-December to March high season in French Alps ski resorts

Shoulder
(Apr–June & Sep)
o Accommodation rates drop in southern France and other traveller hot spots
o Spring is best, with its warm temperatures, flowers and abundance of local produce

o Watching the *vendange* (grape harvest) is reason to visit in Autumn

Low Season
(Oct–Mar)
o Lowest prices – up to 50% less than high season
o Sights, attractions and restaurants open fewer days and shorter hours

Advance Planning

o **Three months before** Book flights and accommodation; book tickets for popular festivals and sporting events such as the Festival d'Avignon and Nice Jazz Festival.

o **One month before** Book train tickets via the SNCF website (www. voyages-sncf.com) to get the cheapest fares. Arrange car hire: French firms such as ADA (www.ada.fr) or discount brokers such as Auto Europe (www.autoeurope.com) often have good deals.

o **Two weeks before** Choose which guided walks and tours you want to do, and book if necessary. Order euros, or charge up your pre-paid card.

Your Daily Budget

Budget up to €100

○ Dorm beds €15–40

○ Double room in budget hotel €50–70

○ Free admission to many museums and monuments first Sunday of month

○ Set lunches €10–15

Midrange €100–200

○ Double room in a midrange hotel €70–175

○ Lunch *menus* (set meals) in gourmet restaurants €20–40

Top End over €200

○ Double room in a top-end hotel €70–175

○ Lower weekend rates in business hotels

○ Top restaurant dinner: *menu* €50, à la carte €100–150

Exchange Rates		
Australia	A$1	€0.71
Canada	C$1	€0.72
Japan	¥100	€0.88
NZ	NZ$1	€0.55
UK	UK£1	€1.17
US	US$1	€0.75

For current exchange rates see www.xe.com

What to Bring

○ **Sunglasses, sunscreen and mosquito repellent** Vital for southern France.

○ **Plug adaptors** France uses two-pin European plugs; UK, US and others will need adaptors.

○ **A corkscrew** Essential for impromptu picnics.

○ **French phrasebook** Choose one with a good food section.

○ **Travel insurance** Check the policy for coverage on snow sports, luggage loss and healthcare.

○ **EHIC Card** Covers healthcare for EU citizens.

○ **ID and passport** Don't forget visas if required.

○ **Driving licence** Your standard home licence should be sufficient.

Arriving in France

○ **Aéroport Roissy Charles de Gaulle, Paris**

Trains, buses and RER – to Paris centre every 15 to 30 minutes, 5.30am to midnight

Night bus – hourly, 12.30am to 5.30am.

Taxis – €45–60; 30 minutes to Paris centre.

○ **Aéroport d'Orly, Paris**

Buses and Orlyval rail – at least every 15 minutes, 6am to 11.30pm

Night bus – hourly, 12.30am to 5.30am

Taxis – €35–50; 25 minutes to Paris centre

Getting Around

○ **Train** France's railway is fast, extensive and efficient. Regular trains travel to practically every town and city.

○ **Car** Having a car buys freedom and flexibility, but driving in big cities can be a nightmare.

○ **Bicycle** A hip way of navigating Paris, Lyon and other big cities.

Accommodation

○ **Hotels** Wide range of budget, midrange and top-end hotels.

○ **Chambres d'Hôtes** Staying in a B&B is particularly popular in rural France.

○ **Châteaux** Some châteaux have been converted into luxurious hotels or B&Bs.

Be Forewarned

○ **Shops** Nearly everywhere shuts on Sunday and public holidays. Shops usually close for lunch from noon to 2pm.

○ **Restaurants** Few serve all day; orders are generally taken between noon and 2pm and 7pm to 10.30pm, six days a week. Sunday evening and all day Monday are popular days to close.

○ **Driving in France** Tolls are charged on many motorways *(autoroutes)*. Automatic cars are very unusual in France.

○ **Crowds** Many sights are at their busiest in July and August, but this can be a good time to visit Paris, as it's when most French people go on holiday.

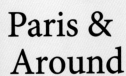

Paris & Around

Paris has all but exhausted the superlatives that can reasonably be applied to any city. Notre Dame, the Eiffel Tower, the Seine – at sunrise, sunset, at night – and Left Bank–Right Bank differences have been described countless times. But what writers haven't quite captured is the grandness and magic of simply strolling the city's broad avenues past impressive public buildings and exceptional museums to parks, gardens and esplanades.

With more famous landmarks than any other city, the French capital evokes all sorts of expectations: of grand vistas, of intellectuals discussing weighty matters in cafés, of Seine-side romance, of naughty nightclub revues. Look hard enough and you'll find them all. Or set aside those preconceptions of Paris and explore the city's avenues and backstreets as though the tip of the Eiffel Tower or the spire of Notre Dame weren't about to pop into view at any moment.

Palais Garnier (p97)
PHOTOGRAPHER: BARBARA VAN ZANTEN

Paris & Around

1 Musée du Louvre
2 Versailles
3 Cathédrale de Notre Dame de Paris
4 Cimetière du Père Lachaise
5 Eiffel Tower
6 Musée d'Orsay
7 Seine

CLICHY
Cimetière Sud

Bd Bessières

Porte de Clichy

17E

See Central Paris – North Map (p72)

Av Bineau

Péreire–Lavallois

Neuilly Porte Maillot Palais des Congrès

R de Rome

Gare St-Lazare

Av Foch

Charles de Gaulle–Étoile

8E

Auber

TRIANGLE D'OR

Lac Inférieur

Jardins du Trocadéro

Jardin des Tuileries

Musée d'Orsay 6

Jardin du Ranelagh

16E

Champ de Mars –Tour Eiffel 5

7E

Bois de Boulogne

Lac Supérieur

Boulain Villiers

LEFT BANK

6E

Av Mozart

Kennedy Radio–France

Av de Saxe

Porte d'Auteuil

Square Henry Paté

Javel

Av Émile Zola

Ste-Périne

Seine

Parc André Citroën

R Lecourbe

Gare Montparnasse

Boulevard Victor

Cimetière du Montparnasse

To 2 (11km)

R de la Convention

R de la Croix Nivert

R de Vouillé

Bd Victor

15E

Denfert Rochereau

Nouveau Cimetière

Parc Georges Brassens

Bd Lefebvre

R d'Alésia

Île St-Germain

Issy–Val de Seine

Square de la Porte de la Plaine

14E

Jacques Henri Lartigue

Square Jean Moulin

Bd Périphérique

Issy Ville

VANVES

Parc Rodin

MALAKOFF

MONTROUGE

N

0   2 km
0   1 miles

Cimetière Parisien de Bagneux

ARCUEIL

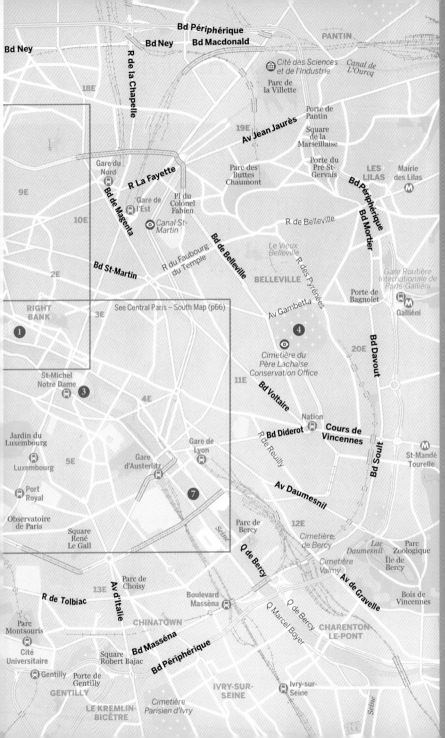

Paris & Around's Highlights

1

The Louvre

I've worked at the Louvre for 10 years and each day I still experience many emotions: it is a magical place, charged with history and very intimate. It was a 12th-century fortress, then a royal palace; today it's one of the most famous art museums in the world.

Need to Know
FACTS 6 hectares of gallery space, 5000 art works, 8 million visitors per year **BRUTAL TRUTH** One visit can't possibly cover it all **PLAN** study www.louvre.fr to optimise your time. **See our author's review, p75.**

Louvre Don't Miss List

BY NIKO SALVATORE MELISSANO,
MUSÉE DU LOUVRE

1 WINGED VICTORY OF SAMOTHRACE

It's impossible to reduce the collections of the Louvre to a hit parade... A definite highlight is the *Winged Victory of Samothrace* atop the Daru Staircase (1st Floor, Denon Wing). I adore her wings. I just cannot stop contemplating her from all angles. She is, moreover, very photogenic.

2 THE SEATED SCRIBE & MONA LISA

I could admire this statuette (Room 22, 1st Floor, Sully Wing) from the ancient Egyptian empire for hours: the face of the scribe (probably that of Saqqara), like his posture (a little 'yoga') and his deep stare, say several things to me: serenity, strength of character, eternal wisdom. Then there is *La Joconde* (Mona Lisa; Room 6, 1st Floor, Salle de la Joconde, Denon Wing) and that amazing fascination of why and how she intrigues spirits with her mysteries.

3 COUR KHORSABAD

With its enormous human-headed winged bulls, this courtyard on the ground floor of the Richelieu Wing is a jump in time into the cradle of one of the oldest cultures in the world: Mesopotamia. During the region of King Sargon II in the 8th century, these bulls carved from alabaster guarded the Assyrian city and palace of Khorsabad (northern Iraq). Their bearded faces with bull ears and a heavy tiara of horns wore a benevolent smile. A mix of force and serenity, perfectly balanced despite their colossal size, these protective monsters with four or five paws were a measure of the power of the Assyrian Empire in its heyday.

4 GRANDE GALERIE

It's a real highlight this gallery (1st Floor, Denon Wing), with masterpieces from the great masters of the Italian Renaissance: Leonardo de Vinci, Raphael, Arcimboldo, Andrea Mantegna... For more on all these works of art, borrow the Louvre's multimedia guide (http://monguide.louvre.fr; adult/under 18yr €6/2), available at the three main entrances (Richelieu, Sully and Denon), which makes for a fun visit at your own pace.

Bottom Right: *Cour Khorsabad*, Musée du Louvre

Versailles

Versailles, as official residence of the kings of France, is magnificent – the only place where the daily life of the monarchy before the French Revolution can really be felt. My favourite moment is the evening, after the crowds have gone, when I quietly walk from room to room lecturing to just a small group...extraordinary.

②

Need to Know
NIGHTMARE QUEUES
Avoid by buying your tickets in advance, arriving first thing in the morning or after 4pm and avoiding Tuesdays, when many Paris museums are closed. **See our author's review, p104.**

Versailles Don't Miss List

BY SYLVAIN POSTOLLE, OFFICIAL
GUIDE, CHÂTEAU DE VERSAILLES

1 KING'S PRIVATE APARTMENT

This is the most fascinating part of the palace as it shows the king as a man and reflects his daily life in the 18th century. Of the 10 or so rooms, the most famous is his bedroom where he not only slept but also held ceremonies. Up to 150 courtiers and people invited from outside the court would watch him have supper here each evening! By the 1780s, the king's life had become more private – he had an official supper just once a week on Sunday.

2 KING LOUIS VXI'S LIBRARY

This is a lovely room – full of books, a place where you can really imagine the king coming to read for hours and hours. Louis XVI loved geography and his copy of *The Travels of James Cook* – in English – is still here.

3 HERCULES SALON

I love one particular perspective inside the palace: from the Hercules Salon you can see all the rooms comprising the King's State Apartment, and to the right, through the gallery leading to the opera house. The salon served as a passageway in fact for the king to go from his state apartment to the chapel to celebrate daily mass.

4 THE ROYAL CHAPEL

This is an exquisite example of the work of a very important architect of the time, Jules Hardouin-Mansart (1646–1708). The paintings, representative of art fashions at the end of the reign of Louis XIV, are also stunning: they evoke the idea that the French king was chosen by God and as such his lieutenant on earth. This is the chapel where, in 1770, the future king Louis XVI wed Marie Antoinette in – the beginning of the French Revolution.

5 ENCELADE GROVE

Versailles' gardens are extraordinary but my favourite spot has to be this grove, typical of the gardens created for Louis XIV by André Le Nôtre. A gallery of trellises surround a pool with a statue of Enceladus, chief of the Titans, who was punished for his pride by the gods from Mount Olympus. When the fountains are on, it's impressive.

Top: Hall of Mirrors (p103); **Bottom Right:** Apollo Salon

Cathédrale de Notre Dame de Paris

France has its share of stunning cathedrals, but none can match the might and majesty of Notre Dame Cathedral (p80), Paris' most-visited monument. Idyllically situated on an island in the middle of the Seine, the cathedral is renowned for its stained glass and soaring Gothic architecture, not to mention an unmissable panorama over the rooftops of Paris.

Eiffel Tower

No Parisian visit would be complete without a trip up the Tour Eiffel (p88). But the 'metal asparagus' was very nearly torn down in the early 20th century (it only survived because it made an ideal radio-antenna platform). Today around 7 million visitors a year venture to the top. Try to time your visit for dusk when the crowds are less and the city lights begin to twinkle.

GLENN BEANLAND

Cimetière du Père Lachaise 4

More sculpture garden than cemetery, this graveyard (p91) in northeastern Paris contains over 69,000 ornate tombs, including those belonging to Molière, Chopin, Oscar Wilde and Jim Morrison. Crisscrossed by wooded paths and winding walkways, it feels a world away from downtown Paris, and makes an ideal refuge when the hustle and bustle of the city gets too much.

Musée d'Orsay 6

It might not be as monumental as the Louvre, but for many people this fine-arts museum (p85) offers a more-rewarding experience. Housed in a turn-of-the-century train station overlooking the Seine, the museum contains France's national collection of art from the 1840s to 1914, including key works by Renoir, Degas, Monet, Cézanne and Vincent van Gogh. Absolutely not to be missed.

The Seine 7

The stately Seine has been a part of Paris' history since Roman times, and the river still plays an integral role in the life of the city. Exploring the Seine is a key part of the Parisian experience, whether that means brunching at a waterfront brasserie, cycling along the riverbanks or strolling across the Pont Neuf – just remember to leave plenty of time for a scenic boat cruise (p78). Pont Neuf (p68)

Paris & Around's Best...

City Views

○ **Eiffel Tower** (p84) Need we say more?

○ **Cathédrale de Notre Dame** (p80) Gargoyles, flying buttresses and an unforgettable view of Paris.

○ **Arc de Triomphe** (p74) Watch the traffic whizz by from the top of the arch.

○ **Tour Montparnasse** (p70) Great views from a 1970s eyesore.

○ **Basilique du Sacré Cœur** (p62) Look out from the dome of Montmartre's basilica.

Traditional Bistros

○ **Le Trumilou** (p89) A century old, with traditional dishes to match.

○ **Bofinger** (p89) Paris' oldest; founded 1864.

○ **Bouillon Racine** (p90) Art-nouveau 'soup kitchen' from 1906.

○ **Le Roi du Pot au Feu** (p93) The address for authentic *pot au feu*.

○ **Le Hide** (p93) Pocket-sized bistro in the heart of Paris.

Places to Chill

○ **Jardin du Luxembourg** (p70) Where Parisians go when the sun shines.

○ **Jardin des Plantes** (p69) A selection of formal gardens to relax in.

○ **Musée Rodin** (p72) This excellent art gallery also boasts one of Paris' loveliest courtyards.

○ **Canal St-Martin** (p81) The city's most-picturesque canal.

○ **Bois de Vincennes** (p90) Swap city for woodland in southeastern Paris.

Need to Know

Quintessential Cafés

o **Les Deux Magots** (p95)
Too famous for its own good,
but still a must-visit.

o **Le Café qui Parle** (p94)
Best for breakfast and
brunch.

o **Café Hugo** (p89) Historic
café on Paris' sweetest
square.

o **Café Marly** (p86)
Priceless views of the Louvre
and the Jardin des Tuileries.

o **Le Cochon à l'Oreille**
(p95) Heritage café with a
flavour of the belle époque.

ADVANCE PLANNING

o **As early as possible**
Book accommodation
and make restaurant
reservations.

o **One week before**
Dodge the queues by
buying tickets online for
Versailles, the Louvre
and exhibitions at the
Grand Palais and Centre
Pompidou.

o **Tickets** (p96) Pick up
concert, musical and
theatre tickets from Fnac
and Virgin Megastore.

RESOURCES

o **Paris Convention &
Visitors Bureau** (www.
parisinfo.com) The city's
central tourist office.

o **Go Go** (www.gogoparis.
com) 'Fashion, food, arts,
gigs, gossip'.

o **Paris.fr** (www.paris.
fr) Comprehensive city
information.

o **My Little Paris** (www.
mylittleparis.com) Insider
secrets from Parisian
writers.

o **Paris by Mouth** (www.
parisbymouth.com) Latest
local tips.

GETTING AROUND

o **Metro & RER** (p101)
Paris' subway system
runs between 5.30am and
midnight. The same tickets
are also valid on buses.

o **Bicycle** (p101) The
capital's bike-rental
scheme, Vélib', has over
1500 stations dotted
across the city.

o **Boats** (p78) Scenic
cruise boats run regularly
along the Seine.

BE FOREWARNED

o **Arrondissements**
Paris addresses are split
into 20 arrondissements
(districts) – 1er for *premier*
(1st), 2e for *deuxième*
(2nd), 3e for *troisième*
(3rd) etc.

o **Museums** Museums
close Monday or Tuesday
and shut their doors 30
minutes to one hour before
listed closing times.

o **Bars & Cafés** A drink
costs more sitting at a
table than standing, more
on a fancy square than
backstreet.

o **Metro stations** Avoid
late at night: Châtelet–
Les Halles, Château
Rouge (Montmartre),
Gare du Nord,
Strasbourg–St-Denis,
Réaumur–Sébastopol and
Montparnasse–Bienvenüe.

Left: Musée Rodin (p72);
Above: Jardin des Plantes (p69)
PHOTOGRAPHERS: (LEFT) BRUCE BI;
(ABOVE) KRZYSZTOF DYDYNSKI

Montmartre Walking Tour

Pretty squares, cobbled streets and city views – not to mention famous cabarets and artistic connections – make Montmartre the quintessential Parisian neighbourhood. Ideal for exploring on foot, as long as you can handle the hills.

WALK FACTS

○ **Start** Ⓜ Blanche

○ **Finish** Ⓜ Abbesses

○ **Distance** 2.5km

○ **Duration** 2½ hours

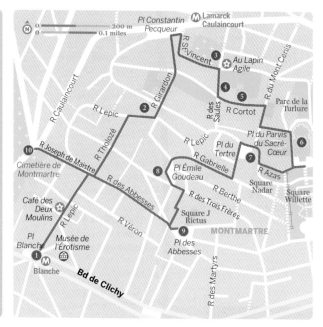

① Place Blanche

Begin outside Blanche metro station. To the northwest is the legendary **Moulin Rouge** beneath its red windmill. To the right is the saucy **Musée de l'Érotisme** (Museum of Erotic Art; 72 bd de Clichy, 18e; adult/student €9/6; ☉10am-2am; Ⓜ Blanche). Halfway along rue Lepic is **Café des Deux Moulins**, where Audrey Tautou worked in the film *Amélie*.

② Montmartre Windmills

Further along rue Lepic are Montmartre's twin windmills: the **Moulin de la Galette** (immortalised in an 1876 painting by Renoir) and the **Moulin Radet** (now a restaurant).

③ Cimetière St-Vincent

This cemetery on rue St-Vincent is the final resting place of Maurice Utrillo (1883–1955), the 'painter of Montmartre'. Just east is the notorious cabaret **Au Lapin Agile**, named after a mural by caricaturist André Gill, which still features on the west wall.

④ Clos Montmartre

South along rue des Saules is Clos Montmartre, a tiny vineyard that produces around 800 bottles of wine a year, which are auctioned for charity in October.

5 Musée de Montmartre

This museum, at 12–14 rue Cortot, is housed in Montmartre's oldest building, a 17th-century house once occupied by Renoir, Utrillo and Raoul Dufy. (www.museedemontmartre.fr; 12 rue Cortot, 18e; adult/child €7/free; ⏱11am-6pm Tue-Sun; Ⓜ Lamarck Caulaincourt)

6 Basilique du Sacré Cœur

This iconic Montmartre landmark is situated on place du Parvis du Sacré Cœur. Inside, 234 steps spiral up to the dome and one of Paris' most spectacular panoramas. (dome admission €5, cash only; ⏱ dome 9am-6 or 7pm)

7 Place du Tertre

Place du Tertre was once the main square of the village of Montmartre. These days it's crammed with cafés, restaurants and tourists, as well as numerous portrait painters who will happily do your likeness.

8 Bateau Lavoir

At No 11b on place Émile Goudeau is the Bateau Lavoir, where the artists Modigliani, Picasso, Kees Van Dongen and Max Jacob lived in an old piano factory (later a laundry). The original building was at No 13 but burned down in 1970 and was rebuilt two doors away in 1978.

9 Abbesses Metro Station

Take the steps from place Émile Goudeau and walk to place des Abbesses, where you can see the famous art-nouveau entrance to the Abbesses metro station, designed in 1912 by Hector Guimard.

10 Cimetière de Montmartre

At the western end of rue des Abbesses is Montmartre's largest cemetery, where you'll find the graves of Émile Zola, Alexandre Dumas, Edgar Degas, François Truffaut and Vaslav Nijinsky, among others. The entrance to the cemetery is on rue Caulaincourt. (⏱8am-5.30pm or 6pm Mon-Fri, from 8.30am Sat, from 9am Sun; Ⓜ Place de Clichy)

Paris In …

TWO DAYS

Start with some of the Parisian icons: **Notre Dame**, the **Eiffel Tower** and the **Arc de Triomphe**. Wander through the **Jardin des Tuileries** and have a coffee or pastis along **av des Champs-Élysées**. In late afternoon, follow our **Montmartre** walking tour before settling down for dinner in a neighbourhood bistro.

On day two factor in visits to the **Musée d'Orsay**, **Ste-Chapelle** and the **Musée Rodin**. Brunch on **place des Vosges** and enjoy an evening exploring the bars and bistros of the **Marais**.

FOUR DAYS

With another two days spare, take a **cruise** along the **Seine** or **Canal St-Martin**, or meander further afield to **Cimetière du Père Lachaise** or the **Bois de Boulogne**. You might also visit the **Musée du Quai Branly** or do a spot of shopping along the **Champs-Élysées**. By night choose from the many restaurants and bars in **Bastille**, **Opéra** and **Montparnasse**. On your final day, squeeze in a side trip to **Fontainebleau** or **Versailles**.

Arc de Triomphe (p74) as seen from the Eiffel Tower (p88)
CHRISTOPHER GROENHOUT

Discover Paris & Around

Sights

Louvre & Les Halles

JARDIN DES TUILERIES   Garden
(Map p66; ⏱7am-7.30, 9 or 11pm; Ⓜ Tuileries or Concorde) Beginning just west of the Jardin du Carrousel, the formal, 28-hectare garden was laid out in its present form – more or less – in the mid-17th century by André Le Nôtre, who also created the gardens at Vaux-le-Vicomte and Versailles. The Tuileries soon became the most fashionable spot in Paris for parading about in one's finery; today it is a favourite of joggers. It forms part of the banks of the Seine World Heritage Site listed in 1991.

PLACE VENDÔME   City Square
(Map p73; Ⓜ Tuileries or Opéra) Octagonal place Vendôme and the arcaded and colonnaded buildings around it were constructed between 1687 and 1721. In March 1796 Napoleon married Josephine, Viscountess Beauharnais, in the building at No 3. Today, the buildings surrounding the square house the posh Hôtel Ritz Paris and some of the city's most fashionable boutiques. The 43.5m-tall **Colonne Vendôme** (Vendôme Column) in the centre of the square consists of a stone core wrapped in a 160m-long bronze spiral made from hundreds of Austrian and Russian cannons captured by Napoleon at the Battle of Austerlitz in 1805. The statue on top depicts Napoleon in classical Roman dress.

Église St-Eustache
PHOTOGRAPHER: RICHARD I'ANSON

ÉGLISE ST-EUSTACHE   Church

(Map p66; www.st-eustache.org, in French; 2 impasse St-Eustache, 1er; ⏰9.30am-7pm Mon-Fri, 10am-7pm Sat, 9am-7.15pm Sun; Ⓜ Les Halles) One of the most beautiful churches in Paris and consecrated to an early Roman martyr who is the patron saint of hunters, this majestic church is just north of the gardens above the Forum des Halles.

Marais & Bastille

The Marais, the area of the Right Bank north of Île St-Louis in the 3e and 4e, was exactly what its name implies – 'marsh' or 'swamp' – until the 13th century, when it was converted to farmland. In the early 17th century, Henri IV built the place Royale (today's place des Vosges), turning the area into Paris' most fashionable residential district and attracting wealthy aristocrats who then erected their own luxurious *hôtels particulier*.

CENTRE POMPIDOU
                    Modern Art Museum

(Map p66; www.centrepompidou.fr; place Georges Pompidou, 4e; Ⓜ Rambuteau) This centre has amazed and delighted visitors since it was inaugurated in 1977, not just for its outstanding collection of modern art, but also for its radical architectural statement.

The open space at ground level has temporary exhibitions and information desks, while the 4th and 5th floors house the **Musée National d'Art Moderne** (MNAM; National Museum of Modern Art; adult/child €10-12/free; ⏰11am-9pm Wed-Mon), France's national collection of art dating from 1905 onwards.

MUSÉE PICASSO   Art Museum

(Map p66; www.musee-picasso.fr, in French; 5 rue de Thorigny, 3e; ⏰9.30am-6pm Wed-Mon; Ⓜ St-Paul or Chemin Vert) One of Paris' best-loved art museums, the Musée Picasso, housed in the mid-17th-century Hôtel Salé, includes more than 3500 of the *grand maître*'s engravings, paintings, ceramic works, drawings and sculptures. It will reopen after extensive renovations in 2012.

PLACE DES VOSGES   City Square

(Map p66; Ⓜ St-Paul or Bastille) Inaugurated in 1612 as place Royale, Place des Vosges is an ensemble of three dozen symmetrical houses with ground-floor arcades, steep slate roofs and large dormer windows arranged around a large square.

The author Victor Hugo lived at the square's Hôtel de Rohan-Guémenée from 1832 to 1848, moving here a year after the publication of *Notre Dame de Paris* (The Hunchback of Notre Dame). His former house, the **Maison de Victor Hugo** (www.musee-hugo.paris.fr, in French; admission adult/child €7/free; ⏰10am-6pm Tue-Sun), is now a municipal museum devoted to the life and times of the celebrated novelist and poet, with an impressive collection of his own drawings and portraits.

PLACE DE LA BASTILLE   City Square

(Map p66; Ⓜ Bastille) The Bastille, built during the 14th century as a fortified royal residence, is probably the most famous monument in Paris that no longer exists; the notorious prison – the quintessential symbol of royal despotism – was demolished by a Revolutionary mob on 14 July 1789 and all seven prisoners were freed. Place de la Bastille in the 11e and 12e, where the prison once stood, is now a very busy traffic roundabout.

The Islands

Paris' twinset of islands could not be more different. Île de la Cité is bigger, full of sights and very touristed (though very few people actually live here). Downstream, villagelike Île St-Louis is residential and much quieter, with just enough boutiques and restaurants – and legendary ice-cream maker Berthillon – to attract visitors.

STE-CHAPELLE   Chapel

(Map p66; 4 bd du Palais, 1er; adult/child €8/free; ⏰9.30am-5 or 6pm; Ⓜ Cité) The most exquisite of Paris' Gothic monuments, Ste-Chapelle is tucked away within the walls of the Palais de Justice (Law Courts).

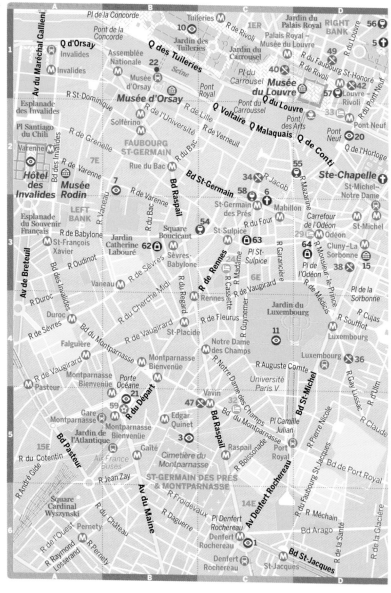

DISCOVER PARIS & AROUND

Built in just under three years (compared with nearly 200 years for Notre Dame), Ste-Chapelle was consecrated in 1248. The chapel was conceived by Louis IX to house his personal collection of holy relics (now kept in the treasury of Notre Dame).

A joint ticket with the Conciergerie (p67) costs €11.

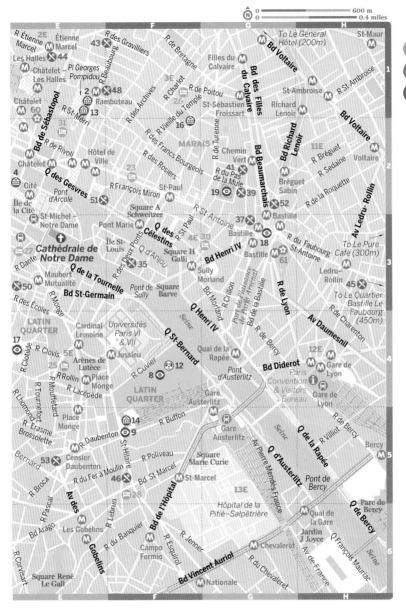

CONCIERGERIE   Monument
(Map p66; 2 bd du Palais, 1er; adult/child €7/free;
⏱9.30am-5 or 6pm; MCité) Built as a
royal palace in the 14th century for the
concierge of the Palais de la Cité, the

Conciergerie was the main prison during
the Reign of Terror (1793–94) and was
used to incarcerate alleged enemies of
the Revolution before they were brought

Central Paris – South

before the Revolutionary Tribunal in the Palais de Justice next door.

A joint ticket for the Conciergerie and Ste-Chapelle costs €11.

PONT NEUF Bridge
(Map p66; **M** Pont Neuf) The sparkling-white stone spans of Paris' oldest bridge, Pont Neuf – literally 'New Bridge' – have linked the western end of the Île de la Cité with both banks of the Seine since 1607. The seven arches, best seen from the river, are decorated with humorous and grotesque figures of barbers, dentists, pickpockets, loiterers etc.

Latin Quarter & Jardin des Plantes

The centre of Parisian higher education since the Middle Ages, the Latin Quarter is so called because conversation between students and professors until the Revolution was in Latin.

MUSÉE NATIONAL DU MOYEN ÂGE
History Museum

(Map p66; www.musee-moyenage.fr; 6 place Paul Painlevé, 5e; adult/child €8.50/free; ☉9.15am-5.45pm Wed-Mon; Ⓜ Cluny–La Sorbonne or St-Michel) The spectacular displays at the city's medieval museum include statuary, illuminated manuscripts, weapons, furnishings, and objets d'art made of gold, ivory and enamel. But nothing compares with *La Dame à la Licorne* (The Lady with the Unicorn), a sublime series of late-15th-century tapestries from the southern Netherlands now hung in circular room 13 on the 1st floor.

PANTHÉON
Monument

(Map p66; place du Panthéon, 5e; adult/child €8/free; ☉10am-6.30pm Apr-Sep, to 6pm Oct-Mar; Ⓜ Luxembourg) The Panthéon is a superb example of 18th-century neoclassicism,

but its ornate marble interior is gloomy in the extreme. The 80-odd permanent residents of the crypt include Voltaire, Jean-Jacques Rousseau, Victor Hugo, Émile Zola, Jean Moulin and Nobel Prize winner Marie Curie, whose remains were moved here in 1995 – the first woman to be interred here.

JARDIN DES PLANTES
Botanical Garden

(Map p66; 57 rue Cuvier & 3 quai St-Bernard, 5e; ☉7.30am-7pm; Ⓜ Gare d'Austerlitz, Censier Daubenton or Jussieu) Paris' 24-hectare Jardin des Plantes was founded in 1626 as a medicinal herb garden for Louis XIII. Here you'll find the Eden-like **Jardin d'Hiver** (Winter Garden), also called the Serres Tropicales (Tropical Greenhouses); the **Jardin Alpin** (Alpine Garden; weekend admission adult/child €1/0.50; ☉8am-4.40pm Mon-Fri, 1.30-6pm Sat, 1.30-6.30pm Sun) with 2000 mountain plants; and the gardens of the **École de Botanique** (admission free; ☉8am-5pm Mon-Fri) where students of Paris' Botany School 'practise'.

The **Ménagerie du Jardin des Plantes** (adult/child €8/6; ☉9am-6 or 6.30pm), a

Musée National du Moyen Âge

medium-size zoo (5.5-hectare, 1000 animals) in the northern section of the garden, was founded in 1794.

A two-day combined ticket covering all the Jardin des Plantes sights, including all the sections of the Musée National d'Histoire Naturelle, costs €20/15.

St-Germain, Odéon & Luxembourg

Centuries ago the Église St-Germain des Prés and its affiliated abbey owned most of today's 6e and 7e. Cafés such as Café de Flore and Les Deux Magots were favourite hang-outs of post-war Left Bank intellectuals and the birthplaces of existentialism.

ÉGLISE ST-GERMAIN DES PRÉS Church
(Map p66; 3 place St-Germain des Prés, 6e; ⏰8am-7pm Mon-Sat, 9am-8pm Sun; Ⓜ St-Germain des Prés) Paris' oldest church, the Romanesque Church of St-Germanus of the Fields, was built in the 11th century on the site of a 6th-century abbey and was the dominant church in Paris until the arrival of Notre Dame.

JARDIN DU LUXEMBOURG City Park
(Map p66; ⏰7.30am to 8.15am-5pm to 10pm according to the season; Ⓜ Luxembourg) When the weather is fine, Parisians of all ages come flocking to the formal terraces and chestnut groves of the 23-hectare Jardin du Luxembourg to read, relax and sunbathe.

Top spot for sun-soaking – there are always loads of chairs here – is the southern side of the palace's 19th-century, 57m-long Orangery (1834) where lemon and orange trees, palms, grenadiers and oleanders shelter from the cold.

Montparnasse
TOUR MONTPARNASSE
Panoramic Tower
(Map p66; www.tourmontparnasse56.com; rue de l'Arrivée, 14e; adult/child €11/8; ⏰9.30am-11.30pm Apr-Sep, to 10.30pm Sun-Thu, 11pm Fri & Sat Oct-Mar; Ⓜ Montparnasse Bienvenüe) A steel-and-smoked-glass eyesore built in 1974, the 210m-high Tour Montparnasse affords spectacular views over the city –

a view, we might add, that does not take in this ghastly oversized lipstick tube.

CIMETIÈRE DU MONTPARNASSE
Cemetery

(Map p66; bd Edgar Quinet & rue Froidevaux, 14e; ⊙8am-5.30 or 6pm Mon-Fri, 8.30am-6pm Sat, 9am-6pm Sun; Ⓜ Edgar Quinet or Raspail) Montparnasse Cemetery received its first 'lodger' in 1824. It contains the tombs of such illustrious personages as the poet Charles Baudelaire, writer Guy de Maupassant, playwright Samuel Beckett, sculptor Constantin Brancusi, painter Chaim Soutine, photographer Man Ray, industrialist André Citroën, Captain Alfred Dreyfus of the infamous Dreyfus Affair, actor Jean Seberg, philosopher Jean-Paul Sartre, writer Simone de Beauvoir and the crooner Serge Gainsbourg.

CATACOMBES
Ossuary

(Map p66; www.catacombes.paris.fr, in French; 1 av Colonel Henri Roi-Tanguy, 14e; adult/ child €8/4; ⊙10am-5pm Tue-Sun; Ⓜ Denfert Rochereau) In 1785 it was decided to solve the hygiene and aesthetic problems posed by Paris' overflowing cemeteries by exhuming the bones and storing them in the tunnels of three disused quarries. After descending 20m (130 steps) from street level, visitors follow 1.7km of underground corridors in which the bones and skulls of millions of former Parisians are neatly stacked along the walls.

Faubourg St-Germain & Invalides

Paris' most fashionable neighbourhood during the 18th century was Faubourg St-Germain in the 7e. **Hôtel Matignon** (Map p66; 57 rue de Varenne, 7e) has been the official residence of the French prime minister since the start of the Fifth Republic in 1958.

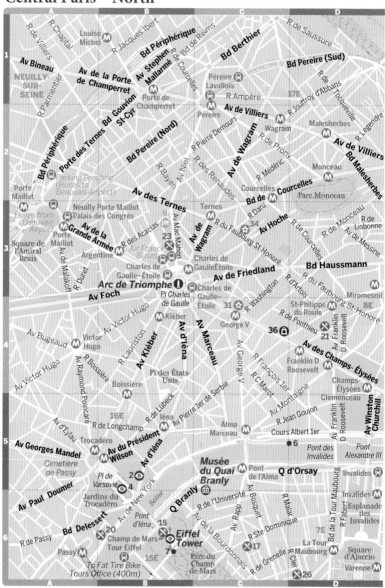

MUSÉE RODIN Garden, Museum
(Map p66; www.musee-rodin.fr; 79 rue de Varenne,
7e; adult/child incl garden €7-10/free, garden only
€1; 10am-5.45pm Tue-Sun; Varenne)

Rooms on two floors of this 18th-century
residence display extraordinarily vital
bronze and marble sculptures by Rodin,
including casts of some of his most

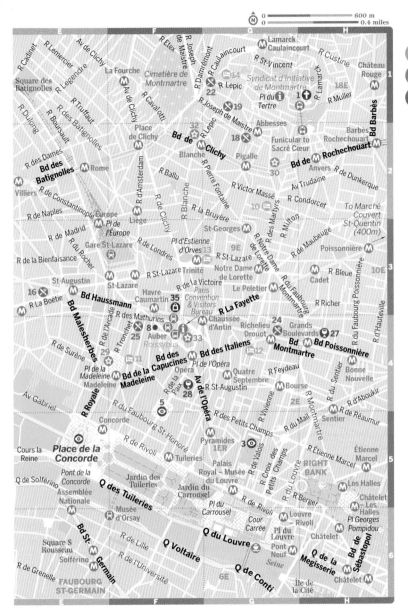

celebrated works: *The Hand of God*, *The Burghers of Calais* (Les Bourgeois de Calais), *Cathedral*, that perennial crowd-pleaser *The Thinker* (Le Penseur) and the incomparable *The Kiss* (Le Baiser).

HÔTEL DES INVALIDES

Monument, Museum

(Map p66; M Varenne or La Tour Maubourg) A 500m-long expanse of lawn known as the Esplanade des Invalides separates

73

Central Paris – North

Faubourg St-Germain from the Eiffel Tower area. At the southern end of the esplanade, laid out between 1704 and 1720, is the final resting place of Napoleon, the man many French people consider to be the nation's greatest hero.

Eiffel Tower Area & 16e

MUSÉE DU QUAI BRANLY   Art Museum
(Map p72; www.quaibranly.fr; 37 quai Branly, 7e; adult/child €8.50/free; ⊙11am-7pm Tue, Wed & Sun, to 9pm Thu-Sat; Ⓜ Pont de l'Alma or Alma-Marceau) The architecturally impressive but unimaginatively named Quai Branly Museum introduces the art and cultures of Africa, Oceania, Asia and the Americas through innovative displays, film and musical recordings. A day pass allowing entry to the temporary exhibits as well as the permanent collection costs adult/concession €10/7; an audioguide is €5.

Étoile & Champs-Élysées

A dozen avenues radiate out from place de l'Étoile – officially called place Charles de Gaulle – and first among them is av des Champs-Élysées.

ARC DE TRIOMPHE   Famous Landmark
(Map p72; viewing platform adult/child €9/free; ⊙10am-10.30 or 11pm; Ⓜ Charles de Gaulle–Étoile) Located 2km northwest of place de la Concorde in the middle of place Charles de Gaulle (or place de l'Étoile), Paris' Triumphal Arch is the world's largest traffic roundabout. It was commissioned by Napoleon in 1806, but not completed until 1836. Since 1920, the body of an **Unknown Soldier** from WWI, taken from Verdun in Lorraine, has lain beneath the arch; his fate and that of countless others is commemorated by a **memorial flame** that is rekindled each evening around 6.30pm.

DISCOVER PARIS & AROUND

IZZET KERIBAR

Don't Miss **Musée du Louvre**

The vast Palais du Louvre was constructed as a fortress by Philippe-Auguste in the early 13th century and rebuilt in the mid-16th century for use as a royal residence.

When the museum opened in the late 18th century, it contained 2500 paintings and objets d'art; today some 35,000 are on display.

The museum's prize piece is da Vinci's *La Joconde,* better known as *Mona Lisa* (room 6, 1st floor, Salle de la Joconde, Denon Wing). Other famous works from antiquity include the *Seated Scribe* (room 22, 1st floor, Sully Wing), the *Code of Hammurabi* (room 3, ground floor, Richelieu Wing) and that armless duo, the *Venus de Milo* (room 7, ground floor, Denon Wing) and the *Winged Victory of Samothrace* (opposite room 1, 1st floor, Denon Wing).

The main entrance and ticket windows in the Cour Napoléon are covered by the 21m-high Pyramide du Louvre, a glass pyramid designed by the Chinese-born American architect IM Pei. Buy your tickets in advance from the ticket machines in the Carrousel du Louvre or from the *billetteries* (ticket offices) of Fnac or Virgin Megastores (see p96) for an extra €1 to €1.60, and walk straight in without queuing. Tickets are valid for the whole day, so you can come and go as you please.

English-language **guided tours** lasting 1½ hours depart from the area under the Grande Pyramide, marked *Acceuil des Groupes* (Groups Reception), at 11am, 2pm and (sometimes) 3.45pm Monday and Wednesday to Saturday. Tickets cost €5 in addition to the cost of admission. Galerie d'Apollon

NEED TO KNOW

(Map p66; www.louvre.fr; permanent collections/permanent collections & temporary exhibitions €9.50/14, after 6pm Wed & Fri €6/12; 🕑9am-6pm Mon, Thu, Sat & Sun, 9am-10pm Wed & Fri; Ⓜ Palais Royal-Musée du Louvre); guided tours (🕿01 40 20 52 63)

The Louvre

A half-day tour

Successfully visiting the Louvre is a fine art. Its complex labyrinth of galleries and staircases spiralling three wings and four floors renders discovery a snakes-and-ladders experience. Initiate yourself with this three-hour itinerary – a playful mix of *Mona Lisa* obvious and up-to-the-minute unexpected.

Arriving by the stunning main entrance, pick up colour-coded floor plans at the lower-ground-floor information desk ❶ beneath IM Pei's glass pyramid, ride the escalator up to the Sully Wing and swap passport for multimedia guide (there are limited descriptions in the galleries) at the wing entrance.

The Louvre is as much about spectacular architecture as masterly art. To appreciate this zip up and down Sully's Escalier Henri II to admire *Venus de Milo* ❷, then up parallel Escalier Henri IV to the palatial displays in Cour Khorsabad ❸. Cross room 1 to find the escalator up to the 1st floor and staircase-as-art *L'Esprit d'Escalier* ❹. Next traverse 25 consecutive galleries (thank you, floor plan!) to flip conventional contemplation on its head with Cy Twombly's *The Ceiling* ❺, and the hypnotic *Winged Victory of Samothrace* sculpture ❻ – just two rooms away – which brazenly insists on being admired from all angles. End with the impossibly famous *Liberty Leading the People* ❼, *Mona Lisa* ❽ and *Virgin & Child* ❾.

TOP TIPS

Cent saver Visit after 3pm or in the evening when tickets are cheaper

Crowd dodgers The Denon Wing is always packed; visit on late nights Wednesday or Friday or trade Denon in for the notably quieter Richelieu Wing

2nd floor Not for first-timers: save its more specialist works for subsequent visits

Multimedia guide Worth it, if only to press the 'Where am I?' button when lost

Mission Mona Lisa

If you just want to venerate the Louvre's most famous lady, use the Porte des Lions entrance, from where it's a five-minute walk. Go up one flight of stairs and through rooms 26, 14 and 13 to the Grande Galerie and adjoining room 6.

L'Esprit d'Escalier
Escalier Lefuel, Richelieu
Discover the 'Spirit of the Staircase' through François Morel-let's contemporary stained glass, which casts new light on old stone. DETOUR» Napoleon III's gorgeous gilt apartments.

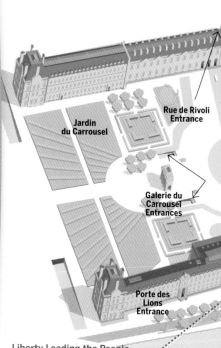

Rue de Rivoli Entrance

Jardin du Carrousel

Galerie du Carrousel Entrances

Porte des Lions Entrance

Liberty Leading the People
Room 77, 1st Floor, Denon
Decipher the politics behind French romanticism in Eugène Delacroix's rousing early 19th-century canvas and Théodore Géricault's *The Raft of the Medusa*.

BILL BACHMANN/ALAMY

Cour Khorsabad
Ground Floor, Richelieu
Time travel with a pair of winged human-headed bulls to view some of the world's oldest Mesopotamian art. **DETOUR»** Night-lit statues in Cour Puget.

ANTOINE MONGODIN/MUSÉE DU LOUVRE

WITOLD SKRYPCZAK

Venus de Milo
Room 7, Ground Floor, Sully
No one knows who sculpted this seductively realistic goddess from Greek antiquity. Naked to the hips, she is a Hellenistic masterpiece.

The Ceiling
Room 32, 1st Floor, Sully
Admire the blue shock of Cy Twombly's 400-sq-metre contemporary ceiling fresco – the Louvre's latest, daring commission. **DETOUR»** *The Braque Ceiling*, room 33.

SULLY WING

Cour Khorsabad

❸

❹

Cour Puget

Cour Marly

Cour Carrée

RICHELIEU WING

❺

Cour Napoléon

❶

❷

Pyramid Main Entrance

Inverted Pyramid

❻

❼ ❽ **Cour Visconti**

❾

Pont des Arts

DENON WING

Pont du Carrousel

Virgin & Child
Room 5, Grande Galerie, 1st Floor, Denon
In the spirit of artistic devotion save the Louvre's most famous gallery for last: a feast of Virgin-and-child paintings by Raphael, Domenico Ghirlandaio, Giovanni Bellini and Francesco Botticini.

Mona Lisa
Room 6, 1st Floor, Denon
No smile is as enigmatic or bewitching as hers. Da Vinci's diminutive *La Joconde* hangs opposite the largest painting in the Louvre – sumptuous, fellow Italian Renaissance artwork *The Wedding at Cana*.

TERRY SMITH/ALAMY

Winged Victory of Samothrace
Escalier Daru, 1st Floor, Sully
Draw breath at the aggressive dynamism of this headless, handless Hellenistic goddess. **DETOUR»** The razzle-dazzle of the Apollo Gallery's crown jewels.

Tickets to the viewing platform of the Arc de Triomphe are sold in the underground passageway that surfaces on the even-numbered side of av des Champs-Élysées.

PLACE DE LA CONCORDE City Square
(Map p72; M Concorde) The 3300-year-old pink granite obelisk with the gilded top in the middle of Place de la Concorde once stood in the Temple of Ramses at Thebes (today's Luxor) and was given to France in 1831 by Muhammad Ali, viceroy and pasha of Egypt.

Tours

FAT TIRE BIKE TOURS Bicycle Tours
(Map p72; 01 56 58 10 54; www.fattirebiketours.com; 24 rue Edgar Faure, 15e; M La Motte Picquet Grenelle) Bike tours by day (€28; four hours) and night; to Versailles, Monet's garden (Giverny) and the Normandy beaches.

BATEAUX MOUCHES Boat Tours
(Map p72; 01 42 25 9610; www.bateauxmouches.com; Port de la Conférence, 8e; adult/child €10/5; Mar-Nov; M Alma Marceau) Based on the Right Bank just east of Pont de l'Alma, Paris's most famous riverboat company runs 1000-seat tour boats, the biggest on the Seine.

PARIS CANAL CROISIÈRES Canal Cruises
(Map p66; 01 42 40 96 97; www.pariscanal.com; Bassin de la Villette, 19-21 quai de la Loire, 19e; adult/child €17/10; Mar-Nov; M Jaurès or Musée d'Orsay) This company runs daily 2½-hour cruises departing from near the Musée d'Orsay (quai Anatole France, 7e) for Bassin de la Villette, 19e, via charming Canal St-Martin and Canal de l'Ourcq.

L'OPEN TOUR Bus Tours
(Map p72; 01 42 66 56 56; www.pariscityrama.com; 13 rue Auber, 9e; 1 day adult/child €29/15; M Havre Caumartin or Opéra) This company runs open-deck buses along four circuits and you can jump on/off at more than 50 stops. Buy tickets from the driver.

PARIS GO Walking Tours
(www.parisgo.fr; €20) Two-hour thematic tours followed by drinks in a local café or bar.

PARIS GREETER Walking Tours
(www.parisiendunjour.fr; donation) See Paris through local eyes with these two- to three-hour city tours. Minimum two weeks' advance notice needed.

PARIS WALKS Walking Tours
(www.paris-walks.com; adult/child €12/8) Long established and highly rated by our readers, Paris Walks offers thematic tours (fashion, chocolate, the French Revolution) in English.

Bateaux mouches, River Seine
PHOTOGRAPHER: JOHN ELK III

Sleeping

The Paris Convention & Visitors Bureau (p98), particularly the Gare du Nord branch, can find you a place to stay for the night of the day you stop by and will make the booking for free.

Louvre & Les Halles

The area encompassing the Musée du Louvre and the Forum des Halles, effectively the 1er and a small slice of the 2e, is very central but don't expect to find tranquillity or many bargains here.

LE RELAIS DU LOUVRE
Boutique Hotel €€

(Map p66; ☎01 40 41 96 42; www.relaisdulouvre.
com; 19 rue des Prêtres St-Germain l'Auxerrois, 1er; s €125, d €170-215, tr €215; ✳️ 🛜 Ⓜ️Pont Neuf) If you're someone who likes style in a traditional sense, pick this lovely 21-room hotel just west of the Louvre and south of Église St-Germain l'Auxerrois.

Marais & Bastille

HÔTEL DU PETIT MOULIN
Boutique Hotel €€€

(Map p66; ☎01 42 74 10 10; www.hoteldu petitmoulin.com; 29-31 rue de Poitou, 3e; r €190-290; ✳️ @ 🛜 Ⓜ️Filles du Calvaire) This scrumptious boutique hotel (OK, we're impressed that it was a bakery at the time of Henri IV) was designed from top to bottom by Christian Lacroix and features 17 completely different rooms.

HÔTEL ST-MERRY
Historic Hotel €€

(Map p66; ☎01 42 78 14 15; www.hotelmarais.
com; 78 rue de la Verrerie, 4e; r €135-230, tr €205-275; ✳️ 🛜 Ⓜ️Châtelet) The interior of this 12-room hostelry, with beamed ceilings, church pews and wrought-iron candelabra, is a neogoth's wet dream. On the downside there is no lift connecting the postage-stamp lobby with the four upper floors, and only some of the rooms have air conditioning.

LE GÉNERAL HÔTEL
Design Hotel €€

(Map p66; ☎01 47 00 41 57; www.legeneralhotel.
com; 5-7 rue Rampon, 11e; s €155-175, d €190-220, tr €220-250; ✳️ 🛜 Ⓜ️République) This hotel

Museum Pass

The **Paris Museum Pass** (www.
parismuseumpass.fr; 2/4/6 days €32/48/64) is valid for entry to some 38 venues in Paris – including the Louvre, Centre Pompidou, Musée d'Orsay and Musée du Quai Branly. Buy the pass online, at participating venues, branches of the Paris Convention & Visitors Bureau (p98), Fnac outlets (p96), RATP (Régie Autonome des Transports Parisians) information desks and major metro stations.

is whiter than pale on the outside and a bonbon box of cherry and chocolate tones within. The décor at 'The General' is fresh and fun, and the 47 rooms are beautifully furnished.

LE QUARTIER BASTILLE LE FAUBOURG
Family Hotel €€

(off Map p66; ☎01 43 70 04 04; www.lequartier hotelbf.com; 9 rue de Reuilly, 12e; s €113-168, d €133-163; ✳️ 🛜 Ⓜ️Gare de Lyon) This warm and welcoming boutique hotel has 42 generously sized rooms with all the comforts and then some, including apples on the bed and free liquorice at reception! Rooms are paired and share an internal hallway.

HÔTEL ST-LOUIS MARAIS
Historic Hotel €€

(Map p66; ☎01 48 87 87 04; www.saintlouis marais.com; 1 rue Charles V, 4e; s €99, d & tw €115-140, tr €150; 🛜 Ⓜ️Sully Morland) This charming hotel sporting wooden beams, terracotta tiles and heavy brocade drapes is in a converted 17th-century convent. Four floors but no lift; wi-fi costs €5.

HÔTEL CARON DE BEAUMARCHAIS
Boutique Hotel €€

(Map p66; ☎01 42 72 34 12; www.carondebeau marchais.com; 12 rue Vieille du Temple, 4e; r €125-162; ✳️ 🛜 Ⓜ️St-Paul) Decorated like an 18th-century private house, this themed hotel has to be seen to be believed.

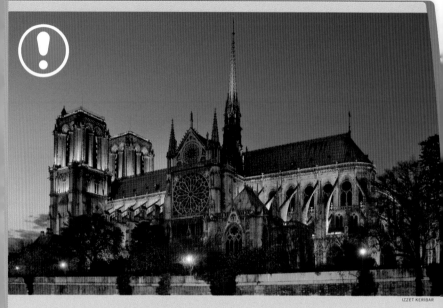

IZZET KERIBAR

Don't Miss **Cathédrale de Notre Dame de Paris**

Notre Dame, the most visited site in Paris, with 10 million people crossing its threshold each year, is not just a masterpiece of French Gothic architecture but has also been the focus of Catholic Paris for seven centuries. Constructed on a site occupied by earlier churches – and, a millennium before that, a Gallo-Roman temple – it was begun in 1163 and largely completed by the mid-14th century. The cathedral is on a very grand scale; the interior alone is 130m long, 48m wide and 35m high and can accommodate more than 6000 worshippers.

Inside, exceptional features include three spectacular **rose windows**, the most renowned of which is the 10m-wide one over the western facade above the 7800-pipe organ, and the window on the northern side of the transept, which has remained virtually unchanged since the 13th century. There are free 1½-hour guided tours of the cathedral in English at noon on Wednesday, at 2pm on Thursday and at 2.30pm on Saturday.

The entrance to the **Tours de Notre Dame**, which can be climbed, is from the North Tower, to the right and around the corner as you walk out of the cathedral's main doorway. The 422 spiralling steps bring you to the top of the west facade, where you'll find yourself face to face with many of the cathedral's most frightening gargoyles, the 13-tonne bell Emmanuel (all the cathedral's bells are named) in the South Tower, and a spectacular view of Paris.

NEED TO KNOW

(Map p66; www.cathedraledeparis.com; 6 place du Parvis Notre Dame, 4e; audioguide €5; ⏰8am-6.45pm Mon-Fri, 8am-7.15pm Sat & Sun; Ⓜ Cité); Tours de Notre Dame (Notre Dame towers; rue du Cloître Notre Dame; adult/child €8/free; ⏰10am-6.30pm Apr-Jun & Sep, 9am-7.30pm Mon-Fri, 9am-11pm Sat & Sun Jul & Aug, 10am-5.30pm Oct-Mar)

Latin Quarter & Jardin des Plantes

There are dozens of attractive midrange hotels in the Latin Quarter, including a cluster near the Sorbonne and another group along the lively rue des Écoles.

HÔTEL LA DEMEURE
Boutique Hotel €€

(Map p66; ☎01 43 37 81 25; www.hotella demeureparis.com; 51 bd St-Marcel, 13e; s/d €165/202; ❄ @ ☎ Ⓜ Gobelins) This elegant little number at the bottom of the 5e is the domain of a charming father–son team (a former professional lawyer and a doctor, no less) who speak perfect English and are always at hand.

HÔTEL HENRI IV RIVE GAUCHE
Hotel €€€

(Map p66; ☎01 46 33 20 20; www.henri-paris-hotel.com; 9-11 rue St-Jacques, 5e; s/d/tr €159/185/210; ❄ @ ☎ Ⓜ St-Michel Notre Dame or Cluny–La Sorbonne) This 'country chic' hotel with 23 rooms awash with antiques, old prints and fresh flowers is just steps from Notre Dame and the Seine – think manor house in Normandy.

HÔTEL DES GRANDES ÉCOLES
Garden Hotel €€

(Map p66; ☎01 43 26 79 23; www.hotel-grandes-ecoles.com; 75 rue du Cardinal Lemoine, 5e; d €1115-140; @ ☎ Ⓜ Cardinal Lemoine or Place Monge) This wonderful, welcoming 51-room hotel is tucked away in a courtyard off a medieval street and has its own garden.

St-Germain, Odéon & Luxembourg

Staying in the chic Left Bank neighbourhoods of St-Germain des Prés (6e) and the quieter 7e *arrondissement* next door is a delight, especially for those mad about boutique shopping.

L'APOSTROPHE
Design Hotel €€

(Map p66; ☎01 56 54 31 31; www.apostrophe-hotel.com; 3 rue de Chevreuse, 6e; d €150-350; ❄ @ ☎ Ⓜ Vavin) As much a street work of art with its stencilled facade featuring the shadowy grey imprint of a leafy tree by French artist Catherine Feff, this art

DISCOVER PARIS & AROUND SLEEPING

Detour:
Canal St-Martin

The shaded towpaths of the tranquil, 4.5km-long **Canal St-Martin** (Map p52; Ⓜ République, Jaurès or Jacques Bonsergent) are a wonderful place for a romantic stroll or a bike ride past nine locks, metal bridges and ordinary Parisian neighbourhoods. The waterbanks here have undergone a real urban renaissance in recent years, and the southern stretch in particular is an ideal spot for café lounging, quayside summer picnics and late-night drinks. Take a tour on a **canal boat** (see p78) to savour the real flavour.

hotel, on a side street off bd du Montparnasse, is style. Its 16 themed rooms, each dramatically different in décor, pay homage to the written word.

HÔTEL RELAIS ST-GERMAIN
Hotel €€€

(Map p66; ☎01 43 29 12 05; www.hotel-paris-relais-saint-germain.com; 9 Carrefour de l'Odéon, 7e; s/d €220/285; ❄ @ ☎ Ⓜ Odéon) What rave reports this elegant top-end hotel with flowerboxes and baby-pink awning gets, and for good reason. Ceilings are beamed, furniture is antique and fabrics are floral (and very fine indeed) inside this 17th-century townhouse.

HÔTEL DE L'ABBAYE SAINT GERMAIN
Patio Hotel €€€

(Map p66; ☎01 45 44 38 11; www.hotelab bayeparis.com; 10 rue Cassette, 6e; d €260-380; ❄ @ ☎ Ⓜ St-Sulpice) It's the delightfully romantic outside areas that set this elegant abode apart from the crowd. Swing through the wrought-iron gates and enjoy a moment in the front courtyard, bedecked with benches, to enjoy its potted plants and flowers.

Notre Dame

A Timeline

1160 Maurice de Sully becomes bishop of Paris. Mission: to grace growing Paris with a lofty new cathedral.

1182–90 The choir with double ambulatory ❶ is finished and work starts on the nave and side chapels.

1200–50 The west facade ❷, with rose window, three portals and two soaring towers, goes up. Everyone is stunned.

1345 Some 180 years after the foundation stone was laid, the Cathédrale de Notre Dame is complete. It is dedicated to *notre dame* (our lady), the Virgin Mary.

1789 Revolutionaries smash the original Gallery of Kings ❸, pillage the cathedral and melt all its bells except the great bell Emmanuel. The cathedral becomes a Temple of Reason then a warehouse.

1831 Victor Hugo's novel *The Hunchback of Notre Dame* inspires new interest in the half-ruined Gothic cathedral.

1845–50 Architect Viollet-le-Duc undertakes its restoration. Twenty-eight new kings are sculpted for the west facade. The heavily decorated portals ❹ and spire ❺ are reconstructed. The neo-Gothic treasury ❻ is built.

1860 The area in front of Notre Dame is cleared to create the *parvis*, an alfresco classroom where Parisians can learn a catechism illustrated on sculpted stone portals.

1935 A rooster bearing part of the relics of the Crown of Thorns, St Denis and St Geneviève is put on top of the cathedral spire to protect those who pray inside.

1991 The architectural masterpiece of Notre Dame and its Seine-side riverbanks become a Unesco World Heritage Site.

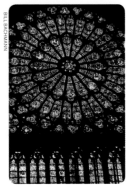

Virgin & Child
Spot all 37 artworks representing the Virgin Mary. Pilgrims have revered the pearly-cream sculpture of her in the sanctuary since the 14th century. Light a devotional candle and write some words to the *Livre de Vie* (Book of Life).

BILL BACHMANN

North Rose Window
See prophets, judges, kings and priests venerate Mary in vivid blue and violet glass, one of three beautiful rose blooms (1225–1270), each almost 10m in diameter.

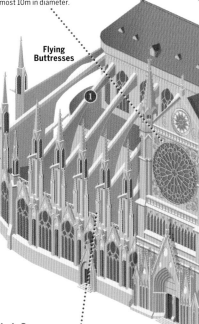

Flying Buttresses

Choir Screen
No part of the cathedral weaves biblical tales more evocatively than these ornate wooden panels, carved in the 14th century after the Black Death killed half the country's population. The faintly gaudy colours were restored in the 1960s.

SIRI/IMAGEBROKER

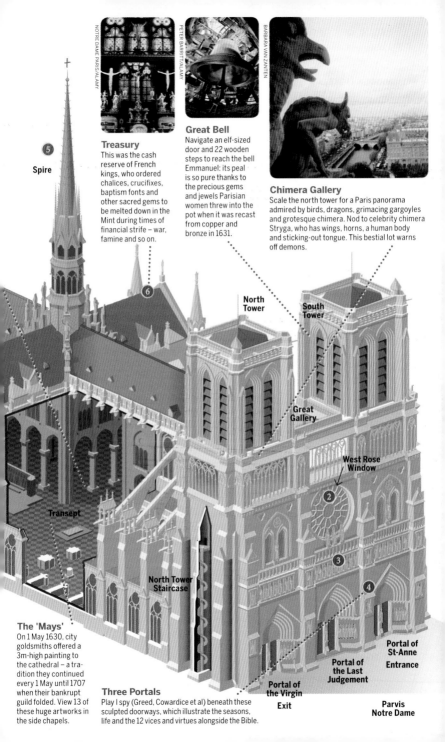

⑤

Spire

Treasury

This was the cash reserve of French kings, who ordered chalices, crucifixes, baptism fonts and other sacred gems to be melted down in the Mint during times of financial strife – war, famine and so on.

⑥

Great Bell

Navigate an elf-sized door and 22 wooden steps to reach the bell Emmanuel: its peal is so pure thanks to the precious gems and jewels Parisian women threw into the pot when it was recast from copper and bronze in 1631.

Chimera Gallery

Scale the north tower for a Paris panorama admired by birds, dragons, grimacing gargoyles and grotesque chimera. Nod to celebrity chimera Stryga, who has wings, horns, a human body and sticking-out tongue. This bestial lot warns off demons.

North Tower

South Tower

Great Gallery

West Rose Window

②

③

④

Transept

North Tower Staircase

The 'Mays'

On 1 May 1630, city goldsmiths offered a 3m-high painting to the cathedral – a tradition they continued every 1 May until 1707 when their bankrupt guild folded. View 13 of these huge artworks in the side chapels.

Three Portals

Play I spy (Greed, Cowardice et al) beneath these sculpted doorways, which illustrate the seasons, life and the 12 vices and virtues alongside the Bible.

Portal of the Virgin

Exit

Portal of the Last Judgement

Portal of St-Anne

Entrance

Parvis Notre Dame

Étoile & Champs-Élysées

This area has some of Paris' finest palace hotels and trendsetters.

HIDDEN HOTEL Boutique Hotel €€€
(Map p72; ☎ 01 40 55 03 57; www.hidden-hotel.com; 28 rue de l'Arc de Triomphe, 17e; s €245, d €285-485; ✻ @ 🕸 Ⓜ Charles de Gaulle–Étoile) The Hidden is one of the Champs-Élysées' best secrets: an ecofriendly boutique hotel, it's serene, stylish, reasonably spacious and even sports green credentials.

HÔTEL DE SÈZE Hotel €€
(☎ 01 47 42 69 12; www.hoteldeseze.com; 16 rue de Sèze, 9e; s €120-150, d €130-150, tr €160; ✻ @ 🕸 Ⓜ Madeleine) This simple but stylish establishment is excellent value for its location – so close to place de la Madeleine.

Opéra & Grands Boulevards

The avenues around bd Montmartre are popular for their nightlife area and it's a lively area in which to stay. It's very convenient for shopping as this is where you'll find Paris' premium department stores.

HÔTEL LANGLOIS Historic Hotel €€
(Map p72; ☎ 01 48 74 78 24; www.hotel-langlois.com; 63 rue St-Lazare, 9e; s €110-120, d €140-150; ✻ @ 🕸 Ⓜ Trinité) If you're looking for a bit of belle époque Paris, the Langlois won't let you down. Built in 1870, this 27-room hotel has kept its charm, from the tiny caged elevator to sandstone fireplaces in many rooms (sadly decommissioned) as well as original bathroom fixtures and tiles.

HÔTEL FAVART Historic Hotel €€
(Map p72; ☎ 01 42 97 59 83; www.hotel-paris-favart.com; 5 rue Marivaux, 2e; s €105-130, d €135-160, tr €145-180, q €155-200; ✻ 🕸 Ⓜ Richelieu Drouot) With 37 rooms facing the Opéra Comique, the Favart is a stylish art nouveau hotel that feels like it never let go of the belle époque.

Paris for Kids

Whether it's wandering around the Jardin du Luxembourg (p70) or descending into the Catacombes (p71), Paris is a great city to explore *en famille*. Museums and attractions are well geared towards kids, and many offer free or discounted entry. For general advice on family travel, see p380.

○ **Eiffel Tower** (p84) Scaling this oversized Lego set should be top of every kid's itinerary.

○ **Cinéaqua** (Map p72; www.cineaqua.com; av des Nations Unies, 16e; adult/child €19.50/12.50; ⏱10am-6 or 7pm; Ⓜ Trocadéro) One of Europe's most-ambitious aquariums, containing over 500 slippery species. The shark tank's a guaranteed winner.

○ **Cité des Sciences et de l'Industrie** (Map p52; www.cite-sciences.fr; 30 av Corentin Cariou, 19e; ⏱10am-6pm Tue-Sat, to 7pm Sun; Ⓜ Porte de la Villette) Hands-on science exhibits, two cinemas, a planetarium and even a 1950s submarine.

○ **Musée National d'Histoire Naturelle** (Map p66; www.mnhn.fr, in French; 57 rue Cuvier, 5e; Ⓜ Censier Daubenton or Gare d'Austerlitz) Paris' excellent Natural History Museum has life-sized stuffed elephants and giraffes in one building, dinosaur skeletons in the other.

○ **Ménagerie du Jardin des Plantes** (p69) Wildlife-watching in the centre of Paris, plus a maze to lose the kids in.

WILL SALTER

Don't Miss **Musée d'Orsay**

Facing the Seine from quai Anatole France, the Musée d'Orsay is housed in a former train station (1900). It displays France's national collection of paintings, sculptures, objets d'art and other works produced between the 1840s and 1914, including the fruits of the Impressionist, post-Impressionist and art nouveau movements.

Many visitors to the museum go straight to the upper level (lit by a skylight) to see the famous Impressionist paintings by Monet, Pissarro, Renoir, Sisley, Degas and Manet and the post-Impressionist works by Cézanne, Van Gogh, Seurat and Matisse, but there's also lots to see on the ground floor, including some early works by such artists as Manet, Monet, Renoir and Pissarro. The middle level has some superb art nouveau rooms.

English-language tours, lasting 1½ hours, include the 'Masterpieces of the Musée d'Orsay' tour. Tickets are valid all day, so you can leave and re-enter the museum as you please. The reduced entrance fee of €5.50 (€7 including temporary exhibition) applies to everyone after 4.15pm (6pm on Thursday). Those visiting the Musée Rodin on the same day save €2 with a combined €12 ticket.

NEED TO KNOW

(Map p66; www.musee-orsay.fr; 62 rue de Lille, 7e; adult/child €8/free; ⊙9.30am-6pm Tue, Wed & Fri-Sun, 9.30am-9.45pm Thu; Ⓜ Musée d'Orsay or Solférino); English-language tours (☏ information 01 40 49 48 48; admission fee plus €6)

Montmartre & Pigalle

Montmartre, encompassing the 18e and the northern part of the 9e, is one of Paris' most charming neighbourhoods and has loads of variety.

HÔTEL AMOUR Boutique Hotel €€
(Map p72; ☏ 01 48 78 31 80; www.hotelamour paris.fr; 8 rue Navarin, 9e; s/d €100/150-280; 🛜 Ⓜ St-Georges or Pigalle) One of the 'in' hotels of the moment, the inimitable

85

black-clad Amour (formerly a love hotel by the hour) features original design and artwork in each of the rooms and is very much worthy of the hype – you won't find a more original place to lay your head in Paris at these prices. Of course, you have to be willing to forgo television (none), but who needs TV when you're in love?

HÔTEL PARTICULIER MONTMARTRE
Boutique Hotel €€€

(Map p72; ☑ 01 53 41 81 40; http://hotel -particulier-montmartre.com; 23 av Junot, 18e; ❄ ☎ Ⓜ Lamarck Caulaincourt) An 18th-century mansion hidden down a private alleyway, this *bijou* (jewel) sparkles from every angle. Much more than an exclusive hotel, staying here is the equivalent of staying in a modern art collector's personal residence. It hosts rotating exhibitions from around the world, and has five imaginative suites designed by top French artists (Philippe Mayaux, Natacha Lesueur), and a lush garden landscaped by Louis Benech of Jardin des Tuileries fame.

Eating

Louvre & Les Halles

CHEZ LA VIEILLE French €€€

(Map p66; ☑ 01 42 60 15 78; 1 rue Bailleul & 37 rue de l'Arbre Sec, 1er; lunch menu €26; ☺ lunch Mon-Fri, dinner to 9.45pm Mon, Tue, Thu & Fri; Ⓜ Louvre-Rivoli) 'At the Old Lady's', a favourite little restaurant south of Bourse, dining is on two floors but don't expect a slot on the more rustic ground floor; that's reserved for regulars.

CAFÉ MARLY Café €€€

(Map p66; ☑ 01 46 26 06 60; cour Napoléon du Louvre, 93 rue de Rivoli, 1er; mains €20-30; ☺ 8am-2am; Ⓜ Palais Royal–Musée du Louvre) This classic venue facing the Louvre's inner courtyard serves contemporary French fare throughout the day under the palace colonnades. Views of the glass pyramid are priceless and depending on how *au courant* (familiar) you are with French starlets and people who appear in *Match*, you should get an eyeful.

Left: Arc de Triomphe du Carrousel at entrance to Jardin des Tuileries (p64);
Below: Les Deux Magots (p95)
PHOTOGRAPHER: (LEFT) CRAIG PERSHOUSE; (BELOW) WILL SALTER

LE PETIT MÂCHON
Lyonnais €€

(Map p66; ☎ 01 42 60 08 06; 158 rue
St-Honoré, 1er; starters €7-12.50, mains €14-22;
⏰ Tue-Sun; Ⓜ Palais Royal–Musée du Louvre)
Close to the Louvre, this upbeat bistro
serves some of the best Lyonnais speci-
alities in town.

JOE ALLEN
American €€

(Map p66; ☎ 01 42 36 70 13; 30 rue Pierre
Lescot, 1er; lunch/dinner menu €14/18.10 &
€22.50; ⏰ noon-1am; 🚻 Ⓜ Étienne Marcel) An
institution since 1972, Joe Allen is a little
bit of New York in Paris. The ribs are
particularly recommended.

Marais & Bastille
The Marais, filled with small restaurants
of every imaginable type, is one of Paris'
premier neighbourhoods for eating out.

CHEZ JANOU
Provençal €€

(Map p66; ☎ 01 42 72 28 41; www.chezjanou.
com; 2 rue Roger Verlomme, 3e; mains €14.50-
19, lunch menu €12.50; Ⓜ Chemin Vert) This
lovely little spot just east of place des
Vosges attracts celebs (last seen: John
Malkovich) and hangers-on with its
inspired Provençal cooking from the
south of France, 80 types of pastis and
excellent service.

LE HANGAR
Bistro €€

(Map p66; ☎ 01 42 74 55 44; 12 impasse
Berthaud, 3e; mains €16-20; ⏰ Tue-Sat; Ⓜ Les
Halles) Unusual for big mouths like us, we
almost baulk at revealing details of this
perfect little restaurant. It serves all the
bistro favourites – rillettes, foie gras,
steak tartare – in relaxing, very quiet
surrounds.

LA GAZZETTA
Brasserie €€€

(Map p66; ☎ 01 43 47 47 05; www.lagazzetta.fr;
29 rue de Cotte, 12e; lunch/dinner menus €16/38
& €50; ⏰ lunch Tue-Sat, dinner Mon-Sat; Ⓜ Le-
dru Rollin) This *néo-brasserie* has gained a
substantial (and international) following
under the tutelage of Swedish chef Peter

87

GLENN BEANLAND

Don't Miss **Eiffel Tower**

When it was built for the 1889 Exposition Universelle (World Fair), marking the centenary of the Revolution, the Tour Eiffel faced massive opposition from Paris' artistic and literary elite. The 'metal asparagus', as some Parisians snidely called it, was almost torn down in 1909 but was spared because it proved an ideal platform for the transmitting antennas needed for the new science of radiotelegraphy. Named after its designer, Gustave Eiffel, the tower is 324m high, including the TV antenna at the tip.

The three levels are open to the public (entrance to the 1st level is included in all admission tickets), though the top level closes in heavy wind. You can take either the lifts (east, west and north pillars) or, if you're feeling fit, the stairs in the south pillar up to the 2nd platform. Buy tickets in advance online to avoid monumental queues at the ticket office.

NEED TO KNOW

(Map p72; ✆ 01 44 11 23 23; www.tour-eiffel.fr; to 2nd fl adult/child €8.10/4, to 3rd fl €13.10/9, stairs to 2nd fl €4.50/3; ⏰ lifts & stairs 9am-midnight mid-Jun–Aug, lifts 9.30am-11pm, stairs 9.30am-6pm Sep–mid-June; Ⓜ Champ de Mars–Tour Eiffel or Bir Hakeim)

Nilsson who is as comfortable producing dishes like scallops with cress and milk-fed lamb confit and ice Bleu d'Auvergne cheese as he is mini anchovy pizzas.

DERRIÈRE   French   €€€
(Map p66; ✆ 01 44 61 91 95; 69 rue des Gravil-liers, 3e; starters €12-15, mains €18-26; ⏰ lunch Tue-Fri, dinner to 11pm; Ⓜ Arts et Métiers)

So secretive it's almost a speakeasy, Behind is just that – set in a lovely courtyard between (and behind) the North African 404 restaurant and Andy Walhoo bar and club. Chilled in a 'shoes-off' kind of way, this place is a lot more serious behind the scenes, serving both classic bistro and more inventive dishes. Vegetarians: more than half

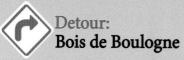

Detour:
Bois de Boulogne

On the western edge of Paris just beyond the 16e, the 845-hectare Bois de Boulogne was inspired by Hyde Park in London. Its attractions include a kids' amusement park, a château, two race-courses and the Stade Roland-Garros, home of the French Open tennis tournament.

Rowing boats can be hired at Lac Inférieur, the largest of the wood's lakes and ponds. Paris Cycles rents bicycles on av du Mahatma Gandhi (Ⓜ Les Sablons), across from the Porte Sablons entrance to the Jardin d'Acclimatation, and near the Pavillon Royal (Ⓜ Av Foch) at the northern end of Lac Inférieur.

Be warned that the Bois de Boulogne becomes a distinctly adult playground after dark, especially along the allée de Longchamp.

NEED TO KNOW

(Map p52; bd Maillot, 16e; Ⓜ Porte Maillot); rowing boats (per hr €15; ⏱ 10am-6pm mid-Mar–mid-Oct); Lac Inférieur (Ⓜ Av Henri Martin); Paris Cycles (per hr €5; ⏱ 10am-7pm mid-Apr–mid-Oct)

of the starts are meatless. Smokers: there's a *fumoir* behind the closet door upstairs.

LE TRUMILOU
Bistro €€

(Map p66; ☎ 01 42 77 63 98; www.letrumilou.com; 84 quai de l'Hôtel de Ville, 4e; menus €16.50 & €19.50; Ⓜ Hôtel de Ville) This no-frills bistro is a Parisian institution in situ for over a century. If you're looking for an authentic menu from the early 20th century and prices (well, almost) to match, you won't do better than this.

BOFINGER
Historic Brasserie €€€

(Map p66; ☎ 01 42 72 87 82; www.bofingerparis.com; 5-7 rue de la Bastille, 4e; menus €20 & €30; ⏱ lunch & dinner to midnight or 12.30am; Ⓜ Bastille) Founded in 1864, Bofinger is reputedly Paris' oldest brasserie and its polished art nouveau medley of mirror, brass and glass is stunning.

CAFÉ HUGO
Café €€

(Map p66; ☎ 01 42 72 64 04; 22 place des Vosges, 4e; mains €10.70-13.30, ⏱ 8am-2am; Ⓜ Chemin Vert) Go for the *plat du jour* (dish of the day) with a glass of wine (€12.50) or brunch (€16.20) at our favourite affordable eatery on Paris' most beautiful square – and you'll love Paris forever.

The Islands

BERTHILLON
Ice-cream €

(Map p66; 31 rue St-Louis en l'Île, 4e; ice cream €2.10-5.40; ⏱ 10am-8pm Wed-Sun; Ⓜ Pont Marie) Berthillon is to ice cream what Château Lafite Rothschild is to wine. While the fruit flavours (eg cassis) produced by this celebrated *glacier* (ice-cream maker) are justifiably renowned, the chocolate, coffee, *marrons glacés* (candied chestnuts), *Agenaise* (Armagnac and prunes), *noisette* (hazelnut) and *nougat au miel* (honey nougat) are even richer. Choose from among 70 flavours.

Latin Quarter & Jardin des Plantes

From cheap-eat student haunts to chandelier-lit palaces loaded with history, the 5e has something to suit every budget and culinary taste.

BISTROY LES PAPILLES
Bistro €€

(Map p66; ☎ 01 43 25 20 79; www.lespapilles paris.com, in French; 30 rue Gay Lussac, 5e; 2-course menu Tue-Fri €22 & €24.50, 4-course menu €31; ⏱ Tue-Sat; Ⓜ Luxembourg) This hybrid bistro, wine cellar and *épicerie* with sunflower-yellow facade is one of

If You Like...
Parks & Gardens

If you enjoy wandering around the Jardin du Luxembourg (p70), here are a few other places to stretch your legs when the sun shines.

1 PARC DE LA VILLETTE
(Map p52; www.villette.com; 🚸 M Porte de la Villette or Porte de Pantin) Opened in 1993, this is one of Paris' largest parks, enlivened by shaded walkways, street furniture and fanciful pavilions, as well as a science museum and concert hall.

2 JARDIN DU PALAIS ROYAL
(Map p72; 6 rue de Montpensier, 1er) Lovely park surrounded by elegant 19th-century shopping arcades.

3 JARDINS DU TROCADÉRO
(Map p72; M Trocadéro) Fronting the Eiffel Tower, the fountains and statues of these gardens are grandly illuminated at night.

4 BOIS DE VINCENNES
(Map p52; bd Poniatowski, 12e; 🚸 M Porte de Charenton or Porte Dorée) This 995-hectare park in southeastern Paris encompasses a château, a zoo, an aquarium and a floral park complete with butterfly garden.

those fabulous dining experiences that packs out the place (reserve a few days in advance to guarantee a table).

L'AGRUME   Bistro   €€
(Map p66; 📞 01 43 31 86 48; 15 rue des Fossés St-Marcel, 5e; starters/mains €14/30, menu lunch €14 & €16, dinner €35; ⏰ Tue-Sat; M Censier Daubenton) Lunching at this much-vaunted, pocket-sized contemporary bistro on a little-known street on the Latin Quarter's southern fringe is magnificent value and a real gourmet experience.

LE PRÉ VERRE   Bistro   €€
(Map p66; 📞 01 43 54 59 47; 25 rue Thénard, 5e; 2-/3-course menu €13.50/28; ⏰ Tue-Sat; 🚸 M Maubert Mutualité) Noisy, busy and buzzing,

this jovial bistro plunges diners into the heart of a Parisian's Paris. At lunchtime join the flock and go for the fabulous-value *formule dejeuner* (€13).

St-Germain, Odéon & Luxembourg

There's far more to this fabled pocket of Paris than the literary cafés of Sartre or the picnicking turf of the Jardin de Luxembourg.

LE COMPTOIR DU RELAIS
Bistro   €€€
(Map p66; 📞 01 44 27 07 97; 9 Carrefour de l'Odéon, 6e; dinner menu €50; M Odéon) Simply known as Le Comptoir (The Counter), this gourmet bistro has provoked a real stir ever since it opened. The culinary handiwork of top chef Yves Camdeborde, it serves seasonal bistro dishes with a creative twist – asparagus and foie gras salad anyone?

AU PIED DE FOUET   Bistro   €
(Map p66; 📞 01 43 54 87 83; 50 rue St-Benoît, 6e; starters €3-5, mains €10; ⏰ Mon-Sat; M St-Germain des Prés) This busy address with Bordeaux facade, tightly packed tables and devout crowd of regulars is an authentic bistro choice. Its classic dishes are astonishingly good value.

BOUILLON RACINE
Traditional French   €€
(Map p66; 📞 01 44 32 15 60; 3 rue Racine, 6e; lunch/dinner menu €14.90/29.50; M Cluny–La Sorbonne) This 'soup kitchen' built in 1906 to feed city workers is an art nouveau palace. Age-old recipes such as roast snails, *caille confite* (preserved quail) and lamb shank with liquorice inspire the menu.

Montparnasse

Since the 1920s, the area around bd du Montparnasse has been one of Paris' premier avenues for enjoying café life, though younger Parisians deem the quarter somewhat *démodé* and touristy these days.

JADIS   Bistro   €€€
(📞 01 45 57 73 20; www.bistrot-jadis.com, in French; 202 rue de la Croix Nivert, 15e; lunch

HUW JONES

Don't Miss **Cimetière du Père Lachaise**

The world's most visited graveyard, Père Lachaise Cemetery opened its one-way doors in 1804. Its 69,000 ornate, even ostentatious, tombs form a verdant, 44-hectare open-air sculpture garden.

Among the 800,000 people buried here are the composer Chopin, the playwright Molière, the poet Apollinaire; the writers Balzac, Proust, Gertrude Stein and Colette; the actors Simone Signoret, Sarah Bernhardt and Yves Montand; the painters Pissarro, Seurat, Modigliani and Delacroix; the *chanteuse* Edith Piaf; the dancer Isadora Duncan; and even those immortal 12th-century lovers, Abélard and Héloïse.

Particularly frequented graves are those of **Oscar Wilde**, interred in division 89 in 1900, and 1960s rock star **Jim Morrison**, who died in an apartment at 17-19 rue Beautreillis, 4e, in the Marais in 1971 and is buried in division 6.

Free maps indicating the location of noteworthy graves are available from the **conservation office** in the southwestern corner of the cemetery.

NEED TO KNOW

(Map p52; www.pere-lachaise.com; ⊙8am-6pm Mon-Fri, from 8.30am Sat, from 9am Sun; Ⓜ Philippe Auguste, Gambetta or Père Lachaise); conservation office (16 rue du Repos, 20e)

---

menus €25 & €32, dinner menus €45 & €65; ⊙Mon-Fri; Ⓜ Boucicaut) This upmarket *néo-bistro* with sober Bordeaux facade and white lace curtains on the corner of a very unassuming street in the 15e is one of Paris' most raved about (reserve in advance to avoid disappointment).

LE DÔME Historic Brasserie €€€
(Map p66; ☎01 43 35 25 81; 108 bd du Montparnasse, 14e; starters/mains €20/40; Ⓜ Vavin) A 1930s art deco extravaganza, Le Dôme is a monumental place for a meal service of the formal white-tablecloth and bow-tied waiter variety.

Top Five Food Markets

o **Marché Bastille** (Map p66; bd Richard Lenoir, 11e; 7am-2.30pm Thu & Sun; MBastille or Richard Lenoir) The best open-air market in Paris.

o **Marché Belleville** (bd de Belleville btwn rue Jean-Pierre Timbaud & rue du Faubourg du Temple, 11e & 20e; 7am-2.30pm Tue & Fri; MBelleville or Couronne) Fascinating entry into the vibrant communities of eastern Paris.

o **Marché Couvert St-Quentin** (off Map p72; 85 bd de Magenta, 10e; 8am-1pm & 3.30-7.30pm Tue-Sat, 8.30am-1pm Sun; MGare de l'Est) Iron-and-glass covered market built in 1866; lots of gourmet and upmarket food stalls.

o **Rue Cler** (Map p72; rue Cler, 7e; 8am-7pm Tue-Sat, 8am-noon Sun; MÉcole Militaire) Fabulous street market that almost feels like a party at weekends when the whole neighbourhood shops en masse.

o **Rue Mouffetard** (Map p66; rue Mouffetard; 8am-7.30pm Tue-Sat, 8am-noon Sun; MCensier Daubenton) Paris' most photogenic market street.

Eiffel Tower Area & 16e

CAFÉ CONSTANT   Modern French €€
(Map p72; 01 47 53 73 34; www.cafeconstant.com, in French; 139 rue Ste-Dominique, 7e; starters/mains/desserts €11/16/7; lunch & dinner to 10.30pm Tue-Sun; MÉcole Militaire or Port de l'Alma) Take a former Michelin-starred chef, a dead-simple corner café and what do you get? Another Christian Constant hit with original mosaic floor, worn wooden tables and a massive queue out the door every meal time. The café doesn't take reservations but you can enjoy a drink at the bar while you wait.

L'ASTRANCE   Gastronomic €€€
(Map p72; 01 40 50 84 40; 4 rue Beethoven, 16e; menus €70-190; Tue-Fri; MPassy) It's been over a decade now since Pascal Barbot's dazzling cuisine at the three-star L'Astrance made its debut, but it has shown no signs of losing its cutting edge. A culinary experience unique to Paris, reserve one/two months ahead for lunch/dinner.

LES COCOTTES   Modern French €€
(Map p72; www.leviolondingres.com; 135 rue Ste-Dominique, 7e; cocottes/starters/mains/desserts €11/16/7; Mon-Sat; MÉcole Militaire

or Port de l'Alma) *Cocottes* are casseroles and that is precisely what Christian Constant's chic space is about. Seating is on bar stools around high tables and the place doesn't take reservations. Get here at noon sharp or 7.15pm (or before) to get a table.

58 TOUR EIFFEL   Modern French €€
(Map p72; 01 45 55 20 04; www.restaurants-toureiffel.com; 1st level, Champ de Mars, 7e; lunch/dinner menus €17.50 & €22.50/65; 11.30am-5.30pm & 6.30-11pm; MChamp de Mars–Tour Eiffel or Bir Hakeim) If you're intrigued by the idea of a meal in the Tower, this is a pretty good choice. It may not be the caviar and black truffles of Jules Verne (on the 2nd level), but Alain Ducasse did sign off on the menu, making it far more than just another tourist cafeteria.

Étoile & Champs-Élysées

The 8e *arrondissement* around the Champs-Élysées is known for its big-name chefs (Alain Ducasse, Pierre Gagnaire, Guy Savoy) and culinary icons (Taillevent), but there are all sorts of under-the-radar restaurants scattered in the back streets where Parisians who live and work in the area dine.

BISTROT DU SOMMELIER

French, Bistro €€€

(Map p72; ☎ 01 42 65 24 85; www.bistrotdu sommelier.com; 97 bd Haussmann, 8e; lunch menu €33, incl wine €43, dinner menus €65-110; ⏲Mon-Fri; Ⓜ St-Augustin) If you're as serious about wine as you are about food, dine here. Indeed the whole point of this attractive eatery is to match wine with food, aided by one of the world's foremost sommeliers, Philippe Faure-Brac.

LE BOUDOIR

Modern French €€€

(Map p72; ☎ 01 43 59 25 29; www.brasseriele boudoir.com; 25 rue du Colisée, 8e; lunch/dinner menu €19/50; ⏲lunch Mon-Fri, dinner Tue-Sat; Ⓜ St-Philippe du Roule or Franklin D Roosevelt) Spread across two floors, the quirky salons here – Marie Antoinette, Palme d'Or and the Red Room – are individual works of art with a style befitting the name. The menu runs from upscale bistro to more adventurous creations such as grilled tandoori scallops and saffron rice with mango.

LE HIDE

French, Bistro €€

(Map p72; ☎ 01 45 74 15 81; www.lehide.fr; 10 rue du Général Lanrezac, 17e; menus €22 & €29; ⏲lunch Mon-Fri, dinner Mon-Sat; Ⓜ Charles de Gaulle–Étoile) A reader favourite, Le Hide is a tiny neighbourhood bistro (seating 33 people) serving scrumptious traditional French fare: snails, baked shoulder of lamb, monkfish in lemon butter. Reserve well in advance.

Opéra & Grands Boulevards

LE J'GO

Southwest French €€

(Map p72; ☎ 01 40 22 09 09; www.lejgo.com; 4 rue Drouot, 9e; menus €15-20; ⏲lunch Mon-Fri, dinner Mon-Sat; 🚼 Ⓜ Richelieu Drouot) This contemporary, Toulouse-style bistro magics diners away to southwestern France. Flavourful regional cooking revolves around a *rôtissoire* (meat on a spit), not to mention other Gascogne standards like cassoulet and foie gras.

LE ROI DU POT AU FEU

Bistro €€

(Map p72; 34 rue Vignon, 9e; menus €24-29; ⏲noon-10.30pm Mon-Sat; Ⓜ Havre Caumartin) The typical Parisian bistro atmosphere adds to the charm of the 'King of Hotpots', but what you really come here for is its *pot au feu,* a stockpot of beef, root vegetables and herbs stewed together, with the stock served as starter and the meat and veg as main course. No bookings.

Scallops from rue Cler market

MARTIN MOOS

HÔTEL DU NORD Modern French €€
(☎ 01 40 40 78 78; www.hoteldunord.org; 102 quai de Jemmapes, 10e; lunch menu €13.50, mains €15-23; ⏲ 9am-2.30am; ☎ M Jacques Bonsergent) The setting for the eponymous 1938 film starring Louis Jouvet and Arletty, the interior of this vintage café feels as if it is stuck in a time warp with its zinc counter, red velvet curtains and old piano. Food is definitely modernist, though.

Montmartre & Pigalle

When you've got Sacré Cœur, place du Tertre and Paris literally at your feet, who needs decent restaurants? But that's not to say that everything is a write-off in this well-trodden tourist area. You just have to pick and choose a bit more carefully than elsewhere in Paris.

LA MASCOTTE Seafood €€
(Map p72; ☎ 01 46 06 28 15; www.la-mascotte -montmartre.com; 52 rue des Abbesses, 18e; lunch/dinner menu €20/38; ⏲ lunch & dinner to midnight; M Abbesses) The Mascot is a small, unassuming spot much frequented by regulars who can't get enough of its seafood and regional cuisine.

CHEZ TOINETTE Traditional French €€
(Map p72; ☎ 01 42 54 44 36; 20 rue Germain Pilon, 18e; mains €17-22; ⏲ dinner Mon-Sat; M Abbesses) In the heart of one of the capital's most touristy neighbourhoods, Chez Toinette has kept alive the tradition of old Montmartre with its simplicity and culinary expertise. *Perdreau* (partridge), *biche* (doe), *chevreuil* (roebuck) and the famous *filet de canard à la sauge et au miel* (fillet of duck with sage and honey) are house specialities.

LE CAFÉ QUI PARLE Modern French €€
(Map p72; ☎ 01 46 06 06 88; 24 rue Caulaincourt, 18e; menus €12.50 & €17; ⏲ lunch & dinner Mon-Sat, lunch Sun; ☎ M Lamarck Caulaincourt or Blanche) We love the Talking Café's wall art and ancient safes below (the building was once a bank), but not as much as we love its weekend brunch (€17).

 **Drinking**

LE FUMOIR Cocktail Bar
(Map p66; 6 rue de l'Amiral Coligny, 1er; ⏲ 11am-2am; M Louvre-Rivoli) This colonial-style bar and restaurant opposite the Louvre's eastern flank is a fine place to sip top-notch gin from quality glassware while nibbling on olives at the vintage mahogany bar.

LE COCHON À L'OREILLE Bar, Café
(Map p66; 15 rue Montmartre, 1er; ⏲ 10am-11pm Tue-Sat; M Les Halles or Étienne Marcel) A Parisian *bijou*, this heritage-listed hole-in-the wall retains its belle époque tiles with market scenes of Les Halles and just eight tiny tables.

Les Deux Magots
PHOTOGRAPHER: BRUCE BI

Moulin Rouge (p96)

BRUCE BI

LE PURE CAFÉ
Café

(14 rue Jean Macé, 11e; ⏱7am-2am; **M**Charonne)** This old café moonlights as restaurant, but we like it as it was intended to be, especially over a *grand crème* (large white coffee) and the papers on Sunday morning.

AU SAUVIGNON
Wine Bar

(Map p66; 80 rue des Saintes Pères, 7e; ⏱8am-midnight; **M**Sèvres-Babylone)** To savour the full flavour of this 1950s wine bar, order a plate of *casse-croûtes au pain Poilâne* – sandwiches made with the city's most famous bread.

CAFÉ LA PALETTE
Historic Café

(Map p66; 43 rue de Seine, 6e; ⏱8am-2am Mon-Sat; **M**Mabillon)** In the heart of gallery land, this café, where Cézanne and Braque drank, attracts fashionable people and art dealers. Its summer terrace is also beautiful.

LES DEUX MAGOTS
Historic Café

(Map p66; www.lesdeuxmagots.fr; 170 bd St-Germain, 6e; ⏱7am-1am; **M**St-Germain des Prés)** St-Germain's most famous café, where Sartre, Hemingway and Picasso hung out.

HARRY'S NEW YORK BAR
Cocktail Bar

(Map p72; 5 rue Daunou, 2e; ⏱10.30am-4am; **M**Opéra)** One of the most popular American-style bars in the pre-war years, Harry's once welcomed such habitués as writers F Scott Fitzgerald and Ernest Hemingway, who no doubt sampled the bar's unique cocktail and creation: the Bloody Mary (€12.50).

AU LIMONAIRE
Wine Bar

(Map p72; ☎01 45 23 33 33; http://limonaire.free.fr; **18 cité Bergère, 9e;** ⏱7pm-midnight Mon, 6pm-midnight Tue-Sun; **M**Grands Boulevards)** This little wine bar is one of the best places to listen to traditional French *chansons* and local singer-songwriters.

Entertainment

Savvy up on what's on when with Pariscope (€0.40), the capital's primary weekly listings guide published every Wednesday, or **L'Officiel des Spectacles** (€0.35; www.offi.fr, in French), the city's other weekly entertainment bible, out on Wednesday too and possibly easier to handle.

If You Like…
Châteaux

If you've fallen for the splendour of Versailles, you might want to seek out some other châteaux around Paris.

1 CHÂTEAU DE FONTAINEBLEAU
(☏01 60 71 50 70; www.musee-chateau -fontainebleau.fr, in French; adult/child & EU resident under 26yr €8/free, admission free 1st Sun of month; ☺9.30am-6pm Wed-Mon summer, to 5pm Wed-Mon winter) Fontainebleau is one of the most stunning châteaux in France, with over 1900 rooms and lavish landscaped gardens to explore. Trains link Paris' Gare de Lyon hourly with Fontainebleau–Avon (€7.90, 35 to 60 minutes).

2 CHÂTEAU DE VAUX-LE-VICOMTE
(☏01 64 14 41 90; www.vaux-le-vicomte.com; adult/child €14/11; ☺10am-6pm Thu-Tue, daily Jul & Aug, closed early Nov-mid-Mar) 61km southeast of Paris, this privately owned château and its magnificent gardens were designed as a precursor to Versailles. To get there, take RER line D2 from Paris (€7.25, 45 minutes) to Melun and catch the **Châteaubus shuttle** (€3.50, four to six times daily weekends early April to early November) or a **taxi** (☏01 64 52 51 50; €15-20).

3 CHÂTEAU DE CHANTILLY
(☏03 44 27 31 80; www.chateaudechantilly. com; adult/child €12/free; ☺10am-6pm Wed-Mon summer, 10.30am-5pm Wed-Mon winter) This heavily restored château consists of two buildings: the **Petit Château** (built around 1560) and the **Grand Château**, whose 19th-century rooms are adorned with paintings and sculptures. Paris' Gare du Nord has regular trains to Chantilly–Gouvieux station (€7.40, 25 to 40 minutes), from where its a further 2km to the château.

Buy tickets for concerts, theatre performances and other cultural events at *billetteries* (box offices) in **Fnac** (☏08 92 68 36 22; www.fnacspectacles.com, in French) or **Virgin Megastores** (☏0825 129 139; www.virginmega.fr, in French). Both accept reservations by phone and the internet, and most credit cards.

Come the day of a performance, snag a half-price ticket (plus €3 commission) for ballet, theatre, opera etc at discount-ticket outlet **Kiosque Théâtre Madeleine** (Map p72; www.kiosquetheatre.com; opp 15 place de la Madeleine, 8e; ☺12.30-8pm Tue-Sat, to 4pm Sun; Ⓜ Madeleine).

Cabaret

Parisians don't tend to watch the city's risqué cabaret revues — tourists do. Tickets cost anything from €55 to €100 per person (€140 to €280 with swish dinner and Champagne).

MOULIN ROUGE   Cabaret
(Map p72; ☏01 53 09 82 82; www.moulin rouge.fr; 82 bd de Clichy, 18e; Ⓜ Blanche) Ooh la la… Paris' most celebrated cabaret was founded in 1889 and its dancers appeared in the celebrated posters by Toulouse-Lautrec.

LE LIDO DE PARIS   Cabaret
(Map p72; ☏01 40 76 56 10; www.lido.fr; 116bis av des Champs-Élysées, 8e; Ⓜ George V) Founded at the close of WWII, this gets top marks for its ambitious sets and lavish costumes, including the famed Bluebell Girls and Lido Boy Dancers.

Live Music

SALLE PLEYEL   Classical
(Map p72; ☏01 42 56 13 13; www.sallepleyel. fr; 252 rue du Faubourg St-Honoré, 8e; concert tickets €10-85; ☺box office noon-7pm Mon-Sat, to 8pm on day of performance; Ⓜ Ternes) Dating from the 1920s, this highly regarded hall hosts many of Paris' finest classical music recitals and concerts, including those by the Orchestre de Paris (www. orchestredeparis.com, in French).

LE VIEUX BELLEVILLE French Chansons
(☏01 44 62 92 66; www.le-vieux-belleville.com; 12 rue des Envierges, 20e; admission free; ☺performances 8pm Thu-Sat; Ⓜ Pyrénées) This old-fashioned bistro at the top of Parc de Belleville is an atmospheric venue for performances of *chansons* featuring accordions and an organ grinder three times a week.

LE BAISER SALÉ
Jazz

(Map p66; ☎ 01 42 33 37 71; www.lebaisersale.com, in French; 58 rue des Lombards, 1er; admission free-€20; ☉ 5pm-6am; Ⓜ Châtelet) One of several jazz clubs located on this street, this relaxed venue hosts concerts of jazz, Afro and Latin jazz and jazz fusion, and is known for discovering new talents.

LA CIGALE
Rock, Jazz

(Map p66; ☎ 01 49 25 81 75; www.lacigale.fr; 120 bd de Rochechouart, 18e; admission €25-60; Ⓜ Anvers or Pigalle) Now classed as a historical monument, this music hall dates from 1887 but was redecorated 100 years later by Philippe Starck.

Opera

OPÉRA BASTILLE
Opera House

(Map p66; ☎ 0 892 899 090; www.opera-de-paris.fr, in French; 2-6 place de la Bastille, 12e; opera €5-172, ballet €5-87, concerts €5-49; Ⓜ Bastille) Despite some initial resistance to this 3400-seat venue, the main opera house in the capital, it's now performing superbly. Ticket sales begin at a precise date prior to each performance, with different opening dates for bookings by telephone, online or from the **box office** (130 rue de Lyon, 11e; ☉ 10.30am-6.30pm Mon-Sat).

PALAIS GARNIER
Opera House

(Map p72; ☎ 08 92 89 90 90; www.opera-de-paris.fr; place de l'Opéra, 9e; Ⓜ Opéra) The city's original opera house is more intimate and glam than its Bastille counterpart, but some seats have limited (or no!) visibility. Ticket prices and conditions (including last-minute discounts) at the **box office** (☉ 11am-6.30pm Mon-Sat, at the corner of rues Scribe and Auber) are identical to those at Opéra Bastille.

Shopping

GALERIES LAFAYETTE
Department Store

(Map p72; 40 bd Haussmann, 9e; ☉ 9.30am-7.30pm Mon-Wed, Fri & Sat, 9.30am-9pm Thu; Ⓜ Auber or Chaussée d'Antin) Paris' famous *grand magasin* is a sight in itself, straddling two adjacent buildings and packed with fashion, accessories and the world's largest lingerie department. A fashion show takes place at 3pm on Fridays.

Galeries Lafayette

BRUCE BI

Flea Markets

Rummaging for bargains in a *marché aux puces* (flea-market) is a quintessentially Parisian pastime.

○ **Marché aux Puces de Montreuil** (av du Professeur André Lemière, 20e; ⊘8am-7.30pm Sat-Mon; Ⓜ Porte de Montreuil) Nineteenth-century, 500-stall *marché aux puces* (flea market) particularly known for its second-hand clothing, designer seconds, engravings, jewellery, linen, crockery, old furniture and appliances.

○ **Marché aux Puces de St-Ouen** (rue des Rosiers, av Michelet, rue Voltaire, rue Paul Bert & rue Jean-Henri Fabre, 18e; ⊘9am-6pm Sat, 10am-6pm Sun, 11am-5pm Mon; Ⓜ Porte de Clignancourt) Founded in the late 19th century and said to be Europe's largest.

○ **Marché aux Puces de la Porte de Vanves** (av Georges Lafenestre & av Marc Sangnier, 14e; ⊘7am-6pm or later Sat & Sun; Ⓜ Porte de Vanves) The smallest and, some say, friendliest of the big three.

SHAKESPEARE & COMPANY Books
(Map p66; 37 rue de la Bûcherie, 5e; ⊘10am-11pm Mon-Fri, 11am-11pm Sat & Sun; Ⓜ St-Michel) Paris' most famous English-language bookshop sells new and used books and is a charm to browse (grab a read and sink into one of the two cinema chairs near the stairs out back).

GUERLAIN Perfume
(Map p72; www.guerlain.com; 68 av des Champs-Élysées, 8e; ⊘10.30am-8pm Mon-Sat, noon-7pm Sun; Ⓜ Franklin D Roosevelt) Guerlain is Paris' most famous *parfumerie,* and its shop, around since 1912, is one of the city's most beautiful.

PIERRE HERMÉ Cakes & Chocolates
(Map p66; www.pierreherme.com; 72 rue Bonaparte, 6e; ⊘10am-7pm Sun-Fri, to 7.30pm Sat; Ⓜ Odéon or Luxembourg) It's the size of chocolate box, but once in your taste-buds will go wild. Pierre Hermé is one of Paris' top *chocolatiers* and his boutique is a veritable feast of perfectly presented petits fours, cakes, chocolate, nougats, macaroons and jam.

LE BON MARCHÉ Department Store
(Map p66; 24 rue de Sèvres, 7e; ⊘10am-8pm Mon-Wed & Fri, 10am-9pm Thu & Sat; Ⓜ Sèvres Babylone) Opened by Gustave Eiffel as Paris' first department store in 1852,

the Good Market (which also means 'bargain' in French) is the Left Bank's chic one-stop shop.

ⓘ Information

Paris Convention & Visitors Bureau (Map p72; www.parisinfo.com; 25-27 rue des Pyramides, 1er; Ⓜ Pyramides; ⊘9am-7pm Jun-Oct, 10am-7pm Mon-Sat & 11am-7pm Sun Nov-May) Main tourist office with a clutch of smaller centres elsewhere in the city.

ⓘ Getting There & Away

Air

Aéroport d'Orly (ORY; ☎ 39 50, 01 70 36 39 50; www.aeroportsdeparis.fr) Older and smaller of Paris' two major airports, 18km south of the city.
Aéroport Roissy Charles de Gaulle (CDG; ☎ 39 50, 01 70 36 39 50; www.aeroportsdeparis.fr) Three terminal complexes – Aérogare 1, 2 and 3 – 30km northeast of Paris in the suburb of Roissy.
Aéroport Beauvais (BVA; ☎ 08 92 68 20 66; www. aeroportbeauvais.com) Used by charter companies and budget airlines, 80km north of Paris.

Train

Gare d'Austerlitz (Map p66; bd de l'Hôpital, 13e; Ⓜ Gare d'Austerlitz) Trains to/from Spain and Portugal; Loire Valley and non-TGV trains to southwestern France (eg Bordeaux and Basque Country).

Gare de l'Est (Map p52; bd de Strasbourg, 10e; Ⓜ Gare de l'Est) Luxembourg, parts of Switzerland (Basel, Lucerne, Zurich), southern Germany (Frankfurt, Munich) and points further east; regular and TGV Est trains to areas of France east of Paris (Champagne, Alsace and Lorraine).

Gare de Lyon (Map p66; bd Diderot, 12e; Ⓜ Gare de Lyon) Parts of Switzerland (eg Bern, Geneva, Lausanne), Italy and points beyond; regular and TGV Sud-Est and TGV Midi-Méditerranée trains to areas southeast of Paris, including Dijon, Lyon, Provence, the Côte d'Azur and the Alps.

Gare Montparnasse (Map p66; av du Maine & bd de Vaugirard, 15e; Ⓜ Montparnasse Bienvenüe) Brittany and places en route from Paris (eg Chartres, Angers, Nantes); TGV Atlantique Ouest and TGV Atlantique Sud-Ouest trains to Tours, Nantes, Bordeaux and other destinations in southwestern France.

Gare du Nord (Map p52; rue de Dunkerque, 10e; Ⓜ Gare du Nord) UK, Belgium, northern Germany, Scandinavia, Moscow etc (terminus of the high-speed Thalys trains to/from Amsterdam, Brussels, Cologne and Geneva and Eurostar to London); trains to the northern suburbs of Paris and northern France, including TGV Nord trains to Lille and Calais.

Gare St-Lazare (Map p72; rue St-Lazare & rue d'Amsterdam, 8e; Ⓜ St-Lazare) Normandy (eg Dieppe, Le Havre, Cherbourg).

ⓘ Getting Around

To/From the Airports

Getting into town is straightforward and inexpensive thanks to a fleet of public-transport options.

AÉROPORT D'ORLY

Air France bus 1 (☏ 0 892 350 820; http://videocdn.

airfrance.com/cars-airfrance; single/return €11.50/18.50; ⏱ 6.15am-11.15pm from Orly, 6am-11.30pm from Invalides) This *navette* (shuttle bus) runs every 30 minutes to/from Gare Montparnasse (rue du Commandant René Mouchotte, 15e; Ⓜ Montparnasse Bienvenüe) and Aérogare des Invalides (Ⓜ Invalides) in the 7e.

Orlybus (☏ 32 46; www.ratp.fr; adult €6.40; ⏱ 6am-11.20pm from Orly, 5.35am-11.05pm from Paris) RATP bus every 15 to 20 minutes to/from metro Denfert Rochereau (20 to 30 minutes) in the 14e.

Orlyval (☏ 32 46; www.ratp.fr; adult €9.85; ⏱ 6am-11pm) This RATP service links Orly with the city centre via a shuttle train and the RER. Automatic rail (€7.60) to the RER B station Antony, then RER B4 north (€2.25; 35 to 40 minutes to Châtelet, every four to 12 minutes).

RER C & shuttle (☏ 32 46; www.ratp.fr; adult €6.20; ⏱ 5.30am-11.30pm) Shuttle bus every 15 to 30 minutes to RER line C station, Pont de Rungis–Aéroport d'Orly RER station, then RER C2 train to Paris' Gare d'Austerlitz (50 minutes).

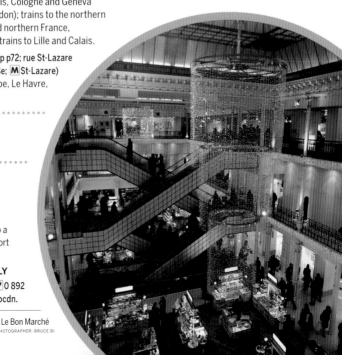

Le Bon Marché
PHOTOGRAPHER: BRUCE BI

AÉROPORT ROISSY CHARLES DE GAULLE

Air France bus 2 (☏0 892 350 820; http://videocdn.airfrance.com/cars-airfrance; single/return €15/24; ⏱5.45am-11pm) Links airport every 30 minutes with the Arc de Triomphe outside 1 av Carnot, 17e, and Porte Maillot metro station, 17e.

Air France bus 4 (☏0 892 350 820; http://videocdn.airfrance.com/cars-airfrance; adult single/return €16.50/27; 45-55min; every 30min ⏱7am-9pm from Roissy Charles de Gaulle, 6.30am-9.30pm from Paris) Links the airport every 30 minutes with train stations Gare de Lyon (20bis bd Diderot, 12e; Ⓜ Gare de Lyon) and Gare Montparnasse (rue du Commandant René Mouchotte, 15e; Ⓜ Montparnasse Bienvenüe).

RATP bus 350 (☏32 46; www.ratp.fr; adult €4.80 or 3 metro tickets ⏱5.30am-11pm) Every 30 minutes to/from Gare de l'Est and Gare du Nord (both one hour).

RER B (☏32 46; www.ratp.fr; adult €8.50; ⏱5.20am-midnight) Under extensive renovation at the time of research, with replacement buses on duty; RER line B3 usually links CDG1 and CDG2 with the city every 30 minutes (10 to 15 minutes).

Roissybus (☏32 46; www.ratp.fr; adult €9.10; ⏱5.30am-11pm) Direct bus every 15 minutes to/from Opéra (corner of rue Scribe and rue Auber, 9e).

Bicycle

Two-wheeling has never been so good in the city of romance thanks to Vélib' (a crunching of *vélo*, meaning bike, and *liberté*, meaning freedom), a self-service bike scheme whereby you pick up a bike for peanuts from one Vélib' station, pedal wherever you're going, and park it right outside at another.

Vélib' (☏01 30 79 79 30; www.velib.paris.fr; day/week/year subscription €1/5/29, bike hire per 1st/2nd/additional half-hr free/€2/4) has revolutionised how Parisians get around. Its almost 1500 *stations* across the city – one every 300m – sport 20-odd bike stands a head (at the last count there were 23,500 bicycles in all flitting around Paris) and are accessible around the clock.

One- and seven-day subscriptions can be purchased at any station with any credit card that has a microchip; as deposit pre-authorise a direct

Left: Metro running along Viaduc de Passy;
Below: Pont des Arts with Institut de France in background
PHOTOGRAPHER: (LEFT) BRUCE BI; (BELOW) RICHARD I'ANSON

debit of €150, all of which is debited if your bike is not returned or is reported as stolen). Bikes are geared to cyclists aged 14 and over, and are fitted with gears, antitheft lock with key, reflective strips and front/rear lights. Bring your own helmet.

Public Transport

Paris' underground network, also run by the RATP, consists of two separate but linked systems: the Métropolitain, or *métro*, with 16 lines and 384 stops; and the RER (Réseau Express Régional), a network of suburban lines, designated A to E and then numbered, that pass through the city centre.

Each metro train is known by the name of its terminus.

The same RATP tickets are valid on the metro, RER (for travel within the city limits), buses, trams and the Montmartre funicular. A single ticket – white in colour and called *un ticket t+* – costs €1.60 (half-price for children aged four to nine years) and a *carnet* of 10 is €11.60 (no carnets for kids).

TOURIST PASSES

The Mobilis card coupon allows unlimited travel for one day in two to six zones (€5.60 to €15.90; €4.55 to €13.70 for children aged four to 11 years). Buy it at any metro, RER or SNCF station in the region.

The Paris Visite pass covers unlimited travel (including to/from airports) and discounted entry to certain museums and activities. The version covering one to three zones costs €8.80/14.40/19.60/28.30 for one/two/three/five days. Children four to 11 years pay half-price.

Taxi

To order a taxi, call Paris' central taxi switchboard (**☎01 45 30 30 30; passengers with reduced mobility ☎01 47 39 00 91; 24hr**). You can also call or book online through the following radio-dispatched taxi companies, on call 24 hours.

Alpha Taxis (**☎01 45 85 85 85; www.alphataxis.com, in French**)

Taxis Bleus (**☎01 49 36 29 48; www.taxis-bleus.com, in French**)

Taxis G7 (**☎01 47 39 47 39; www.taxisg7.fr, in French**)

Versailles

A Day in Court

Visiting Versailles – even just the State Apartments – may seem overwhelming at first, but think of it as a house where people ate, drank, worked, slept and conspired and you'll be on the right path.

Some two decades into his long reign, Louis XIV began turning his father's hunting lodge into a palace large enough to house his entire court (to keep closer tabs on the 6000-strong army of courtiers). Sparing no expense, the Sun King employed the greatest artists and craftspeople of the day and by 1682 he'd created the most extravagant dormitory in history.

The royal schedule was as accurate and predictable as a Swiss watch. By following this itinerary of rooms you can recreate the king's day, starting with the King's Bedchamber ❶ and the Queen's Bedchamber ❷, where the royal couple were roused at about the same time. The royal procession then leads through the Hall of Mirrors ❸ to the Royal Chapel ❹ for morning Mass and returns to the Council Chamber ❺ for late-morning meetings with ministers. After lunch the king might ride or hunt or visit the King's Library ❻. Later he could join courtesans for an 'apartment evening' starting from the Hercules Drawing Room ❼ or play billiards in the Diana Drawing Room ❽ before supping at 10pm.

VERSAILLES BY NUMBERS

Rooms 700 (11 hectares of roof)

Windows 2153

Staircases 67

Gardens and parks 800 hectares

Trees 200,000

Fountains 50 (with 620 nozzles)

Paintings 6300 (measuring 11km laid end to end)

Statues and sculptures 2100

Objets d'art and furnishings 5000

Visitors 5.3 million per year

CHRISTOPHE LEHENAFF/PHOTOLIBRARY

Queen's Bedchamber
Chambre de la Reine

The queen's life was on constant public display and even the births of her children were watched by crowds of spectators in her own bedchamber. **DETOUR »** The Guardroom, with a dozen armed men at the ready.

Lunch Break

Diner-style food at Sister's Café, crêpes at Le Phare St-Louis or picnic in the park.

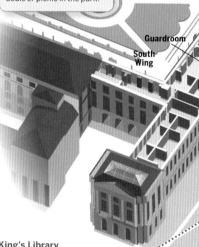

Guardroom

South Wing

King's Library
Bibliothèque du Roi

The last resident, bibliophile Louis XVI, loved geography and his copy of *The Travels of James Cook* (in English, which he read fluently) is still on the shelf here.

RADIUS IMAGES/ALAMY

Savvy Sightseeing

Avoid Versailles on Monday (closed), Tuesday (Paris' museums close, so visitors flock here) and Sunday, the busiest day. Also, book tickets online so you don't have to queue.

Hall of Mirrors
Galerie des Glaces
The solid-silver candelabra and furnishings in this extravagant hall, devoted to Louis XIV's successes in war, were melted down in 1689 to pay for yet another conflict. DETOUR» The antithetical Peace Drawing Room, adjacent.

King's Bedchamber
Chambre du Roi
The king's daily life was anything but private and even his *lever* (rising) at 8am and *coucher* (retiring) at 11.30pm would be witnessed by up to 150 sycophantic courtiers.

Council Chamber
Cabinet du Conseil
This chamber, with carved medallions evoking the king's work, is where the monarch met his various ministers (state, finance, religion etc) depending on the days of the week.

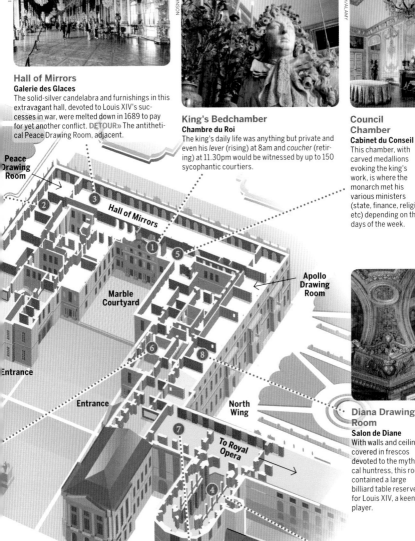

Peace Drawing Room

Hall of Mirrors

Marble Courtyard

Apollo Drawing Room

Entrance

Entrance

North Wing

To Royal Opera

Diana Drawing Room
Salon de Diane
With walls and ceiling covered in frescos devoted to the mythical huntress, this room contained a large billiard table reserved for Louis XIV, a keen player.

Royal Chapel
Chapelle Royale
This two-storey chapel (with gallery for the royals and important courtiers, and the ground floor for the B-list) was dedicated to St Louis, patron of French monarchs. DETOUR» The sumptuous Royal Opera.

Hercules Drawing Room
Salon d'Hercule
This salon, with its stunning ceiling fresco of the strong man, gave way to the State Apartments, which were open to courtiers three nights a week. DETOUR» Apollo Drawing Room, used for formal audiences and as a throne room.

AROUND PARIS
Disneyland Resort Paris

Disneyland Resort Paris, 32km east of Paris, consists of three main areas: Disney Village, with its seven hotels, shops, restaurants and clubs; Disneyland Park, with its five theme *pays* (lands); and Walt Disney Studios Park, which brings film, animation and TV production to life. The first two are separated by the RER and TGV train stations; the studios are next to Disneyland Park. Moving walkways whisk visitors to the sights from the car park.

One-day admission fees at **Disneyland Resort Paris** (✆01 60 30 60 53; www.disneylandparis.com; adult/child €52/44) include unlimited access to all rides and activities in *either* Walt Disney Studios Park or Disneyland Park.

Multiple-day passes are also available: a **one-day pass** (adult/child €65/57) allows entry to both parks for a day; the multiday equivalents – **two-day pass** (€111/94) and **three-day pass** (€138/117) – allow you to enter and leave both parks as often as you like over nonconsecutive days within one year.

Marne-la-Vallée–Chessy, Disneyland's RER station, is served by line A4; trains run every 15 minutes or so from central Paris (€6.50); the last train back to Paris leaves just after midnight.

Versailles
POP 88,930

The prosperous and leafy suburb of Versailles, 28km southwest of Paris, is the site of the grandest and most famous château in France.

Around Paris

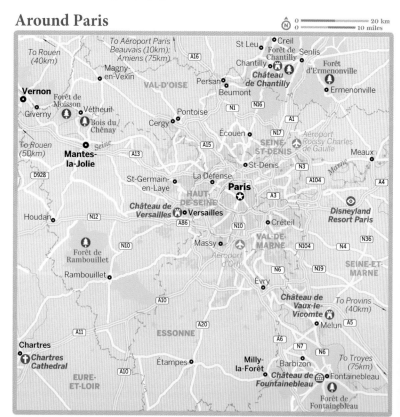

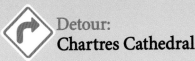

Detour:
Chartres Cathedral

Eighty-eight kilometres southwest of Paris, the 130m-long **Cathédrale Notre Dame de Chartres** (www.diocese-chartres.com, in French; place de la Cathédrale; ⏰8.30am-7.30pm, to 10pm Tue, Fri & Sun) is France's best-preserved medieval cathedral, having been spared postmedieval modifications, the ravages of war and the Reign of Terror.

A visit to the 112m-high **Clocher Neuf** (New Bell Tower; adult/child €7/free; ⏰9.30am-12.30pm & 2-6pm Mon-Sat, 2-6pm Sun), also known as the Tour Nord (North Tower), is worth the ticket price and the climb up the long spiral stairway (350 steps).

The cathedral's 172 extraordinary **stained-glass windows**, almost all of which date back to the 13th century, form one of the most important ensembles of medieval stained glass in the world. The windows are renowned for the depth and intensity of their blue tones, famously called 'Chartres blue'.

Château de Versailles (☎01 30 83 78 00; www.chateauversailles.fr; palace adult/child €15/free, Passeport adult/child €18-25; ⏰9am-6.30pm Tue-Sun) was built in the mid-17th century during the reign of Louis XIV – the Roi Soleil (Sun King) – to project the absolute power of the French monarchy. It is currently undergoing a €400 million restoration program and until it's completed in 2020 at least a part of the palace is likely to be clad in scaffolding when you visit.

The château complex comprises four main sections: the **palais** (palace building), a 580m-long structure with multiple wings, grand halls, sumptuous bedchambers and the Grands Appartements du Roi et de la Reine; the vast gardens, canals and pools to the west of the palace; two much smaller palaces, the **Grand Trianon** and, a few hundred metres to the east, the **Petit Trianon**; and the **Hameau de la Reine** (Queen's Hamlet).

The basic palace ticket and more elaborate Passeport both include an English-language audioguide and allow visitors to freely visit the King's and Queen's State Apartments, Royal Chapel, the **Appartements du Dauphin et de la Dauphine** (Dauphin's and Dauphine's Apartments) and various galleries. The so-called Passeport additionally gets you into the two Trianons and, in high season, the Hameau de la Reine and the Grandes Eaux Musicales fountain displays.

Try to time your visit for the **Grandes Eaux Musicales** (adult/child €8/6; ⏰11am-noon & 3.30-5pm Tues, Sat & Sun Apr-Sep) or the after-dark **Grandes Eaux Nocturnes** (adult/child €21/17; ⏰9-11.30pm Sat & Sun mid-Jun–Aug), truly magical 'dancing water' displays set to music composed by baroque- and classical-era composers throughout the grounds in summer.

The queues are longest on Tuesday, when many of Paris' museums are closed, and on Sunday. Most importantly, buy your château ticket in advance online (www.chateauversailles.fr) or from a branch of Fnac.

ⓘ Getting There & Away

BUS RATP bus 171 (€1.60 or one metro/bus ticket, 35 minutes) links Pont de Sèvres metro station (15e) in Paris with the place d'Armes every six to nine minutes from between 5am and 6.30am to 1am.

TRAIN RER line C5 (€2.95) goes from Paris' Left Bank RER stations to Versailles–Rive Gauche station, 700m southeast of the château and close to the tourist office.

SNCF operates up to 70 trains a day from Paris' Gare St-Lazare (€3.70) to Versailles–Rive Droite, 1.2km from the château.

105

Normandy & Brittany

Stretching along France's northern coastline overlooking La Manche (the English Channel), Normandy has been at the centre of French history for more than 1000 years. And so it's a region awash with historical sights, from the iconic spires of Mont St-Michel and the handwoven epic of the Bayeux Tapestry to the landmark beaches of D-Day. It's also home to three of the nation's favourite 'C's – camembert, cider and the potent apple-flavoured spirit Calvados.

Across the border is Brittany. Once an independent kingdom, it's still governed by its own culture, language and fiery Celtic spirit. This wild and windswept region boasts France's craggiest coastline, as well as a whole host of prehistoric monuments, medieval châteaux and timeless towns – including the corsair city of St-Malo, delightful Dinan and its lovely half-timbered capital, Quimper.

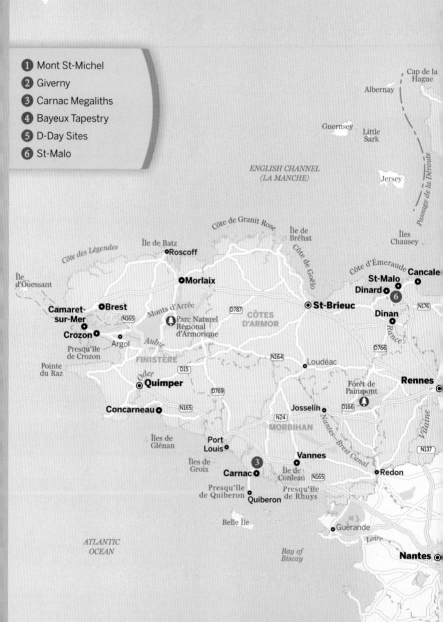

Normandy & Brittany

1 Mont St-Michel
2 Giverny
3 Carnac Megaliths
4 Bayeux Tapestry
5 D-Day Sites
6 St-Malo

Cap de la Hague

Albernay

Guernsey

Little Sark

Jersey

ENGLISH CHANNEL
(LA MANCHE)

Passage de la Déroute

Îles Chausey

Côte de Granit Rose

Île de Bréhat

Côte des Légendes

Île de Batz

Roscoff

Côte de Goëlo

Côte d'Émeraude

St-Malo

Cancale

Dinard 6

Île d'Ouessant

Morlaix

N176

Camaret-sur-Mer

Brest

Monts d'Arrée

D787

CÔTES D'ARMOR

St-Brieuc

Dinan

Rance

Crozon

Parc Naturel Régional d'Armorique

Argol

Aulne

Odet

D766

Presqu'île de Crozon

FINISTÈRE

N164

Loudéac

Pointe du Raz

D15

Quimper

D769

Forêt de Paimpont

Rennes

Concarneau

N165

Josselin

D166

Vilaine

N24

MORBIHAN

Îles de Glénan

Port Louis

N137

Îles de Groix

Carnac 3

Vannes

Île de Conleau

N165

Redon

Presqu'île de Quiberon

Quiberon

Presqu'île de Rhuys

Belle Île

Guérande

Loire

ATLANTIC OCEAN

Bay of Biscay

Nantes

Normandy & Brittany's Highlights

1

Mont St-Michel

The Mount's charm is in the *marais* (salt marshes) and the immense view – so magical, so mysterious. It evokes the crossing of the Red Sea. Pilgrims have trekked across the sand since the 8th century and it's steeped in legend. Top right: Ramparts, Mont St-Michel

Need to Know

DANGER! Take a guide to navigate the swift tides and River Couenson **TOURS** Guided walks (www.decouvertebaie. com); canoe-kayak trips (www. seakayak-fr.com) **See our author's review, p129.**

Mont St-Michel Don't Miss List

BY JACK LECOQ, WALKING GUIDE & STORYTELLER EXTRAORDINAIRE

1 THE BAREFOOT WALK

You can wear plastic shoes, but walking the 13km from Bec d'Andaine in Genêts to Mont St-Michel barefoot is wonderful. We walk across a mix of pitch sand, quicksand, sand flats and endless ripple marks made by the tides. At times we're almost knee-deep in mud.

2 ÎLOT DE TOMBELAINE

After walking for about an hour (3km) this islet, occupied by the English for 35 years (they're very patient) during the Hundred Years' War, pops up. It is now a bird reserve and, from April to July, full of exceptional birdlife. November to March, once the birds have left, you can follow a tiny footpath to the top of the islet from where an exceptional view of Mont St-Michel unfolds – quite, quite astonishing.

3 ABBAYE DU MONT ST-MICHEL

We cross the River Couesnon, the medieval border between Normandy and Brittany, and there is the Mount. The abbey is marvellous. It has beautiful works of art and rooms: the hall where pilgrims gathered is magnificent, as is the Salle des Chevaliers (Knights Hall), where monks spent hours illuminating manuscripts.

4 AVRANCHES

I was born here. After visiting the abbey it's worth going to Avranches' **Scriptoria (Musée des Manuscrits du Mont St-Michel; ☎ 02 33 79 57 00; www.ville-avranches. fr; place d'Estouteville)** where all the historical documents and manuscripts scribed at the abbey are preserved. It illuminates Mont St-Michel's many legends and stories.

5 MEMORABLE MOUNT VIEWS

The view from the Jardin des Plantes (botanical gardens) in Avranches is unique; as are the bay panoramas from Pointe du Grouin du Sud near the fishing village of St-Léonard, 5km southwest, and the clifftops in Carolles, 20km north. If you like oysters, enjoy the view from Cancale in Brittany; if wildlife is your thing, being afloat on a tiny boat in the 365-island archipelago of Îles Chausey is out of this world.

Giverny

Discover your inner Impressionist in the village of Giverny (p120), where Claude Monet lived and worked for 43 years surrounded by the gardens and lilyponds that inspired his most celebrated paintings. Also home to a museum exploring the work of American Impressionists in France, Giverny makes an ideal day trip from either Rouen or Paris. Waterlily pond, Maison et Jardins de Claude Monet (p120)

Bayeux Tapestry

Travel back a thousand years with the world's oldest comic strip, the 68.3m Bayeux Tapestry (p123), which recounts the story of the Norman invasion of England in 1066. It is believed to have been commissioned by Bishop Odo of Bayeux, William the Conqueror's half-brother, to celebrate the opening of Bayeux cathedral in 1077, although opinion is divided on where it was actually made.

HEMIS/ALAMY

JEAN-BERNARD CARILLET

Carnac Megaliths

3

If your imagination's fired by ancient history, you definitely shouldn't miss Carnac (p143). Comprising 3000 menhirs arranged in parallel lines measuring over 6km end to end, it's one of the world's most monumental prehistoric building projects. No one has managed to definitively explain exactly how – or why – the monument was built. Then again, the megalithic mystery is all part of the fun.

JEAN-PIERRE LESCOURRET

D-Day Sites

5

On 6 June 1944, six Allied divisions stormed ashore along the Norman coastline during 'Operation Overlord', otherwise known as the D-Day Landings. Though ultimately successful, the human cost of the invasion was immense; the Cimetière Militaire Américain (p126) above Omaha Beach is one of many memorials dotted along the coastline. For the historical background, head for the fascinating Caen Mémorial (p127).

Omaha Beach (p126)

St-Malo

6

Seaside cities don't come much more spectacular than St-Malo (p133), the 'Corsaire City', which is ringed by defensive walls designed by the great military architect Vauban during the 18th century. Though badly damaged during WWII, St-Malo has been impeccably restored over the last half-century; don't miss a stroll along the ramparts and a cruise to nearby Dinard (p136). Ramparts, St-Malo

Normandy & Brittany's Best...

Museums

- **Musée des Impressionismes Giverny** (p120) American Impressionism in the Norman countryside.

- **Musée de la Tapisserie de Bayeux** (p123) Follow the exploits of William the Conqueror.

- **Musée Eugène Boudin** (p127) Art aplenty in lovely Honfleur.

- **Caen Mémorial** (p127) Immerse yourself in WWII at this audio-visual extravaganza.

- **Musée Départemental Breton** (p142) Quimper's Breton-history museum.

Restaurants

- **Gill** (p121) Book early for a table at Rouen's Michelin-starred wonder.

- **Le Coquillage** (p137) Dine in serious style courtesy of celebrity chef Olivier Roellinger.

- **Restaurant Delaunay** (p135) Didier Delaunay is one of St-Malo's top gastronomic chefs.

- **Le Chalut** (p135) St-Malo's top address for seafood, bar none.

- **Les Nymphéas** (p121) Known for its imaginative take on traditional Norman dishes.

Boat Trips

- **Île de Batz** (p139) Ferries link Roscoff with this offshore escape.

- **Île d'Ouessant** (p139) Brave the waves en route to this craggy, windswept island.

- **Honfleur** (p127) Take a memorable cruise from Honfleur's historic harbour.

- **St-Malo to Dinard** (p135) Catch the water taxi between these seaside neighbours.

- **Dinan** (p144) Canal boats putter along the River Rance to St-Malo.

Things to Try

- **Cider** (p140) The Cider Museum in Argol is a great place to try Breton cider.

- **Oysters** (p137) Eat freshly shucked oysters on Cancale's quayside.

- **Crêpes** (p147) La Ville d'Ys in Rennes is one of our favourite places for Breton pancakes.

- **Calvados** Order this fiery apple brandy in any Norman bar.

- **Camembert** (p128) Sample Normandy's soft cheese at the Président Farm.

ADVANCE PLANNING

- **At least a month before** Book hotels in St-Malo, Dinard, Dinan and Rouen.

- **Two or three weeks before** Reserve your table at the big restaurants.

- **One day before** Reserve ferries to offshore islands such as the Île d'Ouessant, especially in July and August.

RESOURCES

- **Brittany Tourism** (www.brittanytourism.com) Brittany's main tourist site.

- **Normandy Tourism** (www.normandie-tourisme.fr) Normandy's main tourist site.

- **Normandie Mémoire** (www.normandiememoire.com) Multimedia D-Day site.

- **D-Day: Operation Overlord** (www.6juin1944.com) More D-Day context.

- **Cider Route** (www.routeducidre.free.fr) Site for cider-lovers.

GETTING AROUND

- **Budget flights** Fly from the UK to Dinard, Brest and Nantes.

- **Ferries** The main ports for cross-channel ferries are Roscoff, St-Malo and Cherbourg, although some ferries sail to Le Havre, Dieppe and Ouistreham (Caen).

- **Trains & Buses** Trains serve major towns, but you'll be stuck with buses to the smaller villages.

- **Car** Gives you maximum freedom, although be prepared for traffic jams and incomprehensible one-way systems in the big cities.

- **Organised minibus tours** These are an excellent way to visit the D-Day beaches. Book through the Bayeux tourist office.

BE FOREWARNED

- **Mont St-Michel** The climb to the top involves lots of steps, many of them steep. Pay attention to tide times – tides above 13.10m submerge the two car parks closest to the Mont! Arrive early or late in the day to avoid the worst crowds.

- **St-Malo** Accommodation books up fast in summer. If you decide to stay in the old city, be aware that you'll probably have to park outside, beyond the city walls.

Left: Crêpes;
Above: Vieux Bassin, Honfleur (p126)

PHOTOGRAPHERS: (LEFT) GREG ELMS;
(ABOVE) DAVID TOMLINSON

Normandy & Brittany Itineraries

History seems to be etched into the landscape all over Normandy and Brittany. From medieval towns to ancient monuments, these regions offer a smorgasbord of historic sights, not to mention a truly stirring coastline.

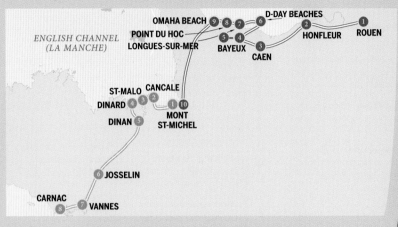

NORMAN HIGHLIGHTS

Rouen to Mont St-Michel

Start with a day exploring the old town of **(1) Rouen**, famous for its half-timbered architecture and Joan of Arc connections (the Maid of Orleáns was burned at the stake here in 1431). Factor in the Musée des Beaux-Arts and the Cathédrale Notre Dame, followed by a slap-up feed at Michelin-starred Gill and a night at Hôtel de Bourgtheroulde.

On day two head west to **(2) Honfleur** for lunch at one of the busy quayside bistros around the Vieux Bassin. Spend the afternoon at the **(3) Caen Mémorial**, which documents the history of WWII in impressive fashion. In the early evening,

arrive in **(4) Bayeux** and check in to the Château de Bellefontaine.

Day three begins with a visit to the **(5) Bayeux Tapestry**, followed by an afternoon tour around the **(6) D-Day beaches**. Detour via the massive cannons of **(7) Longues-sur-Mer** and the **(8) Point du Hoc Ranger Memorial** before finishing up at **(9) Omaha Beach**, where you can pay your respects at the American military cemetery, which featured in the opening shots of *Saving Private Ryan*. If time allows, continue to **(10) Mont St-Michel** for the start of our second tour.

THE BEST OF BRITTANY
Mont St-Michel to Carnac

5 DAYS

This whistle-stop tour of Brittany begins just across the Norman border at **(1) Mont St-Michel**, France's famous island abbey. The crowds can get oppressive in summer, so try and arrive early in the day to dodge the crush; better still, spend the day taking a guided walk across the sands, followed by an unforgettable night-time visit.

On day two spin along the coast to sample fresh oysters in **(2) Cancale** before arriving at the walled city of **(3) St-Malo**, where you can take a walk around the town's ramparts and choose from plenty of excellent restaurants. On day three catch the boat across the water to the elegant resort town of **(4) Dinard**, a favourite seaside getaway for wealthy Parisians since the days of the belle époque.

On day four visit delightfully medieval **(5) Dinan** before cutting across Brittany's centre to visit the **(6) Château de Josselin**. It's a bit of a drive, but you should just about have time to continue to another of Brittany's ancient fortified towns, **(7) Vannes**. Spend your last day exploring the monumental **(8) Alignements de Carnac**, the largest prehistoric structure anywhere on earth.

Chapelle de la Vierge, Cathédrale Notre Dame (p119), Rouen
PHOTOGRAPHER: HANNAH LEVY

Discover Normandy & Brittany

Gros Horloge, Rouen
PHOTOGRAPHER: JOHN ELK III

NORMANDY

Ever since the armies of William the Conqueror set sail from its shores in 1066, Normandy has played a pivotal role in European history, from the Norman invasion of England to the Hundred Years War and the D-Day beach landings of 1944. This rich and often brutal past is what draws travellers to the region today, though the pastoral landscapes, small fishing ports, dramatic coastline and waistline-expanding cuisine are all equally good reasons to include this accessible and beautiful chunk of France in any trip.

Rouen

POP 119,900

With its elegant spires, beautifully restored medieval quarter and soaring Gothic cathedral, the ancient city of Rouen is one of Normandy's highlights. Rouen has had a turbulent history – it was devastated several times during the Middle Ages by fire and plague, and was occupied by the English during the Hundred Years War.

Sights

PLACE DU VIEUX MARCHÉ
Square

The old city's main thoroughfare, rue du Gros Horloge, runs from the cathedral west to this square, where 19-year-old Joan of Arc was executed for heresy in 1431. Dedicated in 1979, the thrillingly bizarre **Église Jeanne d'Arc** (☉10am-noon & 2-6pm Apr-Oct), with its fish-scale exterior, marks the spot where Joan was burned at the stake.

Rouen

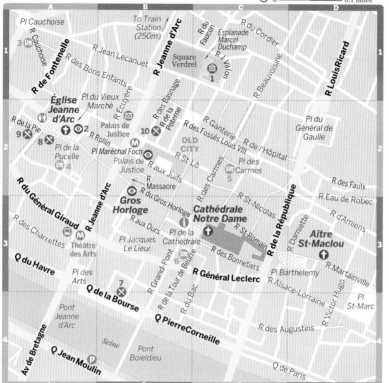

GROS HORLOGE   Clock Tower
(rue du Gros Horloge; adult/child €6/3; ⊙10am-
1pm & 2-7pm Tue-Sun) Rue du Gros Horloge
is spanned by this impressive structure, a Gothic belfry with one-handed
medieval clocks on each side. On the
west side be sure to check out the gilded
Latin inscription dedicated to Ludovico
XV (Louis XV) in 1732 – see if you can
count how many times the suffix -*issimo*
appears.

CATHÉDRALE NOTRE DAME   Cathedral
(place de la Cathédrale; ⊙7.30am-7pm Tue-
Sat, 8am-6pm Sun, 2-7pm Mon) On a site
occupied by churches since the 4th
century, Rouen's magnificent cathedral was painted repeatedly by Claude
Monet, who was fascinated by the
subtle changes of light and colour on
the cathedral's towering French Gothic

Rouen

DIANA MAYFIELD

Don't Miss **Giverny**

The tiny country village of Giverny, 15km south of Les Andelys, is a place of pilgrimage for devotees of Impressionism. Monet lived here from 1883 until his death in 1926 in a rambling house surrounded by flower-filled gardens, which is now the immensely popular **Maison et Jardins de Claude Monet**. Monet bought the **Jardin d'Eau** (Water Garden) in 1895 and set about creating his trademark lily pond, as well as the famous Japanese bridge (since rebuilt).

Giverny's other attraction is the **Musée des Impressionismes Giverny**. Surrounded by beautiful gardens, this museum displays works by American Impressionists, who flocked to France in the late 19th and early 20th centuries. It's 100m down the road from the Maison de Claude Monet.

Shuttle buses (€4 round trip; seven daily Tuesday to Sunday April to October) run by **Veolia** meet most trains to and from Paris.

From Paris Gare St-Lazare there are seven direct daily trains to Vernon (€12.50, 50 minutes), 7km to the west of Giverny. From Rouen (€10.50, 40 minutes), several trains leave for Vernon before noon; to get back to Rouen there's about one train every hour between 5pm and 10pm (till 9pm on Saturday). Jardins de Claude Monet

NEED TO KNOW

Maison et Jardins de Claude Monet (☎ 02 32 51 28 21; www.fondation-monet.com; adult/child under 12yr €6/3.50; ⊙9.30am-6pm Apr-Oct); Musée des Impressionismes Giverny (☎ 02 32 51 94 65; www. museedesimpressionnismesgiverny.com; 99 rue Claude Monet; adult/child under 12yr €6.50/3, free 1st Sun of the month; ⊙10am-6pm Apr-Oct); Veolia (☎08 25 07 60 27; www.mobiregion.net, in French)

facade. Monet would hardly recognise its recently cleaned facade, now almost white.

MUSÉE DES BEAUX-ARTS Museum
(☎ 02 35 52 00 62; esplanade Marcel Duchamp; adult/child €5/3; ⊙10am-6pm Wed-Mon)

This impressive museum is housed in a grand structure erected in 1870 and features a captivating collection of 15th- to 20th-century paintings. Artists include Caravaggio, Rubens, Modigliani, Pissarro, Renoir, Sisley (lots) and (of course) several works by Monet, including a study of Rouen's cathedral (in room 2.33).

AÎTRE ST-MACLOU Historic Quarter
(186 rue Martainville; admission free; ◷8am-8pm Apr-Oct) For a macabre thrill check out the courtyard of this curious ensemble of half-timbered buildings built between 1526 and 1533. Decorated with lurid woodcarvings of skulls, crossbones, gravediggers' tools and hourglasses, it was used as a burial ground for plague victims as recently as 1781.

Sleeping

HÔTEL DE BOURGTHEROULDE
Hotel €€€
(☏02 35 14 50 50; www.hotelsparouen.com; 15 place de la Pucelle; r €215-380; ❊🛜🏊) This stunning conversion of an old private mansion is a worthwhile treat, bringing a dash of glamour and luxury to Rouen's hotel scene. The rooms are large, gorgeously designed and feature beautiful bathrooms.

HÔTEL DANDY Hotel €€
(☏02 35 07 32 00; www.hotels-rouen.net; 93 rue Cauchoise; d €80-105; 🛜) Decorated in a grand Louis XV style, this charming place has individually designed rooms brimming with character (though bathrooms are rather less than exciting) and is passionately run by a friendly family.

HÔTEL DES CARMES Hotel €
(☏02 35 71 92 31; www.hoteldescarmes.com, in French; 33 place des Carmes; d €49-65, tr €67-77; @🛜) This sweet little hotel has 12 rooms decked out with quirky decor and vibrant colours; some even have cerulean-blue cloudscapes painted on the ceilings. You can burn off some Camembert calories by taking one of the less pricey 4th-floor rooms.

HÔTEL LE CARDINAL Hotel €
(☏02 35 70 24 42; www.cardinal-hotel.fr; 1 place de la Cathédrale; s €56-72, d €66-89; 🛜) In a super central spot facing the cathedral, this hotel has 18 simple and unremarkable rooms with lots of natural light and spacious showers. The 4th-floor rooms have fantastic private terraces overlooking the square.

Eating

LES NYMPHÉAS Traditional French €€
(☏02 35 89 26 69; www.lesnympheas-rouen.com, in French; 7-9 rue de la Pie; menus €30-70; ◷12.15-1.45pm & 7.30-9.30pm Tue-Sat) Its formal table settings arrayed under 16th-century beams, this fine restaurant serves cuisine based on fresh local ingredients (including cider and Calvados), giving a Norman twist to dishes such as farm-raised wild duck, scallops and lobster.

GILL Gastronomic €€
(☏02 35 71 16 14; www.gill.fr; 8-9 quai de la Bourse; menus €35-92; ◷Tue-Sat) *The* place to go in Rouen for *gastronomique* French cuisine of the highest order, served in an ultrachic, ultramodern dining room. Specialities include fresh Breton lobster, scallops with truffles, Rouen-style pigeon and, for dessert, *millefeuille à la vanille*.

PASCALINE Bistro €
(☏02 35 89 67 44; 5 rue de la Poterne; lunch menu €13, mains €10-20) A top spot for a great-value *formule midi* (lunchtime fixed-price *menu*), this bustling bistro serves up traditional French cuisine in typically Parisian surroundings – think net curtains, white tablecloths and chuffing coffee machines.

LES MARAÎCHERS Bistro €€
(☏02 35 71 57 73; www.les-maraichers.fr; 37 place du Vieux Marché; menu from €16, mains €11.50-32) All gleaming mirrors, polished wood and colourful floor tiles, this bistro – established in 1912 and classified a *café historique d'Europe* – has a genuine zinc bar and a warm and very-French ambience. Specialities include Normandy-raised beef.

ℹ Information

Tourist office (📞 02 32 08 32 40; www.rouentourisme.com; 25 place de la Cathédrale; ⏰9am-7pm Mon-Sat, 9.30am-12.30pm & 2-6pm Sun & holidays)

ℹ Getting There & Away

From Gare Rouen-Rive Droite (rue Jeanne d'Arc), direct train services include:

Amiens €18.50, 1¼ hours, four or five daily

Caen €23.50, 1½ hours, eight to 10 daily

Paris Gare St-Lazare €20.50, 1¼ hours, 25 daily Monday to Friday, 14 to 19 Saturday and Sunday

Bayeux

POP 14,350

Bayeux has become famous throughout the English-speaking world thanks to a 68m-long piece of painstakingly embroidered cloth: the 11th-century Bayeux Tapestry, whose 58 scenes vividly tell the story of the Norman invasion of England in 1066. A great place to soak up the Norman atmosphere, Bayeux' delightful city centre is crammed with 13th- to 18th-century buildings, including lots of wood-framed Norman-style houses and a fine Gothic cathedral.

◎ Sights

CATHÉDRALE NOTRE DAME   Cathedral
(rue du Bienvenu; ⏰8.30am-6pm) Most of Bayeux' spectacular Norman Gothic cathedral dates from the 13th century, though the crypt (accessible from the north side of the choir), the arches of the nave and the lower portions of the entrance towers are 11th-century Romanesque. The central tower was added in the 15th century; the copper dome dates from the 1860s.

MUSÉE MÉMORIAL DE LA BATAILLE DE NORMANDIE   Museum
(Battle of Normandy Memorial Museum; 📞 02 31 51 46 90; bd Fabien Ware; adult/child €6.50/2.80; ⏰9.30am-6.30pm) Using well-chosen photos (some in original colour), personal accounts, dioramas and wartime objects, this first-rate museum offers an excellent introduction to WWII in Normandy.

BAYEUX WAR CEMETERY   Cemetery
(bd Fabien Ware) This peaceful cemetery, a few hundred metres west of the Musée Mémorial, is the largest of Normandy's 18 Commonwealth military cemeteries.

🛏 Sleeping

CHÂTEAU DE BELLEFONTAINE
Historic Hotel €€
(📞 02 31 22 00 10; www.hotel-bellefontaine.com; 49 rue Bellefontaine; d €125-150, ste €150-230; 📶) Swans and a bubbling brook welcome you to this majestic 18th-century château, which is surrounded by a 2-hectare private park and has 20 enormous rooms, many of which have grand fireplaces and period mouldings.

HÔTEL D'ARGOUGES
Traditional Hotel €€
(📞 02 31 92 88 86; www.hotel-dargouges.com; 21 rue St-Patrice; d €90-120, q €280; 📶) This graceful hotel, in a stately 18th-century residence, has an elegant breakfast room overlooking a private garden, squeaky parquet floors and 28 rooms, some with period features such as marble chimneys.

🍴 Eating

LA REINE MATHILDE   Patisserie €€
(📞 02 31 92 00 59; 47 rue St-Martin; cakes from €2.50; ⏰8.30am-7.30pm Tue-Sun) This sumptuous, c 1900-style *pâtisserie* and *salon de thé* is ideal if you've got a hankering for something soft and sweet.

LE POMMIER   Traditional French €
(📞 02 31 21 52 10; www.restaurantlepommier.com; 38-40 rue des Cuisiniers; menus €14-35; ⏰ closed Sun Nov-Mar & mid-Dec–mid-Jan) Specialities at this smart restaurant include fillet of roast duck, *filet mignon de porc* and a varied selection of imaginative French dishes made with fresh Norman products, including rare heirloom vegetables.

IMAGESEUROPE/ALAMY

Don't Miss **Bayeux Tapestry**

Undoubtedly the world's most celebrated embroidery, the misnamed Bayeux Tapestry (it's actually wool thread embroidered onto linen cloth) vividly recounts the story of the Norman conquest of England in 1066. Divided into 58 scenes briefly captioned in almost-readable Latin, the main narrative – told from an unashamedly Norman perspective – fills up the centre of the canvas, while religious allegories and depictions of daily life in the 11th century unfold along the borders. The final showdown at the Battle of Hastings is depicted in truly graphic fashion, complete with severed limbs and decapitated heads (along the bottom of scene 52). Halley's Comet, which blazed across the sky in 1066, makes an appearance at the top of scene 32, while at the bottom of scene 15 there's – no, it can't be! – an 11th-century 'full Monty'.

Upstairs is an excellent exhibition on the tapestry's creation, its remarkable history and its conservation, as well as a 15-minute film screened alternately in English and French.

NEED TO KNOW

☏ 02 31 51 25 50; www.tapisserie-bayeux.fr; rue de Nesmond; adult/child incl audioguide €8/3.80; ⊙ 9am-6.15pm

---

ⓘ Information

Tourist office (☏ 02 31 51 28 28; www.bayeux -bessin-tourism.com; pont St-Jean; ⊙ 9.30am-12.30pm & 2-6pm) Covers both Bayeux and the surrounding Bessin region, including the D-Day beaches.

ⓘ Getting There & Away

TRAIN Destinations from Bayeux:

Caen €6, 20 minutes, hourly Monday to Saturday, eight Sunday

Cherbourg €15.50, one hour, 14 daily Monday to Friday, three to five on weekends

Coutances €12, 50 minutes, eight daily Monday to Saturday, four Sunday

Pontorson Mont St-Michel €21, 1¾ hours, two or three direct daily

D-Day Beaches

Code-named 'Operation Overlord', the D-Day landings were the largest military operation in history. On the morning of 6 June 1944, swarms of landing craft – part of an armada of over 6000 ships and boats – hit the northern Normandy beaches and tens of thousands of soldiers from the USA, the UK, Canada and elsewhere began pouring onto French soil.

The majority of the 135,000 Allied troops stormed ashore along an 80km stretch of beaches north of Bayeux code-named (from west to east) Utah, Omaha, Gold, Juno and Sword. The landings on D-Day – known as 'Jour J' in French – were followed by the 76-day Battle of Normandy, during which the Allies suffered some 210,000

casualties, including 37,000 troops that were killed. German casualties are believed to have been around 200,000; another 200,000 German soldiers were taken prisoner. About 14,000 French civilians also died.

If you've got wheels, you can follow the D514 along the D-Day coast and several signposted circuits around the battle sites – look for signs for 'D-Day-Le Choc' in the American sectors and 'Overlord-L'Assaut' in the British and Canadian sectors.

For details on D-Day and its context, see www.normandiememoire.com and www.6juin1944.com.

 Tours

An organised minibus tour is an excellent way to get a sense of the D-Day beaches and their place in history. The Bayeux tourist office can handle reservations.

Normandy Sightseeing

Tours D-Day Tours

(☎ 02 31 51 70 52; www.normandy webguide.com) From May to October (and on request the rest of the year), this experienced outfit offers morning (adult/child under 10 years €40/20) and afternoon (€55/35) tours of various beaches and cemeteries. These can be combined into an all-day excursion (€85/45).

Mémorial D-Day Tours

(☎ 02 31 06 06 45; www.memorial-caen. fr; adult/child €75/59) Conducts excellent four- to five-hour minibus tours around the landing beaches. The price includes entry to the Mémorial. You can book online or by telephone.

Arromanches

In order to be able to unload the vast quantities of cargo needed by the invasion forces without having to capture – intact! – one of the heavily defended Channel ports (a lesson learned in the 1942 Dieppe Raid), the Allies set up prefabricated marinas, code-named **Mulberry Harbour**, off two of the landing beaches.

The harbour established at Omaha was completely destroyed by a ferocious gale just two weeks after D-Day, but the remains of the second, **Port Winston** (named after Churchill), can still be seen near Arromanches, 10km northeast of Bayeux.

Longues-sur-Mer

Part of the Nazis' Atlantic Wall, the massive casemates and 150mm German guns near Longues-sur-Mer, 6km west of Arromanches, were designed to hit targets some 20km away, including Gold Beach (to the east) and Omaha Beach (to the west). Over six decades later the mammoth artillery pieces are still in their colossal concrete emplacements – the only in-situ large-calibre weapons in Normandy.

Omaha Beach

The most brutal fighting on D-Day took place on the 7km stretch of coastline around Vierville-sur-Mer, St-Laurent-sur-Mer and Colleville-sur-Mer, 15km northwest of Bayeux, known as 'Bloody Omaha' to US veterans. Sixty years on, little evidence of the carnage unleashed here on 6 June 1944 remains except for concrete German bunkers, though at very low tide you can see a few remnants of the Mulberry Harbour.

On a bluff above the beach the huge **Normandy American Cemetery & Memorial** (Cimetière Militaire Américain; ☏ 02 31 51 62 00; www.abmc.gov; Colleville-sur-Mer; ⏱ 9am-5pm), 17km northwest of Bayeux, is the largest American cemetery in Europe. Featured in the opening scenes of Steven Spielberg's *Saving Private Ryan,* it contains the graves of 9387 American soldiers, including 41 pairs of brothers, and a memorial in 1557 others whose remains were never found.

Opened in 2007, the **visitor center**, mostly underground so as not to detract from the site, has an excellent free multimedia presentation on the D-Day landings, told in part through the stories of individuals.

Pointe du Hoc Ranger Memorial

At 7.10am on 6 June 1944, 225 US Army Rangers commanded by Lt Col James Earl Rudder scaled the 30m cliffs at Pointe du Hoc, where the Germans had a battery of huge artillery guns perfectly placed to rain shells onto the beaches of Utah and Omaha.

Today the **site** (☏ 02 31 51 90 70; admission free; ⏱ 9am-5pm), which France turned over to the US government in 1979, looks much as it did more than half a century ago. The ground is pockmarked with bomb craters, and the German command post (no longer open to the public because it's too close to the eroding cliff) and several of the concrete gun emplacements are still standing, scarred by bullet holes and blackened by flame-throwers.

Utah Beach

Utah beach is marked by memorials to the various divisions that landed here, and the **Musée du Débarquement** (Landing Museum; ☏ 02 33 71 53 35; www.utah-beach.com; Ste-Marie du Mont; adult/6-14yr €6/2.50; ⏱ 9.30am-7pm).

Honfleur

POP 8350

Long a favourite with painters but now more popular with the Parisian jet set, Honfleur is arguably Normandy's most charming seaside town. Even though it can be overrun with tourists in the summer months, it's hard not to love this graceful beauty.

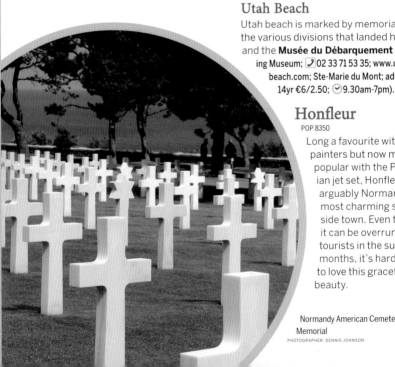

Normandy American Cemetery & Memorial
PHOTOGRAPHER: DENNIS JOHNSON

Detour:
Mémorial – Un Musée pour la Paix

(Memorial – A Museum for Peace; ☏ 02 31 06 06 45; www.memorial-caen.fr; esplanade Général Eisenhower; adult/child under 10yr €17.50/free; ☻9am-7pm, closed Mon Nov-Feb) Situated 3km northwest of Caen's city centre, this innovative memorial-museum provides an insightful and vivid account of the Battle of Normandy and the wider context of WWII.

It's a hugely impressive affair using sound, lighting, film, animation and audio testimony, as well as a range of artefacts and exhibits, to graphically evoke the realities of war, the trials of occupation and the joy of liberation.

Tickets purchased after 1pm can be used to re-enter until 1pm the next day. All signs are in French, English and German.

Its heart is the Vieux Bassin (Old Harbour), from where explorers once set sail for the New World. Now filled with pleasure vessels, this part of the port is surrounded by a jumble of brightly coloured buildings that evoke maritime Normandy of centuries past.

 Sights

ÉGLISE STE-CATHERINE — Church
(place Ste-Catherine; ☻9am-6pm) Initially intended as a temporary structure, this extraordinary church has been standing in the square for over 500 years.

Across the square is the church's free-standing wooden bell tower, **Clocher Ste-Catherine**, supposedly built away from the church in order to avoid damage to the church from lightning strikes and the clock's clanging bells.

MUSEUM EUGÈNE BOUDIN — Art Museum
(☏ 02 31 89 54 00; opposite 50 rue de l'Homme de Bois; adult/child Oct-Jun €5/3.20, Jul-Sep €6.50/5; ☻10am-noon & 2-6pm Wed-Mon) Named in honour of an early Impressionist painter born here in 1824, this museum is three blocks northwest of the Lieutenance. It features a collection of Impressionist paintings from Normandy, including works by Dubourg, Dufy and Monet.

LES MAISONS SATIE — Museum
(☏ 02 31 89 11 11; 67 bd Charles V; adult/child under 10yr €5.50/free; ☻10am-7pm Wed-Mon) The quirky Maisons Satie captures the spirit of the eccentric, avant-garde composer Erik Satie (1866–1925), who lived and worked in Honfleur and was born in the half-timbered house that now contains the museum. Each room is a surreal surprise – winged pears and self-pedalling carousels are just the start.

 Tours

WALKING TOURS — Walking Tour
(€6-7) Some of the tourist office's 1½- to two-hour walking tours of Honfleur are in English, including one that leaves at 3pm every Tuesday and Wednesday in May and June and from September to mid-October. Atmospheric night-time tours begin at 9pm Saturday from May to October.

BOAT TOURS — Boat Tour
(adult/concessions €7.50/5) From about March to mid-October you can take a boat tour from the Avant Port (across the street from the Lieutenance) out to the Seine Estuary and the Pont de Normandie – look for the Cap Christian, L'Évasion III or the larger Jolie France.

127

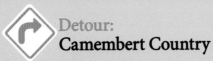

Detour:
Camembert Country

Some of the most enduring names in the pungent world of French *fromage* come from Normandy, including **Pont L'Évêque**, **Livarot** and, most famous of all, **Camembert**, all of which are named after towns south of Honfleur, on or near the D579.

The invention of Camembert is generally credited to Marie Harel, who was supposedly given the secret of soft cheesemaking by an abbot from Brie, on the run from Revolutionary mobs in 1790. The distinctive round wooden boxes in which Camembert is encased have been around since 1890; they were designed by a local engineer by the name of Monsieur Ridel to protect the soft disk during long-distance travel.

If you're interested in seeing how the cheese is made, you can take a guided tour of the **Président Farm** (☏ 02 33 36 06 60; www.fermepresident.com; adult/child €5/2; ⏱10am-noon & 2-6pm Jun-Aug, by reservation Mar-May, Sep & Oct), an early-19th-century farm restored by Président, one of the region's largest Camembert producers. It's in the centre of the town of Camembert, which is about 60km south of Honfleur.

 **Sleeping**

LA MAISON DE LUCIE
Boutique Hotel €€
(☏ 02 31 14 40 40; www.lamaisondelucie.com; 44 rue des Capucins; d €150-220, ste €315; 🛜) Former home of the novelist Lucie Delarue Mardrus (1874–1945), this marvellous little hideaway has just 10 rooms and two suites, the latter decorated with a mixture of antiques and contemporary objets d'art from far-off lands.

HÔTEL L'ÉCRIN
Historic Hotel €€
(☏ 02 31 14 43 45; www.honfleur.com/default -ecrin.htm; 19 rue Eugène Boudin; d €100-180, ste €250; 🛜🏊) This lavish Norman manor house is stuffed with porcelain, oil paintings and antique furniture, re-creating the opulence of times long past. The 30 rooms, which have thoroughly modern bathrooms, retain touches of the 1800s – alongside flat-screen TVs hung on the walls like oil paintings.

LES MAISONS DE LÉA
Traditional Hotel €€
(☏ 02 31 14 49 49; www.lesmaisonsdelea.com; place Ste-Catherine; d €165-205, ste €215; 🛜)

This beautiful old ivy-clad mansion right on Honfleur's main square and facing the church has been converted into a very sleek 30-room hotel.

 Eating

L'HIPPOCAMPE
Modern French €€
(☏ 02 31 89 98 36; 46 quai Ste-Catherine; menus €18-34) This spot is equally great for al fresco dining in the warmer months and dining inside in the cosy interior, a melange of old and new. The food is of very high quality and the evening dinner menus are surprisingly affordable.

L'ABSINTHE
Traditional French €€
(☏ 02 31 89 39 00; 10 quai de la Quarantine; menus €28-64) Facing the Vieux Port, this well-regarded restaurant serves up sumptuous, sophisticated French cuisine – made with seasonally fresh produce – in the finest *gastronomique* tradition.

 **Information**

Tourist office (☏ 02 31 89 23 30; www.ot -honfleur.fr; quai Lepaulmier; ⏱9.30am-12.30pm & 2pm-6pm Mon-Sat) Situated inside the

Médiathèque (library) building. Has a free map detailing a 2km walking circuit; internet access costs €1 for 15 minutes.

Getting There & Around

BUS The bus station (☎02 31 89 28 41) is two blocks east of the tourist office. Bus Verts (☎08 10 21 42 14; www.busverts.fr, in French) services include an express bus to Caen (€10.50, one hour):

Caen €7.50, two hours, 12 daily Monday to Saturday, six Sunday

Deauville & Trouville €2.15, 30 minutes

TRAIN To catch the train (eg to Paris), take the bus to Deauville, Le Havre or Lisieux (€4.25, 50 minutes, four or five daily).

Mont St-Michel
POP 43

It's one of France's most iconic images: the slender towers and sky-scraping turrets of the abbey of Mont St-Michel rising from stout ramparts and battlements, the whole ensemble connected to the mainland by a narrow causeway.

Bishop Aubert of Avranches is said to have built a devotional chapel on the summit of the island in 708, following his vision of the Archangel Michael, whose gilded figure, perched on the vanquished dragon, crowns the tip of the abbey's spire.

Sights

ABBAYE DU MONT ST-MICHEL   Abbey
(☎02 33 89 80 00; www.monuments-nationaux. fr; adult/child incl guided tour €8.50/free; ⊙9am-7pm, last entry 1hr before closing) The Mont's major attraction is the stunning architectural ensemble of the Abbaye du Mont St-Michel. From Monday to Saturday in July and August there are illuminated *nocturnes* (night-time visits) with music from 7pm to 10pm.

Most rooms can be visited without a guide, but it's worth taking the one-hour tour included in the ticket price.

When the tide is out you can walk all the way around Mont St-Michel, a distance of about 1km. Experienced outfits offering guided walks (€6.50) out into – or even across – the bay include **Découverte de la Baie du Mont-Saint-Michel** (☎02 33 70 83 49; www.decouvertebaie. com, in French) and **Chemins de la Baie**

Mont St-Michel

DAVID TOMLINSON

Mont St-Michel

A Timeline

708 Inspired by a vision from St Michael ❶, Bishop Aubert is compelled to 'build here and build high'.

966 Richard I, Duke of Normandy, gives the Mont to the Benedictines. The three levels of the abbey ❷ reflect their monastic hierarchy.

1017 Development of the abbey begins. Pilgrims arrive to honour the cult of St Michael. They walk barefoot across the mudflats and up the Grande Rue ❸ to be received in the almonry (now the bookshop).

1203 The monastery is burnt by the troops of Philip Augustus, who later donates money for its restoration and the Gothic 'miracle', La Merveille ❹, is constructed.

1434 The Mont's ramparts ❺ and fortifications ensure it withstands the English assault during the Hundred Years War. It is the only place in northern France not to fall.

1789 After the Revolution, Monasticism is abolished and the Mont is turned into a prison. During this period the treadmill ❻ is built to lift up supplies.

1878 The causeway ❼ is created. It allows modern-day pilgrims to visit without hip-high boots, but it cuts off the flow of water and the bay silts up.

1979 The Mont is declared a Unesco World Heritage Site.

TOP TIPS

Bring a packed lunch from Pontorson to avoid the poor lunch selection on the Mont

Leave the car – it's a pleasant walk from Pontorson, with spectacular views

Pay attention to the tides – they are dangerous

Take the excellent audioguide – it tells some great stories

JOHN ELK III

Îlot de Tombelaine

Occupied by the English during the Hundred Years War, this islet is now a bird reserve. From April to July it teems with exceptional birdlife.

Treadmill

The giant treadmill was powered hamsterlike by half a dozen prisoners, who, marching two abreast, raised stone and supplies up the Mont.

The West Terrace

Chapelle St-Aubert

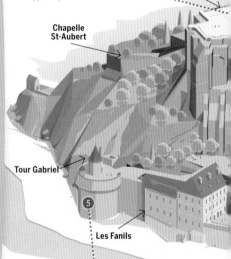

Tour Gabriel

❺

Les Fanils

Ramparts

The Mont was also a military garrison surrounded by machicolated and turreted walls, dating from the 13th to 15th centuries. The single entrance, Porte de l'Avancée, ensured its security in the Hundred Years War. Tip: Tour du Nord (North Tower) has the best views.

ROCCO FASANO

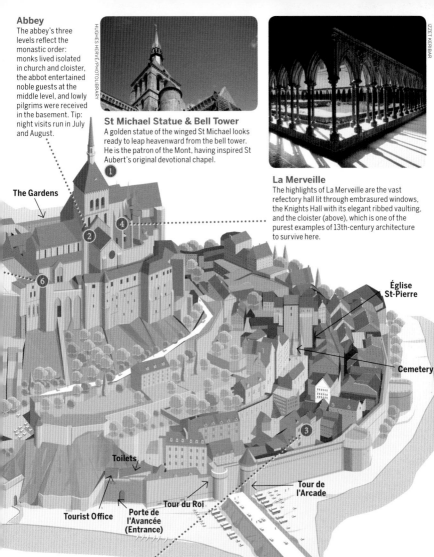

Abbey

The abbey's three levels reflect the monastic order: monks lived isolated in church and cloister, the abbot entertained noble guests at the middle level, and lowly pilgrims were received in the basement. Tip: night visits run in July and August.

St Michael Statue & Bell Tower

A golden statue of the winged St Michael looks ready to leap heavenward from the bell tower. He is the patron of the Mont, having inspired St Aubert's original devotional chapel.

La Merveille

The highlights of La Merveille are the vast refectory hall lit through embrasured windows, the Knights Hall with its elegant ribbed vaulting, and the cloister (above), which is one of the purest examples of 13th-century architecture to survive here.

The Gardens

Église St-Pierre

Cemetery

Toilets

Tour de l'Arcade

Tour du Roi

Tourist Office

Porte de l'Avancée (Entrance)

Grande Rue

The main thoroughfare of the small village below the abbey, Grande Rue has its charm despite its rampant commercialism. Don't miss the famous Mère Poulard shop here, for souvenir cookies.

Causeway

In 2014 the causeway will be replaced by a new bridge, which will allow the water to circulate and will return the Mont to an island. Tip: join a barefoot walking tour and see the Mont as pilgrims would.

Best Views

The view from the Jardin des Plantes in nearby Avranches is unique, as are the panoramas from Pointe du Grouin du Sud near the village of St-Léonard.

(📞 02 33 89 80 88; www.cheminsdelabaie.com, in French), both based across the bay from Mont St-Michel, in Genêts.

ÉGLISE ABBATIALE

The Église Abbatiale (Abbey Church) was built on the rocky tip of the mountain cone. It's famous for its mix of architectural styles: the nave and south transept (11th and 12th centuries) are solid Norman Romanesque, while the choir (late 15th century) is Flamboyant Gothic.

LA MERVEILLE

The buildings on the northern side of the Mont are known as La Merveille (The Marvel). The famous **cloître** (cloister) is surrounded by a double row of delicately carved arches resting on granite pillars. The early-13th-century, barrel-roofed **réfectoire** (dining hall) is illuminated by a wall of recessed windows – remarkable, given that the sheer drop precluded the use of flying buttresses. The Gothic **Salle des Hôtes** (Guest Hall), dating from 1213, has two enormous fireplaces. Look out for the **promenoire** (ambulatory),

with one of the oldest ribbed vaulted ceilings in Europe, and the **Chapelle de Notre Dame sous Terre** (Underground Chapel of Our Lady), one of the abbey's oldest rooms, rediscovered in 1903.

ℹ️ Information

Tourist office – Mont St-Michel (📞 02 33 60 14 30; www.ot-montsaintmichel.com; 🕙 9am-12.30pm & 2-6.30pm Mon-Sat, 9am-noon & 2-6pm Sun)

ℹ️ Getting There & Around

Pontorson, the nearest real town to Mont St-Michel, is 9km to the south.

BUS Mont St-Michel is linked to Beauvoir (eight minutes) and Pontorson (€2, 13 minutes) by bus 6, operated by Manéo (📞 08 00 15 00 50; www.mobi50.com, in French), six to eight times daily (more frequently in July and August). Les Couriers Bretons (📞 02 99 19 70 80) links Pontorson with St-Malo (1¼ hours, one round trip daily); times are coordinated with bus 6.

TRAIN Destinations from Pontorson:

Bayeux €21, 1¾ hours, two or three direct daily

Cherbourg €26, three hours, two to three daily

Coutances €11.50, 40 minutes, three or four daily

Rennes €12.50, 50 minutes, two to four daily

BRITTANY

Brittany is for explorers. Its wild, dramatic coastline, medieval towns and thick forests make an excursion here well worth the detour from the beaten track. This is a land of prehistoric mysticism, proud tradition and culinary wealth, where locals still remain fiercely independent, Breton culture is celebrated and Paris feels a very long way away indeed.

Cathédrale Notre Dame (p119), Rouen
PHOTOGRAPHER: CHRISTOPHER WOOD

ROCCO FASANO

St-Malo

POP 50,200

With one of the world's highest tidal ranges, brewing storms under blackened skies see waves lash over the top of the ramparts ringing St Malo's walled city. The town became a key port during the 17th and 18th centuries as a base for both merchant ships and government-sanctioned privateers (pirates, basically) against the constant threat of the English. These days English arrivals are tourists, for whom St-Malo, a short ferry hop from the Channel Islands, is a summer haven.

 Sights & Activities

For the best views of the walled city, stroll the top of the 1.8km **ramparts**, constructed at the end of the 17th century under military architect Vauban.

Though you'd never guess it from the cobblestone streets and reconstructed monuments in 17th- and 18th-century style, during August 1944 the battle to drive German forces out of St-Malo destroyed around 80% of the old city, lovingly restored since then.

CATHÉDRALE ST-VINCENT Cathedral
(place Jean de Châtillon; ⊙9.30am-6pm except during Mass) The town's centrepiece was constructed between the 12th and 18th centuries, but damage during WWII was severe. A mosaic plaque on the floor of the nave marks the spot where Jacques Cartier received the blessing of the bishop of St-Malo before his 'voyage of discovery' to Canada in 1535.

MUSÉE DU CHÂTEAU City Museum
(☎02 99 40 71 57; adult/child €5/2.80; ⊙10am-noon & 2-6pm, closed Mon Oct-Mar) Within the **Château de St-Malo**, which was built by the dukes of Brittany in the 15th and 16th centuries, is the Musée du Château, also known as the Musée d'Histoire de la Ville (city history museum).

LA MAISON DE CORSAIRE
Historic Mansion
(☎02 99 56 09 40; www.demeure-de-corsaire. com; 5 rue d'Asfeld; adult/child €5.50/4; ⊙10am-noon & 2-6pm, closed Mon in winter) You can visit this 18th-century mansion and historic monument, once owned by corsair (privateer) François Auguste Magon.

133

ROCCO FASANO

ÎLE DU GRAND BÉ Island

At low tide, cross the beach to walk out via the Porte des Bés to the rocky islet of **Île du Grand Bé** (www.petit-be.com, in French), where the great St-Malo-born 18th-century writer Chateaubriand is buried. Once the tide rushes in, the causeway remains impassable for about six hours; check tide times with the tourist office.

About 100m beyond the Île du Grand Bé is the Vauban-built 17th-century **Fort du Petit Bé** (☎06 08 27 51 20), also accessible at low tide.

FORT NATIONAL Fort

(www.fortnational.com; adult/child €5/3; ☺Easter & Jun–mid-Sep) The ramparts' northern stretch looks across to the remains of this former prison, built by Vauban in 1689. Standing atop a rocky outcrop, the fort can only be accessed at low tide.

GRAND AQUARIUM Aquarium

(☎02 99 21 19 00; www.aquarium-st-malo. com; av Général Patton; adult/child €15.50/10; ☺10am-6pm) Allow around two hours to see St-Malo's excellent aquarium. About 4km south of the city centre, it's a great wet-weather alternative for kids, and even has a minisubmarine descent. Bus C1 from the train station passes by every half-hour.

 ## Sleeping

HÔTEL SAN PEDRO Hotel €

(☎02 99 40 88 57; www.sanpedro-hotel.com; 1 rue Ste-Anne; s €52-54, d €63-73; ☎) Tucked away at the back of the old city, the San Pedro has cool, crisp, neutral-toned decor with subtle splashes of colour, friendly service and superb sea views. Breakfast is an €8 feast.

HÔTEL DE L'UNIVERS
Traditional Hotel €

(☎02 99 40 89 52; www.hotel-univers-saintmalo. com; pl Chateaubriand; s/d/tr €77/89/103; ☎) Right by the most frequently used gateway to the old city (Porte St-Vincent), this cream-coloured place with 63 rooms is perfectly poised for all of St-Malo's attractions.

MANOIR DU CUNNINGHAM
Traditional Hotel €€

(☎02 99 21 33 33; www.st-malo-hotel-cunning ham.com; 9 place Monseigneur Duchesne; r €110-

190; 📞) The rather Disneyesque exterior of this hotel outside the city walls belies its very pleasant interior: a 13-room, mahogany-rich guesthouse a stroll from the ferry, with views out to sea. A great spot to be comfortable away from the crowds.

Eating

LE CHALUT
Seafood €€

(📞 02 99 56 71 58; 8 rue de la Corne de Cerf; menus €25-68; 🕙 Wed-Sun) This unremarkable-looking establishment is in fact St-Malo's most celebrated restaurant and a must for any self-respecting seafood lover. Reservations for dinner are advised.

LA BOUCHE EN FOLIE
Modern French €

(📞 06 72 49 08 89; 14 rue du Boyer; menus €13-29; 🕙 closed Mon & Tue) Hidden away from the tourist trail, this sleek joint oozes Gallic gorgeousness from every nook and cranny. The menu gives a modern spin to French staples – lamb is fricas-séed with garlic and artichokes, while monkfish is partnered by peas, black olives and asparagus. Sumptuous.

RESTAURANT DELAUNAY
Gastronomic €€

(📞 02 99 40 92 46; www.restaurant-delaunay.com; 6 rue Ste-Barbe; menus €28-65; 🕙 dinner Mon-Sat, closed Mon in winter) This superb yet unassuming-looking restaurant is where Chef Didier Delaunay creates standout gastronomic cuisine within aubergine-painted walls.

ⓘ Information

Tourist office (📞 08 25 13 52 00, 02 99 56 64 43; www.saint-malo-tourisme.com; esplanade St-Vincent; 🕙 9am-7.30pm Mon-Sat, 10am-6pm Sun) Just outside the city walls.

ⓘ Getting There & Away

BOAT Brittany Ferries (📞 reservations in France 08 25 82 88 28, in UK 0871 244 0744; www.brittany-ferries.com) sails between St-Malo and Portsmouth, and Condor Ferries (📞 in France 08 25 16 54 63, in UK 01202 207 216; www.condorferries.co.uk) runs to/from Poole and Weymouth via Jersey or Guernsey.

From April to September, Compagnie Corsaire (📞 08 25 13 80 35; www.compagniecorsaire.com) and Vedettes de St-Malo (📞 02 23 18 41 08; www.vedettes-saint-malo.com) run a Bus de Mer (Sea Bus; adult/child return €7/4.30) shuttle service (10 minutes, at least hourly) between St-Malo and Dinard.

TRAIN TGV trains run from St-Malo:

Dinan €9, one hour, 10 daily (requiring a change in Dol de Bretagne)

Paris Montparnasse €63, three hours, up to 10 daily

Rennes €13, one hour, roughly hourly

Grand Aquarium
PHOTOGRAPHER: STOCKFOLIO/ALAMY

Dinard

POP 11,180

Visiting Dinard 'in season' is a little like stepping into one of the canvases Picasso painted here in the 1920s. Belle époque mansions built into the cliffs form a timeless backdrop to the beach dotted with blue-and-white striped bathing tents and the beachside carnival.

 ## Sights & Activities

The romantically named **promenade du Clair de Lune** (moonlight promenade) has views across the Rance River estuary to St-Malo's walled city, and nightly sound-and-light spectacles in summer.

Beautiful **seaside trails** extend along the coast in both directions. Walkers can follow the shoreline from Plage du Prieuré to Plage de St-Énogat via Pointe du Moulinet, while cyclists can shadow the coastline on the road.

Framed by fashionable hotels, a casino and neo-Gothic villas, **Plage de l'Écluse** is the perfect place to shade yourself in style by renting one of Dinard's trademark blue-and-white striped **bathing tents** (☎02 99 46 18 12; per half-day €7.50-12, per day €8.50-15.50); you can also hire parasols and deckchairs.

Sleeping

HÔTEL PRINTANIA Traditional Hotel €

(☎02 99 46 13 07; www.printaniahotel.com, in French; 5 av George V; s €67, d €73-104; ☎mid-Mar–mid-Nov; ☎) This charming Breton-style hotel, complete with wood-and-leather furniture, has a superb location overlooking the Baie du Prieuré. Rooms with a sea view cost more; otherwise get your fill of the grand views across the water to St-Servan at breakfast (€8.50).

GRAND HÔTEL BARRIÈRE

Luxury Hotel €€

(☎02 99 88 26 26; www.lucienbarriere.com; 3 bd Féart; s €165-200, d €180-300; ❄☎☎♨) Dinard's most fabulous address is this

old-timer that has been given a very smart facelift and has prices to match. The rooms are spacious, many with balconies and magnificent sea views, though the style is very much anonymous chic.

 ## Eating

Some of Dinard's best restaurants are attached to hotels, such as **Hôtel Printania** (menus €25-38), which serves top-notch fish and seafood.

CHEZ MA POMME   Breton Cuisine €€

(☎02 99 46 81 90; 6 rue Yves Verney; menus €20-26; ☎closed Mon, dinner Sun & Thu Sep-Jun) Codfish roasted in bacon and parmesan is among the innovative twists on local ocean-caught fish, while rich Breton caramel features in the tempting array of desserts.

L'ABRI DES FLOTS   Seafood €€

(☎02 99 16 99 48; 3 place de la République; lunch/dinner menus €23-35) Effortlessly chic, this modern temple to seafood does not disappoint. Its cavernous interior is usually filled to capacity every day when the morning's catch is lovingly transformed into classic French dishes.

Information

Tourist office (☎02 99 46 94 12; www.ot-dinard.com, in French; 2 bd Féart; ☎9.30am-12.15pm & 2-6pm Mon-Sat)

Getting There & Away

AIR Ryanair (www.ryanair.com) has daily flights to and from London Stansted.

BOAT From April to September, Compagnie Corsaire (☎08 25 13 80 35; www.compagniecorsaire.com) and Vedettes de St-Malo (☎02 23 18 41 08; www.vedettes-saint-malo.com) run a Bus de Mer (Sea Bus; adult/child return €7/4.30) shuttle service (10 minutes) between St-Malo and Dinard.

BUS Illenoo (www.illenoo-services.fr) buses connect Dinard and the train station in St-Malo (€1.70, 30 minutes, hourly). Several buses travel to Rennes (€3.90, two hours).

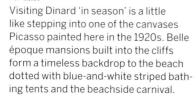

JOHN ELK III

Cancale
POP 5440

The idyllic little fishing port of Cancale, 14km east of St-Malo, is famed for its offshore *parcs à huîtres* (oyster beds).

 Sights

FERME MARINE Oyster Museum
(Marine Farm; www.ferme-marine.com; corniche de l'Aurore; adult/child €7/3.60; ⊘ mid-Feb–Oct) This small museum dedicated to oyster farming and shellfish runs guided tours in English at 2pm from July to mid-September.

 Sleeping & Eating

LA PASTOURELLE B&B €
(✆ 02 99 89 10 09; www.baie-saintmichel.com, in French; Les Nielles, St-Méloir des Ondes; s €56-64, d €62-74; 🛜) The countryside around Cancale shelters some really lovely *chambres d'hôte* (ask the tourist office for a complete list). This vine-covered traditional Breton *longère* (long house) looking out to sea is one of the most delightful.

LE CONTINENTAL Hotel €€
(✆ 02 99 89 60 16; www.hotel-cancale.com, in French; 4 quai Thomas; d €88-148; ⊘ mid-Feb–early Jan; 🛜) Above its portside, red-awning-shaded restaurant (*menus* €19 to €42), this *hôtel de charme* with wheelchair access has beautiful timber-rich rooms. Sea-facing rooms are at a premium, but the views are worth it.

LE COQUILLAGE
Gastronomic, French €€€
(✆ 02 99 89 64 76; www.maisons-de-bricourt. com; 1 rue Duguesclin; menus €26-90; ⊘ closed Jan & Feb) Superchef Olivier Roellinger's latest project is a sumptuous restaurant–hotel housed in the impressive **Château Richeux**, 4km south of Cancale. Roellinger's creations have earned him three Michelin stars and you won't have trouble seeing why if you're lucky enough to get a table here. As well as offering rooms at Château Richeux, Roellinger offers a range of cottages and other deluxe accommodation around Cancale.

MARCHÉ AUX HUÎTRES
Oyster Market €
(⊘ 9am-6pm) Clustered by the Pointe des Crolles lighthouse, stalls sell oysters

from €3.50 per dozen for small *huîtres creuses* to upwards of €20 for saucer-sized *plates de Cancale*.

🛈 Getting There & Around

Keolis Emeraude (www.keolis-emeraude.com) has year-round bus services to and from St-Malo (€2, 30 minutes).

Roscoff

POP 3780

Unlike many of its industrial and less-than-beautiful sister Channel ports, Roscoff (Rosko in Breton) provides a captivating first glimpse of Brittany. Granite houses dating from the 16th century wreathe the pretty docks, which are surrounded by emerald-green fields producing cauliflowers, onions, tomatoes, new potatoes and artichokes.

Roscoff farmers known as 'Johnnies', wearing distinctive horizontally striped tops, used to load up their boats with plaited strings of locally grown pink onions and cross the Channel to the UK, where they peddled – and pedalled – with their onions hanging from their handlebars, thus creating the traditional British stereotype of the French.

◎ Sights & Activities

ÉGLISE NOTRE DAME DE KROAZ-BATZ
Church

(place Lacaze-Duthiers; ⏰9am-noon & 2-6pm) With its Renaissance belfry rising above the flat landscape, this 16th-century Flamboyant Gothic structure is one of Brittany's most impressive churches.

MAISON DES JOHNNIES
History Museum

(📞02 98 61 25 48; 48 rue Brizeux; adult/child €4/2.50) Photographs trace Roscoff's roaming onion farmers from the early 19th century at this popular museum. Tours at 5pm on Tuesdays between mid-June and mid-September include a free hour-long meeting with Johnnies from 6pm to 7pm. Call ahead for tour times as they change frequently.

LE JARDIN EXOTIQUE DE ROSCOFF
Garden

(📞02 98 61 29 19; www.jardinexotiqueroscoff. com; adult/child €5/2; ⏰10am-7pm, closed Dec-Feb) Wander through 3000 species of exotic plants, many from the southern hemisphere, at this impressive exotic garden.

CENTRE DE DÉCOUVERTE
DES ALGUES
Museum

(📞02 98 69 77 05; www.decou vertedesalgues.com, in French; 5 rue Victor Hugo; admission free, walks per adult/child €5/3.50; ⏰10am-7pm) You can learn about local seaweed harvesting at this enthusiastically run museum, which also organises guided walks and gives regular free lectures (often in English and German).

Typical Breton house, Roscoff
PHOTOGRAPHER: JEAN-BERNARD CARILLET

THALASSO ROSCOFF

Seawater Baths

(☎08 25 00 20 99; www.thalasso.com, in French; rue Victor Hugo; ⏱closed Dec) The perfect way to follow a visit to the Centre de Découverte des Algues is to immerse yourself in the stuff at this bathing complex, which offers health-inducing activities including a heated seawater pool, a *hammam* (Turkish bath) and a jacuzzi (€11 for all three).

ÎLE DE BATZ

Island

Bordering what is basically a 4-sq-km vegetable garden fertilised by seaweed, the beaches on the Île de Batz (pronounced ba, Enez Vaz in Breton; www.iledebatz.com) are a peaceful place to bask. The mild island climate tends the luxuriant **Jardins Georges Delaselle** (☎02 98 61 75 65; www.jardin-georgesdelaselle.fr; adult/child €4.60/2; ⏱2-6pm Wed-Mon Apr-Oct, daily Jul & Aug), founded in the 19th century, with over 1500 plants from all five continents.

Ferries (adult/child return €7.50/4, bike €7, 15 minutes each way) between Roscoff and Île de Batz run every 30 minutes between 8am and 8pm from late June to mid-September; there are about eight sailings daily during the rest of the year.

 ## Sleeping & Eating

HÔTEL DU CENTRE

Boutique Hotel €

(☎02 98 61 24 25; www.chezjanie.com; r €69-99; ⏱mid-Feb-mid-Nov; 🛜) Minimal and sleek rooms at this boutique hotel look like they've been lifted out of a magazine, and indeed they've featured in many. But it's perhaps best known for its restaurant, Chez Janie (*menu* €24), serving Breton classics like *kig ha farz* – a farmers' family meal based around the Breton cake *far*, cooked in a linen bag within a boiling bacon and vegetable stew.

If You Like...
Islands

The Île de Batz is just one of many idyllic islands dotted around the Breton coastline. Blessed with beautiful beaches, rich wildlife and stunning coastal walks, the islands make ideal day trips but can get crowded in summer; come in spring or autumn and you might have the scenery all to yourself.

1 ÎLE DE BRÉHAT

This tiny, car-free island measures just 5km from north to south. The best time to visit is in spring, when Mediterranean wildflowers bloom in its gentle microclimate. **Vedettes de Bréhat** (☎02 96 55 79 50; www.vedettesdebrehat.com) operates year-round ferries (adult/child return €8.50/7) from Pointe L'Arcouest, 6km north of Paimpol.

2 ÎLE D'OUESSANT

(☎tourist office 02 98 48 85 83; www.ot-ouessant. fr) Free-roaming sheep and traditional houses give this windswept island an ends-of-the-earth feel. It's a notorious spot for shipwrecks; the black-and-white-striped **Phare de Créac'h** is the world's most powerful lighthouse. **Penn Ar Bed** (☎02 98 80 80 80; www. pennarbed.fr) runs year-round ferries from Brest (adult/child €30.20/18.25, 2½ hours) and Le Conquet (€30.20/18.25, 1½ hours).

3 BELLE ÎLE

(☎tourist office 02 97 31 81 93; www.belle-ile. com) Brittany's largest island (20km by 9km) makes a popular day trip from Quiberon thanks to its fantastic beaches and coastal walks. **Compagnie Océane** (☎08 20 05 61 56; www.compagnie -oceane.fr) operates ferries from Quiberon (adult return €30) and **Navix** (☎02 97 46 60 29; www. navix.fr) operates ferries from Vannes (return €30 to €44).

LE TEMPS DE VIVRE Boutique Hotel €€

(☎02 98 19 33 19; www.tycoz.com/letempsde vivre; 19 place Lacaze Duthiers; d €140-268; 🛜) This glamorous place is hidden away in a lovely stone mansion complete with its own tower just opposite the church. With fantastic sea views from some

139

rooms, decor that is a great blend of modernity and tradition, plus friendly staff, this is one of Roscoff's very best options.

LE SURCOUF Brasserie €
(☎02 98 69 71 89; 14 rue Amiral Réveillère; menus €11-55) A reliable year-round opener, this brasserie-restaurant is unsurprisingly popular with locals. Opening hours and days can vary.

ⓘ Information

Tourist office (☎02 98 61 12 13; www.roscoff -tourisme.com; quai d'Auxerre; ⏰9.15am-noon & 2-6pm Mon-Sat, open Sun Jul-Aug)

ⓘ Getting There & Away

FERRY Brittany Ferries (☎reservations in France 08 25 82 88 28, in UK 0871 244 0744; www.brittany-ferries.com) links Roscoff to Plymouth in England (five to nine hours, one to three daily year-round) and Cork in Ireland (14 hours, once-weekly June to September).

TRAIN There are regular trains and SNCF buses to Morlaix (€5.50, 35 minutes), where you can make connections to Brest, Quimper and St-Brieuc.

Presqu'île de Crozon

The anchor-shaped Crozon Peninsula is part of the **Parc Naturel Régional d'Armorique**, and one of the most scenic spots in Brittany. The partly forested peninsula is criss-crossed by some 145km of signed walking trails.

Argol
POP 830

Argol is a quaint village in its own right, but its main drawcard is the **Musée du Cidre du Bretagne** (Breton Cider Museum; ☎02 98 17 21 87; www.musee-cidre-bretagne. com; adult/child €5/free; ⏰2-7pm Apr-Sep). This former dairy's old stone buildings have been transformed into a working *cidrerie* that produces more than 300,000 bottles annually. A visit (allow around an hour, including a French-language but very visual film) takes you through the

Left: Presqu'île de Crozon; **Below:** Cathedral St-Corentin
PHOTOGRAPHER: (LEFT) JEAN-BERNARD CARILLET; (BELOW) MARTIN MOOS

history of cider in Brittany and present-day production. And, of course, you get to taste it, too.

Camaret-sur-Mer
POP 2600

At the western extremity of the Crozon Peninsula, Camaret (unusually in French, the final 't' is pronounced) is a classic fishing village – or at least it was until early last century, when it was France's biggest crayfish port. Abandoned fishing-boat carcasses now decay in its harbour, but it remains an enchanting place that lures artists. There's an ever-increasing number of galleries dotted around town, particularly along rue de la Marne and around place St-Thomas, one block north of the waterfront.

Three kilometres south of Camaret, **Pointe de Pen-Hir** is a spectacular headland bounded by steep, sheer sea cliffs, with two WWII memorials.

Quimper
POP 67,250

Small enough to feel like a village, with its slanted half-timbered houses and narrow cobbled streets, and large enough to buzz as the troubadour of Breton culture and arts, Quimper (pronounced 'kam-pair') is Finistère's thriving capital.

 Sights

CATHEDRAL ST-CORENTIN Cathedral
(place St-Corentin; ⊙9.30am-noon & 1.30-6.30pm) At the centre of the city stands this impressive cathedral, the distinctive kink built into its soaring light-filled interior said by some to symbolise Christ's head inclined on one shoulder as he was dying on the cross. Begun in 1239, the cathedral wasn't completed

141

until the 1850s, with the seamless addition of its dramatic twin spires.

MUSÉE DES BEAUX-ARTS
Art Museum

(☎ 02 98 95 45 20; 40 place St-Corentin; adult/child €4.50/2.50; ⏰ 10am-7pm) The ground-floor halls are home to some fairly morbid 16th- to 20th-century European paintings, but things lighten up on the upper levels of the town's main art museum. A room dedicated to Quimper-born poet Max Jacob includes sketches by Picasso.

MUSÉE DÉPARTEMENTAL BRETON
Breton Museum

(☎ 02 98 95 21 60; 1 rue du Roi Gradlon; adult/child €4/free; ⏰ 9am-6pm) Recessed behind a magnificent stone courtyard beside the cathedral, this museum is housed in the former bishop's palace. Superb exhibits showcase Breton history, furniture, costumes, crafts and archaeology. Adjoining the museum is the **Jardin de l'Évêché** (Bishop's Palace Garden; admission free; ⏰ 9am-5pm or 6pm).

Tours

VEDETTES DE L'ODET
Boat Tours

(☎ 08 25 80 08 01, 02 98 57 00 58) From June to September, Vedettes de l'Odet runs boat trips (adult/child €25/15, 1¼ hours) from Quimper along the serene Odet estuary to Bénodet, departing from quai Neuf.

Sleeping

HÔTEL GRADLON
Traditional Hotel €€

(☎ 02 98 95 04 39; www.hotel-gradlon.com; 30 rue de Brest; s €101-119, d €109-135; ⏰ closed mid-Dec–mid-Jan; 🛜) This place may not look like much from the street, but its rather bland and modern facade belies a charming country manor interior.

HÔTEL KREGENN
Design Hotel €€

(☎ 02 98 95 08 70; www.hotel-kregenn.fr; 13 rue des Réguaires; s €105, d from €120, ste €150; ❄🛜) A Zen timber-decked courtyard and a guest lounge with outsized mirrors and white leather sofas give you the initial impression that Quimper's coolest hotel is contemporary in style, but the plush rooms (in pistachio green, ocean blue or chocolate) evoke a traditional feel, as does the warm-hearted welcome.

HÔTEL MANOIR DES INDES
Design Hotel €€

(☎ 02 98 55 48 40; www.manoir-hoteldesindes.com; 1 Allée de Prad ar C'hras; s €105-150, d €150-170, ste €180-260; 🛜♿) This stunning hotel conversion just west of Quimper is a hugely impressive labour of love for a couple who have brought an old manor house back to life as a hotel with Indian decor. The hotel is set within its own lovely

Jardin de l'Évêché
PHOTOGRAPHER: CHRIS HELLIER/ALAMY

DAN HERRICK

Don't Miss **Carnac**

Predating Stonehenge by around 100 years, Carnac (Garnag in Breton) also tops it with sheer numbers – it's the world's greatest concentration of megaliths. There are no fewer than 3000 of these upright stones, most around thigh-high, erected between 5000 and 3500 BC.

To see them, sign up for a one-hour guided visit at the **Maison des Mégalithes**, running regularly in French year-round and usually in English at 3pm Wednesday, Thursday and Friday from early July to late August.

The largest menhir field – with 1099 stones – is the **Alignements du Ménec**, 1km north of Carnac-Ville. From here, the D196 heads northeast for about 1.5km to the equally impressive **Alignements de Kermario**. Another 500m further on are the **Alignements de Kerlescan**, a smaller group also accessible in winter.

Between Kermario and Kerlescan, 500m south of the D196, deposit your fee (€1) in an honour box at **Tumulus de Kercado**, dating from 3800 BC and the burial site of a Neolithic chieftain. From the parking area 300m further along the D196, a 15-minute walk brings you to the **Géant du Manio**, the highest menhir in the complex.

For some background, the **Musée de Préhistoire** chronicles life in and around Carnac from the Palaeolithic and Neolithic eras to the Middle Ages.

The main bus stops are in Carnac-Ville, outside the police station on rue St-Cornély, and in Carnac-Plage, beside the tourist office. Keolis Atlantique runs a daily bus to Auray, Vannes and Quiberon (€2). Alignements de Kermario

NEED TO KNOW

Tourist office (☎02 97 52 13 52; www.ot-carnac.fr; 74 av des Druides, Carnac-Plage; ☺9am-7pm Mon-Sat & 3-7pm Sun); Maison des Mégalithes (☎02 97 52 29 81; rte des Alignements; €4; ☺9am-7pm); Musée de Préhistoire (☎02 97 52 22 04; 10 place de la Chapelle, Carnac-Ville; adult/child €5/2.50; ☺10am-6pm); Keolis Atlantique (☎02 97 47 29 64; www.keolis-atlantique.com)

If You Like…
Medieval Towns

If you've been smitten by the olde-worlde charms of the Château de Josselin, you'll love exploring some of the region's other medieval marvels:

1 DINAN
(☎tourist office 02 96 87 69 76; www.dinan-tourisme.com; 9 rue du Château) If you're looking for Brittany's most-authentic medieval town, look no further than Dinan, still encircled by its medieval battlements and watchtowers. The town's main thoroughfare has barely changed since the days when doublet and hose were still in fashion.

2 VANNES
(☎tourist office 08 25 13 56 10; www.tourisme-vannes.com; Quai de Tabarly) Overlooking the Golfe du Morbihan, Vannes' hilly streets are lined with half-timbered houses, and life still revolves around the medieval market square.

3 CONCARNEAU
(☎tourist office 02 98 97 01 44; www.tourismeconcarneau.fr; quai d'Aiguillon; ◷9am-7pm) This salty old port has a long seafaring history. Take a stroll along the ramparts of the Ville Close, followed by a visit to the town's fascinating fishing museum.

4 VITRÉ
(☎tourist office 02 99 75 04 46; www.ot-vitre.fr; place Général de Gaulle) With its winding streets and colossal castle (complete with pointy turrets), Vitré rivals Dinan as one of Brittany's prettiest medieval towns.

2-hectare grounds and is just a short drive from the centre of Quimper.

Eating & Drinking

LE COSY RESTAURANT
Breton Cuisine €
(☎02 98 95 23 65; 2 rue du Sallé; mains €10-14.50; ◷lunch Tue-Sat, dinner Wed, Fri & Sat)

Pas de crêpes! (No crêpes!) the blackboard menu on the street proclaims. Inside, make your way through the *épicerie* (specialist grocer) – crammed with locally canned sardines, ciders and other Breton produce – and up the narrow staircase to the eclectic, artistic dining room, where you can tuck into specialities like gratins and *tartines* (open sandwiches) made from market ingredients.

L'AMBROISIE
Gastronomic €€
(☎02 98 95 00 02; www.ambroisie-quimper.com; 49 rue Elie Fréron; menus €22-63; ◷lunch & dinner Tue-Sat, lunch Sun) Quimper's most-celebrated gastronomic restaurant is sumptuously decorated with contemporary art and elegant china on snow-white tablecloths.

LE PETIT GAVEAU
Bistro €
(☎02 98 64 29 86; 16 rue des Boucheries; mains €8-15; ◷lunch Mon-Sat, dinner Wed-Sat) This charming find is a sleek conversion of an old stone-walled house that plays host to simple yet excellent food (the gourmet burger is superb), and is a world away from the fussy gastronomy and crêpes you'll find elsewhere in town.

❶ Information

Tourist office (☎02 98 53 04 05; www.quimper-tourisme.com, in French; place de la Résistance; ◷9.30am-12.30pm & 1.30-6.30pm) Runs weekly 1½-hour guided city tours in English (€5.20) in July and August, and sells the Pass' Quimper (€10) whereby two people can access four attractions/tours of their choice (from a list of participating organisations).

❶ Getting There & Away

Frequent train services:

Brest €15.50, 1¼ hours, up to 10 daily

Paris Montparnasse €75, 4¾ hours, hourly

Rennes €32, 2½ hours, hourly

Vannes €18, 1½ hours, hourly

Château de Josselin

Guarded by its three round towers, the extraordinary town château at **Josselin** (☏ 02 97 22 36 45; www.chateaujosselin.com; adult/child €7.50/5; ⏱2-5.30pm Apr-Sep) is an incredible sight that remains the home of the Rohan family today. As such, it can only be visited on a guided tour: one English-language tour departs daily from June to September; otherwise you can ask for a leaflet in English. Within the château you will find the **Musée de Poupées** (Doll Museum; adult/child €6.50/4.60); a combination ticket for both costs €12.50/8.50 per adult/child.

Viaoo (www.viaoo29.fr) runs several daily buses to Rennes (€13, 1½ hours).

Rennes

POP 213,100

A crossroads since Roman times, Brittany's vibrant capital sits at the junction of highways linking northwestern France's major cities. It's a beautifully set-out city, with an elaborate and stately centre and a charming old town that's a joy to get lost in.

◉ Sights

CATHÉDRALE ST-PIERRE   Cathedral
(⏱9.30am-noon & 3-6pm) Crowning the old city is the 17th-century cathedral, which has an impressive, if rather dark, neoclassical interior. Much of the surrounding old town was gutted by the great fire of 1720, started by a drunken carpenter who accidentally set alight a pile of shavings. Half-timbered houses that survived line the old city's cobbled streets such as nearby rue St-Michel and rue St-Georges.

PALAIS DU PARLEMENT DE BRETAGNE
     Law Courts
(place du Parlement de Bretagne) This 17th-century former seat of the rebellious Breton parliament has in more recent times been home to the Palais de Justice. In 1994 this building, too, was destroyed by fire, started by demonstrating fishermen. Now restored, it houses the Court of Appeal. In July and August, guided tours in English (adult/child €7/4; book at the tourist office) take you through the ostentatiously gilded rooms.

Château de Josselin

Rennes

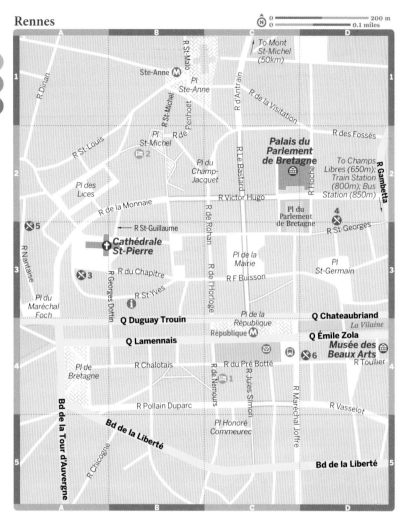

MUSÉE DES BEAUX-ARTS
Art Museum

(02 23 62 17 45; 20 quai Émile Zola; adult/child €6/free; 10am-noon & 2-6pm Tue-Sun) The rooms devoted to the Pont-Aven school are the highlight of the Musée des Beaux-Arts, which also has a 'curiosity gallery' of antiques and illustrations amassed in the 18th century.

CHAMPS LIBRES
Cultural Centre

(02 23 40 66 00; www.leschampslibres. fr; 10 cours des Alliés) Rennes' futuristic cultural centre is home to the **Musée de Bretagne** (02 23 40 66 00; www. musee-bretagne.fr), which offers displays on Breton history and culture. Under the same roof is the **Espace des Sciences** (02 23 40 66 40; www.espace-sciences.org), an interactive science museum; plus you will also find a planetarium, a temporary exhibition space and a library. A combined ticket for all of the different sections costs €7/5 per adult/child.

Rennes

 Sleeping

HÔTEL DE NEMOURS Boutique Hotel €
(☎ 02 99 78 26 26; www.hotelnemours.com; 5 rue de Nemours; r €59-92; ❋ 🛜) Lined with historic black-and-white photographs of Rennes, sumptuous Hôtel de Nemours is elegantly understated, with cream, chocolate and caramel furnishings, high-thread-count white linens, flat-screen TVs and free wi-fi.

HÔTEL DES LICES Hotel €
(☎ 02 99 79 14 81; www.hotel-des-lices.com; 7 place des Lices; r €67-83; ❋ 🛜) You can peer down from the steel balconies or through the floor-to-ceiling glass doors to see the Saturday-morning market, which snakes right past the front door of this modern six-storey hotel. Inside, rooms are small but sleek with pared-down contemporary furnishings and textured walls.

 Eating

LÉON LE COCHON Pork Restaurant €
(☎ 02 99 79 37 54; 1 rue Maréchal Joffre; menu €25, mains €13-24) Basking in the plaudits of almost every French gastronomic guidebook, but still fun and informal,

'Leon the Pig' specialises not just in pork but porcine products in all their many and varied manifestations.

CAFÉ BABYLONE Modern French €
(☎ 02 99 85 82 99; 12 rue des Dames; mains €7-18; ⊘ closed dinner Mon) Despite being virtually built into the walls of Rennes' cathedral, this charming contemporary yet traditional place is a surprisingly tourist-free zone, favoured instead by locals enjoying a plate of oysters or one of the finely produced dishes of rich home cooking on the terrace.

LE CAFÉ BRETON Traditional French €
(☎ 02 99 30 74 95; 14 rue Nantaise; menus €8-18; ⊘ closed dinner Mon) Diminutive rue Nantaise has a handful of top restaurants, including this one, favoured by locals for its tarts, salads and gratins. Definitely book ahead in the evenings.

La Ville d'Ys Crêperie
(☎ 02 99 36 70 28; 5 rue St-Georges; crêpes €2.20-8.40) Probably the town's most famous crêperie, La Ville d'Ys serves up mouth-watering black-wheat pancakes with sublime taste combinations.

 Information

Tourist office (☎ 02 99 67 11 11; www.tourisme-rennes.com; 11 rue St-Yves; ⊘ 9am-7pm Mon-Sat, 11am-1pm & 2-6pm Sun) Offers an audioguide to the city taking you on a walking tour of eight sights for €4.50. Staff can book accommodation for no fee.

 Getting There & Away

Destinations with frequent train services:

Brest €32, two hours

Dinan €13.50, one hour including a change

Nantes €23, 1¼ hours

Paris Gare Montparnasse €48, 2¼ hours

Quimper €32, 2½ hours

St-Malo €13, one hour

Vannes €19, 1½ hours

Champagne & Northern France

Nowhere sums up the effervescent French spirit better than Champagne. This region has been famous for its bubbly since the 17th century, when a monk by the name of Dom Pierre Pérignon added some fizz to his otherwise humdrum wine and discovered he'd created something altogether more exciting.

A couple of centuries on, you'll find famous Champagne houses dotted throughout the region, especially around the elegant towns of Reims and Épernay: a tasting tour of their musty cellars is an absolutely unforgettable experience.

Looking west, the regions of Alsace and Lorraine crackle with a unique blend of French and Germanic cultures. And to the north, the many memorials and cemeteries dotted around Picardy and the Pas-de-Calais recall the region's tragic history as one of the key battlegrounds of WWI.

Champagne vineyards

Champagne & Northern France

Strait of Dover

Calais

Boulogne-sur-Mer

Lille

BELGIUM

⊛ **Brussels**

PAS-DE-CALAIS

Vimy Ridge Canadian National Historical Site 🔖 Lens

Authie

Arras

Beaurains

NORD

Sambre

Baie de Somme

Abbeville

Somme

SOMME

Beamont

Thiepval Memorial 🔖

Albert

🔖 *La Grande Mine*

◉ *Somme American Cemetery*

❻

Péronne

❸ Amiens

St-Quentin

Oise

SEINE-MARITIME

Oise

Laon

AISNE

ARDENNES

Rethel

Aisne

N2

A26

Aisne

OISE

Aisne

❶ ❸

EURE

VAL-D'OISE

Seine

Parc Naturel Régional de la Montagne de Reims

Châtillon-sur-Marne

A4

❶ Reims

Verzenay 🔖

MARNE

Épernay

Paris ⊛

Marne

Le Mesnil-sur-Oger ❶

SEINE-ET-MARNE

❶ Vertus

N3

Châlons-sur-Marne

N44

Vitry-le-François

ESSONNE

Sézanne

N4

Marne

ORLÉANAIS

Romilly-sur-Seine

A26

Seine

N19

AUBE

Lac du Der-Chantecoq

Parc Naturel Régional de la Forêt d'Orient

Troyes 🔖

Lac d'Orient

Baye

A5

Sens

A5

Bar-sur-Seine

N77

Essoyes

A6

LOIRET

Loire

YONNE

Yonne

PAYS D'AUXOIS

Les Riceys

N71

CÔTE D'OR

0 60 km
0 40 miles

1. Wine Tasting in Champagne
2. Centre Pompidou-Metz
3. Reims & Amiens Cathedrals
4. Alsace
5. Fort du Hackenburg
6. WWI Sites

NETHERLANDS

Maas

GERMANY

LUXEMBOURG

Luxembourg

Romagne-sous-Montfaucon

Fort du Hackenberg **5**
Veckring
Saarbrücken

MOSELLE

Douaumont
6 *Fleury*
Forêt d'Argonne
Verdun
A4

Metz
2
Lorraine American Cemetery **1** St-Avold
Metz-Nancy-Lorraine Airport

MEUSE
Lac de Madine
▲ Butte de Montsec

Karlsruhe/Baden Baden Airport

BAS-RHIN

Bar-le-Duc

N4
St-Dizier

Nancy

MEURTHE-ET-MOSELLE

Strasbourg
Strasbourg Airport

Maas

Marne

Colombey-les-Deux-Églises
N19

Chaumont

HAUTE-MARNE

A5 **A31**

A31

Moselle

VOSGES

Épinal

Dambach-la-Ville
Château du Haut Kœnigsbourg
Ribeauvillé ● Sélestat
Col du Bonhomme (949m) ✕ ● Riquewihr
Col de la Schucht (1139m) ▲ Kaysersberg
Col de la Schucht (1140m) ✕ ▲ Petit Ballon (1267m)
Colmar **4**

GERMANY

Saône

Grand Ballon (1424m) ▲
▲ Ballon d'Alsace (1247m)

HAUT-RHIN

TERRITOIRE DE BELFORT

HAUTE-SAÔNE

Basel ● **SWITZERLAND**

Rhine River

Champagne & Northern France's Highlights

① Wine Tasting in Champagne

Champagne is a cold misty land, with the subtle beauty of huge skies, rolling hills and austerely attractive villages. Oh, and the wine, it has a restrained exuberance of flavour of which I never tire, and an exceptional aptitude to age well and mellow.

Need to Know

BEST PANORAMA From the high ridge in the village of Cramant **HARVEST** September – the grapes must be hand-picked **READ** Michael's Wine Diary (http://edwards-onwine. skynetblogs.be)

Wine Tasting in Champagne Don't Miss List

BY MICHAEL EDWARDS, GASTRONOMIC WRITER, RESTAURANT CRITIC & CHAMPAGNE CONNOISSEUR

1 REIMS

This great city is now just 45 minutes from Paris by TGV train. Walk on foot from the station to the splendid cathedral (p165) where the kings of France were crowned for 600 years, and then to the even more beautiful Romanesque Basilique St-Rémi (p161). Reims has a fine range of places to eat and, for me, one of France's best fish restaurants: **Le Foch** (☎ 03 26 47 48 22; www.lefoch.com; 37 blvd Foch), close to central place d'Erlon in the city heart.

2 LE MESNIL-SUR-OGER

Head for the village of Le Mesnil in the Côte des Blancs, the greatest Chardonnay commune in Champagne. Taste with rising star Christophe Constant at **Champagne JL Vergnon** (☎ 03 26 57 53 86; www.champagne-jl-vergnon. com; 1 Grand Rue) in the village centre and lunch afterwards at **Le Mesnil** (☎ 03 26 57 95 57; www.restaurantlemesnil. com; 2 rue Pasteur), five minutes' walk away, where Cedric the chef cooks monkfish beautifully – perfect with one of the fine, fairly priced Champagnes on the list.

3 CHAMPAGNE PRODUCER

My favourite right now is **Veuve Fourny & Fils** (☎ 03 26 52 16 30; www.champagne-veuve-fourny.com; rue du Mesnil, Vertus). They are masters of the bone-dry, non-dosed Champagne; theirs is called Brut Nature and is a wonderful partner for all sorts of shellfish and those great cheese pastry balls called *gougères au fromage*.

4 THE CHAMPENOIS

I love the region so much, mainly because of the people. Reserved but with great inner warmth and a deliciously dry sense of humour, the Champenois are resilient and hard working. But they also know how to play: go to any dance hall and you'll see what I mean.

Top: Cathédrale Notre Dame (p165), Reims

Centre Pompidou-Metz

The capital of the Lorraine region has long been known for its Gothic cathedral (p174), but since 2010 there's been a new attraction in town. The Centre Pompidou-Metz (p174) is a northern offshoot of the Centre Pompidou in Paris. Like its sister institution, it presents major exhibitions of modern art, but it's worth a visit simply for its outlandish architecture designed by architects Shigeru Ban and Jean de Gastines.

Alsace

Alsace is one of France's most underrated regions. Sprinkled with picturesque vineyards, hilltop villages and fortified towns, it's chock-full of rustic charm. Start out with a few days exploring stately **Strasbourg** (p167), then spin south for a couple more days on the peaceful canals of **Colmar** (p172). Finish up with a road trip along the 170km **Route des Vins d'Alsace** (p173), where you can sample local wines and soak up the grandstand views.

BARBARA VAN ZANTEN

Reims and Amiens' Cathédrales Notre Dame

Cathedrals don't get much grander than this Gothic twin set, both Unesco World Heritage Sites. Until the Revolution, French monarchs were crowned at Reims (p165), and it remains one of France's most regal cathedrals. Further north, highlights of Amiens' cathedral (p176) include a famous 'weeping' angel and a jewel-encrusted skull rumoured to be John the Baptist's. Cathédrale Notre Dame, Reims

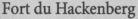

Fort du Hackenberg

Fort du Hackenberg (p177) was one of the largest strongholds on the Maginot Line, the system of fixed defences designed to protect France's eastern border from German invasion. Built at enormous expense to house over 1000 soldiers, the fort proved all but useless in the face of Hitler's blitzkrieg tactics. Its 10km of subterranean tunnels now stand as a fascinating monument to one of the greatest defensive follies of WWII.

WWI Sites

It's been nine decades since the guns of the Western Front fell silent, but the echoes of WWI can still be felt across much of northern France. Dozens of moving memorials and cemeteries commemorate the millions of men who laid down their lives during the course of the conflict, and you can visit many sites associated with the infamous battles of **Verdun** (p178) and the **Somme** (p177). WWI memorial, Verdun

Champagne & Northern France's Best...

Culinary Experiences

◦ **Winstubs** Tuck into hearty fare at these cosy Alsatian restaurants, such as Strasbourg's Maison Kammerzell (p170).

◦ **Sweet treats** (p171) Pick up handmade chocolates and gingerbread in Strasbourg.

◦ **Biscuits Roses** (p163) Try these sweet pink bites with a glass of Champagne.

◦ **Bergamotes de Nancy** (p161) Try Nancy's unique bergamot-flavoured bonbons.

◦ **Alsace Wines** (p173) Sample seven local vintages in Ribeauvillé.

Views

◦ **Reims' Cathedral** (p165) Climb the tower of Reims' Cathédrale de Notre Dame for 360° views.

◦ **Petite Venise** (p172) See the sights around Colmar's prettiest neighbourhood.

◦ **Château du Haut Koenigsbourg** (p173) This fairy-tale castle offers one of Alsace's best panoramas.

◦ **Petite France** (p169) Gaze across the water to Strasbourg's monumental Barrage Vauban.

◦ **Quartier Impérial** (p174) Admire the architecture in Metz' Germanic quarter.

Unusual Museums

◦ **Centre Pompidou-Metz** (p174) Metz' centre for cutting-edge art.

◦ **Maison de Jules Verne** (p176) Visit the sci-fi pioneer's former home in Amiens.

◦ **Musée d'Art Moderne et Contemporain** (p169) More modern art in Strasbourg's glass cube.

◦ **Musée Bartholdi** (p173) Visit Colmar to see where the Statue of Liberty was created.

Need to Know

City Squares

○ **Place des Héros & Grand'Place** (p161) Arras offers a feast for the eyes, especially at night.

○ **Place Notre Dame** (p176) Best viewed in summer when a light show illuminates Amiens' cathedral.

○ **Place Stanislas** (p161) Nancy's neoclassical square is a World Heritage Site.

○ **Place de la République** (p169) Home to Strasbourg's most extravagant buildings.

ADVANCE PLANNING

○ **A month before** Book accommodation as early as possible, especially in Reims, Strasbourg, Épernay and Metz.

○ **Two weeks before** Reserve a guided tour of some Champagne cellars.

○ **One week before** Research money-saving city passes. Strasbourg and Reims both have passes covering sights, museums and public transport.

RESOURCES

○ **Champagne-Ardenne** (www.tourisme-champagne-ardenne.com) Walks, sights and general ideas for the Champagne region.

○ **Northern France Tourist Office** (www.cdt-nord.fr) Offers several themed routes around the region.

○ **Northern Alsace** (www.tourisme67.com) Driving tours, cultural activities and outdoor pursuits.

○ **Southern Alsace** (www.tourisme68.com) Similar info for further south.

○ **Lorraine** (www.tourism-lorraine.com) Main portal for the Lorraine region.

○ **Somme Battlefields** (www.somme-battlefields.co.uk)

GETTING AROUND

○ **Car** Useful for Champagne's more out-of-the-way spots, and pretty much essential in Alsace. Just don't overdo the bubbly.

○ **Train** The big cities can be easily reached by train. Reims, Épernay, Troyes and Metz all make excellent day trips from Paris.

○ **Eurostar** (www.eurostar.com) The high-speed Eurostar connects London with Lille and Strasbourg.

○ **Bus** Buses are limited, but are the best option between Reims and Troyes.

BE FOREWARNED

○ **Champagne** Producers around Reims and Épernay close their doors to visitors during the *vendange* (grape harvest) in September and October.

○ **Hotels** Reims and Épernay are often full at weekends Easter to September and weekdays May, June and September. Hotels in Strasbourg are often booked out during the week when European parliament is in session.

○ **WWI sites** Visitor centres are often closed in January, but cemeteries are open year-round.

Left: Maison Kammerzell (p170);
Above: West door, Reims Cathedral (p165)
PHOTOGRAPHERS: (LEFT) HOLGER LEUE;
(ABOVE) OLIVER STREWE

Champagne & Northern France Itineraries

With its famous fizz houses, chic cities and elegant architecture, Champagne and Northern France encapsulates France's love affair with the finer things in life. It's a treat from start to finish.

3 DAYS

PARIS TO ÉPERNAY

CHAMPAGNE TASTER

This trip provides a perfect introduction to the Champagne region. From **(1) Paris**, it's an easy trip by train or car to **(2) Reims**, home to some of the world's biggest bubbly producers. Spend the first day tasting your way around Mumm, Taittinger and the other big-name Champagne houses. Lunch in art-deco surroundings at Brasserie le Boulingrin before tackling the 250 steps of the city's spectacular cathedral tower. Indulge in a spot of wine and Champagne shopping, before breaking for afternoon tea (actually champagne and pink biscuits) at Waïda. Overnight in the home of a former Champagne merchant at the Grand Hôtel des Templiers.

On day two, catch a train on to **(3) Épernay** and its wealth of subterranean cellars, where 200-million-plus bottles of Champers are being aged, just waiting to be popped open for some sparkling occasion. Take your pick of the city's champagne houses before enjoying a leisurely lunch at La Cave à Champagne, an afternoon's shopping and sightseeing, and an evening at Le Clos Raymi.

Spend day three on a leisurely bike ride or a guided tour of some of the region's smaller vineyards.

ÉPERNAY TO COLMAR
ARCHITECTURE

This trip takes in some of northeast France's top architectural sights. Train is the easiest option between the cities, but you'll have to rely on buses or hiring a car along the Route des Vins d'Alsace. From **(1) Épernay** head to **(2) Metz**, one of France's most-attractive provincial cities. Visit its elegant cathedral and latest modern landmark, the Centre Pompidou-Metz.

Next, move on to **(3) Nancy**. Its splendid 18th-century buildings are best seen around Unesco-listed place Stanislas.

Then head to stately **(4) Strasbourg**, the official home of the EU parliament. It's a suitably grand city, with elements from nearly all of the key periods of French architecture. Step back into the Middle Ages around Grande Île and Petite France, admire the Renaissance at the Palais Rohan, experience 19th-century splendour on the place de la République and marvel at the bold modern statement of the Musée d'Art Moderne et Contemporain.

Spend a couple of days exploring the wider Alsace region. Follow the **(5) Route des Vins d'Alsace** through picturesque vineyards and hilltop villages, before finishing up in atmospheric **(6) Colmar**.

Champagne vineyard near Épernay (p164)
PHOTOGRAPHER: OLIVER STREWE

159

Discover Champagne & Northern France

At a Glance

○ **Champagne** (p160) Famous for its bubbly, Champagne is a must-visit for wine-lovers, with the nation's top fizz houses and a host of smaller *vignerons* to explore.

○ **Northern France** (p167) Often overlooked, France's northern corner is awash with culture and history, from moving WWI battlefields to some of France's most fascinating cities.

Statue to Dom Pierre Pérignon
PHOTOGRAPHER: JULIET COOMBE

CHAMPAGNE

Champagne arouses all of the senses: the eyes feast on vine-covered hillsides and vertical processions of tiny, sparkling bubbles; the nose is tantalised by the damp soil and the heavenly bouquet of fermentation; the ears rejoice at the clink of glasses and the barely audible fizz; and the palate tingles with every sip.

Reims

POP 187,650

Over the course of a millennium (816 to 1825), some 34 sovereigns – among them two dozen kings – began their reigns in Reims' famed cathedral. Along with Épernay (just a half-hour away by train), it is the most important centre of Champagne production and makes an excellent base for exploring the Montagne de Reims Champagne Route.

 Sights

The great-value **Discovery Pass** (€3/free for an adult/ student) gets you into Reims' three municipal museums – Musée des Beaux-Arts, Musée St-Rémi and Musée de la Reddition – and Chapelle Foujita. The **Reims City Card** (€15), available at the tourist office, entitles you to the Champagne house tour of your choice, an audioguide tour of the cathedral and all the benefits of a Discovery Pass.

PALAIS DU TAU Museum
(☑ 03 26 47 81 79; www.palais-du-tau.fr; 2 place du Cardinal Luçon; adult/under 26yr €7/free; ⊙9.30am-12.30pm & 2-5.30pm, closed Mon) This former archbishop's residence,

constructed in 1690, was where French princes stayed before their coronations – and where they hosted sumptuous banquets afterwards. Now a museum, it displays truly exceptional statuary, liturgical objects and tapestries from the cathedral, some in the impressive, Gothic Salle de Tau (Great Hall).

BASILIQUE ST-RÉMI Basilica

(place du Chanoine Ladame; ⊙8am-nightfall, to 7pm summer) This 121m-long former Benedictine abbey church, a Unesco World Heritage Site, mixes Romanesque elements from the mid-11th century (the worn but stunning nave and transept) with early Gothic features from the latter half of the 12th century (the choir, with a large triforium gallery and, way up top, tiny clerestory windows). The basilica is situated about 1.5km south-southeast of the tourist office; take the Citadine 1 or 2 or bus A or F to the St-Rémi stop.

MUSÉE DES BEAUX-ARTS

Art Museum

(Museum of Fine Arts; ☑03 26 35 36 01; 8 rue Chanzy; ⊙10am-noon & 2-6pm, closed Tue) This institution's rich collection, housed in an 18th-century abbey, boasts one of only four versions of Jacques-Louis David's world-famous *Death of Marat* (yes, the bloody corpse in the bathtub), 27 works by Camille Corot (only the Louvre has more), 13 portraits by German Renaissance painters Cranach the Elder and the Younger, lots of Barbizon School landscapes, some art-nouveau creations by Émile Gallé, and two works each by Monet, Gauguin and Pissarro.

MUSÉE DE LA REDDITION Museum

(Surrender Museum; ☑03 26 47 84 19; 12 rue Franklin Roosevelt; ⊙10am-noon & 2-6pm Wed-Mon) The original Allied battle maps are still affixed to the walls of US General Dwight D Eisenhower's headquarters, where Nazi Germany, represented by General Alfred Jodl, surrendered unconditionally at 2.41am on 7 May 1945.

If You Like…
Architecture

If you've been impressed by the architecture of Reims, then you won't want to miss these architectural gems:

1 TROYES

(☑tourist office 03 25 73 36 88; www.tourisme-troyes.com; rue Mignard; ⊙10am-1pm & 2-6pm Mon-Sat, 10am-noon & 2-5pm Sun & holidays, closed Nov-early Apr) This historic city contains some of France's best-preserved medieval buildings. The tiny ruelle des Chats (Alley of the Cats) has barely changed in four centuries.

2 ARRAS

(☑tourist office 03 21 51 26 95; www.ot-arras.fr; place des Héros) Arras' Flemish-inspired architecture is plain to see on the twin market squares, place des Héros and the Grand'Place. For a panoramic perspective, climb the Unesco-listed belltower.

3 LILLE

(☑tourist office 08 91 56 20 04; www.lilletourism.com; place Rihour) Flemish influences are everywhere in industrial Lille, but the city also boasts an attractive old town dotted with art-deco buildings and a trio of art museums.

4 NANCY

(☑tourist office 03 83 35 22 41; www.ot-nancy.fr; place Stanislas; ⊙9am-7pm Mon-Sat, 10am-5pm Sun) The former capital of the Dukes of Lorraine catapults you into 18th-century splendour. The Unesco-listed place Stanislas was laid out in the 1750s.

Tours

The musty *caves* (cellars) and dusty bottles of eight Reims-area **Champagne houses** (known as *maisons* – literally, 'houses') can be visited on guided tours.

MUMM Champagne Cellar

(☑03 26 49 59 70; www.mumm.com; 34 rue du Champ de Mars; tours €10; ⊙tours begin 9am-11am & 2-5pm daily Mar-Oct & Sat Nov-Feb) Mumm (pronounced 'moom'), the only *maison*

161

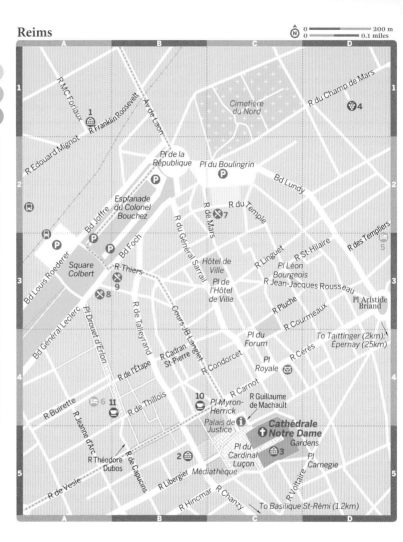

in central Reims, was founded in 1827 and is now the world's third-largest producer (almost eight million bottles a year). Tours that include tutored tastings of special vintages cost €15 to €20.

TAITTINGER   Champagne Cellar

(☎03 26 85 84 33; www.taittinger.com; 9 place St-Niçaise; tours €10; ⏰ tours begin 9.30-11.50am & 2pm-4.20pm, closed Sat & Sun mid-Nov–mid-Mar) The headquarters of Taittinger is an excellent place to come for a clear, straightforward presentation on how Champagne is actually made – there's

no claptrap about the 'Champagne mystique' here. Situated 1.5km southeast of Reims centre; take the Citadine 1 or 2 bus to the St-Niçaise or Salines stops.

 Sleeping

GRAND HÔTEL DES TEMPLIERS

Hotel €€€

(☎03 26 88 55 08; www.grandhoteldestempliers -reims.com; 22 rue des Templiers; r €190-280, ste €350; ❄@🛜🏊) Built in the 1800s

Reims

as the home of a rich Champagne merchant, this neo-Gothic extravaganza retains its original ceilings, stained glass and furnishings.

HÔTEL DE LA PAIX   Hotel €€

(☎03 26 40 04 08; www.bestwestern-lapaix-reims.com; 9 rue Buirette; d €155-205; ❄ @ 🛜 🏊) An island of serenity just steps from hopping place Drouet d'Erlon, this modern, Best Western–affiliated hostelry has 169 classy, comfortable rooms; upgrade to 'Deluxe' for lots more space. To mellow out, you can head to the pool, jacuzzi, hammam and fitness room – or the calming Japanese garden in the courtyard.

Eating

LE FOCH   Modern French €€

(☎03 26 47 48 22; www.lefoch.com; 37 bd Foch; menus €31-80; ❍ closed Mon, lunch Sat & dinner Sun) Described as 'one of France's best fish restaurants' by the food critic Michael Edwards, elegant Le Foch – holder of one Michelin star – serves up classic cuisine that's as beautiful as it is delicious.

BRASSERIE LE BOULINGRIN

 Brasserie €€

(☎03 26 40 96 22; www.boulingrin.fr; 48 rue de Mars; menus €18-28; ❍Mon-Sat) A genuine, old-time brasserie – the decor and zinc bar date back to 1925 – whose ambience and cuisine make it an enduring favourite.

Côté Cuisine

 Traditional French €

(☎03 26 83 93 68; 43 bd Foch; mains €11.80-22.50, weekday lunch menus €12-15.50, dinner menus €32.50; ❍closed dinner Sun) A spacious, semiformal place with white tablecloths, modern chandeliers and well-regarded traditional French cuisine.

Drinking

CAFÉ DU PALAIS   Café

(www.cafedupalais.fr; 14 place Myron-Herrick; ❍10am-8.30pm, to midnight or 1am Fri & Sat, closed Sun) Run by the same family since 1930, this old-time café is *the* place to see and be seen, at least if you're a *bon bourgeois* or a theatre type.

WAÏDA   Tearoom

(5 place Drouet d'Erlon; ❍7.30am-7.30pm Tue-Sun) A good place to pick up a box of *biscuits roses* (€3.90), traditionally nibbled with Champagne (€6 to €7.50 a glass). The *religieuses* (cream-filled puff pastries; €2.75) are divine!

🛈 Information

Tourist office (☎08 92 70 13 51, per minute €0.34; www.reims-tourisme.com; 2 rue Guillaume de Machault; ❍9am-7pm Mon-Sat, 10am-6pm Sun & holidays)

🛈 Getting There & Away

Half the trains to Paris Gare de l'Est (12 to 17 daily) are TGVs (€32 to €41, 45 minutes); the rest are TERs (€24, 1¾ hours). Direct services also go to Épernay (€6, 20 to 36 minutes, 18 daily weekdays, seven to 11 daily weekends), Laon (€9, 35 to 50 minutes, nine daily Monday to Friday, five on Saturday, three on Sunday) and Charles de Gaulle airport (three times a day).

Épernay

POP 25,225

Épernay, self-proclaimed *capitale du champagne* and home to many of the world's most celebrated Champagne houses, is the best place in Champagne for touring cellars and sampling bubbly.

Beneath the streets in 110km of subterranean cellars, more than 200 million bottles of Champagne, just waiting to be popped open on some sparkling occasion, are being aged.

 ## Sights & Activities

Several *maisons* offer informative and engaging cellar tours, followed by a *dégustation* (tasting) and a visit to the factory-outlet shop.

MOËT & CHANDON   Champagne House
(☏03 26 51 20 20; www.moet.com; adult incl 1/2 glasses €14.50/22, 10-18yr €9; 20 av de Champagne; ☉ tours 9.30am-noon & 2-4.30pm, closed Sat & Sun mid-Nov–mid-Mar, also closed Jan) This prestigious *maison* offers frequent one-hour tours that are among the region's most impressive.

Moët & Chandon château

MERCIER   Champagne House
(☏03 26 51 22 22; www.champagnemercier.fr; 68-70 av de Champagne; adult incl 1/3 glasses €9/17, 12-17yr €5; ☉ tours 9.30-11.30am & 2-4.30pm, closed mid-Dec–mid-Feb) Everything here is flashy, including the 160,000L barrel that took two decades to build (for the Universal Exposition of 1889), the lift that transports you 30m underground and the laser-guided touring train.

DE CASTELLANE   Champagne House
(☏03 26 51 19 11; www.castellane.com, in French; 64 av de Champagne; adult incl 1 glass €8.50, under 12yr free; ☉ tours 10-11am & 2-5pm, closed Christmas–mid-Mar) The 45-minute tours, in French and English, take in an informative bubbly museum dedicated to elucidating the *méthode champenoise* and its diverse technologies.

 ## Sleeping

LE CLOS RAYMI   Historic Hotel   €€
(☏03 26 51 00 58; www.closraymi-hotel.com, in French; 3 rue Joseph de Venoge; d from €100, ste €160; 🛜) Staying at this atmospheric

OLIVER STREWE

DANIEL VALLA FRPS/ALAMY

Don't Miss Cathédrale Notre Dame, Reims

Imagine the extravagance, the over-the-top costumes and the egos writ large of a French royal coronation. The structure, a Unesco World Heritage Site since 1991, celebrates its 800th anniversary in 2011.

The finest stained-glass windows are the western facade's 12-petalled **great rose window**; its cobalt-blue neighbour below; and the **rose window** in the north transept (to the left as you walk from the entrance to the high altar), above the Flamboyant Gothic **organ case** (15th and 18th centuries) topped with a figure of Christ.

Feeling as strong as Goliath (look for his worn figure up on the west facade, held in place with metal straps)? Then consider climbing 250 steps up the **cathedral tower** on a one-hour tour. Book at the Palais du Tau.

NEED TO KNOW

(www.cathedrale-reims.culture.fr, www.cathedrale-reims.com, in French; place du Cardinal Luçon; ⊗7.30am-7.30pm, closed during Sun morning Mass); Cathedral tower (adult/under 26yr €7/free, incl the Palais du Tau €9.50; ⊗tours 10am, 11am, 2pm, 3pm & 4pm Tue-Sat & Sun afternoon mid-Mar–Oct, every half-hour 10-11.30am & 2-5pm early May–early Sep)

---

place is like being a personal guest of Monsieur Chandon of Champagne fame, who occupied this luxurious town house over a century ago. The seven romantic rooms – styles include Provençal, Tuscan and colonial – have giant beds, high ceilings, French windows and parquet floors.

HÔTEL LES BERCEAUX   Hotel €€
(☎ 03 26 55 28 84; www.lesberceaux.com; 13 rue des Berceaux; d €95-115; ⊛) Founded in 1889, this institution has 28 comfortable, sound-proofed rooms with lots of dark-wood veneer and all-tile bathrooms.

Eating

RESTAURANT LE THÉÂTRE
Tradtional French €€

(📞 03 26 58 88 19; www.epernay-rest-letheatre.com, in French; 8 place Mendès-France; lunch menus €17-22, dinner menus €28-46; ⏱ closed Wed, dinner Tue & dinner Sun) Refined traditional cuisine is served in a classic corner dining room built a century ago as a brasserie, with 4.2m ceilings and floor-to-ceiling windows. The menu changes every three weeks, depending to what's fresh in the markets.

LA CAVE À CHAMPAGNE
Regional Cuisine €€

(📞 03 26 55 50 70; www.la-cave-a-champagne.com, in French; 16 rue Gambetta; menus €17-32; ⏱ closed Wed & dinner Tue) 'The Champagne Cellar' is well regarded by locals for its *champenoise* cuisine, served in a warm, traditional, bourgeois atmosphere.

BISTROT LE 7
Modern French €€

(📞 03 26 55 28 84; 13 rue des Berceaux; menus €17-23) One of the restaurants at Hôtel Les Berceaux has earned a Michelin star; the other (this one) serves excellent French cuisine amid semiformal, Mediterranean-chic decor.

ℹ Information

Tourist office (📞 03 26 53 33 00; www.ot-epernay.fr; 7 av de Champagne; ⏱ 9.30am-12.30pm & 1.30-7pm Mon-Sat, 11am-4pm Sun & holidays) Has excellent English brochures and maps on cellar visits, walking and cycling options and car touring, and rents out a GPS unit (€7 per day) with self-guided vineyard driving tours in French, English and Dutch.

ℹ Getting There & Around

The **train station** (place Mendès-France) has direct services to Reims (€6, 20 to 36 minutes, 18 daily weekdays, seven to 11 daily weekends) and Paris Gare de l'Est (€21, 1¼ hours, five to 10 daily).

Left: Alsace vineyards; **Below:** Windowbox, Alsace

PHOTOGRAPHER: (LEFT) BARBARA VAN ZANTEN; (BELOW) BARBARA VAN ZANTEN

NORTHERN FRANCE

Many visitors never take the time to explore France's northern regions, but they're missing out. Alsace is a one-off cultural hybrid, with a Germanic dialect and French sense of fashion (not to mention its passion for sauerkraut), fine wine *and* beer.

Next door, Lorraine offers graceful cities, stunning cathedrals and stellar art galleries, while the rest of northern France is strewn with museums and memorials exploring the region's WWI history.

Strasbourg

POP 276,000

Strasbourg is the perfect overture to all that is idiosyncratic about Alsace – walking a fine tightrope between France and Germany, a medieval past and a progressive future, it pulls off its act in inimitable Alsatian style.

Sights

The **Strasbourg Pass** (adult/child €12.50/6), a coupon book valid for three consecutive days, includes a visit to one museum, access to the cathedral platform, half a day's bicycle rental and a boat tour, plus hefty discounts on other tours and attractions.

CATHÉDRALE NOTRE-DAME Cathedral
(place de la Cathédrale; ☺7am-7pm; 🚋Langstross) At once immense and intricate, the cathedral is a riot of filigree stonework and flying buttresses, leering gargoyles and lacy spires.

The west facade, most impressive if approached from rue Mercière, was completed in 1284, but the 142m spire – the tallest of its time – was not in place until 1439; its southern companion was never built.

DISCOVER CHAMPAGNE & NORTHERN FRANCE **NORTHERN FRANCE**

Strasbourg

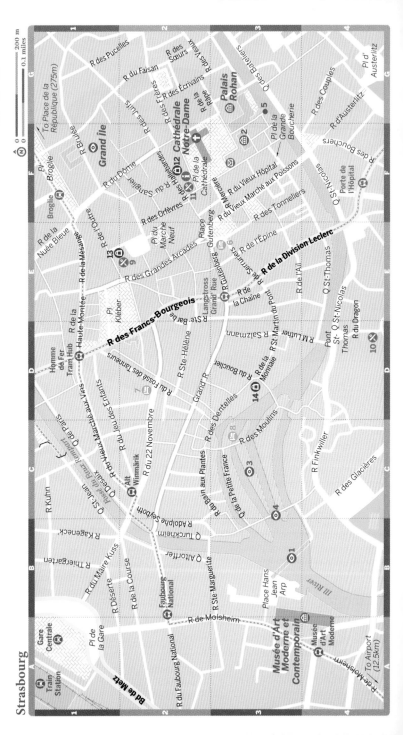

0 0 200 m
0 0 0.1 miles

Gare
Centrale

Train Station

Bd de Metz

Homme de Fer
Tram Hub

Grand Île

To Place de la
République (275m)

Palais
Rohan

Cathédrale
Notre-Dame

R des Francs-Bourgeois

R de la Division Leclerc

Musée d'Art
Moderne et
Contemporain

Musée
d'Art
Moderne

To Airport
(12.5km)

Place Hans
Jean Arp

Ill River

Strabourg

A spiral staircase twists up to the 66m-high **platform (adult/child €4.70/2.30;** ⏱9am-7.15pm) above the facade, from which the tower and its Gothic openwork spire soar another 76m.

GRANDE ÎLE   Historic Quarter
(🚋Langstross) History seeps through winding lanes dotted with candy-coloured half-timbered houses and vibrant café-rimmed squares in the Unesco World Heritage site of Grande Île, a place made for aimless ambling.

PETITE FRANCE   Historic Quarter
(🚋Alt Winmärik) Criss-crossed by narrow lanes, canals and locks, impossibly pretty Petite France is where artisans plied their trades in the Middle Ages. Drink in views of the River Ill and the mighty 17th-century **Barrage Vauban** (Vauban Dam), undergoing renovation at the time of writing, from the much-photographed

Ponts Couverts (Covered Bridges) and their trio of 13th-century towers.

MUSÉE D'ART MODERNE ET CONTEMPORAIN   Art Museum
(place Hans Jean Arp; adult/child €6/free; ⏱noon-7pm Tue, Wed & Fri, noon-9pm Thu, 10am-6pm Sat & Sun; 🚋Musée d'Art Moderne) This striking glass-and-steel cube showcases an outstanding collection of fine art, graphic art and photography. Kandinsky, Picasso, Magritte and Monet canvases hang out alongside curvaceous works by Strasbourg-born abstract artist Hans Jean Arp.

PALAIS ROHAN   Historic Residence
(2 place du Château; adult/child €5/free; ⏱noon-6pm Mon & Wed-Fri, 10am-6pm Sat & Sun; 🚋Langstross) Hailed a 'Versailles in miniature', this opulent 18th-century residence was built for the city's princely bishops, and Louis XV and Marie-Antoinette once slept here.

MUSÉE DE L'ŒUVRE NOTRE-DAME
       Ecclesiastical Museum
(3 place du Château; adult/child €4/free; ⏱noon-6pm Tue-Fri, 10am-6pm Sat & Sun; 🚋Langstross) Occupying a cluster of sublime 14th- and 16th-century buildings, this museum harbours one of Europe's premier collections of Romanesque, Gothic and Renaissance sculptures (including many originals from the cathedral), 15th-century paintings, and stained glass. *Christ de Wissembourg* (c 1060; room two) is the oldest work of stained glass in France.

PLACE DE LA RÉPUBLIQUE   City Square
(🚋République) Many of Strasbourg's grandest public buildings, constructed when the city was ruled by the German Reich, huddle northeast of Grande Île around place de la République.

 Tours

BATORAMA   Boat Trips
(www.batorama.fr, in French; adult/child €8.50/4.50; ⏱tours half-hourly 9.30am-9pm; 🚋Langstross) This outfit's scenic

169

70-minute boat trips glide along the story-book canals of Petite France, past Vauban Dam and the glinting EU institutions.

Sleeping

HÔTEL RÉGENT PETITE FRANCE
Design Hotel €€€

(☎03 88 76 43 43; www.regent-hotels.com; 5 rue des Moulins; r €150-445; ❄ @ 🛜 🚉 Alt Winmärik) Once an ice factory, now Strasbourg's hottest design hotel, this waterfront pile is quaint on the outside and ubercool on the inside. The sleek rooms dressed in muted colours and plush fabrics sport shiny marble bathrooms.

HÔTEL GUTENBERG
Historic Hotel €€

(☎03 88 32 17 15; www.hotel-gutenberg.com; 31 rue des Serruriers; r €75-135; ❄ @ 🛜 🚉 Langstross) Nestled in the flower-strewn heart of Petite France, this hotel is a harmonious blend of 250 years of history and contemporary design – think clean lines, zesty colours and the occasional antique.

HÔTEL HANNONG
Boutique Hotel €€

(☎03 88 32 16 22; www.hotel-hannong.com; 15 rue du 22 Novembre; s €88-108, d €132-197; ❄ 🛜 🚉 Alt Winmärik) Minimalist chic best describes the rooms at this design-focused hotel, kitted out with hardwood floors and colour schemes ranging from space-age silver to chocolate-cream. The skylit bar serves tapas and fine wines.

Eating

LA CHOUCROUTERIE
Alsatian €€

(☎03 88 36 52 87; www.choucrouterie.com, in French; 20 rue St-Louis; choucroute €12-16; 🕐lunch Mon-Fri, dinner daily; 🚉 Porte de l'Hôpital) Naked ladies straddling giant sausages (on the menu, we hasten to add) and eccentric chefs juggling plates of steaming *choucroute garnie* are just the tip of the theatrical iceberg at this inimitable bistro and playhouse double act.

AU CROCODILE
Gastronomic €€€

(☎03 88 32 13 02; www.au-crocodile.com, in French; 10 rue de l'Outre; 3-course lunch menus €35, other menus incl drinks €85/115; 🕐Tue-Sat; 🚉 Broglie) Artistically presented specialities such as smooth foie gras with rhubarb chutney and filet mignon in a mountain-cheese crust have won Au Crocodile a Michelin star. Advance reservations recommended.

MAISON KAMMERZELL
Alsatian €€

(☎03 88 32 42 14; www.maison-kammerzell.com; 16 place de la Cathédrale; menus €27-46; 🚉 Langstross) Slap-bang on Strasbourg's main square, medieval icon Maison Kammerzell serves well-executed Alsatian cuisine like *baeckeoffe* and *choucroute*. A staircase spirals up to

Au Crocodile

DISCOVER CHAMPAGNE & NORTHERN FRANCE

Grand' Rue, Strasbourg

YADID LEVY/ALAMY

frescoed alcoves and the 1st floor where the views – oh the views! – of the floodlit cathedral are sensational.

 Shopping

Strasbourg's swishest shopping street is rue des Hallebardes, whose window displays are real eye candy (**Baccarat** is at No 44). High-street stores punctuate rue des Grandes Arcades and Grand' Rue, while Petite France is crammed with souvenir shops selling stuffed storks and pretzels aplenty.

Strasbourg is also well known for its sweet tooth. Pick up gingerbread at **Mireille Oster** (www.mireille-oster.com, in French; 14 rue des Dentelles; 🚋Langstross) or head for **Christian** (www.christian. fr, in French; 12 rue de l'Outre; 🚋Broglie) for sumptuous truffles, pralines and edible Strasbourg landmarks.

 Information

Main tourist office (📞03 88 52 28 28; www. otstrasbourg.fr; 17 place de la Cathédrale; ⏰9am-7pm; 🚋Langstross)

🛈 **Getting There & Away**

Air

Strasbourg's international **airport** (www. strasbourg.aeroport.fr) is 17km southwest of the city centre (towards Molsheim), near the village of Entzheim.

Train

DOMESTIC Destinations:

Paris Gare de l'Est; €67, 2¼ hours, 17 daily

Lille €94, four hours, 13 daily

Lyon €52, six hours, five daily

Marseille €87, eight hours, five daily

Metz €23, two hours, 20 daily

Nancy €22, 1½ hours, 25 daily

INTERNATIONAL If you take the Eurostar via Paris or Lille, London is just five hours and 15 minutes away.

ROUTE DES VINS From Strasbourg, there are trains to Route des Vins destinations including the following:

Colmar €10.50, 30 minutes, 30 daily

Dambach-la-Ville €8, one hour, 12 daily

Obernai €5.50, 30 minutes, 20 daily

Sélestat €7.50, 30 minutes, 46 daily

171

❶ Getting Around

To/From the Airport

The speedy new shuttle train links the airport to the train station (€3.50, nine minutes, four hourly); the ticket also covers your onward tram journey into the city centre.

Public Transport

Five super-efficient tram lines, A through E, form the backbone of Strasbourg's outstanding public transport network, run by CTS (www.cts-strasbourg.fr, in French).

Tickets, valid on both buses and trams, are sold by bus drivers and ticket machines at tram stops and cost €1.40 (€2.70 return).

Colmar

POP 67,700

Capital of the Alsace wine region and a happy-ever-after fairy-tale of a city if ever there was one, Colmar is a beguiling maze of higgledy-piggledy lanes, where gingerbready half-timbered houses and the tranquil canals of Petite Venise elicit little gasps of wonder.

Colmar's illustrious past is clearly etched in its magnificent churches and

museums, celebrating local legends from Bartholdi to the Issenheim Altarpiece.

Sights

PETITE VENISE   Historic Quarter
One of Colmar's biggest draws is its story-book Little Venice quarter, laced with canals and crammed with half-timbered houses festooned with geraniums. You can almost picture merchants at work in the Middle Ages wandering streets like rue des Tanneurs, with its rooftop verandas for drying hides, and quai de la Poissonnerie, the former fishers' quarter.

MUSÉE D'UNTERLINDEN   Art Museum
(www.musee-unterlinden.com; 1 rue d'Unterlinden; adult/child incl audioguide €7/3; ⏰9am-6pm Mon-Sun) Gathered around a Gothic-style Dominican cloister, this museum hides a prized collection of medieval stone statues, late 15th-century prints by Martin Schongauer and an ensemble of Upper Rhine Primitives.

The star attraction, though, is the late-Gothic **Rétable d'Issenheim** (Issenheim Altarpiece).

Petite Venise, Colmar

BARBARA VAN ZANTEN

MUSÉE BARTHOLDI — Museum

(www.musee-bartholdi.com, in French; 30 rue des Marchands; adult/child €4.50/2.50; ⏱10am-noon & 2-6pm Wed-Mon) In the house where Frédéric Auguste Bartholdi was born, this museum pays homage to the sculptor who captured the spirit of a nation with his Statue of Liberty.

A 12m-high replica of the statue can be seen on the route de Strasbourg (N83), 3km north of the old town.

 ## Sleeping

HÔTEL LES TÊTES — Historic Hotel €€
(☎03 89 24 43 43; www.maisondestetes.com; 19 rue des Têtes; d €91-146; ❄) Luxurious but never precious, this hotel occupies the magnificent Maison des Têtes. Each of its 21 rooms has rich wood panelling, an elegant sitting area, a marble bathroom and romantic views.

HÔTEL ST-MARTIN — Historic Hotel €€
(☎03 89 24 11 51; www.hotel-saint-martin.com; 38 Grand' Rue; s €79, d €89-115; ❄ @ 🛗) What a location! Right on the place de l'Ancienne Douane, this 14th-century patrician house captures the elegance of yesteryear in rooms dressed with handcrafted furniture.

LE MARÉCHAL — Boutique Hotel €€
(☎03 89 41 60 32; www.hotel-le-marechal.com; 46 place des Six Montagnes Noires; s €85-95, d €105-140; @) Peppered with antiques, this 16th-century hotel in Petite Venise cranks up the romance in its cosy (read small) rooms, many with low beams, canopy beds and canal views.

 ## Eating

LE PETIT GOURMAND — Alsatian €€
(☎03 89 41 09 32; 9 quai de la Poissonnerie; menus €23-26; ⏱Tue-Sun) Just a few lucky, lucky diners can eat at this Lilliputian

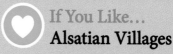

If You Like...
Alsatian Villages

Fallen for the chocolate-box charm of Colmar? Then don't miss visiting some of the other picturesque locations dotted along the 170km Route des Vins d'Alsace, one of France's most-popular driving routes. For online info, see www.alsace-route-des-vins.com.

1 KAYSERSBERG
Ten kilometres northwest of Colmar, Kaysersberg is an instant heart-stealer with its sloping vines, hilltop castle and 16th-century fortified bridge.

2 RIQUEWIHR
With medieval ramparts enclosing a photogenic maze of twisting lanes, hidden courtyards and half-timbered houses, Riquewihr is one of the most-enchanting towns on the Route des Vins. It's 14km northwest of Colmar.

3 RIBEAUVILLÉ
(www.cave-ribeauville.com; 2 rte de Colmar; ⏱8am-noon & 2-6pm Mon-Fri, 10am-noon & 2-6pm Sat & Sun) Sample Alsatian wines at France's oldest wine growers' cooperative (founded 1895), 3km from Riquewihr.

4 SÉLESTAT
Twenty-three kilometres north of Colmar, Sélestat is famous for its **Humanist Library** (1 rue de la Bibliothèque; adult/child €4/2.50; ⏱9am-noon & 2-6pm Mon & Wed-Fri, 9am-noon Sat).

5 DAMBACH-LA-VILLE
Ringed by vines and sturdy ramparts, this flowery village has some 60 wine cellars to visit. It's 32km north of Colmar.

6 CHÂTEAU DU HAUT KOENIGSBOURG
(www.haut-koenigsbourg.fr; adult/child €7.50/free; ⏱9.15am-5.15pm) This château is worth the detour for the wrap-around panorama from its ramparts.

winstub, which has a pontoon on the river for warm nights.

RESTAURANT LE STREUSEL
Alsatian €€

(☎03 89 24 98 02; 4 passage de l'Ancienne Douane; mains €11-16) Dig into good old-fashioned Alsatian cooking, from *fleischnacka* to *choucroute* with stubby pork knuckles, at this beamed 16th-century farmhouse turned restaurant.

ⓘ Information

Tourist office (☎03 89 20 68 92; www.ot-colmar.fr; 4 rue d'Unterlinden; ⊗9am-6pm Mon-Sat, 10am-1pm Sun)

ⓘ Getting There & Away

TRAIN Colmar has train connections to the following:

Basel SNCF €12, 43 minutes, 25 daily

Mulhouse €7.50, 18 minutes, 38 daily

Paris Gare de l'Est; €74, three hours by direct TGV, 17 daily

Strasbourg €11, 35 minutes, 30 daily

Route des Vins destinations from Colmar include Dambach-la-Ville (€5.50) and Obernai (€7.50), both of which require a change of trains at Sélestat (€4.50, 11 minutes, 30 daily).

Metz
POP 125,720

Sitting astride the confluence of the Moselle and Seille rivers, Lorraine's graceful capital Metz (pronounced 'mess') is ready to be fêted. Though the city's Gothic marvel of a cathedral, superlative art collections and Michelin star–studded dining scene long managed to side-step the world spotlight, that all changed with the show-stopping arrival of Centre Pompidou-Metz.

◎ Sights

CATHÉDRALE ST-ÉTIENNE
Cathedral

(place St-Étienne; ⊗8am-6pm) As delicate as Chantilly lace, the golden spires of this Gothic cathedral crown Metz' skyline. Exquisitely lit by kaleidoscopic curtains of 13th- to 20th-century stained glass, the cathedral is nicknamed 'God's lantern'.

Notice the flamboyant **Chagall windows** in the ambulatory, which also harbours the **treasury** (adult/child €2/1; ⊗10am-12.30pm & 2-5pm).

CENTRE POMPIDOU-METZ
Gallery

(www.centrepompidou-metz.fr; 1 parvis des Droits de l'Homme; adult/child €7/free; ⊗11am-6pm Mon, Wed & Sun, 11am-8pm Thu-Sat) Opened in May 2010 to much fanfare, the architecturally innovative Centre Pompidou-Metz is the satellite branch of Paris' Centre Pompidou and the new star of the city's art scene. The gallery draws on Europe's largest collection of modern art to stage ambitious temporary exhibitions, such as the inaugural *Chefs d'oeuvre* (Masterpieces), which presented standouts by Picasso, Matisse and Kandinsky.

MUSÉE LA COUR D'OR
History Museum

(2 rue du Haut Poirier; adult/child €4.60/free; ⊗9am-5pm Mon & Wed-Fri, 10am-5pm Sat & Sun) Delve into the past at this trove of Gallo-Roman antiquities, hiding remnants of the city's Roman baths and a statue of the Egyptian goddess Isis unearthed right here in Metz. Your visit continues with art from the Middle Ages, paintings from the 15th century onwards, and artefacts revealing the history of Metz' ancient Jewish community.

QUARTIER IMPÉRIAL
Historic Quarter

The stately boulevards and bourgeois villas of the German Imperial Quarter, including rue Gambetta and av Foch, are the brainchild of Kaiser Wilhelm II. Built to trumpet the triumph of Metz' post-1871 status as part of the Second Reich, the architecture is a whimsical mix of art deco, neo-Romanesque and neo-Renaissance influences.

🛏 Sleeping

HÔTEL DE LA CATHÉDRALE
Historic Hotel €€

(☎03 87 75 00 02; www.hotelcathedrale-metz.fr; 25 place de Chambre; d €75-110; 🛜) This classy little hotel occupies a 17th-century townhouse opposite the cathedral. Climb the wrought-iron staircase to your classically elegant room, with high ceilings, hardwood floors and antique trappings.

LA CITADELLE   Design Hotel   €€€
(03 87 17 17 17; www.citadelle-metz.com; 5 av Ney; d €205-265; @) A 16th-century citadel given a boutique makeover, luxurious La Citadelle blends history with Zen sleekness. The hotel's pride and joy is its Michelin-starred restaurant, Le Magasin aux Vivres.

HÔTEL MÉTROPOLE   Traditional Hotel €
(03 87 66 26 22; www.hotelmetropole-metz. com; 5 place du Général de Gaulle; s €52, d €58-63;) Beat the crowds to the Centre Pompidou-Metz, five minutes' stroll away, by staying at this German Empire-style townhouse facing the train station. The cheery rooms feature above-par perks like free wi-fi and flatscreen TVs.

Eating

LE MAGASIN AUX VIVRES
Gastronomic   €€€
(03 87 17 17 17; 5 av Ney; mains €40-70; closed Sat lunch, Sun, Mon) Conjurer of textures and seasonal flavours, Michelin-starred chef Christophe Dufossé makes creative use of local produce. Moselle wines work well with specialities like plump scallops sliding into a Lorraine beer emulsion and rack of Limousin lamb in spicy jus.

LA VOILE BLANCHE
Modern French   €€
(03 87 20 66 66; 1 parvis des Droits de l'Homme; menus €25-35; closed dinner Sun, Tue;) Art on a plate is the aim at Centre Pompidou-Metz' kaleidoscope-inspired restaurant, designed by architects

Patrick Jouin and Sanjit Manku. The menu is fresh and seasonal – think summery Camargue rice with red mullet and succulent Charolais beef.

MAIRE   Traditional French   €€
(03 87 32 43 12; www.restaurant-maire.com, in French; 1 rue des Ponts des Morts; menus €37-45; closed Wed lunch, Tue) This smart riverside restaurant serves up moreish views of the cathedral from its window tables and veranda.

ⓘ Information

Tourist office (03 87 55 53 76; http:// tourisme.mairie-metz.fr; 2 place d'Armes; 9am-7pm Mon-Sat, 10am-5pm Sun)

ⓘ Getting There & Away

Metz' ornate early 20th-century **train station** (pl du Général de Gaulle) has a TGV linking Paris with Luxembourg. Direct trains include the following:

Paris Gare de l'Est; €53, 80 minutes, 13 daily

Nancy €9.50, 40 minutes, 48 daily

Verdun €13, 1½ hours, three daily

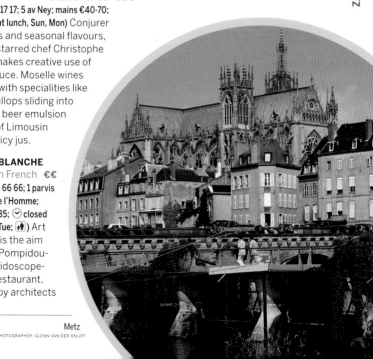

Metz
PHOTOGRAPHER: GLENN VAN DER KNIJFF

Luxembourg €14, 50 minutes, at least 15 daily

Strasbourg €23, 1¾ hours, 14 daily

Amiens

POP 137,800

One of France's most awe-inspiring Gothic cathedrals is reason enough to spend time in Amiens, the comfy, if reserved, former capital of Picardy, where Jules Verne spent the last two decades of his life.

 ## Sights

CATHÉDRALE NOTRE DAME Cathedral
(place Notre Dame; ☉8.30am-6.15pm) The largest Gothic cathedral in France (it's 145m long) and a Unesco World Heritage Site since 1981, this magnificent structure was begun in 1220 to house the **skull of St John the Baptist** (☉on display approx Apr-Oct), on display – framed in gold and jewels – in the northern outer wall of the ambulatory. Connoisseurs rave about the soaring Gothic arches (42.3m high over the transept), unity of style and immense interior, but for

locals, the 17th-century statue known as the **Ange Pleureur** (Crying Angel), in the ambulatory directly behind the over-the-top baroque (18th century) high altar, remains a favourite.

Weather permitting, it's possible to climb the **north tower** (☎03 22 92 03 32; ☉afternoon, closed Tue); tickets are sold in the boutique to the left as you approach the west facade.

MAISON DE JULES VERNE
House Museum
(Home of Jules Verne; ☎03 22 45 45 75; www.jules-verne.net; 2 rue Charles Dubois; adult €7, audioguide €2; ☉10am-12.30pm & 2-6.30pm Mon & Wed-Fri, 2-6.30pm Tue, 11am-6.30pm Sat & Sun) Jules Verne (1828–1905) wrote many of his best-known works of brain-tingling – and eerily prescient – science fiction while living in his turreted Amiens home. Signs are in French and English.

Sleeping

GRAND HÔTEL DE L'UNIVERS Hotel €€
(☎03 22 91 52 51; www.hotel-univers-amiens.com; 2 rue de Noyon; d €75-150; @ 🛜) Offer-

Cathédrale Notre Dame, Amiens

PICTUREPROJECT/ALAMY

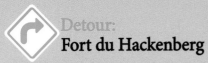

Detour:
Fort du Hackenberg

The largest single Maginot Line bastion in the Metz area was the 1000-man **Fort du Hackenberg** (www.maginot-hackenberg.com; Veckring; adult/child €8/4; ⊘tours in English 2pm Sat & Sun Apr–mid-Nov, 2pm Sat mid-Nov–March), 30km northeast of Metz, whose 10km of galleries were designed to be self-sufficient for three months and, in battle, to fire four tonnes of shells a minute. An electric trolley takes visitors along 4km of tunnels – always at 12°C – past subterranean installations (kitchen, hospital, electric plant etc).

Readers have been enthusiastic about the **tours** (www.maginot-line.com) of Fort du Hackenberg, other Maginot Line sites and Verdun led by Jean-Pascal Speck, an avid amateur historian and owner of the romantic **Hôtel L'Horizon** (☏03 82 88 53 65; www.lhorizon.fr; 5 rte du Crève Coeur; d €98-150) in Thionville. If he's unavailable, he can put you in touch with other English-speaking guides.

ing all the bourgeois comforts, this venerable, Best Western–affiliated hostelry is convenient to both the train station and the city's pedestrianised heart.

Eating

LE T'CHIOT ZINC Bistro €
(☏03 22 91 43 79; 18 rue de Noyon; menus €12-26; ⊘closed Sun, also closed Mon Jul & Aug) Inviting, bistro-style decor reminiscent of the belle époque provides a fine backdrop for the tasty French and Picard cuisine, including fish dishes and *caqhuse* (pork in a cream, wine vinegar and onion sauce).

ⓘ Information

Tourist office (☏03 22 71 60 50; www.amiens-tourisme.com; 40 place Notre Dame; ⊘9.30am-6pm or 6.30pm Mon-Sat, 10am-noon & 2-5pm Sun) Can supply details on the Somme memorials (including minibus tours) and cultural events.

ⓘ Getting There & Around

Train

Amiens is an important rail hub. Accessed through a dramatic modern entrance, the train station offers direct services to Arras (€11, 50 minutes,

six to 12 daily), Lille-Flandres (€19, 1½ hours, six to 121 daily), Paris' Gare du Nord (€19, 1¼ to 1¾ hours, 14 to 30 daily) and Rouen (€18, 1¼ hours, four daily).

Battle of the Somme Memorials

Almost 750,000 soldiers, airmen and sailors from Great Britain, Australia, Canada, the Indian subcontinent, Ireland, New Zealand, South Africa, the West Indies and other parts of the British Empire died during WWI on the Western Front, two-thirds of them in France.

For online information, see www.somme-battlefields.com and www.somme14-18.com.

Tourist offices (including those in Lille, Amiens, Arras and Péronne) can help book tours of battlefield sites and memorials. Respected tour companies include **Battlefield Experience** (☏03 22 76 29 60; www.thebattleofthesomme.co.uk) and **Western Front Tours** (www.westernfronttours.com.au; ⊘mid-Mar–mid-Nov).

La Grande Mine

Some 100m across and 30m deep, the **Lochnagar Crater Memorial** (as it's officially known) was created on the morning of the first day of the First Battle of the Somme (1 July 1916) by about

If You Like...
WWI History

If you've been moved by the Somme memorials, pay your respects at some of the sites of the Battle of Verdun, the longest (and one of the bloodiest) battle of WWI.

The landscape around Verdun is littered with cemeteries, and battlefields still pocked by trenches and artillery craters. By car, take the D913 and D112 and follow signs to 'Douamont', 'Vaux' or the 'Champ de Bataille 14-18'. The **Verdun Tourist Office** (☏ 03 29 84 55 55; www.tourisme-verdun.fr) arranges guided tours.

1 **MÉMORIAL DE VERDUN**
(www.memorial-de-verdun.fr; adult/child €7/3.50; ☺9am-6pm, closed mid-Dec–Jan) The village of Fleury, effectively obliterated during the battle, is now the site of this evocative memorial.

2 **FOSSUAIRE DE DOUAUMONT**
(Douaumont Ossuary; www.verdun-douaumont. com; ☺9am-6pm Mon-Fri, 10am-6pm Sat & Sun) Rising like a gigantic artillery shell above 15,000 crosses, this is one of France's most important WWI memorials.

3 **FORT DE DOUAUMONT**
(adult/child €3/1.50; ☺10am-6pm) Two kilometres northeast of the Douaumont Ossuary, this is the strongest of the 38 fortresses built along a 45km front to protect Verdun.

4 **MEUSE-ARGONNE AMERICAN CEMETERY**
The largest US military cemetery in Europe is in Romagne-sous-Montfaucon, 41km northwest of Verdun.

5 **ROMAGNE '14-'18**
(☏ 03 29 85 10 14; www.romagne14-18.com; 2 rue de l'Andon; guided walks €10; ☺guided walks 9am-noon, museum noon-6pm, closed Wed) This museum displays Jean-Paul de Vries' private collection of war memorabilia. He also conducts guided walks around the battlefields.

6 **LORRAINE AMERICAN CEMETERY**
This is the largest US WWII military cemetery in Europe. It's 45km east of Metz, near St-Avold.

25 tonnes of ammonal laid by British sappers in order to create a breach in the German lines.

La Grande Mine is 4km northeast of Albert along D929.

Péronne

The best place to begin a visit to the Somme battlefields – especially if you're interested in WWI's historical and cultural context – is the outstanding **Historial de la Grande Guerre** (Museum of the Great War; ☏ 03 22 83 14 18; www. historial.org; Château de Péronne; adult/child incl audioguide €7.50/3.80; ☺10am-6pm, closed mid-Dec–mid-Jan). Tucked inside Péronne's massively fortified château, this award-winning museum tells the story of the war chronologically, with equal space given to the German, French and British perspectives on what happened, how and why.

Excellent English brochures on the battlefields can be picked up at Péronne's **tourist office** (☏ 03 22 84 42 38; www.hautesomme-tourisme.com; 18 place André Audinot; ☺10am-noon & 2-5pm or 6.30pm, closed Sun), 100m from the museum entrance.

Péronne (pop 8700) is about 60km east of Amiens.

Somme American Cemetery

In late September 1918, just six weeks before the end of WWI, American units – flanked by their British, Canadian and Australian allies – launched an assault on the Germans' heavily fortified Hindenburg Line.

Some of the fiercest fighting took place near the village of Bony, on the sloping site now occupied by the 1844 Latin crosses and stars of David of the **Somme American Cemetery** (www.abmc. gov; ☺9am-5pm).

The cemetery is 24km northeast of Péronne, mostly along D6, and 18km north of St-Quentin along D1044.

Thiepval Memorial

Dedicated to 'the Missing of the Somme', this Commonwealth memorial – its distinctive outline visible for

Battlefield trench near Verdun

NEIL SETCHFIELD

many kilometres in all directions – is the region's most visited place of pilgrimage. The glass-walled **visitors centre** (☎03 22 74 60 47; admission free; ⏰10am-6pm, closed 2 weeks around New Year) is discreetly below ground level.

Thiepval is 7.5km northeast of Albert, partly along D50 and D151.

Vimy Ridge Canadian National Historic Site

Of the 66,655 Canadians who died in WWI, 3598 lost their lives in April 1917 taking 14km-long **Vimy Ridge** (Crête de Vimy). Its highest point – site of a heavily fortified German position – was later chosen as the site of Canada's **WWI memorial**, designed by Walter Seymour Allward and built from 1925 to 1936.

The rust-coloured **Welcome Centre** (☎03 21 50 68 68; www.vac-acc.gc.ca; ⏰9am or 10am-5pm or 6pm) and its modest exhibits are staffed by bilingual Canadian students. Nearby, visitors can see **mine craters**, visit infantry supply **tunnels** (☎03 22 76 70 86; ⏰tours depart hourly 9am or 10am-5pm or 6pm, closed mid-Dec–mid-Jan) and peer from reconstructed **trenches** (⏰9am or 10am-5pm or 6pm) towards the German front line, a mere 25m away.

Vimy Ridge is 11km north of Arras (towards Lens), partly along N17.

Loire Valley & Central France

In terms of architectural splendour, nowhere tops the Loire Valley. For over a thousand years, this has been the favourite weekend retreat for the cream of French society, and it's littered with lavish châteaux left behind by generations of kings, queens and courtly nobles.

Southeast along the River Loire is Burgundy (Bourgogne in French), France's second-most-famous wine region after Bordeaux. Unsurprisingly, it makes a fantastic place to try and buy wine. The region's elegant capital, Dijon, is also well worth a detour for its historic art and architecture.

Further west, across the mountains of the Massif Central, lies the Dordogne (known to the French as Périgord), known for its rich cuisine and idyllic countryside. It was once home to France's most-ancient settlers, who left behind many stunning prehistoric artworks in the murky caves of the Vézère Valley.

Mansion in autumn, Saumur (p204)
PHOTOGRAPHER: OLIVER STREWE

Loire Valley & Central France

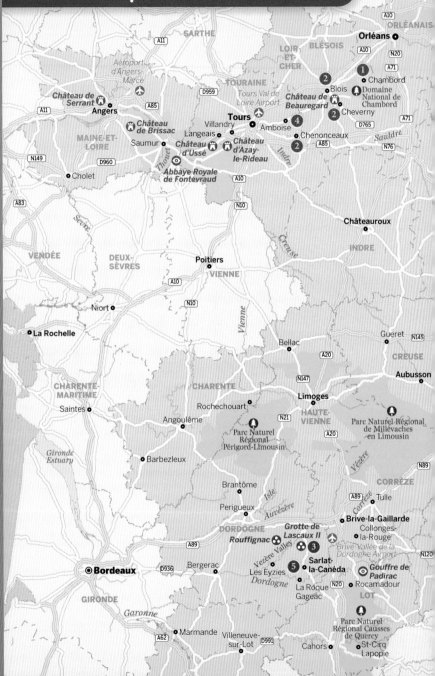

Orléans
ORLÉANAIS

SARTHE

BLÉSOIS

LOIR-ET-CHER

TOURAINE

① Chambord
② Blois
Domaine National de Chambord
Château de Beauregard
② Cheverny

Tours Val de Loire Airport

Château de Serrant
Aéroport d'Angers Marce
Angers
MAINE-ET-LOIRE
Saumur
Château de Brissac
Cholet

Villandry
④ Amboise
Langeais
② Chenonceaux
Château d'Azay-le-Rideau
Château d'Ussé
Abbaye Royale de Fontevraud

Sauldre

Châteauroux
INDRE

VENDÉE

DEUX-SÈVRES
Poitiers
VIENNE
Niort

La Rochelle
Bellac

CHARENTE-MARITIME
Saintes
CHARENTE
Limoges
HAUTE-VIENNE
Gueret
Aubusson
CREUSE

Rochechouart
Parc Naturel Régional de Millevaches en Limousin

Angoulême
Parc Naturel Régional Périgord-Limousin

Gironde Estuary
Barbezieux

Brantôme
CORRÈZE
Tulle
Brive-la-Gaillarde
Collonges-la-Rouge
Brive-Vallée de la Dordogne Airport

Périgueux

Bordeaux
DORDOGNE
Rouffignac
Grotte de Lascaux II
③
⑤ Sarlat-la-Canéda
Gouffre de Padirac
Les Eyzies
La Roque Gageac
Rocamadour
LOT
Bergerac

GIRONDE
Marmande
Villeneuve-sur-Lot
Parc Naturel Régional Causses de Quercy
Cahors
St-Cirq Lapopie

Troyes
AUBE
Chaumont
HAUTE-
MARNE
Seine
A5
A6
Montargis
N60
LOIRET
N7
N60
Forêt
d'Orléans
Auxerre
YONNE
Yonne
Canal de Bourgogne
Forêt de
Châtillon
Abbaye
de Fontenay
HAUTE-
SAÔNE
PAYS D'AUXOIS
Avallon
Vézelay
N6
A6
N71
CÔTE D'OR
A31
A38
Dijon
CHER
D940
D955
Loire
Yonne
Parc Naturel
Régional du
Morvan
Route des
Grande Crus
Côte d'Or
Vineyards
A36
6
N6
Beaune
Bourges
NIÈVRE
A6
Nevers
Bibracte
SAÔNE-ET-LOIRE
JURA
Cher
Allier
N81
N81
Arroux
Saône
Moulins
Canal Latéral à la Loire
Digoin
Tournus
Cluny
ALLIER
N79
A6
A71
AIN
Montluçon
A71
Vichy
Roanne
PUY-DE-
DÔME
Volvic
A72
LOIRE
N141
Thiers
Clermont-
Ferrand
Monts du Forez
La Bourboule
St-Nectaire
Ambert
Montbrison
A89
Le Mont
Dore
D906
D922
Parc Naturel
Régional des
Volcans d'Auvergne
HAUTE-
LOIRE
N88
CANTAL
St-Flour
Le Puy-
en-Velay
D15
A75
Rhône
Lot
Truyère
N140
D921
ARDÈCHE
LOZÈRE
PROVENCE

N
0   60 km
0   40 miles

❶ Chambord
❷ Castle Country
❸ Grotte de Lascaux
❹ Le Clos-Lucé
❺ Sarlat-la-Canéda
❻ Burgundy Wine Road

Loire Valley & Central France Highlights

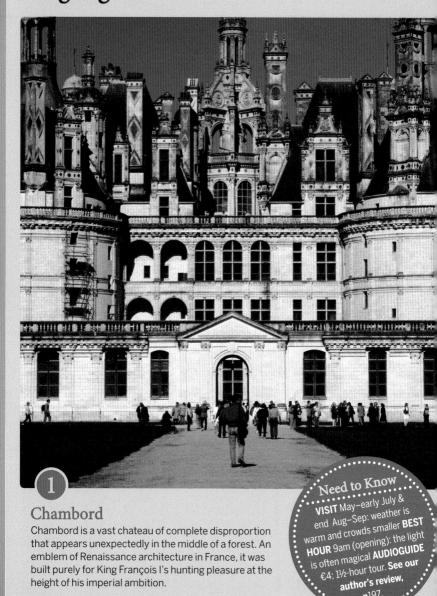

① Chambord

Chambord is a vast chateau of complete disproportion that appears unexpectedly in the middle of a forest. An emblem of Renaissance architecture in France, it was built purely for King François I's hunting pleasure at the height of his imperial ambition.

Need to Know

VISIT May–early July & end Aug–Sep: weather is warm and crowds smaller **BEST HOUR** 9am (opening): the light is often magical **AUDIOGUIDE** €4; 1½-hour tour. **See our author's review, p197.**

Chambord
Don't Miss List

BY ELSA SAUVÉ, CHÂTEAU DE CHAMBORD

1 DOUBLE-HELIX STAIRCASE & ROOFTOP

The double-helix staircase that whisks visitors from the ground floor to the rooftop keep is *the* highlight. This theatrical and majestic staircase is composed of two open parallel flights wrapped around a hollow core, the magic being that two people can see each other go up and down it without their paths ever crossing. A magnificent view of the estate unfolds from the rooftop terraces, an unforgettable place with its sculpted chimney and turrets, really a place of contemplation and daydream.

2 THE 1ST FLOOR

Take time to explore the *premier étage* (1st floor), a historical panorama of the inhabitants of Chambord from François I to Louis XIV and beyond into the 19th century. In the apartments you can really see how château lifestyle evolved over the centuries: all the furniture in Francois I was made to be dismantled and transported with him from château to château.

3 SON ET LUMIÈRE

Every evening in July and August *Chambord, Dream of Lights* is projected on the façade of the castle. The 50-minute sound-and-light show is a voyage through time: It relives the construction of the chateau and the arrival of the court of the king, the balls and banquets he threw. Through beautiful images, music and dance, it very much tugs at the audience's senses and emotions.

4 THE RUTTING SEASON

Chambord is unique in that it is a monument in the middle of a vast forested park. This gives Chambord an additional magic, a place to discover the natural environment as well as culture and history. The park is a wildlife reserve with stags and wild boars. Observatories allow visitors to observe the animals during *le brame,* the rutting or mating season that falls from mid-September to mid-October. The best time to see the animals in action is at sunrise or sunset – bring binoculars.

Top: Middle of Grand Staircase; **Bottom:** Inner courtyard's spiral staircase

Castle Country

Chambord is tough to beat, but it's certainly not the only château worthy of your time in the Loire Valley. From sturdy medieval fortresses to grand Renaissance showpieces, the Loire has enough castles to fill a lifetime of visits. Top honours go to elegant Chenonceau (p202), stately Cheverny (p196) and regal Blois (p195), but there are many more to discover. Château de Chenonceau

Le Clos Lucé

In 1516 the great artist and inventor Leonardo da Vinci upped sticks from Italy and moved into this grand château (p203) just outside Amboise. Though already a ripe old 64 at the time, da Vinci showed no signs of slowing down in retirement, and the château's room and gardens are littered with models of some of his famous inventions.

DIANA MAYFIELD

Grotte de Lascaux

In 1940 four teenage boys out searching for their lost dog discovered the Grotte de Lascaux (p217), a vast network of subterranean chambers adorned with the most extraordinary prehistoric paintings ever found. Though the original cave is now off-limits to avoid damaging these priceless ancient artworks, they have been meticulously recreated in another cave nearby. If you're going to visit only one cave in the Vézère, make sure it's this one.

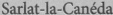

Sarlat-la-Canéda

Few places in France feel as convincingly medieval as Sarlat (p213). With its jumble of alleyways, culs-de-sacs and honey-coloured stone houses, it makes a sublime base for exploring the caves of the Vézère Valley. Don't miss the wonderful Saturday food market, where local producers from all over the Dordogne set up shop on the cobbles of the main square. Place de la Liberté, Sarlat-la-Canéda

Burgundy Wine Road

The best way to explore this world-class wine region is by following the Route des Grands Crus (p210). This signposted route links together the most renowned vineyards along the famous 'Cote d'Or' (Golden Hillside). Tourist offices in Dijon and Beaune can arrange tasting sessions at local châteaux as well as tailored minibus tours. Vineyards near Beaune (p210)

Loire Valley & Central France's Best…

Historic Buildings

○ **Château Royal de Blois** (p195) A whistle-stop tour through French architecture.

○ **Abbaye de Fontenay** (p212) Find inner peace at a Cistercian abbey.

○ **Palais des Ducs et des États de Bourgogne** (p206) Dijon's ducal palace is now a superb arts museum.

○ **Château Royal d'Amboise** (p202) Climb this regal château's spiralling towers.

○ **Hôtel-Dieu des Hospices de Beaune** (p218) Marvel at this medieval hospital.

Places to Get Lost in

○ **Vézelay** (p216) Join the pilgrims (and tourists) at this holy hilltop town.

○ **Collonges-la-Rouge** (p216) This entire village has been classified a historical monument.

○ **La Roque Gageac** (p218) This riverside village makes the perfect place for a cruise aboard a traditional *gabarre*.

○ **Sarlat-la-Canéda** (p213) Lose yourself in the twists and turns of Sarlat's old town.

Photo Opps

○ **St-Cirq-Lapopie** (p216) This tiny clifftop village offers an unparalleled panorama over the Lot Valley.

○ **Jardins de Marqueyssac** (p218) Don't miss the view from the *belvédère* (lookout).

○ **Brantôme** (p216) Look out over Brantôme's waterways from the top of the 11th-century belltower.

○ **Chambord's rooftop** (p197) Get a bird's-eye perspective of the Loire's grandest château.

Curiosities

○ **Chantier Médiéval de Guédelon** (p213) See a 13th-century château being built.

○ **Gouffre de Padirac** (p219) Sail a subterranean river through a breathtaking cave.

○ **Maison de la Magie** (p195) Be befuddled by optical illusions and magic tricks in Blois.

○ **Soupe des Chiens** (p196) Join the dogs' dinner at Cheverny.

○ **École Nationale d'Équitation** (p204) Watch the amazing dressage displays of the Cadre Noir.

Need to Know

ADVANCE PLANNING

○ **As early as possible** Book accommodation, particularly in hotspots such as Saumur, Amboise, Dijon and Sarlat-la-Canéda.

○ **Two weeks before** Book tours for Saumur's École Nationale d'Équitation (p204), Grotte de Lascaux (p217) and Grotte de Font de Gaume (p216).

○ **One week before** Choose your châteaux and buy a combo pass (p195).

RESOURCES

○ **Chateaux Tourisme** (www.chateauxtourisme.com) General info on the Loire Valley.

○ **Randonée en Val de Loire** (www.randonnee-en-val-de-loire.com) Walks and cycling routes in the Loire.

○ **Burgundy Tourism** (www.burgundy-tourism.com) Burgundy's tourist board.

○ **Wines of Burgundy** (www.bourgogne-wines.com) Bone up on your Burgundy vintages.

○ **Espace Tourisme Périgord** (www.dordogne-perigord-tourisme.fr) Comprehensive site covering the Dordogne area.

GETTING AROUND

○ **Train** Regular trains travel from Paris to major cities (including Orléans, Tours, Dijon and Limoges), but regional lines are more limited.

○ **Car** Having a car means more flexibility and freedom; essential for the Vézère Valley.

○ **Organised bus tours** An excellent way of exploring the Loire châteaux (p193) and the Burgundy vineyards (p211).

○ **Bicycle** Cycling is ideal for exploring the flat Loire Valley; see **Châteaux à Vélo** (www.chateauxavelo.com) and **Loire à Vélo** (www.loireradweg.org) for routes, free maps and MP3 guides. For bike-rental outlets contact local tourist offices.

BE FOREWARNED

○ **Vézère Valley** Most caves are closed in winter; visitor numbers are limited in summer. Book ahead.

○ **Grotte de Lascaux** April to October tickets can *only* be bought next to the tourist office in Montignac (p217).

○ **Crowds** Can be a problem, especially in the Loire and the Dordogne and in July and August.

Left: Château Royal de Blois (p195);
Above: St-Cirq-Lapopie (p216)
PHOTOGRAPHERS: (LEFT) DIANA MAYFIELD;
(ABOVE) ANDREW BAIN

Loire Valley & Central France Itineraries

What a variety of experiences this part of France has to offer: with its Renaissance châteaux, tranquil rivers and renowned cave paintings, there's so much to see that you might well find it takes up your entire trip.

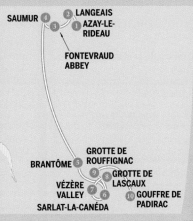

3 DAYS

CHAMBORD TO AZAY-LE-RIDEAU
Château Classics

For maximum freedom you'll want your own car in the Loire, although organised minibus trips can be good if time is short. This tour of the Loire's top châteaux begins with the biggest, boldest and best, **(1) Château de Chambord**. Tour the interior with an audioguide before scaling the double-helix staircase to the rooftop for sweeping views of the grounds, surrounded by a Tolkien-esque jumble of cupolas, domes, chimneys and lightning rods. Overnight in **(2) Blois**.

You should have time to squeeze in at least two châteaux on day two, starting with Renaissance elegance at **(3) Château de Cheverny**, followed by medieval heritage at **(4) Château de Chaumont**. **(5) Amboise** makes an ideal place to end the day, with lots of luxurious sleeps to choose from: one of our favourites is Le Pavillon de Lys.

On day three, visit Château Royal d'Amboise and get to know original Renaissance man Leonardo da Vinci at Le Clos Lucé. In the afternoon, head west to see the remarkable ornamental gardens of **(6) Château de Villandry**. Wrap up with a night-time visit to the Loire's oldest and best *son-et-lumière* (sound and light show), projected directly onto the walls of moat-encircled **(7) Château d'Azay-le-Rideau**.

190

AZAY-LE-RIDEAU TO SARLAT-LA-CANÉDA

Castles to Cave Art

Head west from **(1) Azay-le-Rideau** along the Loire. You'll find a quintessential medieval castle at **(2) Langeais**, ramparts, drawbridge and all. Spend the afternoon at **(3) Fontevraud Abbey** and overnight in **(4) Saumur**.

On day two, head south towards the Dordogne. You'll reach the riverside village of **(5) Brantôme** by afternoon, where you could stop for a late lunch or a canal cruise before heading on to **(6) Sarlat-la-Canéda**. Sarlat makes an ideal base for exploring the Dordogne region, but it deserves a day in its own right – don't miss its buzzy morning market and medieval architecture.

On day four, head off to view the amazing Stone Age art in the **(7) Vezère Valley**. Book guided visits to the Grotte de Font de Gaume and the Grotte des Combarelles before heading over to the famous **(8) Grotte de Lascaux** in the afternoon.

On the last day, you should be able to fit in two unforgettable underground adventures: a trip aboard the rattling train deep into the **(9) Grotte de Rouffignac** and a punt along the spooky subterranean river at the **(10) Gouffre de Padirac**.

Château de Villandry (p200)
PHOTOGRAPHER: BARBARA VAN ZANTEN

Discover Loire Valley & Central France

LOIRE VALLEY

In centuries past, the Loire River was a key strategic area, one step removed from the French capital and poised on the crucial frontier between northern and southern France. Kings, queens, dukes and nobles established their feudal strongholds and country seats along the Loire, and the broad, flat valley is sprinkled with many of the most extravagant castles and fortresses in France.

Orléans

POP 116,490

There's a definite big-city buzz around the boulevards, flashy boutiques and elegant buildings of Orléans, 100km south of Paris. It's a city with enduring heritage: already an important settlement by the time of the Romans' arrival, Orléans sealed its place in history in 1429 when a young peasant girl by the name of Jeanne d'Arc (Joan of Arc) rallied the armies of Charles VII and staged a spectacular rout against the besieging English forces, a key turning point in the Hundred Years War.

Statue of Jeanne d'Arc, Chinon
PHOTOGRAPHER: DIANA MAYFIELD

◎ Sights & Activities

MUSÉE DES BEAUX-ARTS
Art Museum

(☏ 02 38 79 21 55; 1 rue Fernand Rabier; adult/child incl audio guide €4/2.50; ☉10am-6pm Tue-Sun) Orléans' five-storeyed fine-arts museum is a treat, with an excellent selection of Italian, Flemish and Dutch paintings (including works by Correggio, Velázquez and Bruegel), as well as a huge collection by such French artists as

CHÂTEAU TOURS

Most companies (listed below) offer a choice of well-organised itineraries, taking in various combinations of Azay-le-Rideau, Villandry, Cheverny, Chambord and Chenonceau (plus wine-tasting tours). Half-day trips cost between €18 and €33; full-day trips range from €43 to €50. Entry to the châteaux isn't included, although you'll get a discount on tickets. Reserve via the tourist office in Tours, from where most tours depart.

Acco-Dispo (☏ 06 82 00 64 51; www.accodispo-tours.com)

Alienor (☏ 06 10 85 35 39; www.alienor.com)

Loire Valley Tours (☏ 02 54 33 99 80; www.loire-valley-tours.com) Tours including château admission (€125)

Luxury Tours (☏ 06 66 64 20 08; www.luxurytours.fr) Private town cars (€105–256)

Quart de Tours (☏ 06 30 65 52 01; www.quartdetours.com)

St-Eloi Excursions (☏ 02 47 37 08 04; www.saint-eloi.com)

Touraine Evasion (☏ 06 07 39 13 31; www.tourevasion.com)

Léon Cogniet (1794–1880) and Orléans-born Alexandre Antigna (1817–1878).

CATHÉDRALE STE-CROIX   Cathedral
(place Ste-Croix; ⏰ 9.15am-noon & 2.15-5.45pm) Towering above place Ste-Croix, Orléans' Flamboyant Gothic cathedral was originally built in the 13th century. Inside, slender columns soar skywards towards the vaulted ceiling and 106m spire, completed in 1895, while a series of vividly coloured stained-glass windows relate the life of St Joan, who was canonised in 1920.

HÔTEL GROSLOT   Historic Mansion
(☏ 02 38 79 22 30; place de l'Étape; ⏰ 9am-noon & 2-6pm Mon-Fri, 5-7pm Sat, 10am-6pm Sun) Opposite the fine arts museum, the Renaissance Hôtel Groslot was built in the 15th century as a private mansion for Jacques Groslot, a city bailiff, and later used as Orléans' town hall during the Revolution.

MAISON DE JEANNE D'ARC
  History Museum
(☏ 02 38 52 99 89; www.jeannedarc.com.fr, in French; 3 place du Général de Gaulle; adult/child €2/1; ⏰ 10am-noon & 2-6pm Tue-Sun) This reconstruction of a 15th-century house

that hosted the Maid between April and May 1429 (the original was destroyed by British bombing in 1940, something the locals politely avoid mentioning) displays manuscripts, flags and vintage swords, plus a scale model recreating the siege of Orléans.

 Sleeping

HÔTEL DE L'ABEILLE   Historic Hotel   €€
(☏ 02 38 53 54 87; www.hoteldelabeille.com; 64 rue Alsace-Lorraine; s €47, d €64-89, 5-people €120; 🛗 🛜) Bees buzz, floorboards creak and vintage Orléans posters adorn the walls at this gorgeous turn-of-the-century house. It's deliciously old-fashioned, from the scuffed pine floors and wildly floral wallpapers to the hefty dressers and bee-print curtains. For breakfast (€9) there's a choice of coffees, teas, pâtisserie and exotic jams.

HÔTEL ARCHANGE   Boutique Hotel   €
(☏ 02 38 54 42 42; www.hotelarchange.com; 1 bd de Verdun; d €47-57) Gilded mirrors, cherub murals and sofas shaped like giant hands greet you at this station hotel aiming for boutique status.

193

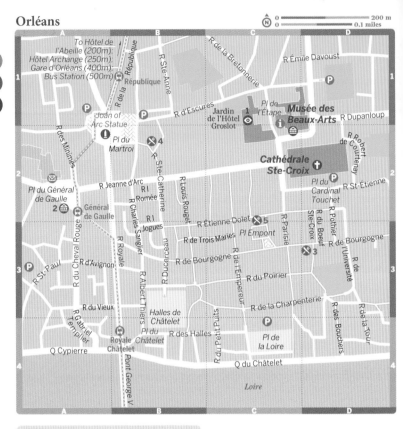

Orléans

 Eating

CHEZ NOÉ   Brasserie €€

(☎ 02 38 53 44 09; 195 rue de Bourgogne; lunch menus €12, dinner menus €21-32; ⏰ lunch Tue-Fri, dinner Tue-Sat) Characterful – think hardwood floors, checked tablecloths and Louis Prima on the stereo – cheery and crammed at lunchtime and on weekends, this lively brasserie is about uncomplicated food at fair prices, from garlic snails to salmon steak.

LE BRIN DE ZINC   Bistro €€

(☎ 02 38 53 38 77; 62 rue St-Catherine; lunch menus €16, dinner menus €22-27) Battered signs, old telephones and even a vintage scooter decorate this old-world bistro, serving up lashings of mussels and oysters at lunchtime and platters of rich bistro food till late.

Le Dariole   Tea House €€

(☎ 02 38 77 26 67; 25 rue Étienne Dolet; menus €17.50-22; ⏰ lunch Mon-Fri, dinner Tue-Fri, salon de thé 2.30-7pm Mon-Sat) This rustic *salon de thé* carries loads of teas from rare Jasmine to

Georgian and Chinese Dragon, as well as home-made cakes and pâtisserie. After nightfall it transforms into a smart restaurant specialising in regional food.

Information

Tourist office (☏ 02 38 24 05 05; www.tourisme-orleans.com; 2 place de l'Étape; ☺9am-1pm & 2-6pm Mon-Sat)

Getting There & Away

The city's two train stations, Gare d'Orléans and Gare des Aubrais-Orléans (the latter is 2km to the north), are linked by tram and frequent shuttle trains.

Blois €13 to €20, 45 minutes, hourly

Paris Gare d'Austerlitz €24 to €37, 70 minutes, hourly

Tours €24 to €35, one to 1½ hours, hourly

Blois
POP 40,057

Looming on a rocky escarpment on the northern bank of the Loire, Blois' historic château (formerly the feudal seat of the powerful counts of Blois) provides a whistle-stop tour through the key periods of French history and architecture.

Sights

Many of the châteaux in the Blésois are covered by the Pass' Châteaux, which offers savings of between €1.20 and €5.30 depending on which châteaux you visit; contact the tourist offices in Blois, Cheverny and Chambord.

CHÂTEAU ROYAL DE BLOIS Castle

(☏ 02 54 90 33 32; www.chateaudeblois.fr; place du Château; adult/child €8/4; ☺9am-6.30pm) Blois' château and the former royal seat was intended more as an architectural showpiece than a military stronghold, and successive French kings have left their creative mark over the centuries. From the château's huge **central courtyard** you can view four distinct periods of French architecture: the Gothic

Salle des États and original medieval castle; François I's Renaissance north wing (1515–24); the classical west wing (1635–38) constructed under Gaston d'Orléans, brother to Louis XIII; and Louis XII's red-brick Flamboyant Gothic east wing (1498–1503).

The impressive **Salle des États Généraux** (Estates General Hall, c1220) has a soaring double barrel-vaulted roof decorated in royal blues and golden fleurs-de-lys. Blois' medieval lords meted out justice here in the Middle Ages, and Luc Besson used it for the dramatic trial scene in his 1999 biopic *Jeanne d'Arc*.

The most famous feature of the **Renaissance wing**, the royal apartments of François I and Queen Claude, is the **loggia staircase**, decorated with salamanders and curly Fs (heraldic symbols of François I).

The château hosts a 45-minute **son et lumière** (☏ 02 54 55 26 31; adult/child €7/4; ☺ mid-Apr–late Sep) featuring huge projections on the walls (English version Wednesdays).

MAISON DE LA MAGIE Magic Museum

(House of Magic; ☏ 02 54 90 33 33; www.maisondelamagie.fr, in French; 1 place du Château; adult/child €9/5; ☺10am-12.30pm & 2-6.30pm, closed mornings Mon-Fri Sep) Opposite the château you can't miss the former home of watchmaker, inventor and conjurer Jean Eugène Robert-Houdin (1805–71) when, on the hour, dragons emerge roaring from the windows. It has entertaining live magic shows (three to four daily), exhibits on the history of magic and loads of optical trickery including a mysterious 'Hallucinoscope'. It's goofy good fun! The great Harry Houdini named himself after Houdin, and there is a short historical film about the American magician.

MUSÉE DE L'OBJET Art Museum

(☏ 02 54 55 37 45; www.museedelobjet.org, in French; 6 rue Franciade; adult/child €4/2; ☺1.30-6.30pm Fri-Sun, closed Dec-Feb) This brilliant modern arts museum is based on the collection of the artist Eric Fabre, and concentrates on artworks made using everyday materials.

Sleeping

CÔTÉ LOIRE Hotel €
(📞02 54 78 07 86; www.coteloire.com; 2 place de la Grève; d €55-76; 🛜) If it's charm and colours you want, head for the centrally located Loire Coast, with rooms decked out in cheery checks, bright pastels and the odd bit of exposed brick.

HÔTEL ANNE DE BRETAGNE Hotel €
(📞02 54 78 05 38; http://annedebretagne.free.fr; 31 av du Dr Jean Laigret; s €45-51, d €54-56, tr €60-72; 🛜♿) This creeper-covered hotel has friendly staff and a bar full of polished wood and vintage pictures. Modern rooms are finished in flowery wallpaper and stripy bedspreads; some adjoin for families.

Eating

L'ORANGERIE Gastronomic €€€
(📞02 54 78 05 36; www.orangerie-du-chateau.fr; 1 av du Dr Jean Laigret; menus €33-77) Polish up those heels and dust off that suit! Tucked behind wrought-iron gates opposite the château, the Orangery is cloud nine for connoisseurs of *haute cuisine*. Plates are artfully stacked (duck liver, langoustine, foie gras) and the sparkling *salon* would make Louis XIV green with envy.

LES BANQUETTES ROUGES
Traditional French €€
(📞02 54 78 74 92; 16 rue des Trois Marchands; lunch menus €14.50, dinner menus €26-32; 🕐Tue-Sat) Handwritten slate menus and wholesome food distinguish quiet, charming Red Benches: rabbit with marmalade, duck with lentils and salmon with apple vinaigrette, all done with a spicy twist and a smile.

AU BOUCHON LYONNAIS Lyonnais €€
(📞02 54 74 12 87; 25 rue des Violettes; lunch menus €12.50, dinner menus €20) Classic neighbourhood bistro with a flavour of bygone days. The food is straight out of the Lyonnais cookbook: snails and duck steaks.

ℹ Information

Tourist office (📞02 54 90 41 41; www.bloispaysdechambord.com; 23 place du Château; 🕐9am-7pm)

ℹ Getting There & Away

BUS TLC (📞02 54 58 55 44; www.tlcinfo.net) runs a château shuttle and buses departing from Blois' train station (tickets €2 on board):

Beaugency Line 16, 55 minutes, four Monday to Saturday, one Sunday.

Chambord Line 3, 40 minutes, four Monday to Saturday, one Sunday.

Cheverny Line 4, 45 minutes, six to eight Monday to Friday, two Saturday, one Sunday.

TRAIN The train station is at the top of the hill on av Jean Laigret.

Amboise €11, 20 minutes, 10 daily.

Orléans €13-20, 45 minutes, hourly.

Paris Gares d'Austerlitz and Montparnasse €34-57, two hours, 26 daily.

Tours €13–19, 40 minutes, 13 daily.

Château de Cheverny

Thought by many to be the most perfectly proportioned château of all, **Cheverny** (📞02 54 79 96 29; www.chateau-cheverny.fr; adult/child €7.50/3.60; 🕐9.15am-6.45pm Jul & Aug, 9.15am-6.15pm Apr-Jun & Sep, 9.45am-5.30pm Oct, 9.45am-5pm Nov-Mar) represents the zenith of French classical architecture, the perfect blend of symmetry, geometry and aesthetic order.

Since its construction between 1625 and 1634 by Jacques Hurault, an intendant to Louis XII, the castle has hardly been altered, and its interior decoration includes some of the most sumptuous furnishings, tapestries and objets d'art anywhere in the Loire Valley.

Behind the main château, the 18th-century **Orangerie**, where many priceless artworks, including the *Mona Lisa*, were stashed during WWII, is now a tearoom.

Near the château's gateway, the **kennels** house pedigreed French pointer/English foxhound hunting dogs still used by the owners of Cheverny:

JOHN BANAGAN

Don't Miss **Château de Chambord**

For full-blown château splendour, you can't top **Chambord**, one of the crowning examples of French Renaissance architecture, and by far the largest, grandest and most visited château in the Loire Valley. It's worth picking up the multilingual audioguide (adult/child version €4/2), if only to avoid getting lost around the endless rooms and corridors.

Begun in 1519 as a weekend hunting lodge by François I, it quickly snowballed into one of the most ambitious (and expensive) architectural projects ever attempted by any French monarch. By the time Chambord was finally finished 30-odd years later, the castle boasted some 440 rooms, 365 fireplaces and 84 staircases, not to mention a cityscape of turrets, chimneys and lanterns crowning its rooftop, and a famous **double-helix staircase**, reputedly designed by the king's chum, Leonardo da Vinci. Ironically, François ultimately found his elaborate palace too draughty, preferring the royal apartments in Amboise and Blois; he only stayed here for 42 days during his entire reign from 1515 to 1547.

Several times daily there are 1½-hour **guided tours** (€4) in English, and during school holidays **costumed tours** entertain the kids. *Son et lumière* shows, known as **Chambord, Rêve de Lumières**, are projected onto the château's facade nightly from July to mid-September (adult/child €12/10). Outdoor spectacles held throughout summer include a daily **equestrian show**.

Chambord is 16km east of Blois, 45km southwest of Orléans and 17km northeast of Cheverny. For transport see p196.

NEED TO KNOW

(☏ 02 54 50 50 20; www.chambord.org; adult/under-25yr €9.50/free; ⏰ 9am-7.30pm mid-Jul–mid-Aug, 9am-6.15pm mid-Mar–mid-Jul & mid-Aug–Sep, 9am-5.15pm, Jan–mid-Mar & Oct-Dec; 👪); equestrian show (☏ 02 54 20 31 01; www.ecuries-chambord.com, in French; adult/child €9.50/7; ⏰ May-Sep)

feeding time, known as the **Soupe des Chiens**, takes place daily at 5pm April to September and 3pm October to March.

ℹ Getting There & Away

Cheverny is 16km southeast of Blois and 17km southwest of Chambord. For transport see p196.

Château de Chaumont

Set on a defensible bluff behind the Loire, **Chaumont-sur-Loire** (☎ 02 54 20 99 22; www.domaine-chaumont.fr, in French; adult/child €9/3.50; ⏰10am-6.30pm Apr-Sep, to 5pm or 6pm Oct-Mar) presents a resolutely medieval face, with its cylindrical corner turrets and sturdy drawbridge, but the interior mostly dates from the 19th century.

The most impressive room is the **Council Chamber**, with its original maiolica-tiled floor, plundered from a palace in Palermo, but the château's finest architecture is arguably reserved for the **Écuries** (stables), built in 1877 to house the Broglies' horses in truly sumptuous style (the thoroughbreds all had their own personal padded stalls). A collection of vintage carriages is now displayed inside.

ℹ Getting There & Away

Chaumont-sur-Loire is 17km southwest of Blois.

Tours

POP 139,958

Bustling Tours has a life of its own despite being one of the hubs of castle country. It's a smart, vivacious kind of place, filled with wide 18th-century boulevards, parks and imposing public buildings, as well as a busy university of some 25,000 students.

◎ Sights & Activities

The old city encircles place Plumereau (locally known as place Plum), about 400m west of rue Nationale.

Left: Château de Chaumont; **Below:** Bas-relief at Basilique St-Martin

PHOTOGRAPHER: (LEFT) JOHN ELK III; (BELOW) RUSSELL MOUNTFORD

MUSÉE DES BEAUX-ARTS
Art Museum

(☎ 02 47 05 68 73; 18 place François Sicard; adult/child €4/2; ☉ 9am-6pm Wed-Mon) Originally the archbishop's gorgeous palace, the Musée des Beaux-Arts is now a fine example of a French provincial arts museum, with grand rooms decorated to reflect the period of the artworks on display. Look out for works by Delacroix, Degas and Monet, as well as a rare Rembrandt miniature and a Rubens *Madonna and Child*.

CATHÉDRALE ST-GATIEN   Cathedral
(place de la Cathédrale; ☉ 9am-7pm) With twin west towers stretching skyward through a latticework of Gothic decorations, flying buttresses and gargoyles, this cathedral's a show-stopper – especially known for its intricate stained glass, particularly the rose windows above the organ. On the north side, the **Cloître de la Psallette** (adult/child €2.50/free; ☉ 9.30am-12.30pm & 2-6pm Mon-Sat, 2-6pm Sun, closed Mon & Tue Oct-Mar) was built from 1442 to 1524.

MUSÉE DU COMPAGNONNAGE
Craft Museum

(☎ 02 47 21 62 20; 8 rue Nationale, in Cloître St-Julien; adult/child €5/3.30; ☉ 9am-noon & 2-6pm, closed Tue mid-Sep–mid-Jun) In addition to traditional professions such as stonemasonry, carpentry and blacksmithing, the *compagnonnages* (guild organisations) welcome in many metiers, including pastry chefs, coopers and locksmiths. Works range from exquisitely carved chests and staircases, to handmade tools, booby-trapped locks and enormous cakes (one took 800 hours to make, in the shape of Hospices de Beaune, with 20kg of dough and tiny sheets of gelatin for windows).

BASILIQUE ST-MARTIN   Church
Tours was once an important pilgrimage city thanks to the soldier-turned-evangelist St Martin (c 317–97), bishop of Tours in the 4th century. After his death a Romanesque basilica was

199

If You Like…
Châteaux

Once you've done the big three – Chambord, Chenonceau and Cheverny – it's worth taking the time to discover some of the Loire's lesser-known châteaux.

1 VILLANDRY

(☎ 02 47 50 02 09; www.chateauvillandry.com; château & gardens adult/child €9/5, gardens only €6/3.50; ⊙château 9am-6pm, to 5.30pm Mar, to 5pm Feb & early Nov, gardens 9am-btwn 5pm & 7.30pm year-round) Completed in 1756, Villandry is famous for its lavish **landscaped gardens**, which are at their blooming best between April and October. Villandry is 17km southwest of Tours and 11km northeast of Azay-le-Rideau.

2 BEAUREGARD

(☎ 02 54 70 40 05; www.beauregard-loire.com; adult/child €8/6.50; ⊙9.30am-6.30pm Jun-Aug, 9.30am-12.30pm & 2-6.30pm Apr-May & Sep-Oct, 9.30am-noon & 2-5pm Nov, Feb & Mar, closed Dec & Jan & Wed Oct-Mar) This little-visited château contains an amazing **portrait gallery** depicting 327 historical figures, including Christopher Columbus, Francis Drake, Cardinal Richelieu, Catherine de Médicis and a host of French kings.

3 LANGEAIS

(☎ 02 47 96 72 60; adult/child €8.50/5; ⊙9.30am-6.30pm, to 5.30pm Feb & Mar, 9am-7pm Jul & Aug) Built in the 1460s, this classic medieval stronghold comes complete with drawbridge, crenellated ramparts and watchtowers. Langeais is 14km west of Villandry and about 31km southwest of Tours.

4 USSÉ

(☎ 02 47 95 54 05; www.chateaudusse.fr; adult/child €13/4; ⊙10am-7pm Apr-Aug, to 6pm Sep–mid-Nov & mid-Feb-Mar, closed mid-Nov–mid-Feb) This turret-topped castle inspired Charles Perrault's classic fairy tale, *La Belle au Bois Dormant* (Sleeping Beauty). It's also said to have been the model for the Disney logo. Ussé is about 14km north of Chinon.

constructed above his tomb, but today only the north tower, the **Tour Charlemagne**, remains. A **replacement basilica** was built in 1862 on a new site a short distance south along rue Descartes to house his relics, while the small **Musée St-Martin** (☎ 02 47 64 48 87; 3 rue Rapin; adult/concession €2/1; ⊙9am-12.30pm & 2-5.30pm Wed-Sun) displays artefacts relating to the lost church.

Tours

Walks   Walking Tours
The tourist office offers an **audioguide** (€5) for a two-hour self-guided tour or various **guided tours** (adult/child €5.60/4.60) in French.

Sleeping

HÔTEL RONSARD   Boutique Hotel €
(☎ 02 47 05 25 36; www.hotel-ronsard.com; 2 rue Pimbert; s €53-67, d €59-72; ❄ @ 🛜)
Completely renovated in 2010 with sleek modern rooms, the Ronsard is centrally located, comfortable and good value, with perks like air-con in summer.

HÔTEL L'ADRESSE
        Boutique Hotel €€
(☎ 02 47 20 85 76; www.hotel-ladresse.com; 12 rue de la Rôtisserie; s €50, d €70-100; ❄ 🛜) On a walking street in the old quarter lies a boutique bonanza, with rooms finished in slates, creams and ochres, topped off with flat-screen TVs, designer sinks and reclaimed rafters.

🍴 Eating

Place Plumereau is crammed with cheap eats, but the quality can be variable.

CAP SUD   Gastro Bistro €€
(☎ 02 47 05 24 81; 88 rue Colbert; lunch menus €14.50-17, dinner menus €19.50-36; ⊙Tue-Sat)

Sensitive, refined creations are made from the freshest ingredients presented in style. Dishes are along the lines of tender braised pork with creamy polenta and baby vegetables. Reserve ahead.

LE ZINC Traditional French €€
(✆ 02 47 20 29 00; 27 place du Grand Marché; menus €19-26; ☺ closed Wed & lunch Sun) One of the new breed of French bistros, more concerned with simple, classic staples and market-fresh ingredients (sourced direct from the local Halles) than Michelin stars and *haute cuisine* cachet. Country dishes (duck breast, beef fillet, river fish) shine in a buzzy dining room.

COMME AUTRE FOUÉE Regional Cuisine €€
(✆ 02 47 05 94 78; 11 rue de la Monnaie; lunch menus €10, dinner menus €16-21; ☺ lunch Tue-Thu, Sat & Sun, dinner Tue-Sat) For local flavour, you can't top this place, which churns out the house speciality of *fouées,* a pita-like disc of dough stuffed with pork rillettes, white beans or goat's cheese.

ⓘ Information

Tourist office (✆ 02 47 70 37 37; www.ligeris. com) main office (78-82 rue Bernard Palissy; ☺8.30am-7pm Mon-Sat, 10am-12.30pm & 2.30-5pm Sun) place Plumereau (**Tout Le Val de Loire; 1 place Plumereau**) Buy château tickets at a slight reduction. The annexe at place Plumereau gives info but doesn't sell tickets.

ⓘ Getting There & Away

Tours is the Loire Valley's main rail hub. The train station is linked to St-Pierre-des-Corps, Tours' TGV train station, by frequent shuttle trains.

Amboise €11, 20 minutes, 12 daily

Blois €9.10, 40 minutes, 12 daily

Chenonceau €11, 30 minutes, eight daily

Orléans €24 to €35, one to 1½ hours, hourly

Paris Gare d'Austerlitz €41 to €62, two to 2¾ hours, five daily, slow trains

Paris Gare Montparnasse €44 to €83, 1¼ hours, 30 daily, high-speed TGVs

Saumur €14 to €21, 35 minutes, hourly

TGVs also serve Bordeaux (€40 to €62, 2¾ hours), La Rochelle (€35 to €48, 2½ to 3¼ hours) and Nantes (€28 to €55, 1½ hours).

Château de Villandry

DIANA MAYFIELD

GREG GAWLOWSKI

Château de Chenonceau

Spanning the languid Cher River via a series of supremely graceful arches, the castle of **Chenonceau** (📞02 47 23 90 07; www.chenonceau.com; adult/child €10.50/8, audioguide €4.50; 🕐9am-8pm Jul & Aug, 9am-7.30pm Jun & Sep, 9am-7pm Apr & May, 9.30am-5pm or 6pm rest of year) is one of the most elegant and unusual in the Loire Valley.

This architectural fantasy land is largely the work of several remarkable women (hence its alternative name, Le Château des Dames: 'Ladies' Château'). The initial phase of construction started in 1515 for Thomas Bohier, a court minister of King Charles VIII, although much of the work and design was actually overseen by his wife, Katherine Briçonnet.

Chenonceau had a heyday under the aristocratic Madame Dupin, who made the château a centre of fashionable 18th-century society and attracted guests including Voltaire and Rousseau (the latter tutored her son).

The *pièce de resistance* is the 60m-long window-lined **Grande Gallerie** spanning the Cher, scene of many a wild party hosted by Catherine de Médicis or Madame Dupin.

In July and August the illuminated château and grounds are open for the **Promenade Nocturne** (adult/child €5/ free).

The château is 34km east of Tours, 10km southeast of Amboise and 40km southwest of Blois. There are trains and buses from all three towns.

Amboise

POP 12,929

The childhood home of Charles VIII and the final resting place of the great Leonardo da Vinci, elegant Amboise is pleasantly perched on the southern bank of the Loire and overlooked by its fortified 15th-century château.

 Sights

CHÂTEAU ROYAL D'AMBOISE Castle
(📞02 47 57 00 98; place Michel Debré; adult/child €10/6.50; 🕐9am-6pm, 9am-5.30pm Mar, 9am-12.30pm & 2-4.45pm Jan-Feb & mid-Nov–Dec) Sprawling across a gor-

geously situated, rocky escarpment with panoramic views of the river and surrounding countryside, the easily defendable castle presented a formidable prospect to would-be attackers, but in fact saw little military action. Charles VIII (r 1483–98), was born and brought up here, and was responsible for the château's Italianate remodelling in 1492. François I (r 1515–47), who constructed Chambord, also grew up here alongside his sister Margaret of Angoulême, and later invited da Vinci to work at nearby Clos-Lucé under his patronage.

Today, just a few of the original 15th- and 16th-century structures survive, notably the **Flamboyant Gothic wing** and the **Chapelle St-Hubert**, a small chapel dedicated to the patron saint of hunting (note the carved stag horns and hunting friezes outside) and believed to be the final resting place of da Vinci.

Exit the château through **Tour Hurtault** on an ingenious sloping spiral ramp designed to allow carriages and horses to easily ascend to the château from the town below.

LE CLOS LUCÉ   Historic Mansion
(02 47 57 00 73; www.vinci-closluce.com; 2 rue du Clos Lucé; adult/child €12.50/7.50; 9am-7pm) Leonardo da Vinci (pronounced van-see in French) took up residence in the grand manor house at Le Clos Lucé in 1516 on the invitation of François I, who was greatly enamoured with the Italian Renaissance. Already 64 by the time he arrived, da Vinci spent his time sketching, tinkering and dreaming up new contraptions: the house is jammed with scale models of many of his inventions. The expansive, beautiful **gardens** wind through forest and stream and are dotted with full-size replicas of his inventions including a protoautomobile, tank, bridges, hydraulic turbine and even a primitive helicopter. He died here on 2 May 1519.

 Sleeping

LE PAVILLON DES LYS
     Boutique Hotel   €€
(02 47 30 01 01; www.pavillondeslys.com; 9 rue d'Orange; d €98-160;) Take a cappuccino-coloured 18th-century town house and fill it with designer lamps, just-so furniture, roll-top baths, hi-fis and deep sofas, and you're halfway there; then chuck in a locally renowned restaurant, an elegant patio garden and boutiquey treats.

VILLA MARY   B&B   €€
(02 47 23 03 31; www.villa-mary.fr; 14 rue de la Concorde; d incl breakfast €90-120) Four tip-top rooms in an impeccably furnished 18th-century town house, crammed with beeswaxed antiques, glittering chandeliers and antique rugs.

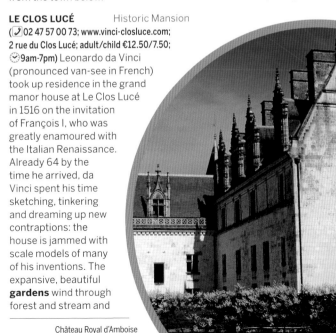
Château Royal d'Amboise
PHOTOGRAPHER: JENNY JONES

LE CLOS D'AMBOISE Historic Hotel €€
(☎ 02 47 30 10 20; www.leclosamboise.com; 27 rue Rabelais; r €97-149; ☒) Another posh pad finished with style and luxurious fabrics, from wood panelling to antique beds and original fireplaces.

 Eating & Drinking

CHEZ BRUNO Regional Cuisine €
(☎ 02 47 57 73 49; place Michel Debré; menus from €12; ☾ lunch Tue-Sun, dinner Tue-Sat) Uncork a local vintage in a coolly contemporary setting, accompanied by honest, inexpensive regional cooking. If you're after Loire Valley wine tips, this is the place.

L'ÉPICERIE Traditional French €€
(☎ 02 47 57 08 94; 46 place Michel Debré; menus €22-34; ☾ Wed-Sun) A more time-honoured atmosphere with rich wood and neo-Renaissance decor matched by filling fare like *cuisse de lapin* (rabbit leg) and *tournedos de canard* (duck fillet).

BIGOT Tea House €
(☎ 02 47 57 59 32; 2 rue Nationale; ☾ 9am-7.30pm Tue-Fri, 8.30am-7.30pm Sat & Sun) Since 1913 this award-winning chocolatier and pâtisserie has been whipping up some of the Loire's creamiest cakes and gooiest treats: multicoloured *macarons*, handmade chocolates, éclairs and *petits fours*.

ⓘ Information

Tourist Office (☎ 02 47 57 09 28; www.amboise-valdeloire.com; ☾ 9am-7pm Mon-Sat, 10am-1pm & 2-6pm Sun) In a riverside building opposite 7 quai du Général de Gaulle.

ⓘ Getting There & Around

Amboise is 34km southwest of Blois and 23km northeast of Tours. The **train station** (bd Gambetta) is across the river from the centre.

Blois €11, 20 minutes, 14 daily

Paris Gare d'Austerlitz €38 to €56, 2¼ hours, 14 daily

Paris Gare Montparnasse €107, 1¼ hours, 10 daily, TGV

Tours €11, 20 minutes, 10 daily

Château d'Azay-le-Rideau

Romantic, moat-ringed **Azay-le-Rideau** (☎ 02 47 45 42 04; adult/child €7.50/free; ☾ 9.30am-6pm, to 7pm Jul & Aug, 10am-12.30pm & 2-5.30pm Oct-Mar) is wonderfully adorned with slender turrets, geometric windows and decorative stonework and is surrounded by a shady landscaped park. Built in the 1500s on a natural island in the River Indre, the château is one of the Loire's loveliest: Honoré de Balzac called it a 'multi-faceted diamond set in the River Indre'.

Its most famous feature is its open **loggia staircase**, in the Italian style, overlooking the central courtyard and decorated with the salamanders and ermines of François I and Queen Claude. The interior is mostly 19th century, remodelled by the Marquis de Biencourt from the original 16th-century château. In July and August, a **son et lumière** (one of the Loire's oldest and best) is projected onto the castle walls nightly. Multi-language audioguides cost €4.50 and seven daily guided tours in French are free.

ⓘ Getting There & Away

Château d'Azay-le-Rideau is 26km southwest of Tours.

BUS Touraine Fil Vert's (p201) bus V travels from Tours to Azay-le-Rideau (€1.70, 50 minutes) twice daily June to August.

Saumur

POP 29,587

There's an air of Parisian sophistication around Saumur, but also a sense of laidback contentment. The town is renowned for its École Nationale d'Équitation, a national cavalry school that's been home to the crack riders of the Cadre Noir since 1828.

 Sights

ÉCOLE NATIONALE D'ÉQUITATION
Riding School
(National Equestrian School; ☎ 02 41 53 50 60; www.cadrenoir.fr; rte de Marson; adult/child

€7/5) Three kilometres west of town, outside of sleepy St-Hilaire-St-Florent, the École Nationale d'Équitation is one of France's foremost riding academies.

Advance reservations are essential for the one-hour guided visits (four to 10 per day; enquire about the availability of English-language tours). If you happen to be in town for one of the semi-monthly **Cadre Noir presentations (adult/child €16/9)** do not miss it: they are like astonishing horse ballets.

 ## Sleeping

CHÂTEAU DE VERRIÈRES
Castle Hotel **€€€**

(✆ 02 41 38 05 15; www.chateau-verrieres. com; 53 rue d'Alsace; r €150-210, ste €260-290; 🛜⛲) Every one of the 10 rooms in this impeccably wonderful 1890 château, ensconced within the woods and ponds of a 1.6-hectare English park, is different.

HÔTEL SAINT-PIERRE
Historic Hotel **€€**

(✆ 02 41 50 33 00; www.saintpierresaumur.com; 8 rue Haute St-Pierre; r €70-155; ❄🛜) Squeezed down a minuscule alleyway opposite the cathedral, this effortlessly smart hideaway mixes heritage architecture with modern-day comfort: pale stone, thick rugs and vintage lamps sit happily alongside minibars and satellite TV.

 ## Eating

LE POT DE LAPIN
Modern French **€€**

(✆ 02 41 67 12 86; 35 rue Rabelais; tapas €1.50-5, mains €11-19; ⏱Tue-Sat) The jaunty strains of Django Reinhardt's guitar waft from the cheery dining room through the wine bar and onto the streetside terrace. Chef Olivier serves the tables himself, proposing perfect wine pairings, and the food – well, the food is decadent.

LE GAMBETTA
Gastronomic **€€**

(✆ 02 41 67 66 66; www.restaurantlegambetta. com, in French; 12 rue Gambetta; lunch menus €20-27, other menus €27-82; ⏱lunch Thu-Tue, dinner Mon-Tue & Thu-Sat) OK, prepare yourself. This is another place to write home about: a fantastic regional restaurant combining refined elegance and knock-your-socks-off creative food.

Château d'Azay-le-Rideau

DIANA MAYFIELD

ⓘ Information

Tourist office (📞 02 41 40 20 60; www.saumur-tourisme.com; place de la Bilange; 🕐9.15am-12.30pm & 2-6pm)

ⓘ Getting There & Around

Train services connect Tours (€15 to €23, 50 minutes, 15 daily) and Angers (€11 to €19, 25 minutes, nine daily).

BURGUNDY

Burgundy (Bourgogne in French) offers some of France's most gorgeous countryside: rolling green hills dotted with medieval villages, and mustard fields blooming in bright contrast. Two great French passions, wine and food, come together here in a particularly enticing form.

Dijon

POP 250,000

Dijon is one of France's most appealing cities. Filled with elegant medieval and Renaissance buildings, the lively centre is wonderful for strolling, especially if you like to leaven your cultural enrichment with excellent food, fine wine and shopping.

 Sights

PALAIS DES DUCS ET DES ÉTATS DE BOURGOGNE
Palace

(Palace of the Dukes and States of Burgundy) Once home to Burgundy's powerful dukes, this monumental palace is the focal point of old Dijon. Given a neoclassical facade in the 17th and 18th centuries while serving as the seat of the States-General (Parliament) of Burgundy, it overlooks **place de la Libération**, a magnificent semicircular public square designed by Jules Hardouin-Mansart (one of the architects of Versailles) in 1686.

Just off the **Cour d'Honneur**, the 46m-high, mid-15th-century **Tour Philippe le Bon** (Tower of Philip the Good; 📞03 80 74 52 71; adult/child €2.30/free; 🕐 accompanied climbs every 45min 9am-noon & 1.45-5.30pm, Wed pm-Sun, closed Thu-Fri late Nov-Easter) affords fantastic views over the city.

MUSÉE DES BEAUX-ARTS
Art Museum

(📞 03 80 74 52 09; audioguide €4, tours adult/child €6/3; 🕐9.30am-6pm Wed-Mon) Housed in the eastern wing of the Palais des Ducs, these sprawling galleries make up one of the most outstanding museums in France. The star is the wood-panelled **Salle des Gardes** (Guards' Room), once warmed by a gargantuan Gothic fireplace.

The modern and contemporary art section, with works by Manet and Monet

Palais des Ducs
PHOTOGRAPHER: ANDREW BAIN

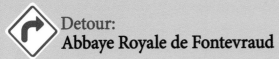

Detour:
Abbaye Royale de Fontevraud

(📞 02 41 51 71 41; www.abbaye-fontevraud.com; adult/child €8.50/7, tour or audioguide €4; ⏰ 9.30am-6.30pm) Until its closure in 1793 this huge 12th-century complex was one of the largest ecclesiastical centres in Europe. Unusually, both nuns and monks were governed by an abbess (generally a lady of noble birth retiring from public life). The extensive grounds include a **chapter room** with murals of the Passion of Christ by Thomas Pot, dormitories, workrooms and prayer halls, as well as a spooky underground sewer system and a wonderful barrel-vaulted **refectory**, where the monks and nuns would eat in silence while being read the scriptures.

The highlight is undoubtedly the massive, movingly simple **abbey church**, notable for its soaring pillars, Romanesque domes, and the polychrome tombs of four illustrious Plantagenets: Henry II, King of England (r 1154–89); his wife Eleanor of Aquitaine (who retired to Fontevraud following Henry's death); their son Richard the Lionheart; and his wife Isabelle of Angoulême.

The abbey is 15km southeast of Saumur. Public transport is limited, so you'll need a car.

and sculptures by Matisse and Rodin, harbours a particular delight: the **Pompon Room**. Tucked off a back staircase, this room is packed with stylised modern sculptures of animals by François Pompon (1855–1933).

In the courtyard, the **ducal kitchens** (1433) often host exhibitions of works by local artists.

ÉGLISE NOTRE DAME   Church
A block north of the Palais des Ducs, Église Notre Dame was built between 1220 and 1240. High atop the church, the 14th-century **Horloge à Jacquemart** (Jacquemart Clock) was transported from Flanders in 1383 by Philip the Bold, who claimed it as a trophy of war.

HÔTELS PARTICULIERS
                        Historic Mansions
Many of Dijon's finest houses lie north of the Palais des Ducs on and around rue Verrerie, rue Vannerie and rue des Forges, whose names reflect the industries that once thrived there (glassmaking, basket-weaving and metalsmithery, respectively). The early 17th-century **Maison des Cariatides**

(28 rue Chaudronnerie), its facade a riot of stone caryatids, soldiers and vines, is particularly fine.

CATHÉDRALE ST-BÉNIGNE   Cathedral
(place St-Philibert) Situated above the tomb of St Benignus (who is believed to have brought Christianity to Burgundy in the 2nd century), this Gothic-style church with multicoloured roof tiles was built around 1300 as an abbey church. Some of Burgundy's great figures are buried here.

 Tours

MP3 Tour   History Tour
(€6, incl MP3 player with images €12) From the main tourist office.

Walking Tours   History Tour
(adult/child €6/3) A slew of different tours depart from the main tourist office.

Vineyard Tours   Wine Tours
Minibus tours in English introduce the Côte d'Or vineyards. Operators include: **Alter & Go** (📞 06 23 37 92 04; www.alterandgo.fr; tours €60-80) with an emphasis on history and winemaking methods; **Authentica Tour** (📞 06 87 01 43

208

Dijon

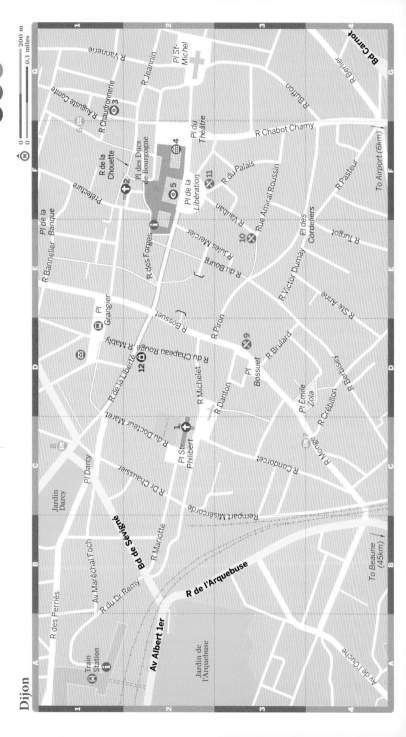

0   200 m
0   0.1 miles

To Airport (6km)

R Chabot Chamy

Bd Carnot

To Beaune
(45km)

Av de l'Ouche

Train
Station

Jardin
Darcy

Jardin de
l'Arquebuse

Av Albert 1er

R de l'Arquebuse

Bd de Sévigné

Pl Darcy

Av Maréchal Foch

R du Dr Remy

R Mariotte

R des Perriès

R de la Liberté

R du Docteur Maret

R D'r Chaussier

Pl St-
Philbert

R Monge

R Condorcet

Rempart Miséricorde

R Crébillon

R Berbisey

Pl Emile
Zola

R Danton

R Michelet

Pl
Bossuet

R Brulard

R Piron

R Ste-Anne

R Victor Dumay

R Vauban

Rue Amiral Roussin

Pl des
Cordeliers

R Turgot

R Pasteur

R Berlier

R Buffon

R du Palais

Pl du
Théâtre

Pl de la
Libération

Pl des Ducs
de Bourgogne

Pl des Forges

Pl du Bourg

Pl Jules Mercier

R Bossuet

R du Chapeau Rouge

R Mably

Pl
Grangier

R Bannelier

Pl de la
Banque

Préfecture

R de la
Chouette

R Auguste Comte

R Chaudronnerie

R Jeannin

R Vannerie

Pl St-
Michel

78; www.authentica-tour.com; tours €55-95); and **Wine & Voyages** (☎03 80 61 15 15; www. wineandvoyages.com; 2/3hr tours €48/58).

Sleeping

HÔTEL LE JACQUEMART   Hotel €
(☎03 80 60 09 60; www.hotel-lejacquemart.fr; 32 rue Verrerie; d €49-65; @ 🛜) Right in the heart of old Dijon, this basic hotel has 31 tidy, comfortable rooms; the pricier ones are quite spacious and some come with marble fireplaces.

HÔTEL LE SAUVAGE   Hotel €
(Hostellerie du Sauvage; ☎03 80 41 31 21; www. hotellesauvage.com, in French; 64 rue Monge; s €46-55, d €51-61, tr €80; 🛜) In a 15th-century *relais de poste* (mail staging post) set around a cobbled, vine-shaded courtyard, this good-value budget hotel is just off lively rue Monge. Parking €5.

HÔTEL SOFITEL LA CLOCHE
   Hotel €€€
(☎03 80 30 12 32; www.hotel-lacloche.com; 14 place Darcy; d €190-240, ste €300-800; ❄ @ 🛜) This venerable hostelry, built in 1884, boasts a huge lobby chandelier, an immaculate back garden, a sauna and a small fitness room.

Eating

LE PRÉ AUX CLERCS
   Gastronomic French €€€
(☎03 80 38 05 05; www.jeanpierrebilloux.com; 13 place de la Libération; lunch menus €35, dinner menus €50-95; 🕑lunch Tue-Sun, dinner Tue-Sat) From the luscious lunch menu (which includes a glass of wine) to the nine-course *dégustation* menu, every detail is cared for at this top-notch restaurant looking out onto the Palais des Ducs.

LA DAME D'AQUITAINE Burgundian €€
(☎03 80 30 45 65; 23 place Bossuet; lunch menus €21, dinner menus €28-43; 🕑lunch Tue-Sat, dinner Mon-Sat, closed lunch mid-July–mid-Aug) Excellent Burgundian and southwestern French cuisine is served under the sumptuously lit bays of a 13th-century *cave*.

LE PETIT ROI DE LA LUNE Bistro €€
(☎03 80 49 89 93; 28 rue Amiral Roussin; lunch menu €10, mains €15-18; 🕑lunch Tue-Sat, dinner Mon-Sat) A hip, younger crowd comes for French cuisine that, explains the chef, has been *revisitée, rearrangée et decalée* (revisited, rearranged and shifted).

Shopping

Moutarde Maille   Mustard
(☎03 80 30 41 02; 32 rue de la Liberté; 🕑10am-7pm Mon-Sat) Thirty-six kinds of mustard, like cassis or truffle and celery, include three on tap that you can sample (from €2.40 per 200ml).

🛈 Information

Tourist office (☎08 92 70 05 58; www. visitdijon.com; 🕑9am-6.30pm Mon-Sat, 10am-6pm Sun) main office (11 rue des Forges); station annexe (train station) The one- to three-day Dijon Côte de Nuits Pass may save you some cash.

🛈 Getting There & Away

For train destinations within Burgundy, see town listings in this chapter. Trains leave the **train station** (rue du Dr Remy) for the following:

BETHUNE CARMICHAEL

Don't Miss Côte d'Or Vineyards

The villages of the Côte d'Or offer innumerable places to sample and purchase world-class wines a short walk from where they were made! See Dijon or Beaune for tours of the vineyards.

Burgundy's most renowned vintages come from the vine-covered Côte d'Or (literally Golden Hillside, but it is actually an abbreviation of Côte d'Orient or Eastern Hillside), the narrow, eastern slopes of a range of hills made of limestone, flint and clay that runs south from Dijon for about 60km.

Burgundy's most famous wine route, the **Route des Grands Crus**, and its often-narrow variants wend their way between stone-built villages with steeple-topped churches or the turrets of a château peeping above the trees. The Côte's lower slopes are seas of vineyards; on the upper slopes, vines give way to forests, cliffs and breathtaking views. Signposted in brown, the Route des Grands Crus generally follows the tertiary roads west of the N74.

For details on public transport around Côte d'Or wine villages, see p212 and p212.

NEED TO KNOW
www.road-of-the-fine-burgundy-wines.com

Lyon-Part Dieu €34, two hours, 25 daily

Nice €90, 6¼ hours by TGV, two direct daily

Paris Gare de Lyon €61, 1¾ hours by TGV; €44, three hours non-TGV; 20 daily

Strasbourg €49, 3½ hours by TGV, 4½ hours non-TGV; nine daily.

Beaune
POP 22,720

Beaune (pronounced similarly to 'bone'), 44km south of Dijon, is the unofficial capital of the Côte d'Or. This thriving town's *raison d'être* and the source of its *joie de vivre* is wine: making it, tasting it, selling it but, most of all, drinking it. Consequently Beaune is one of the best places in all of France for wine tasting.

Sights & Activities

HÔTEL-DIEU DES HOSPICES DE BEAUNE
Historic Hospital

(☎ 03 80 24 45 00; rue de l'Hôtel-Dieu; adult/child €6.50/2.80; ⏱9am-6.30pm, interior closes 1hr later) Built in 1443 by Nicolas Rolin, the chancellor to Philippe-le-Bon, and used as a hospital until 1971, this magnificent Gothic hospital building is famously topped by stunning turrets and pitched rooftops covered in multicoloured tiles. Do not miss the brilliant **Polyptych of the Last Judgement** by the Flemish painter Rogier van der Weyden.

MARCHÉ AUX VINS
Wine Tasting

(☎ 03 80 25 08 20; www.marcheauxvins.com, in French; 2 rue Nicolas Rolin; admission €10; ⏱9.30-11.45am & 2-5.45pm, no midday closure mid-Jun–Aug) Using a *tastevin*, sample an impressive 15 wines in the candle-lit former Église des Cordeliers and its cellars.

PATRIARCHE PÈRE ET FILS
Wine Tasting

(☎ 03 80 24 53 78; www.patriarche.com; 5 rue du Collège; audioguide tour €10; ⏱9.30-11.30am & 2-5.30pm) The largest cellars in Burgundy, they are lined with about five million bottles of wine. Visitors sample 13 wines and take the *tastevin* home.

Tours

The tourist office handles reservations for **hot-air-balloon rides**, and **vineyard tours** (per adult/child €38-42/19-21) run by **Chemins de Bourgogne** (www.chemins-de-bourgogne.

Hôtel-Dieu des Hospices de Beaune
PHOTOGRAPHER: CHRISTOPHER WOOD

com), **Safari Tours** (www.burgundy-tourism-safaritours.com) and **Vinéatours** (www.vineatours.com).

Sleeping

HÔTEL DE LA POSTE
Historic Hotel €€€

(☎ 03 80 22 08 11; www.hoteldelapostebeaune.com; 1 bd Georges Clemenceau; d €160-220; ✳🛜) This swank establishment sits on a site that's been home to a hostelry since 1660. The old-time wooden lift carries you to spacious, soothing rooms; no bling here, just impeccable understated elegance.

ABBAYE DE MAIZIÈRES
Historic Hotel €€

(☎ 03 80 24 74 64; www.beaune-abbaye-maizieres.com; 19 rue Maizières; d €112; @) An idiosyncratic hotel inside a 12th-century abbey whose 13 tastefully converted rooms, with modern bathrooms, make creative use of the old brickwork and ancient wooden beams.

Eating

LOISEAU DES VIGNES
Gastronomic €€€
(📞03 80 24 12 06; 31 rue Maufoux; lunch menus €20-28, dinner menus €59-75; ⏱Tue-Sat) Wines are served only by the glass (€3 to €80) from snazzy sleek red degustation contraptions ringing the hushed but relaxed dining room. Service is knowledgeable and attentive, making a meal here a true pleasure.

CAVES MADELEINE
Burgundian €€
(📞03 80 22 93 30; 8 rue du Faubourg Madeleine; menus €14-24; ⏱closed Thu, Sun & lunch Fri) A convivial Burgundian restaurant, much appreciated by locals who prize good value; regional classics include *boeuf bourguignon* and *cassolette d'escargots*. Join fellow diners at long communal wooden tables surrounded by wine racks.

Information

Tourist office (📞03 80 26 21 30; www.beaune-tourisme.fr); branch (1 rue de l'Hôtel-Dieu; ⏱10am-1pm & 2-6pm); main office (6 bd Perpreuil; ⏱9am-7pm Mon-Sat, 9am-6pm Sun) Sells Pass Beaune ticket combos.

Getting There & Away

BUS Transco (📞08 00 10 20 04) bus 44 links Beaune with Dijon (€1.50, 1½ hours, two to seven daily), stopping at Côte d'Or villages such as Vougeot, Nuits-St-Georges and Aloxe-Corton.

TRAIN Trains connect the following places:

Dijon €11, 25 minutes, 40 daily.

Nuits-St-Georges €11, 10 minutes, 40 daily.

Paris Gare de Lyon €64–118, 2¼ hours by TGV (non-TGV 4½ hours), 20 daily, two direct TGVs daily.

Lyon-Part Dieu €31–46, 1¾ hours, 16 daily.

Abbaye de Fontenay

Founded in 1118 and restored to its medieval glory a century ago, **Abbaye de Fontenay** (Fontenay Abbey; 📞03 80 92 15 00; www.abbayedefontenay.com; adult/child €9.50/5.50; ⏱10am-6pm Apr-11 Nov, 10am-noon & 2-5pm 12 Nov-Mar) offers a fascinating glimpse of the austere, serene surroundings in which Cistercian monks lived lives of contemplation, prayer and manual labour. Set in a bucolic wooded

Abbaye de Fontenay

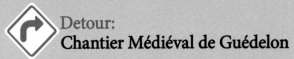

Detour:
Chantier Médiéval de Guédelon

A team of skilled artisans, aided by archaeologists, has been hard at work building a fortified **castle** (☎ 03 86 45 66 66; www.guedelon.fr; D955 near Treigny; adult/child €9/7; ⏰ 10am-5.30pm or 6pm Thu-Tue, closed Oct–mid-Mar; 🚻) here since 1997 using only 13th-century techniques. No electricity or power tools here...stone is quarried on site using iron hand tools forged by a team of blacksmiths, who also produce vital items like door hinges.

A very worthwhile guided tour, sometimes in English, costs €2 per person. Wear closed shoes, as the site is often a sea of muck. Child-oriented activities include stone carving (using especially soft stone).

Located 45km southwest of Auxerre.

valley along a stream called Ru de Fontenay, the abbey, a Unesco World Heritage Site, includes an unadorned Romanesque church, a barrel-vaulted monks' dormitory, landscaped gardens and the first metallurgical factory in Europe, which has a forge from 1220.

Fontenay is 25km north of Semur-en-Auxois.

THE DORDOGNE

With its rich food, heady history and rolling countryside strewn with countless historic castles, the Dordogne has long been a favourite place of escape for second-homing Brits and French families on *les grandes vacances*. But the castle-builders weren't the first to settle on the riverbanks; Cro-Magnon man was here long before, and the Vézère Valley shelters the most spectacular series of prehistoric cave paintings anywhere in Europe.

Sarlat-la-Canéda

POP 9943

A picturesque tangle of honey-coloured buildings, alleyways and secret squares make up Sarlat-la-Canéda. Ringed by forested hilltops, its heart-shaped Cité Médiévale (medieval town) is home to some of the country's best-preserved architecture from the Middle Ages.

 Sights & Activities

Part of the fun of wandering around Sarlat is losing yourself – literally – in its network of twisting alleyways and back streets.

CATHÉDRALE ST-SACERDOS Cathedral
Whichever street you take, sooner or later you'll end up at the cathedral on place du Peyrou, once part of Sarlat's Cluniac abbey.

MAISON DE LA BOÉTIE Architecture
This 16th-century timber-framed house opposite the cathedral is the birthplace of the writer Étienne de la Boétie (1530–63).

ÉGLISE STE-MARIE Architecture
A few steps south of place du Marché aux Oies is the Église Ste-Marie, ingeniously converted by acclaimed architect Jean Nouvel, whose parents still live in Sarlat. Not only does it now house Sarlat's mouthwatering **Marché Couvert** (covered market) but also, by the time you read this, a **panoramic lift** (elevator) will have been installed by Nouvel in its belltower.

HISTORIC QUARTER Architecture
Two medieval courtyards, the **Cour des Fontaines** and the **Cour des Chanoines**, can be reached via an alleyway off rue Tourny.

Nearby is the **Jardin des Enfeus**, Sarlat's first cemetery, and the rocket-shaped **Lanterne des Morts** (Lantern of the Dead), built to honour a visit by St Bernard, one of the founders of the Cistercian order, in 1147.

Sleeping

HÔTEL LES RÉCOLLETS   Hotel €
(☎ 05 53 31 36 00; www.hotel-recollets-sarlat. com; 4 rue Jean-Jacques Rousseau; d €45-69; ❄ 🛜 👪) Lost in the medieval maze of the old town, the Récollets is a budget beauty. Nineteen topsy-turvy rooms and a charming vaulted breakfast room are rammed in around the medieval *maison*.

CLOS LA BOËTIE   Boutique Hotel €€€
(☎ 05 53 29 44 18; www.closlaboetie-sarlat.com; 95-97 av de la Selves; d €210-280, ste €300-340; ❄ @ 🛜 🏊) Each of the 11 rooms at this 19th-century mansion is a jewel, right down to the high thread-count linen and super-soft pillows.

HÔTEL ST-ALBERT   Boutique Hotel €€
(☎ 05 53 31 55 55; www.hotel-saintalbert.eu; place Pasteur; d from €60; 🛜) At this pared back, stylish hotel with the barest of boutique touches, individually deco-rated rooms in chocolate-and-cream tones and posh bath goodies make it feel closer to a metropolitan crash pad than an old-town *auberge*.

Eating

BISTRO DE L'OCTROI
Regional Cuisine €€
(☎ 05 53 30 83 40; www.lebistrodeloctroi.fr, in French; 111 av de Selves; menus €18-26) This locals' tip is a little way out of town, but don't let that dissuade you. Sarladais pack into this cosy townhouse for the artistically presented, accomplished cooking that doesn't sacrifice substance for style.

Left: Maison de la Boétie (p213) on place du Peyrou;
Below: Lanterne des Morts

PHOTOGRAPHER: (LEFT) CRAIG PERSHOUSE; (BELOW) CRAIG PERSHOUSE

LE GRAND BLEU
Gastronomic   €€€

(📞05 53 29 82 14; www.legrandbleu.
eu, in French; 43 av de la Gare; menus €33-90;
🕙lunch Thu-Sun, dinner Tue-Sat; 👫) Near
the train station, every menu at this
Michelin-starred temple to fine dining
includes a choice of meat (like veal
sweetbreads with truffles) or seafood
(such as lobster risotto with roast eggplant and truffle mousse), with a *'petit
gourmet'* menu for little gourmands,
and an upcoming program of cooking
courses.

LE PRÉSIDIAL
Regional Cuisine   €€

(📞05 53 28 92 47; 6 rue Landry; menus from
€29; 🕙lunch Tue-Sat, dinner Mon-Sat Apr-Nov)
Housed in one of Sarlat's most historic
buildings (originally a 17th-century
courthouse), Le Présidial's stout gates
swing back to reveal the city's most
romantic terrace, filled with summer
flowers and climbing ivy – the perfect
place to sit back and enjoy authentic
saveurs de terroir (country flavours).

SATURDAY MARKET
Market   €

(place de la Liberté & rue de la République;
🕙8.30am-6pm Sat) For the full-blown
French market experience, you absolutely mustn't miss Sarlat's chaotic
Saturday market, which takes over the
streets around the cathedral.

ⓘ Information

Tourist office (📞05 53 31 45 45; www.sarlat
-tourisme.com; rue Tourny; 🕙9am-6pm Mon-
Sat, 10am-1pm & 2-5pm Sun)

ⓘ Getting There & Away

Sarlat's train station is 1.3km south of the old city
along av de la Gare. Destinations include Périgueux
(change at Le Buisson; €13.90, 1¾ hours, three
daily), Les Eyzies (change at Le Buisson; €8.60, 50
minutes to 2½ hours depending on connections,
three daily) and Bergerac (€11.20, 2½ hours, six
daily), as well as a direct service to Bordeaux
(€23.90, 2¾ hours, seven daily).

215

Picturesque Villages

If you've had your soul stirred by Sarlat, you won't want to miss these other picture-perfect villages.

1 **VÉZELAY**
(tourist office 03 86 33 23 69; www.vezelaytourisme.com) Perched on a rocky spur surrounded by vineyards, fields and grazing cows, hilltop Vézelay seems to have been lifted from another age. Cobbled streets wind uphill to the **Basilique Ste-Madeleine**, which houses the relics of St Mary Magdalene and hosts concerts of sacred music from June to September. Vézelay is 15km from Avallon.

2 **ROCAMADOUR**
(tourist office 05 65 33 22 00; www.rocamadour.com) Clinging to the side of a sheer cliff 51km east of Sarlat, this otherworldy town looks like it's tumbled from *The Da Vinci Code*. It's been an important pilgrimage site since the Middle Ages thanks to its supposedly miraculous *Vierge Noire* (Black Madonna).

3 **BRANTÔME**
(tourist office 05 53 05 80 63; www.ville-brantome.fr) With its five medieval bridges arcing over the River Dronne, Brantôme is often known as the 'Venice of the Périgord'. The abbey's 11th-century belltower is allegedly the oldest in France. It's 27km north of Périgueux.

4 **ST-CIRQ-LAPOPIE**
(tourist office 05 65 31 29 06; www.saint-cirqlapopie.com) Teetering high above the River Lot, this minuscule clifftop village has one of the most magical settings in the Lot, but beware the crowds in summer. It's 25km east of Cahors.

5 **COLLONGES-LA-ROUGE**
(tourist office 05 55 25 47 57; www.ot-collonges.fr) With its skyline of conical turrets and rust-red buildings, this entire village has been classed as a historic monument. It's 18km southeast of Brive-la-Gaillarde.

Vézère Valley

Flanked by limestone cliffs, subterranean caverns and ancient woodland, the Vézère Valley is world famous for its prehistoric sites, notably its incredible collection of cave paintings – the highest concentration of Stone Age art found in Europe. Most of the key sites are around the towns of Les Eyzies-de-Tayac-Sireuil and Montignac, which are both well set up for visitors. Visitor numbers to most caves are strictly limited to avoid damaging the paintings, so it's wise to book at least a couple of days in advance, especially in high summer.

MUSÉE NATIONAL DE PRÉHISTOIRE
Prehistory Museum

(www.musee-prehistoire-eyzies.fr, in French; 1 rue du Musée adult/child €5/free, 1st Sun of month free; 9.30am-6pm Wed-Mon) Housing the most comprehensive collection of prehistoric finds in France, highlights include a huge gallery of Stone Age tools, weapons and jewellery, and skeletons of some of the animals that once roamed the Vézère (including bison, woolly rhinoceros, giant deer and cave bears), as well as a collection of carved reliefs on the 1st floor – look out for an amazing frieze of horses and a bison licking its flank.

GROTTE DE FONT DE GAUME
Prehistoric Site

(05 53 06 86 00; http://eyzies.monuments-nationaux.fr; adult/child €7/free; 9.30am-12.30 & 2-5.30pm Sun-Fri) An astounding testament to the breadth and complexity of prehistoric art, this extraordinary cave 1km northeast of Les Eyzies on the D47 contains the only original 'polychrome' (as opposed to single-colour) paintings still open to the public. About 14,000 years ago, the prehistoric artists created the gallery of over 230 figures, including bison, reindeer, horses, mammoths, bears and wolves, although only about 25 are on permanent display. The 45-minute guided tours are generally in French; ask about the availability of English tours when you book.

GROTTE DES COMBARELLES

Prehistoric Site

(☎05 53 06 86 00; http://eyzies.monuments-na
tionaux.fr; adult/child €7/free; ☺9.30am-12.30 &
2-5.30pm Sun-Fri) Rediscovered in 1901, this
narrow cave 1.5km east of Font de Gaume
is renowned for its animal engravings,
many of which cleverly use the natural
contours of the rock to sculpt the animals'
forms. Six- to eight-person group tours
last about an hour and can be reserved
through the Font de Gaume ticket office.

ABRI DU CAP BLANC

Prehistoric Site

(☎05 53 06 86 00; http://eyzies.monuments
-nationaux.fr; adult/child €7/free; ☺9.30am-12.30
& 2-5.30pm Sun-Fri) While most of the
Vézère's caves contain a combination of
engravings and paintings, unusually, this
rock shelter contains carved sculptures
that were hollowed out, shaped and
refined using simple flint tools some
14,000 years ago. It's peacefully situated
about 7km east of Les Eyzies.

GROTTE DE ROUFFIGNAC

Prehistoric Site

(www.grottederouffignac.fr; adult/child €6.30/4;
tours in French ☺10-11.30am & 2-5pm) Hidden
in woodland 15km north of Les Eyzies,
this cave is one of the most complex and
rewarding to see in the Dordogne. The
massive cavern plunges 10km into the
earth through a mind-boggling maze of
tunnels and sub-shafts – luckily, you visit
aboard a somewhat ramshackle **electric
train**, so there's no chance of getting lost.

Rouffignac is sometimes known as the
'Cave of 100 Mammoths' and you'll see
many painted pachyderms on your trip
into the underworld, including a frieze of
10 mammoths in procession, one of the
largest cave paintings ever discovered.

Tickets are sold at the cave entrance
but can't be reserved in advance so
arrive early – and wrap up warmly as it's
chilly below ground.

GROTTE DE LASCAUX & LASCAUX II

Prehistoric Site

(☎Lascaux II 05 53 51 95 03; www.semitour.
com; adult/child €8.80/6, joint ticket with Le Thot
€12.50/8.50; ☺9.30am-6pm) France's most
famous prehistoric **cave paintings** are
at the Grotte de Lascaux, 2km southeast
of Montignac. Far from the comparative-
ly crude etchings of some of the Vézère's
other caves, Lascaux' paintings are
renowned for their astonishing artistry:

Musée National de Préhistoire

SALLY DILLON

the 600-strong menagerie of animal figures are depicted in Technicolor shades of red, black, yellow and brown, and range from reindeer, aurochs, mammoths and horses to a monumental 5.5m-long bull, the largest cave drawing ever found.

The original cave was opened to visitors in 1948, and public interest was unsurprisingly massive. But within a few years it became apparent that human breath and body heat was causing irreparable damage to the paintings, and the cave was closed just 15 years later in 1963. In response to public demand, a replica of the most famous sections of the original cave was meticulously recreated a few hundred metres away – a massive undertaking that required the skills of some 20 artists and took over 11 years.

There are several guided tours every hour; ask at the ticket office about the availability of tours in languages including English. From April to October, tickets are sold *only* in Montignac at the ticket office next to Montignac's tourist office (☏ 05 53 51 82 60; www.tourisme-lascaux.com; place Bertrand de Born; ☉ 9.30am-12.30pm & 2-6pm Mon-Sat).

❶ Information

Tourist office (☏ 05 53 06 97 05; www.tourisme-terredecromagnon.com; ☉ 9am-noon & 2-6pm Mon-Sat, 10am-noon & 2-5pm Sun)

❶ Getting There & Away

Les Eyzies is on the D47, 21km west of Sarlat. The train station is 700m north of town, with connections to Périgueux (€7.20, 30 minutes, 10 daily) and Sarlat (change at Le Buisson; €8.60, 50 minutes to 2½ hours depending on connections, three daily).

La Roque Gageac & Around
POP 431

La Roque Gageac's jumble of amber buildings crammed into the cliff-face above the Dordogne have earned it recognition as another of France's *plus beaux villages*, with flourishing gardens thanks to its microclimate.

◉ Sights

JARDINS DE MARQUEYSSAC　Gardens
(www.marqueyssac.com; adult/child €7.20/3.60; ☉ 10am-7pm) Signposted walkways wind through Marqueyssac's manicured overhanging gardens, 3km west of La Roque, to a breathtaking *belvédère* (lookout).

CHÂTEAU DE CASTELNAUD　Castle
(www.castelnaud.com; adult/child €7.80/3.90; ☉ 10am-7pm) The massive ramparts and metre-thick walls of this quintessential castle 4.5km southwest of La Roque are topped by crenellations and sturdy towers. The castle's **museum of medieval warfare** dis-

Château de Castelnaud
PHOTOGRAPHER: BARBARA VAN ZANTEN

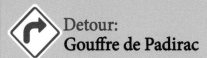

Detour:
Gouffre de Padirac

Gouffre de Padirac (05 65 33 64 56; www.gouffre-de-padirac.com; adult/child €9.20/6; ⏰10am-7pm) has glittering caverns that are among the most breathtaking in France. Discovered in 1889, the cave's navigable river, 103m below ground level, is reached through a 75m-deep, 33m-wide chasm. Boat pilots ferry visitors along 1km of the subterranean waterway, visiting a series of glorious floodlit caverns en route, including the soaring **Salle de Grand Dôme** and the **Lac des Grands Gours**, a 27m-wide subterranean lake. From Rocamadour, the caverns are 15km to the northeast.

plays daggers, spiked halberds and huge trebuchets. If you fancy seeing them in action, **mock battles** are staged from mid-July to August, as well as one-hour guided **evening tours** by costumed actors (adult/child €9.60/5) – check the events diary on the website.

CHÂTEAU DES MILANDES Castle
(www.milandes.com; Castelnaud-la-Chapelle; adult/child €8.50/5.50; ⏰10am-7pm) This 15th-century château, 8.5km southwest of La Roque, is less famous for its architecture (impressive though it is) than its former owner: glamorous African-American dancer, singer and music-hall star **Josephine Baker** (1906–75), who took the Parisian cultural scene by storm in the 1920s with her raunchy performances.

Baker purchased the castle in 1936 and lived here until 1958.

The château houses a **museum** documenting the life of the great Ms Baker, and her famous tunes tinkle out from the speaker system as you stroll around. Between May and October there are also 30-minute-long daily displays by the château's **birds of prey**.

😃 Activities

GABARRE CRUISES
A timeless way to explore the region's scenery is aboard a *gabarre*, a flat-bottomed, wooden boat traditionally used to transport freight up and down the rivers of the Périgord and Lot Valley. Trips generally last about 55 minutes and cost €8.50/6 per adult/child; advance reservations are recommended.

Operators in and around La Roque Gageac include **Gabarres Caminade** (✆05 53 29 40 95; gabarrescaminade@wanadoo. fr Le Bourg, La Roque Gageac); **Gabarres de Beynac** (✆05 53 28 51 15; www.gabarre -beynac.com, in French; Le Port, Beynac-et-Cazenac) and **Gabarres Norbert** (✆05 53 29 40 44; www.norbert.fr; Le Bourg, La Roque Gageac).

Lyon & the French Alps

The French Alps is a place of boundless natural beauty. Whether it's virgin snow in Chamonix, the rhythm of boots on a lonely mountain pass, or the silence of a summer's morning as the first rays illuminate Mont Blanc, these colossal mountains offer a symphony of unforgettable experiences. Needless to say, the Alps are a paradise for hikers, bikers and wildlife spotters, but it's the epic pistes and après-ski that keep people coming back year after year.

At the foothills of the Alps lies grand old Lyon, France's third-largest metropolis and arguably its gastronomic capital. It's a place to savour, with Roman amphitheatres, romantic parks and a delightful old town, but for many people nothing beats tucking into some hearty Lyonnais dishes in a traditional city *bouchon* (small bistro) – old-world atmosphere, checked tablecloths, clattering pans and all.

French Alps behind La Clusaz ski resort

PHOTOGRAPHER: GLENN VAN DER KNIJFF

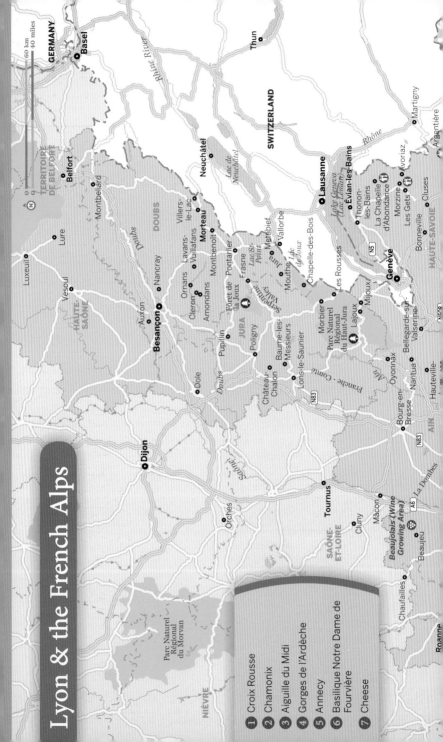

Lyon & the French Alps

1. Croix Rousse
2. Chamonix
3. Aiguille du Midi
4. Gorges de l'Ardèche
5. Annecy
6. Basilique Notre Dame de Fourvière
7. Cheese

Lyon & the French Alps' Highlights

Croix Rousse

I simply love its village feel, windy roads and cosy shops, daily market and beautiful setting, perched on top of the hill overlooking downtown Lyon. Croix Rousse is also a living museum that tells the story of the former silk-weavers and social revolutions that happened here.

Need to Know

HOT TIP Wear sturdy shoes to tackle Croix Rousse's endless steps and stairs **TRABOULES** Pick up a free map from the tourist office **For our author's review, see p239.**

Croix Rousse Don't Miss List

BY LISE PEDERSEN, FRENCH TV JOURNALIST

1 MARCHÉ DE LA CROIX

This market fills bd de la Croix Rousse daily (except Mondays) and brims with fresh produce, including fruit and veg from local farms. There's an organic market every Saturday morning at the boulevard's far end.

2 CAFÉ TERRACES

Two stand out for their remarkable view: the terrace at **Le Montana** (http://restaurantlemontana. fr) towers over Lyon, offering a splendid panorama of Fourvière (p238) and the city's two rivers. The other is **Le Gros Caillou (180 blvd de la Croix Rousse)**, right by the eponymous Gros Caillou (literally 'large rock'). On a clear day there's an absolutely spectacular view of Mont Blanc, creating the illusion that the Alps are but a few miles away.

3 LE CRIEUR

On Sunday morning around 11am you can't miss *le crieur* (town crier), aka born-and-bred Croix Roussien actor Gerald. Centre stage is place de la Croix Rousse where he reads out messages, poems and pamphlets people have left in post boxes at bars and cafés around town during the week. He encourages people to loosen up, shake each other's hands; he is unique, entertaining and heart-warming.

4 LYONNAIS CUISINE

Croix Rousse has become very 'bo-bo' in recent years, with lots of expensive, molecular cuisine places and so on. But you really can't go wrong at **Le Comptoir du Vin** (☎ **04 78 39 89 95; 2 rue Belfort**) if you fancy tucking into decently priced, excellent Lyonnais food in a genuine Croix Rousse atmosphere. If you like your meat raw, order the steak tartare, but be warned – it's not for the faint-hearted!

5 TRABOULES

On your way up to Croix Rousse or on your way down, follow the *traboules* (secret underground passages). A trip back in time, they take you through the famous secret passageways built through the city's buildings by local 19th-century silk-weavers to avoid the long windy roads when transporting their silk.

Action Chamonix!

Ever since Mont Blanc, the highest peak in the Alps, was first climbed in 1786, Chamonix has attracted travellers worldwide. Not only does it sit amid extremely condensed mountaineering potential; it is also a perfectly balanced combination of pure landscape alignment and dramatic mountain views.

②

Need to Know

OFF-PISTE Hire a local certified mountain guide **ESSENTIAL STOP** Maison de la Montagne: weather office, ski school and the world's oldest mountain-guide company **For more, see p245.**

Local Knowledge

Chamonix Don't Miss List

BY ERIC FAVRET, MOUNTAIN GUIDE, COMPAGNIE DES GUIDES DE CHAMONIX

1 SKIING IN GRANDS MONTET

Chamonix has six main ski areas. Grands Montets is particularly heavenly, with long off-piste glacial runs, easily accessible from lifts and offering over 6000ft of vertical drop! Its north-facing aspect combined with altitude, moreover, keeps the snow really good all winter long.

2 AIGUILLE DU MIDI

The Aiguille du Midi, with one of the highest cable cars in the world, cannot be missed. Beyond the summit ridge is a world of snow and ice offering some of the greatest intermediate off-piste terrain in the Alps.

3 OFF-PISTE THRILLS

The Vallée Blanche (p247) has to be seen. But the Aiguille du Midi also has amazing off-piste runs, such as Envers du Plan, a slightly steeper and more advanced version of Vallée Blanche, offering dramatic views in the heart of the Mont-Blanc range. There is also the less frequented run of the 'Virgin' or 'Black Needle': a striking glacial run, offering different views and a close-up look at the Giant's seracs.

4 SUMMER HIKES ON MONT BUET

Mont Buet is a favourite. It is a summit in itself and offers outstanding 360-degree panoramas over the Mont Blanc massif and its surrounding range. It requires a good level of fitness to do in a day, but there is a hut to split the trip into two days, which also takes you into a wildlife sanctuary.

5 BEST-EVER MONT BLANC VIEW

No hesitation: the Traverse from Col des Montets to Lac Blanc. It's as popular as the Eiffel Tower, for hikers in summer. I love swimming in mountain lakes, so I like to stop at Lac des Chéserys, just below, where it is quieter: what's better than a swim in pure mountain water, looking at Mont Blanc, the Grandes Jorasses and Aiguille Verte? This is what I call mountain landscape perfection!

227

Aiguille du Midi

Be blown away by views of Mont Blanc atop the Aiguille du Midi (p246). A jagged pinnacle of rock rising above snowfields and rocky crags, 8km from the domed summit of Europe's highest mountain, this 3842m-high peak is Chamonix's iconic landmark. Don't miss lunch at Le 3842, which claims to be the highest café anywhere in Europe.

3

5

Annecy

Criss-crossed by canals and set around the shores of a gleaming lake, Annecy (p251) is blessed with one of the loveliest settings in the Alps. It's a town that's tailor-made for unwinding wander the peaceful backstreets, pac a picnic for the Champ de Mars, snap your picture on the famous Lover's Bridge or just soak up the Alpine atmosphere.

JOHN ELK III

Gorges de l'Ardèche

These fabulous river canyons make a fantastic day trip from Lyon. The best way to explore them is by kayak or canoe (p245) – you'll find outdoors operators all along the course of the River Ardèche. The best views are from the lookout points dotted along the Haute Corniche (D290) – but be prepared for traffic jams in summer.

ANDREW BAIN

GREG ELMS

Basilique Notre Dame de Fourvière

Set high on a hilltop above Lyon, this 18th-century basilica (p238) commands a panoramic position overlooking the city's rooftops. Fourvière was once the site of the Roman settlement of Lugdunum, and an intriguing museum near the basilica explores the city's Roman connections. If you don't fancy the uphill climb, catch the creaky funicular from Vieux Lyon instead.

Cheese Feast

Cheese is an essential component in several classic Alpine dishes, including *raclette* (Raclette melted over potatoes, cold meats and gherkins) and *tartiflette* (Reblochon baked with potatoes, cream, onions and bacon). They're a staple feature on most Alpine restaurant menus – try L'Etage (p253) in Annecy or Le Chaudron (p249) in Chamonix – just don't blame us for the calorie count...

LYON & THE FRENCH ALPS' HIGHLIGHTS ● ● ● 229

Lyon & the French Alps' Best...

Alpine Experiences

◦ **Mer de Glace** (p245) Catch the rack-and-pinion train to Chamonix' 'sea of ice'.

◦ **Télécabine Panoramic Mont Blanc** (p246) Dangle above glaciers and crevasses in the dizzying cable-car ride from the Aiguille du Midi to Pointe Helbronner.

◦ **La Vallée Blanche** (p247) Brave the Alps' legendary ski descent.

◦ **Parc Naturel Régional du Vercors** (p250) Spot some wildlife on a nature walk through the park's pastures and peaks.

Hiking

◦ **Parc National de la Vanoise** (p250) Hit the trails in France's oldest national park between June and September.

◦ **Le Brévent** (p245) A multitude of routes cover this 2525m peak, offering breathtaking views of Mont Blanc.

◦ **Annecy** (p251) Walk or rollerblade round the shores of Lac d'Annecy.

◦ **Parc National des Écrins** (p250) Escape the crowds in France's second-largest national park.

Cultural Sights

◦ **Musée des Beaux-Arts** (p238) Lyon's art museum is a showstopper.

◦ **Musées Gadagne** (p235) Two museums in one, covering local history and Lyon's famous puppet, Guignol.

◦ **Musée Lumière** (p240) Visit the boyhood home of cinematic pioneers Auguste and Louis Lumière.

◦ **Château d'Annecy** (p251) Savoyard history in a château setting.

◦ **Route des Ducs de Savoie** (p253) Castles, abbeys and historic sites.

Need to Know

Dining

o **Le Bec** (p242) Top chef Nicolas Le Bec has two shiny Michelin stars and three Lyonnais eateries.

o **Café des Fédérations** (p242) The quintessential Lyonnais *bouchon*.

o **La Nouvelle Maison de Marc Veyrat** (p253) Classy fine-dining within driving distance of Annecy.

o **Le Bistrot** (p248) Chamonix' best restaurant by a mile.

o **Chalet la Pricaz** (p252) Our tip for Alpine cooking *par excellence*.

ADVANCE PLANNING

o **As early as possible** Book accommodation and/or ski packages, especially if you're planning on hitting the slopes.

o **Two weeks before** Arrange hiking, cycling, skiing and activity tours with local guides.

o **One week before** Book for well-known restaurants. Buy ski passes online, get weather forecasts and snow conditions and download piste maps.

RESOURCES

o **Lyon** (www.lyon.fr) Official city website.

o **Rhône-Alpes Tourisme** (www.rhonealpes-tourisme.com) Regional tourist information.

o **Compagnie des Guides** (www.chamonix-guides.com) Mountain guides, leading the way since 1821.

o **France Montagnes** (http://ski-resort-france.co.uk) Guides, maps, snow reports and more.

GETTING AROUND

o **Airports** The region's major airports are **Lyon St-Exupéry** (www.lyon.aeroport.fr), **Grenoble** (www.grenoble-airport.com) and **Geneva** (www.gva.ch) in Switzerland.

o **Car & Motorcycle** Traffic on mountain roads can be hellish, especially at weekends. Road signs indicate if mountain passes are blocked. Carry snow chains and/or winter tyres in winter.

o **Train** Lyon has excellent rail connections to anywhere in France. Eurostar ski trains travel to some resorts in winter.

o **Satobus Alpes** (http://satobus-alpes.altibus.com) Bus shuttle between Lyon St-Expéry airport and major ski resorts.

BE FOREWARNED

o **Opening times** *Bouchons* (small bistros) in Lyon tend to shut on weekends; many restaurants close on Mondays.

o **High-Season Prices** Over Christmas, New Year and during French school holidays in late February/early March.

o **Weather** Snow covers most ski stations from December to April. Weather can change rapidly, and avalanches are a serious danger – resorts announce the daily risk through signs and coloured flags.

Left: Montenvers train (p246);
Above: Mont Blanc and Chamonix Valley (p245)

PHOTOGRAPHERS: (LEFT) JOHN ELK III; (ABOVE) GRANT DIXON

Lyon & the French Alps Itineraries

For sheer natural drama, nowhere in France tops the Alps. Its snowy peaks and icy glaciers are essential terrain for skiers, hikers, boarders and bikers, as well as anyone who likes their views big and wild.

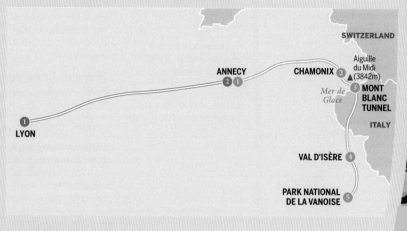

LYON TO ANNECY
3 DAYS
BIG CITY, LITTLE CITY

No city demands a weekend getaway more than **(1) Lyon**, a place most travellers arrive in unexpectedly, are pleasantly surprised by and yearn to return to.

You'll need at least a couple of days to do it justice. Devote the first to exploring the Presqu'île and Vieux Lyon, and allow a leisurely couple of hours for that quintessential long French lunch in a homely Lyonnais *bouchon* such as the Café des Fédérations.

With downtown Lyon under your belt, day two's for exploring further afield. Delve into the city's insider heart in Croix Rousse, with its lush morning market, mysterious maze of *traboules* and vibrant café life. In the afternoon catch the funicular to Fourvière for a peek at the Roman ruins and the basilica, before descending back to the old town for an alfresco drink on one of the city's grand squares. Reward yourself with dinner at one of the Michelin-starred establishments belonging to Nicolas Le Bec.

On day three, quit the big city for the altogether more-tranquil setting of **(2) Annecy**, a chic lakeside town with a sparkling lake to swim in and another beautiful old town to get lost in.

ANNECY TO CHAMONIX

ALPINE ADVENTURES

5 DAYS

(1) Annecy makes the ideal springboard for venturing into the spectacular peaks and valleys of the French Alps. In winter France's main playground for skiers and snowboarders, come summer it's a paradise for hikers and mountain-bikers. The following trip traverses some high Alpine passes, so it's a summer-only adventure.

From Annecy, head straight for the source – **(2) Chamonix**, renowned as one of Europe's top spots for mountain sports. Don't miss the *télécabine* up to the Aiguille du Midi, where you can enjoy a high-altitude lunch with views over Mont Blanc. Another key Chamonix sight is the

Mer de Glace, the aptly named 'Sea of Ice', where you can step inside an ice cave that has to be recarved every year due to the movement of the glacier.

After a couple of days trying out the activities in Chamonix, head out of town via the **(3) Mont Blanc tunnel**. Detour briefly into Italy before crossing back into France en route to **(4) Val d'Isère**, another of the Alps' classic mountain resorts. To the south sprawls the glorious **(5) Parc National de la Vanoise**, where you can spend the remainder of your trip hiking the trails and spotting wildlife.

Parc National de la Vanoise (p250)

Discover Lyon & the French Alps

LYON
POP 480,660

Commercial, industrial and banking powerhouse for the past 500 years, today Lyon is the focal point of a prosperous area of some 1,748,271 people.

Outstanding museums, a dynamic cultural life, busy clubbing and drinking scenes, a thriving university and fantastic shopping lend the city a distinctly sophisticated air, and adventurous gourmets can indulge their wildest gastronomic fantasies.

Lyon comprises nine *arrondissements* (neighbourhoods); the *arrondissement* number appears after each street address.

 Sights

The **Lyon City Card** (www.lyon-france.com; 1/2/3 days adult €20/30/40, child €11/15/20) covers admission to every Lyon museum and the roof of Basilique Notre Dame de Fourvière, as well as a guided city tour, a river excursion (April to October) and discounts for Le Grand Tour, the Aquarium du Grand Lyon and other selected attractions, exhibitions and shops.

The card also includes city-wide transport, offering unlimited travel on buses, trams and the funicular and metro (cheaper cards not incorporating transport are also available).

Vieux Lyon

Lyon's Unesco-listed old town, with its narrow streets and medieval and Renaissance houses, is divided into three quar-

Relief sculpture on a church wall, Lyon
PHOTOGRAPHER: GREG ELMS

GLENN VAN DER KNIJFF

ters: St-Paul (north), St-Jean (middle) and St-Georges (south).

CATHÉDRALE ST-JEAN
Cathedral

(place St-Jean, 5e; ⏰8am-noon & 2-7.30pm Mon-Fri, 8am-noon & 2-7pm Sat & Sun; Ⓜ Vieux Lyon) This partly Romanesque cathedral, seat of Lyon's 133rd bishop, was built between the late 11th and early 16th centuries. The portals of its Flamboyant Gothic facade (completed in 1480) are decorated with 280 square stone medallions. Don't miss the **astronomical clock** in the north transept, which chimes at noon, 2pm, 3pm and 4pm daily.

MEDIEVAL & RENAISSANCE ARCHITECTURE
Architecture

Lovely old buildings line rue du Bœuf, rue St-Jean and rue des Trois Maries. Crane your neck upwards to see gargoyles and other cheeky stone characters carved on window ledges along rue Juiverie, home to Lyon's Jewish community in the Middle Ages.

MUSÉES GADAGNE
Museums

(www.museegadagne.com; place du Petit Collège, 5e; 1 museum adult/child €6/free, both museums €8/free; ⏰11am-6.30pm Wed-Sun; Ⓜ Vieux Lyon) Housed in a 16th-century mansion built for two rich Florentine bankers, this newly reopened museum incorporates an excellent **local history museum** covering the city's layout as its silk-weaving, cinema and transportation evolved, and an **international puppet museum** paying homage to Lyon's iconic puppet, Guignol. On the 4th floor a **café** adjoins tranquil, terraced **gardens**, here since the 14th century and laid out two centuries later.

LE PETIT MUSÉE FANTASTIQUE DE GUIGNOL
Puppet Museum

(www.lamaisondeguignol.fr, in French; 6 rue St-Jean, 5e; adult/child €5/3; ⏰11am-6.30pm Tue-Sun; Ⓜ Vieux Lyon) Guignol is the star of this tiny, two-room museum with cute, sensor-activated exhibits; ask staff to set up the English soundtrack.

MUSÉE DES MINIATURES ET DÉCORS DU CINÉMA
Film Museum

(www.mimlyon.com, in French; 60 rue St-Jean, 5e; adult/child €7/5.50; ⏰10am-6.30pm Tue-Fri, 10am-7pm Sat & Sun; Ⓜ Vieux Lyon) This mazelike museum on tourist-busy rue St-Jean provides an unusual insight into the making of movie sets and special effects achieved with the use of miniatures.

235

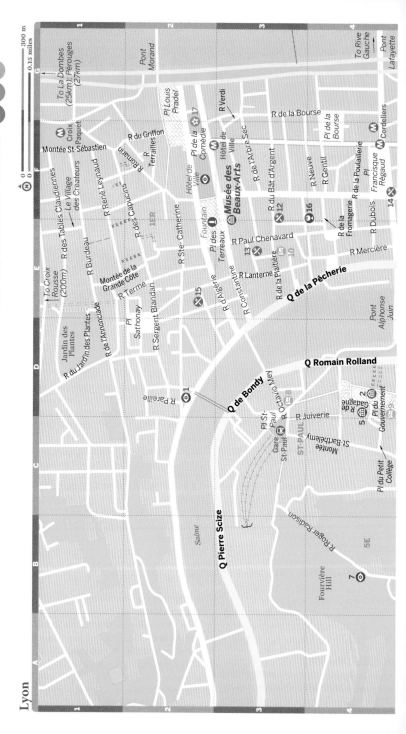

0 300 m
0 0.15 miles

To La Dombes
(25km); Pérouges
(27km)

Pont
Morand

To Croix
Rousse (200m)

To Rive
Gauche

Pont
Lafayette

Croix
Paquet

Montée St-Sébastien

Le Village
des Créateurs

R des Tables Claudiennes

R René Leynaud

R du Griffon

Pl Louis
Pradel

R Verdi

R de la Bourse

R Burdeau

R des Capucins

R Romarin

R
Terrailles

Pl de la
Comédie

17

Hôtel de
Ville

Hôtel de
Ville

Musée des
Beaux-Arts

R de l'Arbre Sec

R de la Bourse

Pl de la
Bourse

Cordeliers

1ER

Montée de la
Grande Côte

Fountain

Pl des
Terreaux

R du Bât d'Argent

R Neuve

R Gentil

Francisque
Régaud
Pl

R de la Poulaillerie

R Terme

R d'Annonciade

R Ste-Catherine

13

R Paul Chenavard

12

16

R de la
Fromagerie

R Dubois

14

Jardin des
Plantes

Pl
Sathonay

R du Jardin des Plantes

R d'Algérie

R Constantine

R Lanterne

10

R de la Plâtrière

R Mercière

Q de la Pêcherie

R Sergent Blandan

15

Q Romain Rolland

Pont
Alphonse
Juin

Saône

R Pareille

Q de Bondy

1

Gare
St-Paul

Pl St-
Paul

R Octavio Mey

8

R Juiverie

Montée St-Barthélemy

ST-PAUL

5E

Pl du
Gouvernement

R de
Gadagne

Pl du
Gadagne

2

5

9

Pl du Petit
Collège

Q Pierre Scize

R Roger Radisson

Fourvière
Hill

7

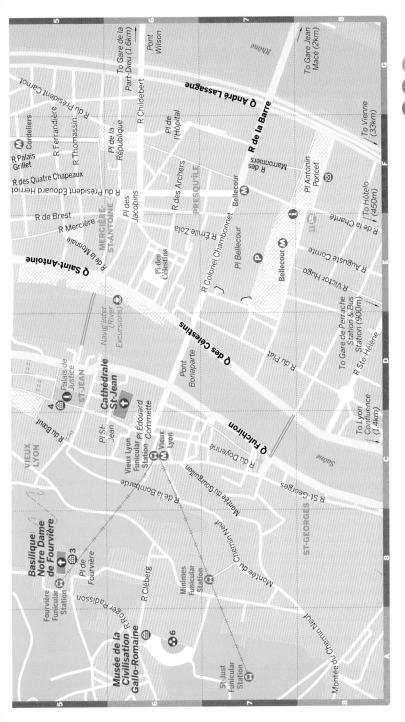

Basilique
Notre Dame
de Fourvière

Musée de la
Civilisation
Gallo-Romaine

Fourvière
Funicular
Station

R Roger Radisson

Pl de
Fourvière

R Cléberg

VIEUX
LYON

Minimes
Funicular
Station

St-Just
Funicular
Station

R du Bœuf

Palais de
Justice

ST-JEAN

Cathédrale
St-Jean

Pl St-
Jean

Vieux Lyon
Funicular
Station

Vieux
Lyon

Pl Édouard
Commette

R de la Bombarde

Montée du Gourguillon

Chemin Neuf

Montée du Chemin Neuf

R du Doyenne

Q Fulchiron

Pont
Bonaparte

Q des Célestins

Navig Inter
(River
Excursions)

Q Saint-Antoine

R de la Monnaie

MERCIÈRE-
ST-ANTOINE

R Mercière

R de Brest

R du Président Édouard Herriot

R des Quatre Chapeaux

R Palais
Grillet

Cordeliers

R Ferrandière

R Thomassin

R du Président Carnot

Pl de la
République

To Gare de la
Part-Dieu (1.6km)

Pont
Wilson

R Childebert

Q André Lassagne

Rhône

Pl de
l'Hôpital

R de la Barre

R des
Marronniers

PRESQU'ÎLE

R des Archers

R Émile Zola

Pl des
Jacobins

Pl des
Célestins

R Colonel Chambonnet

Pl Bellecour

Bellecour

Bellecour

Pl Antonin
Poncet

R de la Charité

R Auguste Comte

R Victor Hugo

R du Plat

R Ste-Hélène

ST-GEORGES

R St-Georges

Saône

To Gare de Perrache
Station & Bus
Station (900m)

To Lyon
Confluence
(1.4km)

To Vienne
(33km)

To Gare Jean
Macé (2km)

To Hôtelo
(450m)

237

Lyon

Fourvière

Over two millennia ago the Romans built the city of Lugdunum on the slopes of Fourvière. Today it's topped by the **Tour Métallique**, an Eiffel Tower–like structure (minus its bottom two-thirds) built in 1893 and used as a TV transmitter.

Footpaths wind uphill, but the **funicular** (return ticket €2.40; M Vieux Lyon) is a less-taxing way up.

BASILIQUE NOTRE DAME DE FOURVIÈRE
Basilica

(☎04 78 25 86 19; www.fourviere.org; ⊙ chapel 7am-7pm, basilica 8am-7pm) Crowning the hill – with stunning city panoramas

from its terrace – this 66m-long, 19m-wide and 27m-high basilica is lined with intricate mosaics and a superb example of late-19th-century French ecclesiastical architecture. One-hour **discovery visits** (adult/child €2/1; ⊙ several times daily Apr-Nov) take in the main features of the basilica and crypt; **rooftop tours** (adult/child €5/3; ⊙2.30pm & 4pm daily Apr-Oct, 2.30pm & 3.30pm Wed & Sun Nov) climax on the stone-sculpted roof.

MUSÉE D'ART RELIGIEUX   Art Museum

(www.fourviere.org; 8 place de Fourvière, 5e; adult/child €5/free; ⊙10am-12.30pm & 2-5.30pm; M Fourvière funicular station) Works of sacred art and worth-the-trip temporary exhibitions are showcased adjacent to the basilica.

MUSÉE DE LA CIVILISATION GALLO-ROMAINE
Archaeological Museum

(www.musees-gallo-romains.com; 17 rue Cléberg, 5e; adult/child €4/free, Thu free; ⊙10am-6pm Tue-Sun; M Fourvière funicular station) Ancient artefacts found in the Rhône Valley are displayed at the city's Roman museum. Next door, the **Théâtre Romain** (M Fourvière funicular station or Minimes funicular station), built around 15 BC and enlarged in AD 120, sat an audience of 10,000. Romans held poetry readings and musical recitals in the smaller, adjacent **odéon**.

Presqu'île

Lyon's city centre lies on this 500m- to 800m-wide peninsula bounded by the rivers Rhône and Saône.

MUSÉE DES BEAUX-ARTS   Art Museum

(www.mba-lyon.fr; 20 place des Terreaux, 1er; adult/child €7/free; ⊙10am-6pm Wed, Thu & Sat-Mon, 10.30am-6pm Fri; M Hôtel de Ville) This stunning and eminently manageable museum showcases France's finest collection of sculptures and paintings outside Paris from antiquity on. Highlights include works by Rodin, Rubens, Rembrandt, Monet, Matisse and Picasso.

PLACE DES TERREAUX   City Square

(M Hôtel de Ville) The centrepiece of the Presqu'île's beautiful central square is a 19th-century **fountain** made of 21 tonnes of lead and sculpted by Frédéric-Auguste Bartholdi (of Statue of Liberty fame). The four horses pulling the chariot symbolise rivers galloping seawards. The **Hôtel de Ville** (town hall) fronting the square was built in 1655 but given its present ornate facade in 1702.

PLACE BELLECOUR   City Square
(Ⓜ Bellecour) One of Europe's largest public squares, place Bellecour was laid out in the 17th century. In the centre is an equestrian **statue of Louis XIV**.

OPÉRA DE LYON   Opera House
(Ⓜ Hôtel de Ville) Lyon's neoclassical, 1831-built opera house was modernised in 1993 by renowned French architect Jean Nouvel, who added the striking semi-cylindrical glass-domed roof.

FRESQUE DES LYONNAIS   Mural
(cnr rue de la Martinière & quai de la Pêcherie, 1er; Ⓜ Hôtel de Ville) Well-known Lyonnais peer out from this seven-storey mural, including loom inventor Joseph-Marie Jacquard (1752–1834), Renaissance poet Maurice Scève (c 1499–1560), superstar chef Paul Bocuse (b 1926),

puppet Guignol, and the yellow-haired Little Prince, created by author/aviator Antoine de St-Exupéry (1900–44).

Croix Rousse

Independent until it became part of Lyon in 1852, and retaining its own distinct character with its bohemian inhabitants and lush outdoor food market, the hilltop quarter of Croix Rousse slinks north up the steep *pentes* (slopes).

Following the introduction of the mechanical Jacquard loom in 1805, Lyonnais *canuts* (silk-weavers) built tens of thousands of workshops in this area, with large windows to let in light and hefty wood-beamed ceilings more than 4m high to accommodate the huge new machines.

MAISON DES CANUTS   Silk Museum
(☏ 04 78 28 62 04; www.maisondescanuts. com; 10-12 rue d'Ivry, 4e; adult/child €6/3; ⏱ 10am-6pm Tue-Sat, guided tours 11am & 3.30pm; Ⓜ Croix Rousse) On a guided tour, learn about weavers' labour-intensive life and the industry's evolution, see manual looms in use and browse its silk boutique.

Riverside Rejuvenation

The Rhône's Rive Gauche (left bank), once the domain of high-speed traffic and car parks, has been extensively redeveloped in the past decade to provide Lyon with a fabulously landscaped walkway and cycling and inline-skating tracks, spanning 10 hectares over 5km of riverfront known as the **Berges du Rhône**.

Further downriver, the former industrial area of the **Lyon Confluence** (www.lyon -confluence.fr) is now the focus of another multimillion-euro rejuvenation project. **Maison de La Confluence** (☏ 04 78 38 74 00; 28 rue Casimir Perier, 2e; admission free; ⏱ 2-6.30pm Wed-Sat; 🚊 tramline 1, Montrochet stop), with a bird's eye view of construction from its rooftop terrace, displays scale models of the area's ongoing development.

The **Musée des Confluences** (www.museedesconfluences.fr), an ambitious science-and-humanities museum to be housed in a futuristic steel-and-glass transparent crystal, is estimated to open in 2014, about half a decade behind schedule. Until then, the **Local d'Information du Musée des Confluences** (☏ 04 78 37 30 00; www.museedesconfluences.fr; 86 quai Perrache, 2e; admission free; ⏱ 1-6pm Wed-Sat, 10am-noon & 1-6pm Sun) offers sneak previews of the Musée des Confluences' future collection.

Atelier de Passementerie Silk Workshop
(☎04 78 27 17 13; www.soierie-vivante.asso.fr;
21 rue Richan, 4e; guided tour adult/child €5/3;
⌚2-6.30pm Tue, 9am-noon & 2-6.30pm Wed-Sat,
guided tours & loom demonstrations 2pm & 4pm
Tue-Sat; MCroix Rousse) Trimmings workshop
that functioned until 1979.

Rive Gauche

MUSÉE LUMIÈRE Film Museum
(www.institut-lumiere.org; 25 rue du Premier Film,
8e; adult/child €6/5, audioguide €3; ⌚11am-
6.30pm Tue-Sun; MMonplaisir-Lumière) Cinema's glorious beginnings are showcased
at the art nouveau home of Antoine Lumière, 3km southeast of place Bellecour
along cours Gambetta, who moved to
Lyon with sons Auguste and Louis in 1870.
The brothers shot the first reels of the
world's first motion picture, *La Sortie des
Usines Lumières* (Exit of the Lumières Factories) in one of their father's photographic factories in the grounds on 19 March
1895. Today the former factory houses
the Hangar du Premier Film cinema.

 Tours

WALKING TOURS Walking Tour
(adult/child €9/5) The tourist office organises a variety of English-language tours
through Vieux Lyon and Croix Rousse,
and several others in French.

NAVIG'INTER Cruises
(☎04 78 42 96 81; www.naviginter.fr, in French;
13bis quai Rambaud, 2e; MBellecour or Vieux
Lyon) From April to October, Navig'inter
runs **river excursions** (adult/child €9/6; 1
or 1¼ hr) from its **dock** (3 quai des Célestins,
2e; MBellecour or Vieux Lyon). Advance
bookings are essential for its **lunch and
dinner cruises** (23 quai Claude Bernard, 7e;
transport €20-25, plus menus €26-34; MAmpère
or Guillotière).

Le Grand Tour Bus tour
(☎04 78 56 32 39; www.pariscityrama.com/fr/
visiter_lyon; adult 1-/2-day ticket €17/20, child 1
or 2 days €5; ⌚10am-6.30pm) Hop-on, hop-off
double-decker bus tours.

Left: Place des Terreaux (p238); **Below:** Silk loom, Atelier de Passementerie
PHOTOGRAPHER: (LEFT) CORINNE HUMPHREY; (BELOW) RODNEY ZANDBERGS

🛏 Sleeping

Lyon has a wealth of accommodation to suit every taste and budget. The tourist-office-run **reservation office** (☎04 72 77 72 50; www.lyon-france.com) offers a free booking service and good-value package deals.

COUR DES LOGES   Hotel   €€€
(☎04 72 77 44 44; www.courdesloges.com; 2-8 rue du Bœuf, 5e; d/ste from €240/505; ❄ @ 🛜 ≋ Ⓜ Vieux Lyon) Four 14th- to 17th-century houses wrapped around a *traboule* (secret underground passage) and with preserved features like Italianate loggias make this an exquisite place to stay. Individually designed rooms woo with Philippe Starck bathroom fittings and a bounty of antiques, while decadent facilities include a spa, an elegant **restaurant** (menus €60 to €85), swish **café** (mains €18 to €24) and cross-vaulted bar.

COLLÈGE HOTEL   Hotel   €€
(☎04 72 10 05 05; www.college-hotel.com; 5 place St-Paul, 5e; d €115-145; ❄ @ 🛜 Ⓜ Vieux Lyon) The ultrastark white-on-white minimalism of this hotel's guestrooms is quite startling (which is to say, not everyone will appreciate it). Breakfast can be taken on your balcony; in the *salle de classe petit dejeuner*, which is bedecked like a classroom of yesteryear; or in the rooftop garden.

LE ROYAL   Hotel   €€€
(☎04 78 37 57 31; www.lyonhotelroyal.com; 20 place Bellecour, 2e; d around €250; ❄ @ 🛜 Ⓜ Bellecour) In business since 1895, this timeless visiting card offers Lyon's ultimate in luxury, enveloping you in its stylish *salons* (lounges) and exquisite fabrics and furnishings. Rates vary wildly depending on dates and availability.

241

HÔTEL DE PARIS
Hotel €€

(☎ 04 78 28 00 95; www.hoteldeparis-lyon.com; 16 rue de la Platière, 1er; s €49-59, d €65-90; ❄ @ 🛜 Ⓜ Hôtel de Ville) At this fantastic-value hotel in a 19th-century bourgeois building, the funkiest rooms' retro '70s decor incorporates a palette of chocolate and turquoise or candyfloss pink. Rooms on the 4th and 5th floors have air conditioning (€2 extra per night).

HOTELO
Hotel €€

(☎ 04 78 37 39 03; www.hotelo-lyon.com; 37 cours de Verdun, 2e; d from €70; ❄ 🛜 ♿ Ⓜ Perrache) With a refreshingly contemporary design throughout, one of Hotelo's 17 rooms is equipped for travellers with disabilities, while another can sleep a family of four.

 Eating

A flurry of big-name chefs presides over a sparkling restaurant line-up that embraces all genres: French, fusion, fast and international, as well as traditional Lyonnais *bouchons*.

CAFÉ DES FÉDÉRATIONS
Bouchon €€

(☎ 04 78 28 26 00; www.lesfedeslyon.com, in French; 8 rue Major Martin, 1er; lunch menus €19, dinner menus €24-42; ⏰ Mon-Sat; 🛜 Ⓜ Hôtel de Ville) Black-and-white photos of old Lyon speckle the wood-panelled walls at this treasure of a *bouchon* where nothing has changed for decades – including the heaping portions, the warm service and the convivial atmosphere among diners (and, yes, the Turkish toilet. No matter, this is *bouchon* dining at its best).

LE BEC
French, Fusion €€€

(☎ 04 78 42 15 00; www.nicolaslebec.com, 2e; 14 rue Grolée; lunch menus €40, dinner menus €90-135; ⏰ Tue-Sat, closed 3 weeks August) With two Michelin stars, this is the flagship restaurant of Lyon's hottest chef, Nicolas Le Bec, famed for his seasonal, world-influenced cuisine. Le Bec is also the force behind the innovative new concept space **Rue Le Bec** (☎ 04 78 92 87 87; 43 quai Rambaud, 2e; mains €9-30, Sunday brunch €45; ⏰ Tue-Sun; 🚋 tramline 1, Montrochet stop), an airy restaurant set amid a covered-market-like layout of shops and eateries.

THOMAS
French €€

(☎ 04 72 56 04 76; www.restaurant-thomas.com, in French; 6 rue Laurencin, 2e; lunch/dinner menus €18/41; ⏰ Mon-Fri; Ⓜ Ampère) Ingenious chef Thomas Ponson gives taste buds the choice between formal dining at his eponymous restaurant, more casual fare in his à la carte wine bar, **Comptoir Thomas** (3 rue Laurencin; mains €14-25; ⏰ Mon-Fri), and more casual still at his tapas-inspired **Café Thomas** (1 rue Laurencin; tapas €1-5; ⏰ Tue-Sat).

Le Bec

GRAND CAFÉ DES NÉGOCIANTS

Brasserie €€

(☎04 78 42 50 05; www.cafe-des-negociants.com, in French; 2 place Francisque Regaud, 2e; lunch menus €17.90-21.90, mains €17.50-34; ⏰7am-3am; Ⓜ Cordeliers) Dubbed Les Négos by locals, this café-style brasserie with mirror-lined walls and a tree-shaded terrace has been a favourite meeting point with Lyonnais since 1864.

BRASSERIE GEORGES

Brasserie €€

(☎04 72 56 54 54; www.brasseriegeorges.com; 30 cours de Verdun, 2e; menus €18.50-24; ⏰11.30am-11.15pm Sun-Thu, 11am-midnight Fri & Sat; Ⓜ Perrache) Opened as a brewery in 1836 and still in the business (with four brews on tap), Georges' enormous 1924 art deco interior can feed 2000 a day! Famous customers have included Rodin, Balzac, Hemingway, Zola, Jules Verne and Piaf; food spans onion soup, sauerkraut, seafood and Lyonnais specialities.

BRASSERIE LÉON DE LYON

Brasserie €€

(☎04 72 10 11 12; www.leondelyon.com; 1 rue Pléney, 1e; menus €19.50-34; Ⓜ Hôtel de Ville) Renowned Lyonnais chef Jean-Paul Lacombe has turned his Michelin-starred gastronomic restaurant into a relaxed brasserie – same 1904 decor, same impeccable service, more-affordable prices.

MAGALI ET MARTIN

Lyonnais €€

(☎04 72 00 88 01; 11 rue Augustins, 1er; lunch/dinner menus €19.50/35; ⏰ lunch & dinner Mon-Fri, closed 3 weeks Aug & late Dec–mid Jan; Ⓜ Hôtel de Ville) Peep into the third of the trio of large glass windows fronting this fantastic eating space to watch the chefs turning out traditional but lighter, more-varied *bouchon*-influenced cuisine.

🍸 Drinking & Entertainment

Weekly 'what's on' guides include **Lyon Poche** (www.lyonpoche.com, in French; at newsagents €1) and **Le Petit Bulletin** (www.petit-bulletin.fr, in French; free on street corners).

Lyon Food Markets

Food shopping in Lyon is an unmissable part of the city's experience. And with so many urban spaces and parks, there are plenty of picnic spots too.

Lyon's famed indoor food market **Les Halles de Lyon** (http://halledelyon.free.fr, in French; 102 cours Lafayette, 3e; ⏰8am-7pm Tue-Sat, 8am-noon Sun; Ⓜ Part-Dieu) has over 60 stalls selling their renowned wares.

Lyon has two main **outdoor food markets**: Croix Rousse (bd de la Croix Rousse, 4e; ⏰Tue-Sun morning; Ⓜ Croix Rousse); Presqu'île (quai St-Antoine, 2e; ⏰Tue-Sun morning; Ⓜ Bellecour or Cordeliers).

PLACE DES TERREAUX

Cafés

(12 rue Ste-Catherine, 1er; Ⓜ Hôtel de Ville) The bounty of café terraces on the Presqu'île's central square buzz with drinkers all hours.

LE WINE BAR D'À CÔTÉ

Wine Bar

(☎04 78 28 31 46; www.cave-vin-lyon.com, in French; 7 rue Pleney, 1er; ⏰Tue-Sat; 📶 Ⓜ Cordeliers) Hidden in a tiny alleyway, this cultured wine bar is furnished like a rustic English gentlemen's club, with leather sofa seating and library.

OPÉRA DE LYON

Opera House

(☎08 26 30 53 25; www.opera-lyon.com, in French; place de la Comédie, 1er; ⏰mid-Sep–early Jul; Ⓜ Hôtel de Ville) Lyon's landmark opera house is the premier place to catch opera, ballet and classical concerts.

ℹ Information

Emergency

Police station (Commissariat de Police) place Sathonay (☎04 78 28 11 87; 5 place Sathonay, 1er; Ⓜ Hôtel de Ville); rue de la Charité (☎04 78 42 26 56; 47 rue de la Charité, 2e; Ⓜ Perrache or Ampère)

Medical Services

Hôpital Édouard Herriot (☎ 08 20 08 20 69; www.chu-lyon.fr, in French; 5 place d'Arsonval, 3e; ⊙ 24hr; Ⓜ Grange Blanche) Has an emergency room.

Tourist information

Tourist office (☎ 04 72 77 69 69; www.lyon-france.com; place Bellecour, 2e; ⊙ 9am-6pm; Ⓜ Bellecour)

❶ Getting There & Away

Air

Lyon-St-Exupéry Airport (☎ 08 26 80 08 26; www.lyon.aeroport.fr; 📶) Located 25km east of the city, serving 120 direct destinations across Europe and beyond, including many budget carriers.

Train

Lyon has two main-line train stations: Gare de la Part-Dieu (Ⓜ Part-Dieu), 1.5km east of the Rhône, and Gare de Perrache (Ⓜ Perrache). Some local trains stop at Gare St-Paul (Ⓜ Vieux Lyon) and Gare Jean Macé (Ⓜ Jean Mace). Buy tickets at the stations or at the SNCF Boutique (2 place Bellecour, 2e; Ⓜ Bellecour).

Destinations by direct TGV include the following:

Beaune €23.10, 2¼ hours, up to nine daily

Dijon €30.20, two hours, at least 12 daily

Lille-Europe €92, 3¼ hours, nine daily

Marseille €58.60, 1¾ hours, every 30 to 60 minutes

Paris Gare de Lyon €64.30, two hours, every 30 to 60 minutes

Strasbourg €55.90, 4¾ hours, five daily

❶ Getting Around

To/From the Airport

The Rhonexpress (☎ 04 72 68 72 17; www.rhonexpress.fr, in French) tramway links the airport with the Part-Dieu train station in under 30 minutes. Trams depart approximately every 15 minutes between 6am and 9.30pm, and every 30 minutes from 5am to 6am and 9.30pm to midnight. One-way tickets cost €13/free per adult/child (kids over 12 years of age pay €11).

By taxi, the 30- to 45-minute trip between the airport and the city centre costs around €40 during the day and €55 between 7pm and 7am.

Village at the base of Mont Blanc

RICHARD NEBESKY

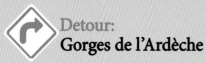

Detour:
Gorges de l'Ardèche

The serpentine Ardèche River slithers between towering mauve, yellow and grey limestone cliffs from near **Vallon Pont d'Arc** (population 2512) to **St-Martin de l'Ardèche** (population 830), a few kilometres west of the Rhône. En route it passes beneath the **Pont d'Arc**, a stunning natural stone bridge created by the river's torrents. Eagles nest in the cliffs and there are numerous caves to explore.

Souvenir-shop-filled Vallon Pont d'Arc is the area's main hub; its **tourist office** (📞 04 75 88 04 01; www.vallon-pont-darc.com; place de la Gare; ⏰9am-12.15pm & 1.30-6pm Mon-Fri, to 5pm Sat) is in the village centre. The scenic D579 from the village out along the gorges is lined by **campgrounds** and **canoeing** and **kayaking rental outlets**. Alternatively, arrange hire through **Base Nautique du Pont d'Arc** (📞04 75 37 17 79; www.canoe-ardeche.com; rte des Gorges de l'Ardèche; ⏰Apr-Nov).

About 300m above the gorge's waters, the **Haute Corniche** (D290) has a dizzying series of *belvédères* (panoramic viewpoints), but turns into a chaotic traffic jam in summer. On the plateaux above the gorges, typical Midi villages are surrounded by *garrigue* (aromatic scrub land), lavender fields and vineyards.

Public Transport

Buses, trams, a four-line metro and two funiculars linking Vieux Lyon to Fourvière and St-Just are operated by TCL (www.tcl.fr).

Tickets valid for all forms of public transport cost €1.60 (€13.70 for a *carnet* of 10) and are available from bus and tram drivers and machines at metro entrances.

THE FRENCH ALPS

The French Alps are a place of boundless natural beauty. Whether you dream of gliding over virgin snow, tramping over lonesome mountain passes or watching the first rays of a summer's morning illuminate Mont Blanc – these mountains have got you covered. Here a symphony of colossal peaks and glaciers, epic drops and climbs will elevate you, seduce your senses, make your heart pound and leave you crying 'encore!' like few other places on earth.

Chamonix
POP 9400 / ELEV 1037M

With the pearly white peaks of the Mont Blanc massif as its sensational backdrop, being an icon comes naturally to Chamonix. First 'discovered' by Brits

William Windham and Richard Pococke in 1741, this is the mecca of mountaineering, its birthplace, its flag-bearer. It is also a wintertime playground of epic proportions that entices Olympic champions and hard-core skiers and boarders to its pistes, and party-mad aprés-ski bunnies to its boot-stompin' bars.

 Sights

LE BRÉVENT   Viewpoint
The highest peak on the western side of the valley, Le Brévent (2525m) has tremendous views of the Mont Blanc massif, myriad hiking trails, ledges to paraglide from and summit restaurant Le Panoramic. Reach it via the **Télécabine du Brévent** (29 rte Henriette d'Angeville; adult/child return €24/19.50; ⏰8.50am-4.45pm), from the end of rue de la Mollard to midstation **Planpraz** (2000m), then continuing to the top.

MER DE GLACE   Glacier
France's largest glacier, the glistening 200m-deep Mer de Glace (Sea of Ice), snakes 7km through mighty rock spires and turrets. The glacier moves up to 90m a year and has become a popular

245

CHRISTIAN ASLUND

Don't Miss **Aiguille du Midi**

A jagged needle of rock rearing above glaciers, snowfields and rocky crags, 8km from the hump of Mont Blanc, the Aiguille du Midi (3842m) is one of Chamonix' most distinctive landmarks. If you can handle the height, the 360-degree views of the French, Swiss and Italian Alps from the summit are (quite literally) breathtaking.

Year-round the vertiginous **Téléphérique de l'Aiguille de Midi** cable car links Chamonix with the Aiguille du Midi. Halfway Plan de l'Aiguille (2317m) is a terrific place to start hikes or paraglide. In summer you will need to obtain a boarding card in addition to a ticket – note that advance phone reservations incur a €2 booking fee. Bring warm clothes as even in summer the temperature rarely rises above -10°C at the top.

From the Aiguille du Midi, between mid-May and mid-September, the unrepentant can continue for a further 30 minutes of mind-blowing scenery – think suspended glaciers and spurs, seracs and shimmering ice fields – in the smaller bubbles of the **Télécabine Panoramic Mont Blanc** to Pointe Helbronner (3466m) on the French-Italian border. From here another cable car descends to the Italian ski resort of Courmayeur.

NEED TO KNOW

Téléphérique de l'Aiguille de Midi (☎advance reservations 24hr 04 50 53 22 75; place de l'Aiguille du Midi; adult/child return to Aiguille du Midi €41/33, Plan de l'Aiguille €24/19.20; ⊗8.30am-4.30pm); Télécabine Panoramic Mont Blanc (adult/child return from Chamonix €65/52; ⊗8.30am-3.45pm)

attraction thanks to the rack-and-pinion railway line opened in 1908.

Wrap up warm to experience the **Grotte de la Mer de Glace** (⊗late Dec-May & mid-Jun–Sep) ice cave, where frozen tunnels and ice sculptures change colour like mood rings.

A quaint red mountain train trundles up from **Gare du Montenvers** (35 place de la Mer de Glace; adult/child €24/19; ⊗10am-4.30pm) in Chamonix to Montenvers (1913m), from where a cable car takes you down to the glacier and cave.

Activities

Winter Activities

MAISON DE LA MONTAGNE
Outdoor Activities

(190 place de l'Église; ☺8.30am-noon & 3-7pm)
Get the **Mont Blanc** lowdown here, opposite the tourist office.

SKIING & SNOWBOARDING
Chamonix skiing is the stuff of legend: glorious off-piste terrain, thrilling descents and unbeatable Mont Blanc views. Of Chamonix' nine main areas, Le Tour, Les Planards and Les Chosalets are best for beginners. For speed and challenge, it has to be Brévent-Flégère, above Chamonix, and Les Grands Montets, accessible from Argentière, 9km north of Chamonix.

LA VALLÉE BLANCHE   Off-Piste Route
(per person/group of 4 incl guide €75/283) This mythical descent is *the* off-piste ride of a lifetime. A veritable obstacle course, La Vallée Blanche takes four to five hours, leading from Aiguille du Midi over the crevasse-riddled Mer de Glace glacier

and back through forest to Chamonix, covering 2800m of jaw-dropping vertical. It must *only* be tackled with a guide.

Summer Activities

WALKING
When the snow melts, hikers can take their pick of 350km of spectacular high-altitude trails, many reached by cable car. There's enough light to walk until at least 9pm in June and July.

CYCLING
Lower-altitude trails such as the Petit Balcon Sud (250m) from Argentière to Servoz are perfect for biking. Most outdoor-activity specialists arrange guided mountain-biking expeditions.

PARAGLIDING
Come summer, the sky above Chamonix is dotted with paragliders wheeling down from the heights. Tandem flights from Planpraz (2000m) cost €100 per person (€220 from the Aiguille du Midi). Paragliding schools include **Summits** (☎04 50 53 50 14; www.summits.fr; 27 allée du Savoy) and **Les Ailes du Mont Blanc** (☎04 50 53 96 72; www.lesailesdumontblanc.com; 24 av de la Plage).

Aiguille du Midi

JOHN ELK III

Sleeping

Many places close from mid-April to May and from November to mid-December. Room rates nosedive in the low season and summer; expect discounts of up to 50% on high-season prices.

HOTEL SLALOM   Boutique Hotel €€

(☎ 04 50 54 40 60; www.hotelslalom.net; 44 rue de Bellevue, Les Houches; r €158; 🛜) Tracy, Heather and Justin are your affable hosts at this gorgeous chalet-style hotel, right at the foot of the slopes in Les Houches (8km west of central Chamonix). Rooms are the epitome of boutique chic – sleek, snowy white and draped with Egyptian cotton linen.

HOTEL L'OUSTALET   Family Hotel €€

(☎ 04 50 55 54 99; www.hotel-oustalet.com; 330 rue du Lyret; d/q €140/180; 🛜🚠👪) You'll pray for snow at this alpine chalet near Aiguille du Midi cable car, just so you can curl up by the fire with a *chocolat chaud* or unwind in the sauna and whirlpool.

The rooms, including family ones, are snugly decorated in solid pine, and open onto balconies with Mont Blanc views.

HÔTEL FAUCIGNY   Small Hotel €€

(☎ 04 50 53 01 17; www.hotelfaucigny -chamonix.com; 118 place de l'Église; s/d/tr/q €55/86/98/124; @🛜) Jacqueline and Guy Écochard run this bijou hotel, one of the sweetest deals in town. Rooms are comfortable and quiet, and guests can relax by an open fire in winter and on the flower-clad terrace with Mont Blanc views in summer.

GRAND HÔTEL DES ALPES

Historic Hotel €€€

(☎ 04 50 55 37 80; www.grandhoteldesalpes. com; 75 rue du Docteur Paccard; r €330-390, ste €580-750; ❄@🛜🚠) This grand old dame goes down in the chronicles of Chamonix history as one of the resort's first (built in 1840) and finest. The wood-panelled rooms exude timeless elegance.

Eating

LA PETITE KITCHEN

Modern European €

(80 place du Poilu; plat du jour €7-13, mains €14-19.50; 🕐 closed Tue) The Little Kitchen is just that: a handful of tables for the lucky few who get to indulge on its locally sourced feel-good food. Filling English break-fasts, steaks with home-made *frites* (hot chips) and the stickiest of toffee puddings will send you rolling happily out the door.

LE BISTROT

Gastronomic €€€

(☎ 04 50 53 57 64; www. lebistrotchamonix.com, in French; 151 av de l'Aiguille du Midi; lunch menus €17, dinner menus €42-65; 👪) Michelin-starred chef

Mont Blanc (p226)
PHOTOGRAPHER: GARETH MCCORMACK

Mickey experiments with textures and seasonal flavours to create taste sensations such as pan-seared Arctic char with chestnuts, and divine warm chocolate macaroons with raspberry and red pepper coulis.

LE GOUTHÉ   Tea Room   €

(95 rue des Moulins; menus €9; ⊙9am-6.30pm Fri-Mon; 🎵) Welcome to the sweetest of tea rooms. Philippe's smooth hot chocolates with pistachio and gingerbread infusions, startlingly bright macaroons and crumbly homemade tarts (such as mirabelle plum with liquorice) are just the sugar fix needed for the slopes.

LE CHAUDRON

Savoyard Cuisine   €€

(🕿04 50 53 57 64; 79 rue des Moulins; menus €20-23; ⊙dinner) On a cold winter's day this chic alpine chalet is guaranteed to give you that warm inner glow. Funky cowskin-clad benches are the backdrop for a feast of Savoyard fondues and lamb slow-cooked in red wine to melting perfection.

🍷 Drinking & Entertainment

Chamonix nightlife rocks. Quaint old riverside rue des Moulins touts a line-up of drinking holes.

CHAMBRE NEUF   Bar

(272 av Michel Croz; 🛜) Cover bands, raucous après-ski drinking and Swedish blondes dancing on the tables make Chambre Neuf one of Chamonix' liveliest party haunts.

MBC   Microbrewery

(www.mbchx.com; 350 rte du Bouchet; ⊙4pm-2am) This trendy microbrewery run by four Canadians is fab. Be it with their burgers, cheesecake of the week, live music or amazing locally brewed and named beers (Blonde de Chamonix, Stout des Drus, Blanche des Guides etc), MBC delivers.

❤ If You Like...
Skiing

If you've caught the downhill bug in Chamonix, you'll love the world-class skiing found throughout the Alps. Here's a quick run-down of our favourite resorts.

1 TROIS VALLÉES

(elevation 1450-2300m; www.les3vallees.com) The Three Valleys covers the world's largest ski area, comprising three side-by-side resorts: snow-sure **Val Thorens**, Europe's highest ski area at 2300m; **Méribel** (1450m), intermediate heaven and a favourite for Brits abroad; and ritzy **Courchevel** (1550m to 1850m), which includes some knee-trembling black couloirs for the brave and excellent off-piste terrain, and is favoured by the rich and royal.

2 VAL D'ISÈRE

(1850m; www.valdisere.com) Unlike many resorts, Val d'Isère has a community feel that remains long after the snows have melted. Along with nearby **Tignes** (elevation 2100m), Val d'Isère forms part of the huge **Espace Killy** skiing area, named after triple Olympic gold medallist Jean-Claude Killy.

3 LES PORTES DU SOLEIL

(1000-2466m; www.portesdusoleil.com) The Gates of the Sun covers 12 villages along the French-Swiss border, including charming **Morzine** (1000m), trendy, car-free **Avoriaz** (1800m) and family-friendly **Les Gets** (1172m).

4 LES DEUX ALPS

(1600m; www.les2alps.com) Year-round skiing on the **Glacier du Mont de Lans**, glorious powder and a party atmosphere make Les Deux Alpes a resort with altitude. Hardcore skiers come from far and wide to tackle the near-vertical Vallons de la Meije descent in **La Grave**, 21km east.

5 ALPE D'HUEZ

(1860m; www.alpedhuez.com) This purpose-built resort has 245km of groomed pistes that range from dead-easy to death-defying: at 16km **La Sarenne** is Europe's longest black run. Alpe d'Huez also provides one of the most notorious stages of the Tour de France, with an average slope gradient of 7.9%.

If You Like…
The Great Outdoors

Enjoyed the scenery in Annecy? Then how about exploring one of the Alps' spectacular national parks, where you'll find huge tracts of untouched wilderness and some of France's rarest wildlife.

1 PARC NATIONAL DE LA VANOISE
(www.parcnational-vanoise.fr; Maison du Val Cénis ☏04 79 05 23 66; www.valcenis.com; Bonneval-sur-Arc tourist office ☏04 79 05 95 95; www.bonneval-sur-arc.com) Rugged peaks, mirror-like lakes and vast glaciers are just the tip of the superlative iceberg in the 530-sq-km **Parc National de la Vanoise**, designated France's first national park in 1963. Marmots, chamois and Alpine ibexes graze the slopes, and if you're lucky you might even spy a bearded vulture or a golden eagle. Walking trails are accessible June to September.

The **Grand Tour de Haute Maurienne** (www.hautemaurienne.com), a hike of five days or more around the upper reaches of the valley, takes in national park highlights. The **GR5** and **GR55** cross it, and other trails snake south to the Parc National des Écrins and east into Italy's Grand Paradiso National Park.

2 PARC NATUREL RÉGIONAL DU VERCORS
(http://parc-du-vercors.fr; Villard de Lans tourist office ☏04 76 95 10 38; www.villarddelans.com; place Mure Ravaud) The gentle pastures and chiselled peaks of this 1750-sq-km nature park, southwest of Grenoble, are great for soft adventure. This wildlife-rich park is also a magnet for family-friendly activities such as cross-country skiing, snowshoeing, caving and hiking. Nature walks and guided treks can be arranged with **Les Accompagnateurs Nature et Patrimoine** (☏04 76 95 08 38; www.accompagnateur-vercors.com).

3 PARC NATIONAL DES ÉCRINS
(☏Bourg d'Oisans tourist office 04 76 80 00 51; www.les-ecrins-parc-national.fr; rue Gambetta) Created in 1973, this is France's second-largest national park (918 sq km). 700km of footpaths provide prime hiking, while the lofty passes are ideal for mountain biking, rock-climbing, paragliding and other activities.

MONKEY BAR Music Bar
(81 place Edmond Desailloud; ☺1pm-2am; 🔊) Slightly grungy, very cool, this party hotspot has live gigs and DJs several times a week.

LA TERRASSE Music Bar
(www.laterrassechamonix.com; 43 place Balmat; ☺4pm-2am; 🔊) Race the clock for cheap drinks (5pm €5, 6pm €6 etc) and take position on the strategically placed terrace on Chamonix' main square.

ℹ Information

Tourist office (☏04 50 53 00 24; www.chamonix.com; 85 place du Triangle de l'Amitié; ☺8.30am-7pm)

ℹ Getting There & Away

Bus

From Chamonix bus station (www.sat-montblanc.com; place de la Gare), located next to the train station, two to three buses run daily to/from Geneva airport and bus station (one way/return €33/55, 1½ to two hours) and Courmayeur (one way/return €13/20, 45 minutes). Advance booking is required for both.

Car & Motorcycle

Approaching Chamonix from Italy, you arrive via the 11.5km-long Tunnel de Mont Blanc (www.atmb.net; toll one way/return €35/44), which enters town in the southern suburb of Les Pélerins. From France the A40 toll motorway – the Autoroute Blanche – hooks up with the Chamonix-bound N205 dual carriageway for the last leg.

Train

From Chamonix–Mont Blanc train station (place de la Gare) the Mont Blanc Express narrow-gauge train trundles from St-Gervais–Le Fayet station, 23km west of Chamonix, to Martigny in Switzerland, stopping en route in Les Houches, Chamonix and Argentière. There are nine to 12 return trips between Chamonix and St-Gervais (€9.50, 40 minutes).

From St-Gervais–Le Fayet, there are trains to most major French cities.

RUSSELL MOUNTFORD

Annecy

POP 53,000 / ELEV 447M

Annecy paints the prettiest of pictures. Caressed by sapphire Lac d'Annecy, ringed by lushly wooded mountains and spiralling around a medieval old town, it makes visitors – all two million of them a year – stop in wonder and reach for their cameras on every glorious corner.

 Sights

PALAIS DE L'ISLE   Museum

(3 passage de l'Île; adult/child €3.60/1.30; ☻10.30am-6pm) Sitting on a triangular islet in the Canal du Thiou, the whimsically turreted, 12th-century Palais de l'Isle has been a lordly residence, courthouse, mint and prison (lucky inmates!) over the centuries. Today Annecy's most visible landmark hosts local-history displays.

VIEILLE VILLE & LAKEFRONT
Historic Quarter

It's a pleasure simply to wander aimlessly around Annecy's medieval old town, a photogenic jumble of narrow streets, turquoise canals and colonnaded passageways. Continue down to the tree-fringed lakefront and the flowery **Jardins de l'Europe**, linked to the popular picnic spot **Champ de Mars** by the poetic iron arch of the **Pont des Amours** (Lovers' Bridge).

CHÂTEAU D'ANNECY   Castle

(rampe du Château; adult/child €4.90/2.30; ☻10.30am-6pm) Rising dramatically above the old town, this perkily turreted castle was once home to the Counts of Geneva. The oldest part is the 12th-century **Tour de la Reine** (Queen's Tower). Its **museum** takes a romp through traditional Savoyard art, crafts and alpine natural history.

 Tours

COMPAGNIE DES BATEAUX   Cruises

(www.annecy-croisieres.com; 2 place aux Bois; 1-/2-hr lake cruise €12.50/16; ☻mid-Mar–Oct) Cruises depart from quai Bayreuth; tickets are sold 15 minutes before departure. From May to September boats also sail across the lake to Menthon-St-Bernard (€5.50), Talloires (€6.50) and other villages.

251

Sleeping

You'll need to book months ahead if you're planning to visit Annecy in July or August when rooms are gold-dust rare.

HÔTEL ALEXANDRA Family Hotel €
(☎ 04 50 52 84 33; www.hotelannecy-alexandra. fr; 19 rue Vaugelas; s/d/tr/q €48/59/70/89; 🛜🚷) Nice surprise: Annecy's most charming hotel is also one of its most affordable. The welcome is five star, rooms are fresh and spotless – a few extra euros get you a balcony and canal view – and breakfast is a generous spread with fresh pastries.

LE PRÉ CARRÉ Boutique Hotel €€€
(☎ 04 50 52 14 14; www.hotel-annecy.net; 27 rue Sommeiller; s/d €172/202; ❄ @ 🛜) One of Annecy's chicest hotels, Le Pré Carré keeps things contemporary with Zen colours in rooms with balconies or terraces, a jacuzzi and a business corner.

Eating

CHALET LA PRICAZ
Traditional French €€
(☎ 04 50 60 72 61; Col de la Forclaz, mains €18-30; ⊙ closed Wed; 🅿) On its fairy-tale perch above Lake Annecy, this is prime romantic sunset material. Tangy *tartiflettes* (Reblochon cheese with potatoes, crème fraîche, onions and diced bacon) and farm-fresh charcuterie go brilliantly with the first-rate selection of Savoyard wines. The tucked-away restaurant is off the D42, 13km south of Annecy.

LA CUISINE DES AMIS Bistro €€
(☎ 04 50 10 10 80; 9 rue du Pâquier; mains €16.50-25) Here locals and all-comers are treated like one big jolly *famille*. Pull up a chair, *prendre un verre* (have a drink), dine well on regional fare, pat the dog and, finally, see if your snapshot ends up on the wall of merry *amis*.

LA CIBOULETTE Modern French €€
(☎ 04 50 45 74 57; www.laciboulette-annecy. com; cour du Pré Carré, 10 rue Vaugelas; menus €31-46; ⊙ Tue-Sat) Such class! Crisp white linen and gold-kissed walls set the scene at this surprisingly affordable Michelin-starred place, where chef Georges Paccard cooks fresh seasonal specialities such as slow-roasted Anjou pigeon with Midi asparagus. Reservations are essential.

CONTRESENS Fusion €€
(☎ 04 50 51 22 10; 10 rue de la Poste; mains €15; ⊙ Tue-Sat; 🚼) The menu reads like a mathematical formula but it soon becomes clear: starters are A, mains B, sides C and desserts D. The food is as experimental as the menu – sun-dried tomato, Beaufort cheese and rocket salad burger, mussel ravioli, 'deconstructed' Snickers – and totally divine. Kid nirvana.

A Lofty Lunch

Feast on fine cuisine and even finer mountain views at these high-altitude favourites.

Le 3842 (☎ 04 50 55 82 23; Aiguille du Midi; mains €12-21; ⊙ restaurant mid-Jun–mid-Sep, snack bar all year) offers stylish summit dining and drinking with knockout views at the top of the Aiguille du Midi in what claims to be Europe's highest café.

At Le Panoramic (☎ 04 50 53 44 11; Le Brévent; menus from €15; ⊙ mid-Dec–Apr & late Jun-Sep), views of Mont Blanc are included with a menu of cheeses, cured meats and BBQ fare. For something a little more frugal, a *vin chaud* (hot mulled wine) on the terrace will do just fine.

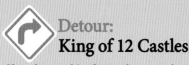

Detour:
King of 12 Castles

If you love nothing better than a castle, you'll love following in the footsteps of gallant dukes and feudal lords on the **Route des Ducs de Savoie** (Road of the Dukes of Savoy; www.chateaux-france.com/route-savoie). The route weaves through pristine alpine landscapes from Thonon-les-Bains to Avressieux, 30km west of Chambéry, and ticks off 12 castles, abbeys and historic sites, including Château de Ripaille, Château d'Annecy and Château des Ducs de Savoie.

For acting out fairy-tale fantasies, there's little that beats the silver-turreted, high-on-a-hillside **Château de Menthon-St-Bernard** (www.chateau-de-menthon. com; Menthon-St-Bernard; guided tour adult/child €7.50/4.50; ☺2-6pm Fri-Sun May-Sep), the birthplace of St Bernard (1008). Tours of the medieval interior, taking in tapestry-adorned salons and a magnificent library, are intriguing, but it's the sparkling Lake Annecy panorama that leaves visitors spellbound.

L'ÉTAGE   Traditional French   €€
(☏04 50 51 03 28; 13 rue du Pâquier; mains €14-22, 3-course menus €18) Cheese, glorious cheese... *Fromage* is given pride of place in spot-on fondues and *raclette* (a combination of melting cheese, boiled potatoes, charcuterie and baby gherkins) at L'Étage, where a backdrop of mellow music and cheerful staff keep the ambience relaxed.

LA NOUVELLE MAISON DE MARC VEYRAT   Gastronomic   €€€
(☏04 50 09 97 49; www.marcveyrat.fr; 13 vieille rte des Pensières, Veyrier-du-Lac; d €200-300, menu €92; ☺Thu-Sun late May-Sep) French celebrity chef Marc Veyrat has handed over his stove, culinary flamboyance and signature use of wild herbs to his capable successor Yoann Conte at this Michelin-starred restaurant. In Veyrier-du-Lac, 5km southeast of Annecy, the baby-blue house by the lake also has a handful of wonderful rooms.

ℹ Information

Tourist office (☏04 50 45 00 33; www.lac-annecy.com; 1 rue Jean Jaurès, Centre Bonlieu; ☺9am-6.30pm Mon-Sat, 10am-1pm Sun)

ℹ Getting There & Away

From Annecy's train station (place de la Gare), there are frequent trains to/from Aix-les-Bains (€7, 30 minutes), Chambéry (€9, 45 minutes), St-Gervais (€13.50, 1½ hours), Lyon (€23, 2¼ hours) and Paris Gare de Lyon (€75, four hours).

Bordeaux & French Basque Country

For wine aficionados, nowhere lights up the imagination quite like Bordeaux. For centuries this has been the undisputed heartland of French *viticulture* (winemaking), and the region is littered with some of the most illustrious names from the world of wine. But while the fruits of the vine are undoubtedly the main reason for a visit to the Bordeaux region, they're far from the only one.

South of Bordeaux, France's Atlantic Coast unfurls through a string of sandy beaches, sparkling bays and beautiful towns, all of which are worth a visit in their own right. There's Arcachon – famous for producing some of France's finest oysters – and Biarritz, a seaside getaway since the belle époque, now the centre of a thriving surf culture. And then there's the French Basque Country, a fiery and independent region that fizzes with a passion, energy and culture all of its own.

Biarritz (p279)
PHOTOGRAPHER: JOHN KING

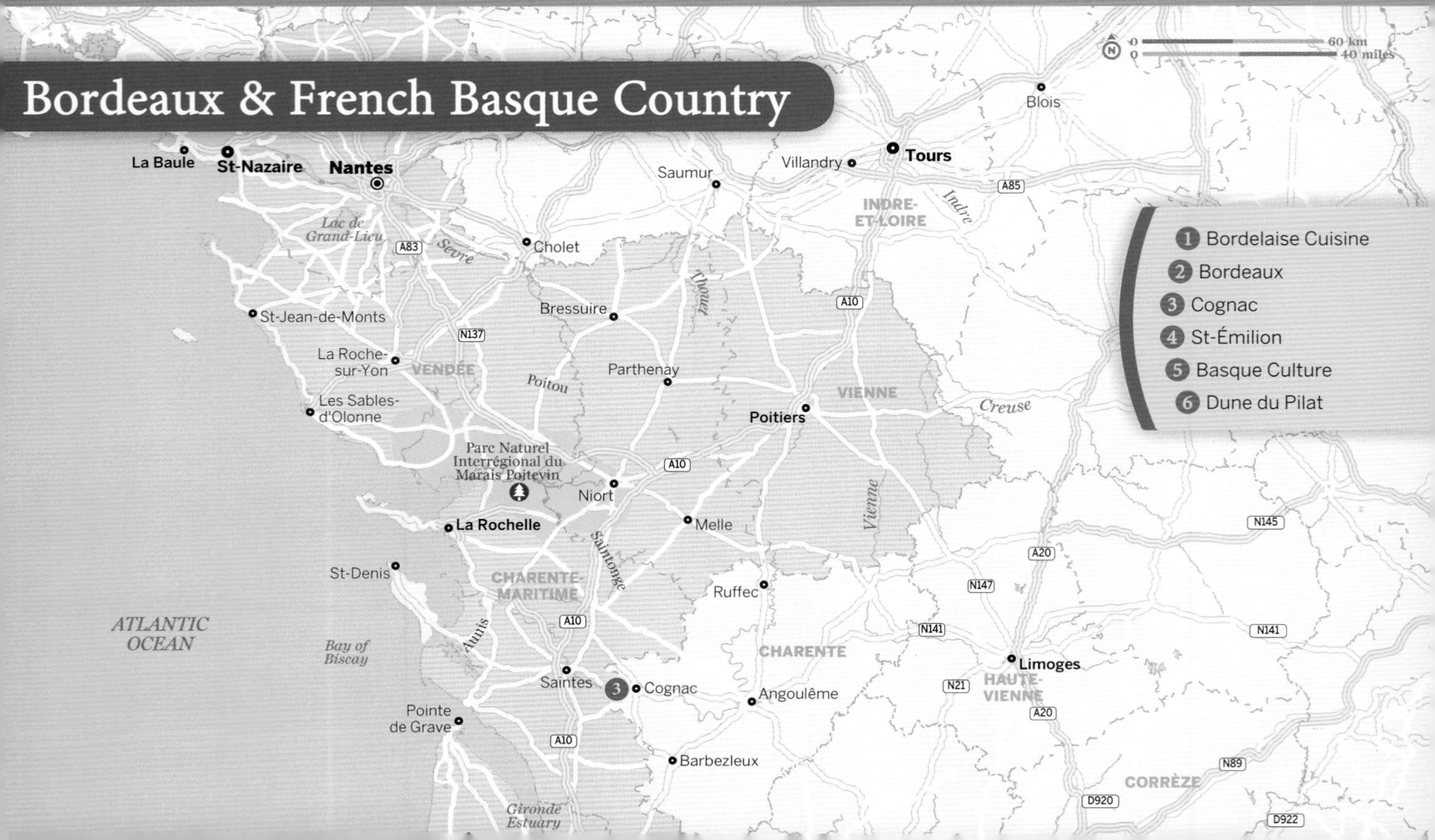

Bordeaux & French Basque Country
1 Bordelaise Cuisine
2 Bordeaux
3 Cognac
4 St-Émilion
5 Basque Culture
6 Dune du Pilat
0 60 km
0 40 miles
La Baule
St-Nazaire
Nantes
Saumur
Villandry
Tours
Blois
A85
INDRE-ET-LOIRE
Indre
Lac de Grand-Lieu
A83
Sevre
Cholet
Thouet
A10
Bressuire
St-Jean-de-Monts
N137
La Roche-sur-Yon
VENDÉE
Poitou
Parthenay
Poitiers
VIENNE
Creuse
Les Sables-d'Olonne
Parc Naturel Interrégional du Marais Poitevin
Niort
La Rochelle
Melle
Vienne
Saintonge
St-Denis
CHARENTE-MARITIME
Ruffec
N145
A20
N147
ATLANTIC OCEAN
Bay of Biscay
Aunis
N141
CHARENTE
Limoges
HAUTE-VIENNE
N21
Saintes
Cognac
Angoulême
Pointe de Grave
Barbezieux
N89
CORRÈZE
D920
D922
Gironde Estuary

Bordeaux & French Basque Country's Highlights

① Bordelaise Cuisine

The best moment is when I catch the *bonheur* (happiness) in people's eyes as they are eating a particular dish. I was born in Blaye, 50km from Bordeaux, and my cuisine is *paysanne* (a country cuisine); using only the best products and traditional recipes from the southwest.

Bordelaise Cuisine Don't Miss List

BY JEAN-PIERRE XIRADAKI, CULINARY
WRITER & CELEBRITY RESTAURANT OWNER
SINCE 1968

1 MARCHÉ DES CAPUCINS

Cuisine bordelaise (Bordeaux cuisine) originates from the south, from Basque-country women who came to work in the great Bordelaise houses. And the diversity of produce is enormous. We have river and sea fish, shellfish, oysters, fowl (duck and geese), lamb, beef, mushrooms, vegetables, poultry, truffles … We really have everything, although we miss cheese. I buy my produce from local producers and markets: Marché des Capucins (see image below; www. marchedescapucins.fr) in Bordeaux and the twice-weekly market in Blaye (Wednesday and Saturday mornings).

2 CASSOULET, MACARONADE & EELS

I love *cassoulet,* typical to the rural southwest and traditionally eaten to celebrate; it's a heart-warming haricot bean stew with a few giblets, bit of sausage and pork thrown in. Then there's *macaronade aux cèpes et au foi gras*, fresh macaroni with local *cèpes* (boletus mushrooms), foie gras and cream. It is very rich, very delicious and demands a healthy appetite! *Lamproie à la Bordelaise* (eel-like lamprey), a migratory river fish cooked with wine and leeks, is very typical of our local cuisine.

3 LA SOUPE

In winter at La Tupina (p270) we always have a cauldron of soup cooking in the fireplace; the fire burns all day just as it did at my grandparents'. We throw in cabbage, carrots, beans, a bit of duck or pork to give it taste and so on, just as peasants did centuries ago. For them it provided all the daily nutrition they needed – water, vegetables and a little meat.

4 WINE & OYSTERS

L'Essentiel (☎05 57 24 39 76; 6 rue Guadel) in St-Émilion is *the* place to taste wine and **La Boîte à Huitres** (☎05 56 81 64 97; 35 cours du Chapeau Rouge), a restaurant in Bordeaux, is the *dégustation* (tasting) address for oysters. Favourite wine producers include **Château Mayne Lalande** (7 route du Mayne) and **Château Lestage** (☎05 56 58 02 43; www.chateau -lestage.com), both 35km north of Bordeaux in Listrac.

Bordeaux

Since 2007 half of Bordeaux (p266) – 18 sq km, from the outer boulevards to the banks of the Garonne – has been Unesco listed, making it the largest urban World Heritage site anywhere on earth. Sprinkled with grand buildings, stately monuments and enticing restaurants, it's a city that more than lives up to its billing, and makes an ideal launchpad for visiting the region's world-famous vineyards (p267). Cathédrale St-André (p266)

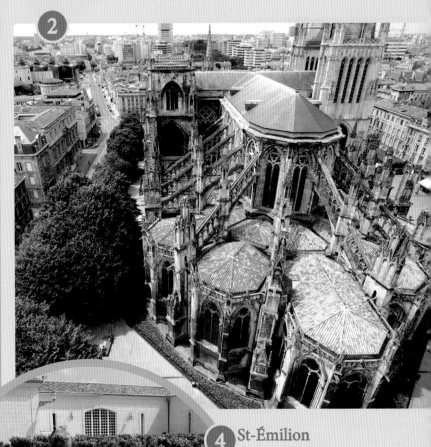

2

4 St-Émilion

Perched on a limestone ridge 40km east of Bordeaux, the honey-hued town of St-Émilion (p271) is a must for wine connoisseurs. Surrounded by vines as far as the eye can see, it's also home to some of France's most hallowed châteaux – so it's a fantastic place to try and buy wines. But don't forget to leave time for a tour into the murky catacombs beneath the town's cathedral.

LEE FOSTER

Cognac

OLIVER STREWE

3

While Bordeaux is mainly known for its fine wines, it's not the region's only alcoholic tipple. The double-distilled spirit cognac (p270) is produced according to a strict set of rules that have remained largely unchanged for the last three centuries. You can quaff it in musty cellars all around town, but at a minimum of 40% proof, you'll definitely need to name a designated driver...

ANDREW BAIN

5

Basque Culture

A passion for bullfighting, pelota, peppers and spicy ham make the French Basque Country (p276) feel closer to Spain than to the rest of France. Governed by its own culture, costumes and language, it's very much a region in its own right. The lively towns of Bayonne and St-Jean de Luz both make great bases for further exploration, situated within easy reach of the sparkling beaches of Biarritz. St-Jean de Luz (p282)

6

Dune du Pilat

This colossal sand dune (p275) stretches for almost 3km to the south of Arcachon and is still spreading eastwards at up to 4.5m a year (swallowing trees, roads and even a hotel in the process). Hum the theme tune from *Lawrence of Arabia* as you scale it for a memorable panorama over the Bassin d'Arcachon – it's the closest you'll get to the Sahara without leaving Europe.

Bordeaux & French Basque Country's Best…

Bird's-Eye Views

○ **Bordeaux city panorama** (p266) Best seen from the cathedral belfry.

○ **St-Émilion rooftops** (p271) Slog up the bell tower for views of this hilltop hamlet.

○ **Biarritz** (p282) Biarritz' lighthouse offers coast and city vistas.

○ **Pic du Jer** (p286) Look out over Lourdes from this rocky outcrop.

○ **Pic du Midi** (p287) Catch the funicular to this former observatory for eye-popping Pyrenean views.

Souvenir Shopping

○ **L'Intendant, Bordeaux** (p270) 15,000 bottles of wine, and counting.

○ **La Winery, Arsac-en-Médoc** (p275) Ground-breaking winery with 1000 different Bordeaux wines.

○ **St-Émilion** (p273) With one wine shop for every eight residents, wine shopping in St-Émilion's a breeze.

○ **Bayonne** (p279) For Bayonne's famous ham, visit Pierre Ibaïalde or the covered market.

○ **Cognac** (p270) Take home some of this superb brandy.

Beach Retreats

○ **Biarritz** (p279) A classic beach resort since the belle époque, now the destination of choice for French surfers.

○ **Arcachon** (p274) Sandy beaches pepper the beautiful Bassin d'Arcachon.

○ **Cap Ferret** (p276) Cruise past oyster beds and bird reserves to this peaceful peninsula across the bay from Arcachon.

○ **St-Jean de Luz & Ciboure** (p282) Kick back on the golden sands of these twin Basque towns.

Need to Know

Local Hangouts

○ **Le Cheverus Café**
(p269) Be prepared to
queue at Bordeaux's best
neighbourhood bistro.

○ **Bar-Restaurant du
Marché** (p278) Practise
your Basque in this Bayonne
restaurant.

○ **Casa Juan Pedro** (p281)
This Biarritz fishing shack is
a locals' tip for seafood.

○ **Buvette des Halles**
(p283) Teeny café with big,
bold flavours in St-Jean de
Luz.

○ **Bar Jean** (p281) Tip-top
for tapas in Biarritz.

ADVANCE PLANNING

○ **As early as possible**
Book accommodation,
particularly for Bayonne
and Biarritz in July and
August.

○ **Two weeks before**
Ask at the Bordeaux
tourist office (p270)
about the Découverte
hotel package, which
includes accommodation,
admissions, a city tour, a
vineyard tour and a bottle
of wine.

○ **One week before**
Book visits at Cognac
houses (p270), Bordeaux
vineyards (p267) and big-
name restaurants.

RESOURCES

○ **Loire Atlantique** (www.
ohlaloireatlantique.com)
General traveller info for
the Loire Atlantique region.

○ **Bordeaux** (www.bordeaux.
com) Excellent online
resource for oenophiles.

○ **Cognac World** (www.
cognac-world.com) All you
ever wanted to know
about Cognac, and more
besides.

○ **PNR Pyrenees** (www.
pnr-pyrenees.com) Main
web portal for the
Pyrenees National Park.

GETTING AROUND

○ **Air** The region's main
airports are in Bordeaux
(p270), Biarritz-Anglet-
Bayonne (p282) and Pau
(www.pau.aeroport.fr), all
served by budget flights.

○ **Train** Speedy TGVs
serve Bordeaux, Biarritz
and several other cities.
Most smaller towns and
villages can be reached via
regional trains.

○ **Car** Allows maximum
freedom, but be careful
not to overtipple if you're
tasting wine or cognac.

BE FOREWARNED

○ **St-Émilion** Wear flat
comfy shoes: the village's
steep, uneven streets are
hard going.

○ **Bassin d'Arcachon** Take
care swimming in this area:
powerful currents swirl out
to sea from the deceptively
tranquil *baïnes* (little bays).

○ **Bordeaux wine
châteaux** Generally
close their doors during
October's grape harvest.

○ **Finding a hotel bed**
Bayonne is tough from
mid-July to mid-August
and near impossible during
the Fêtes de Bayonne.

○ **Lourdes** So quiet in
winter that most hotels
shut down.

Left: Pic du Midi (p287) ;
Above: Biarritz (p279)

PHOTOGRAPHERS: (LEFT) GARETH MCCORMACK;
(ABOVE) VERONICA GARBUTT

Bordeaux & French Basque Country Itineraries

The southwest is one of France's most perennially popular regions. There's lots to pack in, but don't rush – life here cruises along at its own laid-back pace.

3 DAYS

BORDEAUX TO ST-ÉMILION

A VINTAGE TRIP

If you're going to get to grips with Bordeaux wine, there's only one place to start. **(1) Bordeaux** is one of France's most impressive cities – so impressive, in fact, that Unesco has planted most of it on the World Heritage list. You should devote at least a day to sight-seeing – don't miss the Cathédrale St-André and a climb up the Tour Pey-Beyland, a visit to CAPC Musée d'Art Contemporain and a river cruise, followed by supper at Le Cheverus Café or La Tupina.

On day two take a guided tour of some of the region's celebrated vineyards, including the illustrious names of the **(2) Médoc**. There will be plenty of opportunities to buy some bottles en route, or you could wait to stock up back at Bordeaux's top wine shop, L'Intendant.

On day three travel east to beautiful **(3) St-Émilion**. Perched on a limestone ridge surrounded by seemingly endless green vines, the town has umpteen wine shops and châteaux to visit. Don't miss a guided tour into the musty caverns hollowed out beneath the 11th-century Église Monolithe.

Top Left: Vineyards, Bordeaux;
Top Right: Cathédrale St-André (p266)

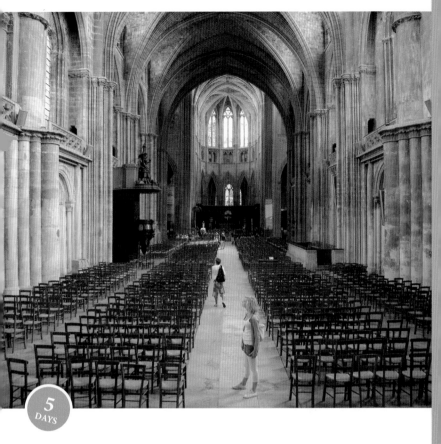

5 DAYS

BORDEAUX TO BIARRITZ
INTO THE BASQUE COUNTRY

After **(1) Bordeaux**, it's time to head south into the fiery heartland of the French Basques. First stop is **(2) Arcachon**, a popular seaside town that's famous for its oysters and the nearby, enormous sand dune, Dune du Pilat. If you have time, you won't regret a boat trip across the bay to the pretty peninsula of Cap Ferret.

Further south, the Basque Country begins in earnest at **(3) Bayonne**, where you can watch a game of *pelote*, buy some delicious Basque ham and dine at delightful riverside restaurants, such as La Criée Bayonaisse.

On day three head to hip **(4) Biarritz**, a quick trip from Bayonne, where you'll find fantastic beaches, a thriving surf culture and invigorating views of the coast from the Rocher de la Vierge. It's also a great place to try some classic Basque cuisine – for seafood try the ramshackle beach shack Casa Juan Pedro, or for authentic tapas head for Bar Jean.

On days four and five, make time for some beach-lounging in **(5) St-Jean de Luz**, chilli-eating in **(6) Espelette** and village-wandering in **(7) St-Jean Pied de Port**. Got the Basque bug? Don't fret – the Spanish border's just 8km away...

Discover Bordeaux & French Basque Country

ATLANTIC COAST

With quiet country roads winding through vine-striped hills and wild stretches of coastal sands interspersed with misty islands, the Atlantic coast is where France gets back to nature. Much more laid-back than the Med (but with almost as much sunshine), this is the place to slow the pace right down.

The one thing that unites the people of this area is a love of the finer things in life. The region's exceptional wine is famous worldwide, and to wash it down you'll find fresh-from-the-ocean seafood wherever you go and plenty of regional delicacies including crêpes in the north, snails in the centre and foie gras in the south.

Bordeaux
POP 229,500

The new millennium was a major turning point for the city long known as La Belle au Bois Dormant (Sleeping Beauty). The mayor, ex-Prime Minister Alain Juppé, roused Bordeaux, pedestrianising its boulevards, restoring its neoclassical architecture and implementing a high-tech public transport system.

In mid-2007 half of the entire city (18 sq km, from the outer boulevards to the banks of the Garonne) was Unesco-listed, making it the largest urban World Heritage Site.

 Sights & Activities

CATHÉDRALE ST-ANDRÉ   Cathedral
Lording over the city, and a Unesco World Heritage Site prior to the city's classification, the cathedral's oldest sec-

Old Bordeaux
PHOTOGRAPHER: DENNIS JONES

On the Wine Trail

Thirsty? The 1000-sq-km winegrowing area around the city of Bordeaux is, along with Burgundy, France's most important producer of top-quality wines.

The Bordeaux region is divided into 57 *appellations* (production areas whose soil and microclimate impart distinctive characteristics to the wine produced there) that are grouped into seven *familles* (families), and then subdivided into a hierarchy of designations (eg premier grand cru classé, the most prestigious) that often vary from *appellation* to *appellation*. The majority of the Bordeaux region's reds, rosés, sweet and dry whites and sparkling wines have earned the right to include the abbreviation AOC (Appellation d'Origine Contrôlée) on their labels, indicating that the contents have been grown, fermented and aged according to strict regulations that govern such viticultural matters as the number of vines permitted per hectare and acceptable pruning methods.

Bordeaux has over 5000 châteaux (also known as domaines, *crus* or *clos*), referring not to palatial residences but rather to the properties where grapes are raised, picked, fermented and then matured as wine. The smaller châteaux sometimes accept walk-in visitors, but at many places, especially the better-known ones, you have to make advance reservations. Many close during the *vendange* (grape harvest) in October.

Whet your palate with the tourist office's informal introduction to wine and cheese courses (adult €24), held every Thursday at 4.30pm, where you sip three different wines straight from the cellar and sup on cheese.

Serious students of the grape can enrol at the **École du Vin** (Wine School; ☏ 05 56 00 22 66; www.bordeaux.com/Ecole-du-Vin), within the **Maison du Vin de Bordeaux** (Bordeaux House of Wine; 3 cours du 30 Juillet), across the street from the tourist office. Introductory two-hour courses are held Monday to Saturday from 10am to noon between June and September (adult €25).

tion dates from 1096; most of what you see today was built in the 13th and 14th centuries. Even more imposing than the cathedral itself is the gargoyled, 50m-high Gothic belfry, **Tour Pey-Berland** (adult/child €5/free; ⏰10am-1.15pm & 2-6pm). Scaling the tower's 232 narrow steps rewards you with a spectacular panorama of the city.

MUSEUMS   Museums

(permanent collections/temporary exhibits free/€5 unless stated otherwise below; ⏰11am-6pm Tue-Sun) Bordeaux has a healthy collection of museums and galleries. Gallo-Roman statues and relics dating back 25,000 years are among the highlights at the impressive **Musée d'Aquitaine** (20 cours Pasteur; temporary exhibitions €3).

Built in 1824 as a warehouse for French colonial produce like coffee, cocoa, peanuts and vanilla, the cavernous Entrepôts Lainé creates a dramatic backdrop for cutting-edge modern art at the **CAPC Musée d'Art Contemporain** (Entrepôt 7, rue Ferrére).

The evolution of Occidental art from the Renaissance to the mid-20th century is on view at Bordeaux' **Musée des Beaux-Arts** (20 cours d'Albret; ⏰Wed-Sun). Occupying two wings of the 1770s-built Hôtel de Ville, either side of the **Jardin de la Mairie** (an elegant public park), the museum was established in 1801; highlights include 17th-century Flemish, Dutch and Italian paintings.

PARKS   Parks

Landscaping is artistic as well as informative at the **Jardin Public** (cours de Verdun). Established in 1755 and laid out in the English style a century later, the

Bordeaux

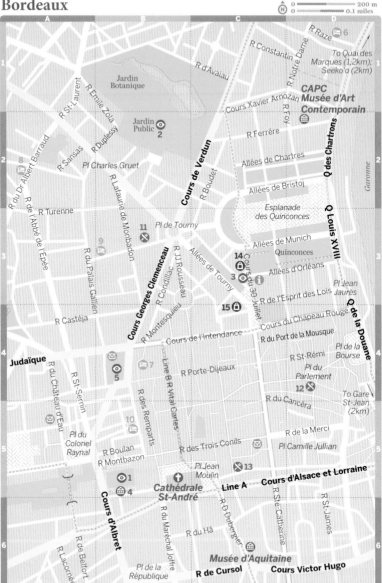

grounds incorporate the meticulously catalogued **Jardin Botanique** founded in 1629 and at this site since 1855.

Pretty **place Gambetta**, a central open area ringed by shaded benches,

also has its share of history – during the Reign of Terror that followed the Revolution, a guillotine placed here severed the heads of 300 alleged counter-revolutionaries.

Bordeaux

 Tours

The tourist office runs a packed program of bilingual city tours, including a wheelchair-accessible two-hour **morning walking tour** (adult/child €8/7, plus optional wine tasting €3.50; ⏲10am, plus 3pm mid-Jul–mid-Aug); a **night-time walking tour** (adult/child €15/10) takes in Bordeaux' floodlit buildings and monuments. Contact the tourist office for details of dozens of other tour options, including **gourmet** and **wine tours** as well as **river cruises** in the warmer months.

 Sleeping

ECOLODGE DES CHARTRONS
B&B €€

(📞05 56 81 49 13; www.ecolodgedeschartrons. com; 23 rue Raze; s/d incl breakfast €98/110) Hidden away in a little side street off the quays in Bordeaux' Chartrons wine merchant district, this *chambre d'hôte* is blazing a trail for ecofriendly sleeping in the city. Owner–hosts Veronique

and Yann have added a solar-powered hot-water system, energy-efficient gas heating and hemp-based soundproofing, while preserving the soul of this old wine merchant's house.

LA MAISON BORD'EAUX
Historic Hotel €€

(📞05 56 44 00 45; www.lamaisonbordeaux. com; 113 rue du Docteur Albert Barraud; s/d from €130/150; 🛜) You'd expect to find a sumptuous 18th-century château with a conifer-flanked courtyard and stable house in the countryside, but this stunning *maison d'hôte* is right in the middle of the city.

UNE CHAMBRE EN VILLE
Boutique Hotel €€

(📞05 56 81 34 53; www.bandb-bx.com; 35 rue Bouffard; s/d €103/115, ste s/d €126/138) On a street full of antique and art shops, this stylish place blends in well because each of the five rooms is an individual work of art in its own right.

LA MAISON DU LIERRE
Boutique Hotel €€

(📞05 56 51 92 71; www.maisondulierre.com; 57 rue Huguerie; d €68-128; 🛜🚼) The delightfully restored 'House of Ivy' has a welcoming *chambre d'hôte* feel. A beautiful Bordelaise stone staircase (no lift) leads to sunlit rooms with polished floorboards, rose-printed fabrics and sparkling bathrooms.

HÔTEL DE LA TOUR INTENDANCE
Boutique Hotel €€

(📞05 56 44 56 56; www.hotel-tour-intendance. com; 14-16 rue de la Vieille Tour; s €78, d €88-148; ❄🛜) Wake up to exposed-sandstone walls, stone-laid floors and wood-beamed ceilings at this stylish boutique hotel tucked into a quiet corner of the city.

 Eating

LE CHEVERUS CAFÉ
Brasserie €

(📞05 56 48 29 73; 81-83 rue du Loup; menu from €10.50; ⏲closed Sun) In a city full of neighbourhood bistros, this one, smack in the city centre, is one of the most impres-

Detour:
The Home of Cognac

On the banks of the River Charente amid vine-covered countryside, **Cognac** is known worldwide for the double-distilled spirit that bears its name, and on which the local economy thrives. Made of grape *eaux-de-vie* (brandies) of various vintages, Cognac is aged in oak barrels and blended by an experienced *maître de chai* (cellar master).

The best-known **Cognac houses** are open to the public, running tours of their cellars and production facilities ending with a tasting session. Opening times vary annually; it's a good idea to reserve in advance.

Hennessey (☎05 45 35 72 68; www.hennessey.com; 8 rue Richonne; adult/12-18yr/under 12 €9/7/free; ⊙closed Jan & Feb) Situated 100m uphill from quai des Flamands, tours include a film (in English) and a boat trip across the Charente to visit the cellars.

Martell (☎05 45 36 33 33; www.martell.com; place Édouard Martell; adult/child €7.50/3) Found 250m northwest of the tourist office; last entry is one hour prior to closing.

Rémy Martin (☎05 45 35 76 66; www.visitesremymartin.com) Two locations: the **estate** (adult/child €15/7; ⊙closed Oct-Apr), 4km southwest of town towards Pons; and, in town, the **house** (adult/12-18yr/under 12yr €25/14/7; ⊙by appointment), for intimate tastings in groups of eight.

---

sive. It's friendly, cosy and chaotically busy (be prepared to wait for a table at lunchtime). The lunch menus, which include wine, are an all-out bargain.

LA TUPINA　　　Gastronomic　€€
(☎05 56 91 56 37; 6 rue Porte de la Monnaie; menus €16/60, mains €18-40) Filled with the aroma of soup simmering inside an old *tupina* ('kettle' in Basque) over an open fire, this white-tableclothed place is feted far and wide for its seasonal southwestern French specialities such as a minicasserole of foie gras and eggs, milk-fed lamb or goose wings with potatoes and parsley.

BAUD ET MILLET　　Cheese & Wine　€€
(☎05 56 79 05 77; 19 rue Huguerie; menus €23-25, mains €16-18) If you like cheese or wine, or both of them, then this cute neighbourhood place with over 250 different cheeses served in myriad forms (including a cheese *tajine*!) and almost as many wines is unmissable.

KARL　　　　International　€€
(☎05 56 81 01 00; place du Parlement; brunch €20; ⊙8.30am-7.30pm; 👶) Simply *the* place in town for a morning after the night

before brunch. These range from a light continental-style affair to the full works with salmon, cheeses, hams and eggs.

🛍 Shopping

Bordeaux Magnum　　　　　Wine
(3 rue Gobineau) Speciality wine shop.

L'Intendant　　　　　　Wine
(2 allées de Tourny). A central spiral staircase climbing four floors is surrounded by cylindrical shelves holding 15,000 bottles of regional wine.

❶ Information

Main tourist office (☎05 56 00 66 00; www.bordeaux-tourisme.com; 12 cours du 30 Juillet; ⊙9am-7pm Mon-Sat, 9.30am-6.30pm Sun)

❶ Getting There & Away

AIR Bordeaux airport (☎05 56 34 50 00; www.bordeaux.aeroport.fr) is in Mérignac, 10km west of the city centre, with domestic and increasing numbers of international flights to most west European and North African destinations.

TRAIN The train station, Gare St-Jean, is about 3km from the city centre at the southern terminus of cours de la Marne.

Paris Gare Montparnasse €70, three hours, at least 16 daily

Bayonne €28, two hours

Nantes €45, four hours

Poitiers €36, 1¾ hours

Toulouse from €33, 2¼ hours

Getting Around

To/From the Airport

The train station, place Gambetta and the main tourist office are connected to the airport (one way €7) by **Jet'Bus** (☎05 56 34 50 50).

St-Émilion
POP 2345

The medieval village of St-Émilion perches above vineyards renowned for producing full-bodied, deeply coloured red wines and is easily the most alluring of all the region's wine towns. Named after Émilion, a miracle-working Benedictine monk who lived in a cave here between 750 and 767, it soon became a stop on pilgrimage routes, and the village and its vineyards are now Unesco-listed.

Sights

CLOCHER Tower
(bell tower; admission €1.25) For captivating views of the hilltop hamlet, collect the key from the tourist office to climb above the church.

CASTEL DAOU REY Castle
(admission €1.25; ⊙11am-7.15pm) The 13th-century donjon known as the Tour du Roi (King's Tower) has exceptional views of the town and the Dordogne Valley.

Activities

Blind tastings and games (available in English) are a fun and informative introduction to wine tasting at **L'École du Vin de St-Émilion** (www.vignobleschateaux.fr; 4 rue du Clocher; tasting courses €29; ⊙3pm Apr-Oct, by reservation Nov-Mar). The adjacent **Maison du Vin** (place Pierre Meyrat; classes

Wine tasting in St-Émilion

GREG ELMS

€21; mid-Jul–mid-Sep) also offers bilingual 1½-hour classes starting at 11am.

Eight hiking circuits, from 4km to 14km, loop through the greater World Heritage jurisdiction; the tourist office has maps.

 Tours

The only (but highly worthwhile) way to visit the town's most interesting historical sites is with one of the tourist office's **guided tours** (adult/child €11/free). French-language tours leave from the tourist office daily at 11am, while English tours are at 11am weekends only. The **St-Émilion Souterrain** (Underground St-Émilion; adult/child €7/free) tour takes you beneath the pretty streets and into a fascinating labyrinth of catacombs – highlights are the hermit saint's famous cave, **Grotte de l'Ermitage**, and the 11th-century church **Église Monolithe**, carved out of limestone between the 9th and the 12th centuries. Tours in French depart regularly throughout the day.

The tourist office organises two-hour afternoon **château visits** (adult/child €12/free; May-Sep) in French and English. It also runs various events throughout the year, such as **La Journée Viticole** (Winemakers' Day; minimum 2 people €385; 11am-5pm Jun-Sep) that combines a vineyard visit, lunch, town tour and wine tasting course.

Sleeping & Eating

HÔTEL-RESTAURANT DU PALAIS CARDINAL Historic Hotel €€
(05 57 24 72 39; www.palais-cardinal.com; place du 11 Novembre 1918; s/d from €71/88, menus from €28;) Run by the same family for five generations, this hotel puts a little more thought into its dress sense than the other 'cheap' St-Émilion hotels. The heated pool is set in rambling flower-filled gardens and framed by sections of the original medieval town-wall fortifications, dating from the 13th century.

AUBERGE DE LA COMMANDERIE

Traditional Hotel €€

(☎ 05 57 24 70 19; www.aubergedelacommand erie.com; 2 rue Porte Brunet; r from €76; ⊗ mid-Feb–mid-Jan; 🛜 👬) Inside this hotel's 13th-century walls, rooms are modernised with massive murals depicting a Technicolorised pop-art version of an old black-and-white postcard of the village.

GRAND BARRAIL   Historic Hotel €€€

(☎ 05 57 55 37 00; www.grand-barrail.com; rte de Libourne/D243; r from €290, menus from €28; ❄ 🛜 ≋) Grand doesn't even begin to describe this immense 1850-built château, 3km from the village, with its decadent on-site spa, stone-flagged heated swimming pool, free state-of-the-art fitness room, wheelchair access and its own helipad on the front lawns.

RESTAURANT HOSTELLERIE DE PLAISANCE   Gastronomic €€€

(☎ 05 57 55 07 55; www.hostellerie-plaisance. com; place du Clocher; menus €95-130; ⊗ closed Sun-Mon) Award-winning chef Philippe Etchebest cooks up food like you've never had before at his double-Michelin-starred restaurant housed in a dining room of eggshell blue and white gold inside the hotel of the same name. Advance reservations essential.

Shopping

St-Émilion's sloping streets and squares are lined with about 50 wine shops – one for every eight of the old city's residents. The largest is the **Maison du Vin** (place Pierre Meyrat; ⊗ 9.30am-12.30pm & 2-6pm), which is owned by the 250 châteaux whose wines it sells at cellar-door prices.

ℹ Information

Tourist office (☎ 05 57 55 28 28; www.saint -emilion-tourisme.com; place des Créneaux; ⊗ 9.30am-12.30pm & 1.45-6.30pm)

273

Getting There & Away

There are around half a dozen train services a day from Bordeaux (€8, 35min). St-Émilion station is a kilometre south of town.

Arcachon

POP 11,800

A long-time oyster-harvesting area on the southern side of the tranquil, triangular Bassin d'Arcachon (Arcachon Bay), this seaside town lured bourgeois Bordelaise at the end of the 19th century. Its four little quarters are romantically named for each of the seasons, with villas that evoke the town's golden past amid a scattering of 1950s architecture.

Sights

TOWN & BEACHES   Town, Beaches
In the **Ville d'Été** (Summer Quarter), Arcachon's sandy beach, **Plage d'Arcachon**, is flanked by two piers. Lively **Jetée Thiers** is at the western end. In front of the eastern pier, **Jetée d'Eyrac**, stands the town's tur-

reted **Casino de la Plage**, built by Adalbert Deganne in 1953 as an exact replica of Château de Boursault in the Marne.

On the tree-covered hillside south of the Ville d'Été, the century-old **Ville d'Hiver** (Winter Quarter) has over 300 villas, many decorated with delicate wood tracery, ranging in style from neo-Gothic through to colonial. It's an easy stroll or a short ride up the **art deco public lift** (admission free) in Parc Mauresque.

Tours

LES BATELIERS ARCACHONNAIS
    Boat Tours
(UBA; ☏05 57 72 28 28; www.bateliers-arcachon. com, in French; ⁂) Year-round cruises sail around **Île aux Oiseaux** (adult/child €14/10), the uninhabited 'bird island' in the middle of the bay. In summer there are regular all-day excursions (11am to 5.30pm) to the **Banc d'Arguin** (adult/child €16/11), the sand bank off the Dune du Pilat.

Sleeping

HÔTEL LE DAUPHIN
    Historic Hotel   €€
(☏05 56 83 02 89; www.dauphin-arcachon. com; 7 av Gounod; s/d from €198/108; ❄☏⊠⁂) Don't miss this late 19th-century gingerbread place with patterned red-and-cream brickwork. An icon of its era, it's graced by twin semicircular staircases, magnolias and palms. Plain but spacious rooms are well set up for families. Parking is free.

Eating

The bay's oysters (served raw and accom-

Oyster ports, Bassin d'Arcachon
PHOTOGRAPHER: SALLY DILLON

DISCOVER BORDEAUX & FRENCH BASQUE COUNTRY

Detour:
The Médoc

Northwest of Bordeaux, along the western shore of the Gironde Estuary, lie some of Bordeaux' most celebrated vineyards. To their west, fine-sand beaches, bordered by dunes and *étangs* (lagoons), stretch from Pointe de Grave south along the Côte d'Argent (Silver Coast) to the Bassin d'Arcachon and beyond, with some great surf. On the banks of the Gironde, the town of **Pauillac** (population 1300) is at the heart of the wine country, surrounded by the distinguished Haut-Médoc, Margaux and St-Julien appellations. The Pauillac wine appellation encompasses 18 *crus classés*, including the world-renowned Mouton Rothschild, Latour and Lafite Rothschild. The town's tourist office houses the **Maison du Tourisme et du Vin** (☏05 56 59 03 08; www.pauillac-medoc.com; La Verrerie; ☻9.30am-7pm Mon-Sat, 10am-1pm & 2-6pm Sun), which has information on the châteaux.

Bordeaux Excursions (www.bordeaux-excursions.com) customises private wine-country tours, starting from €190 for one to five people (excluding châteaux fees) for a half-day trip.

If you're travelling under your own steam, the Maison du Vin de Bordeaux supplies free, colour-coded maps of production areas, details on châteaux and the addresses of local *maisons du vin* (tourist offices that mainly deal with winery visits).

While you're in the area, don't miss Philippe Raoux' **La Winery** (☏05 56 39 04 90; www.lawinery.fr, in French; Rond-point des Vendangeurs, D1, Arsac-en-Médoc). A first for France, this vast glass-and-steel wine centre mounts concerts and contemporary-art exhibits alongside various fee-based tastings, including innovative tastings that determine your *signe œnologique* ('wine sign') costing from €16 (booking required), and stocks over 1000 different wines.

panied by the local small, flat sausages, *crepinettes*) appear on *menus* everywhere.

Aux Mille Saveurs Traditional French €€ (☏05 56 83 40 28; 25 bd du Général Leclerc; menus €19-48; ☻closed dinner Sun &Tue) In a light-filled space of flowing white tablecloths, this genteel restaurant is renowned for its traditional French fare artistically presented on fine china.

❶ Information

Tourist office (☏05 57 52 97 97; www.arcachon.com; Esplanade Georges Pompidou; ☻9am-7pm)

❶ Getting There & Away

There are frequent trains between Bordeaux and Arcachon (€10, 50 minutes).

Dune du Pilat

This colossal sand dune (sometimes referred to as the Dune de Pyla because of its location in the resort town of Pyla-sur-Mer), 8km south of Arcachon, stretches from the mouth of the Bassin d'Arcachon southwards for almost 3km. Already the largest in Europe, it's spreading eastwards at 4.5m a year – it has swallowed trees, a road junction and even a hotel.

The view from the top (approximately 114m above sea level) is magnificent. To the west you can see the sandy shoals at the mouth of the Bassin d'Arcachon, including the **Banc d'Arguin bird reserve** and Cap Ferret. Dense pine forests stretch eastwards.

Take care swimming in this area: powerful currents swirl out to sea from the deceptively tranquil *baïnes* (little bays).

275

If You Like...
Gourmet Food

If you've developed a taste for the finer things while touring around Bordeaux's vineyards, you'll definitely want to indulge yourself at these gastronomic landmarks:

1 LA RIBAUDIÈRE

(☎ 05 45 81 30 54; www.laribaudiere.com; Bourg-Charente; menus from €42; ☺ lunch Wed-Sun, dinner Mon-Sat) Find this gastronomic haven among orchards overlooking the River Charente in the tiny village of **Bourg-Charente**, 11km east of Cognac. Chef Thierry Verrat grows his own vegetables to accompany his seasonally changing, Michelin-starred creations. If the food sends your taste buds into whirls of excitement, you can keep them happy by joining one of the restaurants **cookery courses** (€110). See the website for details.

2 ITHURRIA

(☎ 05 59 29 92 11; www.ithurria.com; Ainhoa; s €85-105, d €105-120, menus €35-58; ❄ P ☎ ⌖) For an unforgettable Basque meal, don't miss the Michelin-starred establishment in pretty **Ainhoa**, about 27km south of Biarritz. Established by the Isabal family in an old pilgrims' hostel, and now run by Maurice Isabal's two sons (one the sommelier, the other the chef), it's simply *the* address for modern Basque cuisine.

3 LE VISCOS

(☎ 05 62 97 02 28; www.hotel-leviscos.com; d €85-126; ☺ closed 2 weeks Jan)

Paulo Coelho, Michael and Kirk Douglas and Nicolas Sarkozy are just some of the celebs who have dined at this divine Pyrenean hotel, 16km south of Lourdes in **St-Savin** – officially 'one of France's prettiest villages'. Run by ex–TV chef Jean-Pierre St-Martin, it's one of the most respected tables in southwest France, known for its blend of Basque, Breton and Pyrenean flavours. Plump for the €89 *menu gastronomique*, which features a belt-busting tour through Jean-Pierre's trademark cuisine, and you'll be treated to a personal introduction from the chef for each dish.

Cap Ferret
POP 6392

Hidden within a canopy of pine trees at the tip of the Cap Ferret peninsula, the tiny village of Cap Ferret spans a mere 2km between the tranquil bay and the crashing Atlantic waves. It's crowned by its 53m-high, red-and-white **lighthouse** (adult/child €4.50/3; ☺ 10am-7.30pm), with interactive exhibits and stunning views of the surf from the top.

Les Bateliers Arcachonnais (UBA; www.bateliers-arcachon.com, in French) runs ferries from Arcachon to Cap Ferret (adult/child return €11.50/8) year-round.

FRENCH BASQUE COUNTRY

Gently sloping from the foothills of the Pyrenees into the deep sapphire-blue Bay of Biscay, the Basque Country straddles France and Spain. Yet this feisty, independent land remains profoundly different from either of the nation states that have adopted it.

The Basque Country is famed for the glitzy beach resort of Biarritz, where surfers strut their stuff in the waves, and oiled sun-seekers pack its beaches like glistening sardines. Nearby Bayonne is a chocolate box of narrow winding streets full of Basque culture, and St-Jean de Luz, further south, is a delightful seaside fishing port.

Inland, up in the lush hills, little one-street villages and green valleys traversed by hiking trails fan out from the walled town of St-Jean Pied de Port, an age-old stop for pilgrims heading over the Spanish border to Santiago de Compostela.

Bayonne
POP 44,200

Surrounded by sturdy fortifications and splashed in red and white paint, Bayonne (Baiona in Basque), capital of the French Basque Country, is one of the most at-

Cathédrale Ste-Marie

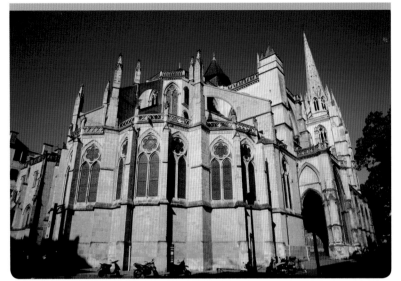

RUSSELL MOUNTFORD

tractive towns in southwest France. Its perfectly preserved old town (until 1907 it was actually forbidden to build outside the town's fortifications) and shoals of riverside restaurants are an absolute delight to explore.

In addition to its chocolates, which you'll see sold throughout France, Bayonne is famous for its prime cured ham and for the *baïonnette* (bayonet), developed here in 1640 on rue des Faures ('Blacksmiths' Street').

◉ Sights & Activities

MUSÉE BASQUE ET DE L'HISTOIRE DE BAYONNE   Museum
(www.musee-basque.com, in French; 37 quai des Corsaires; adult/child €5.50/free, with Musée Bonnat €9; ⏱10am-6.30pm) The seafaring history, traditions and cultural identity of the Basque people are all explored at this superb museum through exhibits including a reconstructed farm and the interior of a typical *etxe* (home). Labelling is in French, Spanish and Basque only but English information sheets are available.

MUSÉE BONNAT   Museum
(www.museebonnat.bayonne.fr; 5 rue Jacques Lafitte; adult/child €5.50/free, with Musée Basque €9; ⏱10am-6.30pm Wed-Mon) Unexpected treasures are crammed into the Musée Bonnat, including canvases by El Greco, Goya, Ingres and Degas, and a roomful of works by Rubens. Nearby is the **Le Carré Musée Bonnat (9 rue Frédéric Bastiat; admission free)**, which houses the Bonnat museum's ever-changing collection of works by the Basque artists of today.

CATHÉDRALE STE-MARIE   Cathedral
(⏱10-11.45am & 3-5.45pm Mon-Sat, 3.30-6pm Sun) The twin towers of Bayonne's Gothic cathedral soar above the city. Construction began in the 13th century, and was completed in 1451; the mismatched materials in some ways resemble Lego blocks. Above the north aisle are three lovely stained-glass windows; the oldest, in the Chapelle Saint Jérôme, dates from 1531.

RAMPARTS   Parks
You can walk the stretches of the old ramparts that rise above bd Rempart Lachepaillet and rue Tour de Sault.

277

Cheeses at Bayonne's Saturday market

RUSSELL MOUNTFORD

 ## Sleeping

Even outside the Fêtes de Bayonne, it's tough to find a bed from mid-July to mid-August.

HÔTEL DES ARCEAUX
Boutique Hotel €€

(05 59 59 15 53; www.hotel-arceaux.com, in French; 26 rue Port Neuf; d from €79;) If this hotel, which is located on one of the prettiest streets in the old town, were a pop star it would surely have to be Lady Gaga or some other flamboyant and over-the-top personality. It easily has more flair and character than all the other hotels in Bayonne put together and is very well run.

LE GRAND HÔTEL   Historic Hotel €€
(05 59 59 62 00; www.legrandhotelbayonne. com; 21 rue Thiers; s/d from €106/111;) This old building was once a convent, but when they ran out of nuns someone turned it into a hotel. Now its cream-toned, wheelchair-accessible rooms and cosy on-site bar (which probably didn't exist when it was a convent) make this friendly business-class hotel a fine place to rest up.

 ## Eating

CHILOA GURMENTA RESTAURANT
Basque €

(7 rue des Tonneliers; menu/mains €12.50/10;) As Basque as a game of *pelota*, this simple and rustic little restaurant, located inside a former brothel, serves one thing and one thing only: *axoa*. A Basque farmers' dish, *axoa* originates from the nearby village of Espelette and consists of minced veal with Espelette peppers, rice, potato and whatever else is lying around.

BAR-RESTAURANT DU MARCHÉ
Basque €

(05 59 59 22 66; 39 rue des Basques; menu/mains €13/7.50; lunch Mon-Sat) Run by a welcoming Basque-speaking family, this unpretentious place is an absolute institution where everyone knows everyone (and therefore some people may find it slightly intimidating, but don't worry, just dive right in – nobody cares!) and simple but ample home-cooked dishes full of the flavours of the neighbouring market are dished up to all comers.

LA CRIÉE BAYONNAISE Seafood €€

(☎ 05 59 59 56 60; 14 quai Chaho; menus from €15, mains €13-15; ⏱ lunch Mon-Sat, dinner Tue-Sat) Decked out in marine colours, this unassuming little find does delicious Basque seafood specialities (such as *les chipirons à l'espagnole* – squid with sweet peppers served with finely ground rice), but you can also get fresh mussels and even fish and chips.

Shopping

PIERRE IBAÏALDE Food

(41 rue des Cordeliers) To buy Bayonne's famous ham at the lowest prices, visit the covered market or, for the best quality, visit a specialist shop such as Pierre Ibaïalde, where you can taste before you buy.

❶ Information

Tourist office (☎ 08 20 42 64 64; www.bayonne-tourisme.com; place des Basques; ⏱ 9am-7pm Mon-Sat, 10am-1pm Sun)

❶ Getting There & Away

Air

Biarritz-Anglet-Bayonne airport (☎ 05 59 43 83 83; www.biarritz.aeroport.fr) is 5km southwest of central Bayonne and 3km southeast of the centre of Biarritz.

Bus 6 links both Bayonne and Biarritz with the airport (€1.20, buses depart roughly hourly). A taxi from the town centre costs around €15 to €20.

Train

TGVs run between Bayonne and Paris Gare Montparnasse (€97, five to six hours, eight daily).

There are five trains daily to St-Jean Pied de Port (€9,

1¼ hours) and fairly frequent services to St-Jean de Luz (€4.50, 25 minutes) via Biarritz (€2.50, nine minutes), plus the French and Spanish border towns of Hendaye (€7, 40 minutes) and Irún (from €7, 45 minutes).

❶ Getting Around

STAB buses link Bayonne, Biarritz and Anglet. Buses 1 and 2 run between Bayonne and Biarritz about 50 times daily, stopping at the *hôtels de ville* (town halls) and stations of both towns.

Biarritz
POP 30,700

As ritzy as its name suggests, this stylish coastal town, 8km west of Bayonne, took off as a resort in the mid-19th century when Napoléon III and his Spanish-born wife, Eugénie, visited regularly. Along its rocky coastline are architectural hallmarks of this golden age, and the belle époque and art deco eras that followed. Although it retains a high glamour quotient (and high prices to match), it's also a magnet for vanloads of surfers, with some of Europe's best waves.

Biarritz
PHOTOGRAPHER: ANDREW BAIN

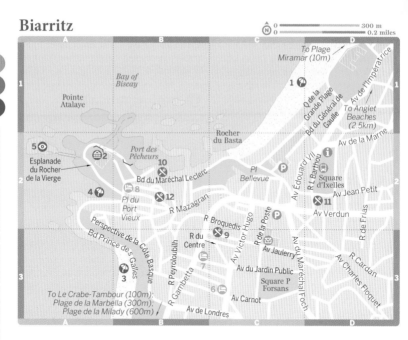

◉ Sights & Activities

BEACHES   Beaches

Biarritz' raison d'être is its fashionable beaches, particularly the two central **Grande Plage** and **Plage Miramar**, which are lined end to end with sunbathing bodies on hot summer days. Stripy 1920s-style beach tents can be hired for €9.50 per day. The other central Biarritz beach is the tiny cove of **Plage du Port Vieux**, which – thanks to its lack of swell – is the best one for young children to splash about on. North of Pointe St-Martin, the adrenaline-pumping surfing beaches of **Anglet** (the final 't' is pronounced) continue northwards for more than 4km.

To the south, beyond the long, exposed **Plage de la Côte des Basques**, some 500m south of Port Vieux, are **Plage de Marbella** and **Plage de la Milady**.

MUSÉE DE LA MER   Aquarium
(www.museedelamer.com; Esplanade du Rocher de la Vierge; adult/child €8/5.50; ⏲9.30am-midnight) Housed in a wonderful art deco building, Biarritz' Musée de la Mer is seething with underwater life from the Bay of Biscay and beyond, as well as exhibits on fishing recalling Biarritz' whaling past. It's the seals that steal the show though (feeding time, which is always a favourite with children, is at 10.30am and 5pm). In high season it's possible to have the place almost to yourself by visiting late at night.

ROCHER DE LA VIERGE   Viewpoint

If the swell's big, you might get a drenching as you cross the footbridge at the end of Pointe Atalaye to Rocher de la Vierge (Rock of the Virgin), named after its white statue of the Virgin and child. Views from this impressive outcrop extend to the mountains of the Spanish Basque Country.

PHARE DE BIARRITZ   Lighthouse

Climbing the 258 twisting steps inside the 73m-high **Phare de Biarritz** (admission €2.50; ⏲10am-12.30pm & 2.30-7pm), the town's 1834 lighthouse, rewards you with sweeping views of the Basque coast.

Biarritz

Sleeping

Inexpensive hotels are a rarity in Biarritz, and any kind of room is at a premium in July and August.

HÔTEL MIRANO Boutique Hotel €€
(☎ 05 59 23 11 63; www.hotelmirano.fr, in French; 11 av Pasteur; d €100-110, ste €140) Squiggly purple, orange and black wallpaper and oversize orange perspex light fittings are some of the rad '70s touches at this boutique retro hotel, a 10-minute stroll from the town centre.

VILLA LE GOËLAND Historic Hotel €€€
(☎ 05 59 24 25 76; www.villagoeland.com; 12 plateau de l'Atalaye; r from €170; 🛜) This stunning family home with its château-like spires perched high on a plateau above Pointe Atalaye is one of the most notable buildings in town. Rooms, tastefully furnished with antiques, family photos and mementos, have panoramic views of the town, sea and across to Spain.

HÔTEL ÉDOUARD VII Historic Hotel €€
(☎ 05 59 22 39 80; www.hotel-edouardvii.com; 21 av Carnot; d from €118; 🛜 👪) From the ornate dining room full of gently tick-tocking clocks to the pots of lavender carefully colour coordinated to match the floral wallpaper, everything about this beautiful and intimate hotel screams 1920s Biarritz chic.

MAISON GARNIER Boutiique Hotel €€
(☎ 05 59 01 60 70; www.hotel-biarritz.com; 29 rue Gambetta; r from €115) The seven boutique 'rooms' (suites would be a better description) of this elegant mansion are tastefully decorated and furnished in cool, neutral tones; those up at attic level are especially romantic.

Eating

CASA JUAN PEDRO Seafood €
(☎ 05 59 24 00 86; Port des Pêcheurs; mains €5-15) Down by the old port, which is something of a hidden little village of wooden fishing cottages and old-timers, is this cute little fishing shack restaurant. The gregarious atmosphere ensures that you can wash down your tuna, sardines or squid with plenty of friendly banter from both the staff and other customers.

LE CRABE-TAMBOUR Seafood €€
(☎ 05 59 23 24 53; 49 rue d'Espagne; lunch menu €13, dinner menus from €18) Named after the famous 1977 film of the same name (the owner was the cook for the film set), this friendly local place, a little way out of the centre, offers great seafood for a price that is hard to fault.

LE CLOS BASQUE Basque €€
(☎ 05 59 24 24 96; 12 rue Louis Barthou; menus €24; ☺ lunch Tue-Sun, dinner Tue-Sat) With its tiles and exposed stonework hung with abstract art, this tiny place could have strayed in from Spain. The cuisine, however, is emphatically Basque, traditional with a contemporary twist or two, such as sirloin with green mustard, or stuffed eggplant with saffron.

BAR JEAN Tapas €
(5 rue des Halles; tapas €1-2) The most original, and delicious, selection of tapas in the city is served up with a flamenco soundtrack and a backdrop of blue and white Andalucian tiles.

MIREMONT
Café €

(1bis place Georges-Clemenceau; tea & cake €7-9; ⏲9am-8pm) Operating since 1880, this *grande dame* of a place harks back to the time when belle-époque Biarritz was simply the beach resort of choice for the rich and glamorous of Europe.

❶ Information

Tourist office (☎05 59 22 37 00; www.biarritz. fr; square d'Ixelles; ⏲9am-6pm Mon-Sat, 10am-5pm Sun)

❶ Getting There & Away

BUS To reach Biarritz-Anglet-Bayonne airport (p279), take STAB bus 6 or, on Sunday, line C to/from Biarritz' *hôtel de ville*.

TRAIN Biarritz-La Négresse train station is about 3km south of the town centre; walking to the centre isn't advised due to busy roads without footpaths, so catch buses 2 or 9 (B and C on Sundays).

St-Jean de Luz & Ciboure
POP 13,600

If you're searching for the quintessential Basque seaside town – with atmospheric narrow streets and a lively fishing port pulling in large catches of sardines, tuna and anchovies that are cooked up at authentic restaurants – you've found it.

St-Jean de Luz, 24km southwest of Bayonne, sits at the mouth of the River Nivelle and is overlooked by the lush Pyrenean foothills.

Its sleepy, smaller alter ego, Ciboure, is on the western curve of the bay, separated from St-Jean de Luz by the fishing harbour.

◉ Sights

A superb panorama of the town unfolds from the promontory of **Pointe Ste-Barbe**, at the northern end of the Baie de St-Jean de Luz and about 1km beyond the town beach.

BEACHES
Beaches

St-Jean de Luz' beautiful banana-shaped sandy beach sprouts stripy bathing tents from June to September. Ciboure has its own modest beach, **Plage de Socoa**.

ÉGLISE ST-JEAN BAPTISTE
Church

(rue Gambetta; ⏲8.30am-noon & 2-7pm) The plain facade of France's largest and finest Basque church conceals a splendid interior with a magnificent baroque altarpiece. It was in front of this very altarpiece that Louis XIV and María Teresa, daughter of King Philip IV of Spain, were married in 1660.

MAISON LOUIS XIV
Historical Building

(www.maison-louis-xiv.fr, in French; adult/child €5.50/3; ⏲10.30am-12.30pm & 2.30-6.30pm, closed Tue & mid-Oct–Easter) Built in 1643 by a wealthy shipowner and furnished in period style, this is where Louis XIV lived out his last days of bachelorhood before marrying María Teresa.

SOCOA
Old Town

The heart of Socoa is about 2.5km west of Ciboure along the continuation of quai Maurice Ravel (named for the *Boléro* composer, who was born in Ciboure in 1875). Its prominent **fort** was built in 1627 and later improved by Vauban. You can walk out to the Digue de Socoa breakwater or climb to the **lighthouse** via rue du Phare, then out along rue du Sémaphore for fabulous coastal views.

🛏 Sleeping

LA DEVINIÈRE
Boutique Hotel €€

(☎05 59 26 05 51; www.hotel-la-deviniere.com; 5 rue Loquin; r with street/garden view €120/160; 🚹) You have to love a place that forsakes TVs for antiquarian books (room 11 even has its own mini-library). It's a truly charming place that feels like a little old country cottage that has somehow been sucked into the town centre.

ZAZPI
Design Hotel €€€

(☎05 59 26 07 77; www.zazpihotel.com; 21 bd Thiers; r/ste from €205/400; ❄🛜🛟) Seriously hip, this wonderful old mansion-turned-designer-hotel is one of the most stylish hotels in southwest France.

Waterfront fort, Socoa

GREG JOHNSTON

There's a rooftop terrace complete with pool and sensational views over an ocean of terracotta roof tiles to the fairytale green Basque hills.

 Eating

BUVETTE DES HALLES Seafood €
(☎ 05 59 26 73 59; bd Victor Hugo; dishes €7-14; ⏱ 6am-2pm & dinner) Tucked into a corner of the covered market, this minuscule restaurant serves goat's cheese, Bayonne ham, grilled sardines, fish soup, mussels and much more, outside beneath the plane trees on the small square between June and September.

GRILLERIE DU PORT Seafood €
(☎ 05 59 51 18 29; quai du Maréchal Leclerc; ⏱ mid-Jun–mid-Sep) In this old shack by the port, join the crowds gorging on fresh sardines, salads and slabs of tuna steak fresh off the boat. It's informal and economical; prices depend on the day's catch but are always reasonable.

LE PEITA Seafood €
(☎ 05 59 26 86 66; 21 rue Tourasse; mains €14.50-20, menus from €16; ⏱ Wed-Sun) Dried

Espelette chillies and hams hang from the ceiling at this authentic place with crushed-silk tablecloths and friendly owners. For a taste of the local produce on display, order one of the combination plates accompanied by fresh local cheese.

❶ Information

Tourist office (☎ 05 59 26 03 16; www.saint-jean-de-luz.com; 20 bd Victor Hugo; ⏱ 9am-12.30pm & 2.30-6.30pm Mon-Sat, 10am-1pm Sun, extended hrs Jul & Aug)

❶ Getting There & Away

There are frequent trains to Bayonne (€4.50, 25 minutes) via Biarritz (€3, 15 minutes) and to Hendaye (€2.90, 15 minutes), with connections to Spain.

St-Jean Pied de Port
POP 1700

At the foot of the Pyrenees, the walled town of St-Jean Pied de Port, 53km southeast of Bayonne, was for centuries the last stop in France for pilgrims heading south over the Spanish border, a mere 8km away, and on to Santiago de

283

Compostela in western Spain. Today it remains a popular departure point for hikers attempting the pilgrim trail, but there are plenty of shorter hikes and opportunities for mountain biking in the area.

St-Jean Pied de Port makes an ideal day trip from Bayonne, particularly on Monday when the market is in full swing.

 Sights & Activities

OLD TOWN
Old Town

The walled old quarter is an attractive place of cobbled streets, geranium-covered balconies and lots of quirky boutiques. Specific sights worth seeking out include the **Église Notre Dame du Bout du Pont**, with foundations as old as the town itself but thoroughly rebuilt in the 17th century. Beyond Porte de Notre Dame is the photogenic **Vieux Pont** (Old Bridge), the town's best-known landmark, from where there's a fine view of whitewashed houses with balconies leaning out above the water.

Rue de la Citadelle is edged by substantial, pink-granite 16th- to 18th-century houses. A common motif is the scallop shell, symbol of St Jacques (St James or Santiago) and of the Santiago de Compostela pilgrims.

LA CITADELLE
Fortress

From the top of rue de la Citadelle, a rough cobblestone path ascends to the massive citadel itself, from where there's a spectacular panorama of the town and the surrounding hills. Constructed in 1628, the fort was rebuilt around 1680 by military engineers of the Vauban school. Nowadays it serves as a secondary school and is closed to the public.

If you've a head for heights, descend by the steps signed *escalier poterne* (rear stairway). Steep and slippery after rain, they plunge beside the moss-covered ramparts to **Porte de l'Échauguette** (Watchtower Gate).

ⓘ Information

Tourist office (☎ 05 59 37 03 57; www. pyrenees-basque.com; place Charles de Gaulle; ◷ 9am-7pm Mon-Sat, 10am-4pm Sun Jul & Aug, 9am-noon & 2-6pm Mon-Sat Sep-Jun)

Homage to the Sanctuaires Notre Dame de Lourdes

MARTIN MOOS

ℹ Getting There & Away

Train is the best option to travel to or from Bayonne (€9, 1¼ hours, up to five daily) since the irregular bus service makes a huge detour (and drops you at the station, rather than the centre of town, despite passing right through it – go figure).

Lourdes

POP 15,700 / ELEVATION 400M

If you've ever wondered what a religious theme park would look like, chances are it'd turn out pretty close to Lourdes. This provincial town, 43km southeast of Pau, has been one of the world's most important pilgrimage sites since 1858, when 14-year-old Bernadette Soubirous (1844–79) saw the Virgin Mary in a series of 18 beatific visions, which came to her in a rocky grotto just outside town.

Each year, around 70,000 invalids make the spiritual pilgrimage to Lourdes in the hope of finding a cure for all manner of afflictions and ailments, and while the town itself can be a pretty disheartening experience, the sanctuaries themselves are refreshingly free of commercial clutter.

◎ Sights

SANCTUAIRES NOTRE DAME DE LOURDES   Sacred Caves

The development of the Sanctuaries of Our Lady of Lourdes began within a decade of Ste Bernadette's apparitions in 1858.

The most dramatic approach is via the Port St-Joseph, from where a broad boulevard sweeps west towards the Byzantine **Basilique du Rosaire** (Basilica of the Rosary), topped by lavishly gilded turrets and tiled frescoes depicting Bernadette's visions. Beneath the basilica is Lourdes' most revered site, the **Grotte de Massabielle** (sometimes known as the Grotte Miraculeuse or

♥ If You Like…
Basque Culture

Once you've visited the Musée Basque in Bayonne, here are some more tips for getting to grips with the unique culture of the Basque Country.

1 FÊTES DE BAYONNE
(www.fetes.bayonne.fr) This Basque festival in early August attracts up to a million people to Bayonne for a five-day orgy of drinking, dancing, processions and fireworks, culminating in the town's own version of Pamplona's 'Running of the Bulls' ceremony (only here the bulls are replaced by heifers).

2 PELOTA
The national Basque sport of *pelota* (*pelote basque* in French) encompasses sixteen different games, all played with a hard ball (the *pelote*) using bare hands (*mains nues*), a wooden paddle (*pala*) or a scooplike racket (*chistera*). Nearly every village has its own court (*fronton*); you can catch matches in Biarritz, Bayonne and St-Jean de Luz between June and September.

3 PIMENTS D'ESPELETTE
This spicy chilli pepper is an essential accompaniment to Basque meals (it even has its own AOC, just like fine wine). The village of **Espelette** (✎ tourist office 05 59 93 95 02; www.espelette.fr) hosts its own chilli festival on the last weekend in October, culminating in the crowning of a *chevalier du piment* (knight of the chilli).

4 AXOA
This classic Basque dish of tender minced veal simmered with onions and chilli peppers is a staple on Basque menus, including Bayonne's Chiloa Gurmenta Restaurant.

5 DANSES DES SEPT PROVINCES BASQUES
Folk dancers from all across the Spanish and French Basque Country meet in early summer for this annual festival in St-Jean de Luz.

the Grotte des Apparitions), where Bernadette allegedly experienced her famous visions.

The Esplanade des Processions, lined with enormous flickering candles left by previous pilgrims, leads along the river to the grotto's entrance, where people line up patiently for the chance to enter the cave itself, or take a chilly dip in one of the sacred **baths** (⊙9-11am & 2.30-4pm Mon-Sat, 2-4pm Sun & holy days).

CHÂTEAU FORT   Castle, Museum
(Fortified Castle; adult/child €5/2.30; ⊙9am-noon & 1.30-6.30pm) On a rocky pinnacle above town squats this imposing castle. There's been some kind of stronghold on this site since Roman times, but the present building is largely medieval, including the stout walls and the central keep.

Since the 1920s, the castle has housed the **Musée Pyrénéen**, which owns one the region's largest collection of folk art, rural artefacts, tools and other exhibits.

Take the free lift (elevator) from rue Baron Duprat or walk up the ramp at the northern end of rue du Bourg.

PIC DU JER   Mountain Viewpoint
(bd d'Espagne) When the crowds of pilgrims get too much, you can take refuge on the rocky 94m-high pinnacle of the Pic du Jer, which offers panoramic views of Lourdes and the central chain of the Pyrenees.

There are two routes to the top: a punishing three-hour slog along a signed trail, or a speedy six-minute ride on the century-old **funicular** (bd d'Espagne; adult/child return €9/6; ⊙10am-6pm Mar-Nov & winter holidays, 9am-8pm mid-Jul–Aug). We'll leave it up to you to decide which is the more rewarding.

Take bus 2 from place Monseigneur Laurence.

Sleeping

Unsurprisingly, considering the hordes of pilgrims who descend on the town every year, Lourdes is awash with hotels (it actually has more accommodation than anywhere in France outside Paris).

CITEA ST JEAN   Hotel   €€
(☎05 62 46 30 07; lourdes@citea.com; 1 av du Paradis; s €48-60, d €68-90; 🛜) If you're determined to stay in Lourdes, this town hotel is just about the best bet, offering plain, modern rooms with nary a Madonna or crucifix in sight. It's part of the Citea chain, so it's businesslike, but even in summer the rates stay reasonable.

BESTWESTERN BEAUSÉJOUR   Hotel   €€
(☎05 62 94 38 18; 16 av de la Gare; d €78-105; 🛜) The

Château Fort
PHOTOGRAPHER: MARTIN MOOS

Detour: The Pyrenees

They might not be on quite the same lofty scale as the Alps, but the Pyrenees still pack a mighty impressive mountain punch. Crested by snow for much of the year, these high, wild peaks form a natural frontier between southwest France and northern Spain. End to end, they cover a total distance of around 430km, including the 100km-strip of protected land known as the **Parc National des Pyrénées**. The park was created in 1967 and is now an important haven for rare wildlife such as eagles, griffon vultures, izards (a type of goat) and some of France's last remaining wild brown bears.

Needless to say, if you're a hiker, biker or skier, or if you're simply a sucker for grandstand views, you'll be in seventh heaven in the Pyrenees. Hemmed in by snowy peaks, **Cauterets** is a superb summertime base; numerous high-altitude trails leave from the **Pont d'Espagne**, reached via the 6.5km switchbacking D920 from Cauterets.

Also, don't miss the dizzying ascent to the **Pic du Midi de Bigorre** (www.picdumidi.com; adult/student/child €25/22/15; ⊙daily Feb & Jun-late Sep, closed last 3 weeks Nov, call for closing days rest of yr), which affords one of the most eye-popping panoramas in the entire Pyrenees. A cable car climbs right to the top of the mountain in around 15 minutes from the ski resort of La Mongie (1800m).

Park visitor centres can be found at Etsaut, Laruns, Arrens-Marsous, Cauterets, Luz-St-Sauveur, Gavarnie and St-Lary-Soulan. The park's official website, **PNR Pyrenees** (www.parc-pyrenees.com), is also packed with info.

attractive heritage facade and glossy lobby promises big things at this Best Western – sadly the rooms are as bland and generic as ever. Still it's business-like and efficient, handy for the station and it's a lot tidier than many places round town.

ℹ Information

Forum information office (☏05 62 42 78 78; www.lourdes-france.com; Esplanade des Processions; ⊙8.30am-6.30pm) For information on the Sanctuaires.

Tourist office (☏05 62 42 77 40; www.lourdes-infotourisme.com; place Peyramale; ⊙9am-6.30pm)

ℹ Getting There & Away

Lourdes has regular train connections, including TGVs to Pau and Paris Montparnasse. Destinations served:

Bayonne €21, 1¾ hours

Paris Montparnasse €89.30, 6½ hours

Pau €7.10, 30 minutes

Toulouse €25.10, two hours

Provence & the French Riviera

There is no more sunny and celebrity-rich part of France than the south. So get set for heart and soul seduction. Travelling here means sensual sauntering through scented lavender fields and vineyards, around vibrant morning markets groaning with fresh produce, and along paradisaical shores lapped by clear turquoise waters.

Roughly speaking, this region splits into three: east is the iconic French Riviera, wedged between glitzy star-spangled Cannes and megalomaniacal Monte Carlo in the millionaire principality of Monaco. In the middle is Provence, hinged on the coast by the wildly contrasting fishing ports of St-Tropez and Marseille, and tethered inland by a stash of Roman vestiges, hilltop villages and exceptional natural landscapes. Languedoc lies west, an upcoming region that travellers tramp to first and foremost for the walled city of Carcassonne and its bewitching witch's-hat turrets.

Lavender fields, Provence
PHOTOGRAPHER: DAVID TOMLINSON

Provence & the French Riviera

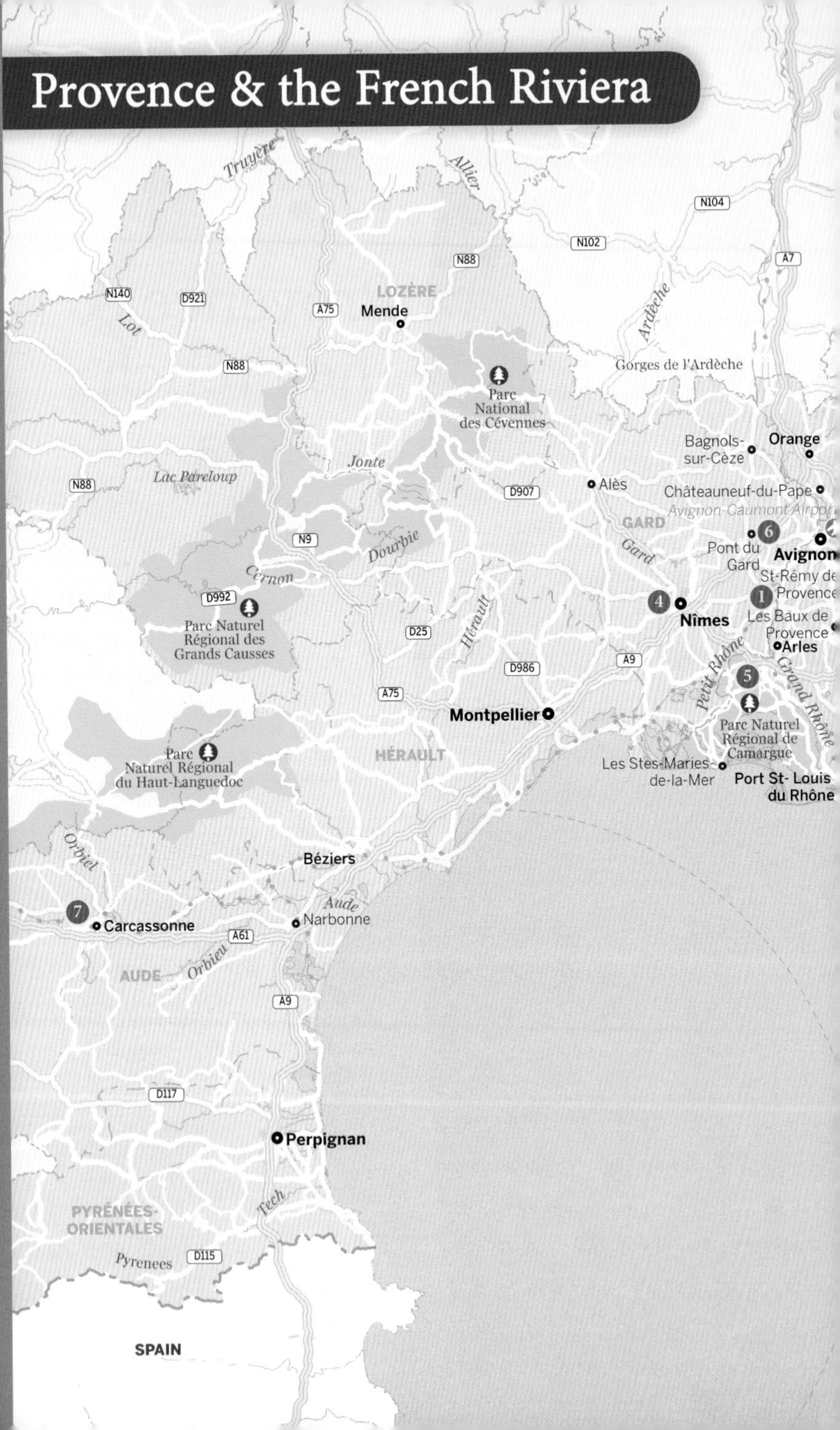

Truyère
Allier
N104
N102
A7
N88
LOZÈRE
N140
D921
A75
Mende
Lot
Ardèche
N88
Gorges de l'Ardèche
Parc National des Cévennes
Bagnols-sur-Cèze
Orange
Jonte
Lac Pareloup
N88
D907
Alès
Châteauneuf-du-Pape
Avignon-Caumont Airport
GARD
6
Gard
N9
Dourbie
Pont du Gard
Avignon
Cernon
St-Rémy de Provence
1
D992
4
Nîmes
Les Baux de Provence
Parc Naturel Régional des Grands Causses
D25
Hérault
Arles
A9
D986
Petit Rhône
Grand Rhône
5
A75
Montpellier
Parc Naturel Régional de Camargue
Parc Naturel Régional du Haut-Languedoc
HÉRAULT
Les Stes-Maries-de-la-Mer
Port St- Louis du Rhône
Orbiel
Béziers
Aude
7
Carcassonne
Narbonne
A61
AUDE
Orbieu
A9
D117
Perpignan
Tech
PYRÉNÉES-ORIENTALES
Pyrenees
D115
SPAIN

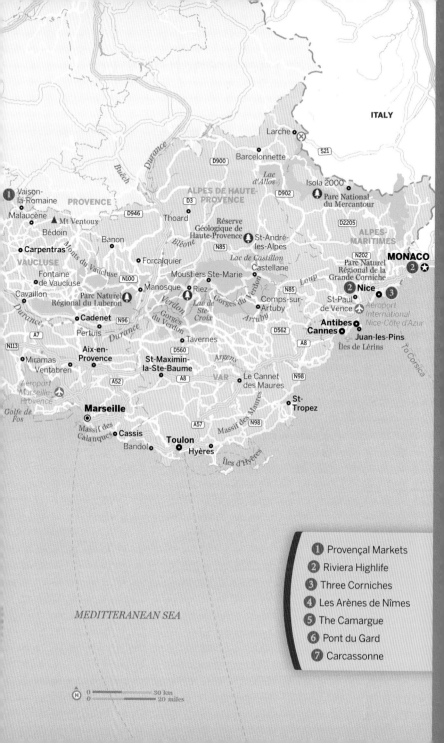

ITALY

Larche

Barcelonnette

1 Vaison-la-Romaine

PROVENCE

Malaucène

▲ Mt Ventoux

Bédoin

Carpentras

VAUCLUSE

Banon

Thoard

ALPES DE HAUTE-PROVENCE

Lac d'Allos

Isola 2000

4 Parc National du Mercantour

ALPES-MARITIMES

Réserve Géologique de Haute-Provence

4 St-André-les-Alpes

Fontaine de Vaucluse

Forcalquier

Moustiers Ste-Marie

Lac de Castillon

Castellane

MONACO 2

Parc Naturel Régional de la Grande Corniche

Cavaillon

Parc Naturel Régional du Luberon

Manosque

Riez

Lac de Ste-Croix

Gorges du Verdon

Comps-sur-Artuby

2 Nice

3

St-Paul de Vence

Cadenet

Gorges du Verdon

Aéroport International Nice-Côte d'Azur

Pertuis

Tavernes

Antibes

Cannes

Aix-en-Provence

Juan-les-Pins

Îles de Lérins

Miramas

Ventabren

St-Maximin-la-Ste-Baume

Argens

VAR

Le Cannet des Maures

Aéroport Marseille-Provence

To Corsica

Marseille

Massif des Maures

St-Tropez

Golfe de Fos

Massif des Calanques

Cassis

Toulon

Bandol

Hyères

Îles d'Hyères

MEDITERRANEAN SEA

1 Provençal Markets

2 Riviera Highlife

3 Three Corniches

4 Les Arènes de Nîmes

5 The Camargue

6 Pont du Gard

7 Carcassonne

0 — 30 km
0 — 20 miles

Provence & the French Riviera's Highlights

① Provençal Markets

Provence is the source of so many good, fresh ingredients, from black truffles to artichokes and asparagus, strawberries, melons, heirloom tomatoes, baby Delicatesse potatoes, and superb lamb, poultry and sausages. Not to mention truly bargain-priced wines and outstanding cheeses. What more does one need in life?

Need to Know

GET UP EARLY Markets run around 7am to noon **READ** At Home in Provence (Patricia Wells) for ideas on cooking your purchases **COOKING CLASSES** Sign up a year in advance at www.patriciawells. com

Provençal Markets Don't Miss List

BY PATRICIA WELLS, COOKBOOK
AUTHOR & COOKING TEACHER

. . . .

1 VAISON-LA-ROMAINE

The Tuesday market in Vaison-la-Romaine might be 'my' market but it is truly one of Provence's greats. It has the freshest local produce around, especially asparagus, strawberries, melons and heirloom tomatoes. Go to Lou Canesteou for cheese and Peyrerol for chocolate.

. . . .

2 ST-RÉMY DE PROVENCE

My other favourite is St-Rémy on Wednesday: I love the town, the ambience. Perhaps it is more a market to buy trinkets than food, but whatever you are there for, you just always feel as though you are in the right place at the right time. (Pictured far left and below)

. . . .

3 UZÈS

The third in my top three is also on Wednesday, in Uzès, west of Nîmes. The organic market on place aux Herbes, one of the prettiest little squares in all of France, is stunning – great goat's cheeses, *confitures* (jams) from the nuns and wonderful local olives and olive oil.

. . . .

4 RICHERENCHES

My favourite speciality market is on Saturday in Richerenches, November through February. It is a fresh black truffle market – VERY mysterious and you can't figure out what is going on, with lots of people selling pillow cases bulging with black truffles from the trunks of their cars. Stay until lunchtime and have a truffle omelette at one of the two cafés in the village.

. . . .

5 THE BEST PRODUCE

Tip 1 When looking for the best meat, look for a line of elderly French women. They know how to shop! **Tip 2** Look at the vendors: just as people often resemble their dogs, produce vendors resemble their produce. If the vendor is neat, trim, clean, so will his produce be neat, trim, clean. Dirty fingernails usually mean ugly produce! **Tip 3** Take time to tour the entire market before you buy. Nothing is worse that a quick, rash purchase at the beginning of the market, only to find better, better-priced produce later on.

Riviera High Life

Monaco and the Riviera *are* glam and glitzy; it's simply impossible to tire of the exceptional beauty of the place. I wander around and I'm constantly noticing it, the architecture, the beaches... To me it is very important to live in a beautiful place, which is why I've spent the best part of 20 years here. Casino de Monte Carlo (p343)

Need to Know

GLAMOUR TIP Most Riviera bars aren't glam; they're just full of glam people **DRESS CODE** Smart **TIMELESS ADDRESS** Monaco's Stars 'n' Bars (p346) and neighbouring terrace cafés at Monaco port

②

Riviera High Life Don't Miss List

BY ELIZABETH LEWIS, RADIO PRESENTER
AT 106.5 RIVIERA RADIO

1 LIVE JAZZ
My favourite summer festival is Nice Jazz Festival (p44). I've seen everyone from BB King to Kool and The Gang there, dancing under olive trees as the moon rises over the outdoor stages. Then there's **La Note Bleue** (www.lanotebleue.mc), a Monaco beach club where the best jazz musicians play. Spend the afternoon on a sun lounger sipping rosé, dine on the best seafood risotto on the Riviera and jive until the wee hours.

2 CELEBRITY SPOTTING
So many famous people live or have second homes on the Riviera that it's hard *not* to see them! At Monte Carlo Sporting Club's **Salle des Étoiles** (www.sportingmontecarlo. com) I've chatted to Shirley Bassey (she lives next door to it) at a Liza Minnelli concert, stood behind Elton John (another celebrity resident) at a Grace Jones concert and spotted Julian Lennon at the next table when seeing Steely Dan live.

3 ROOFTOP SPAS & BARS
Rooftops are prime Riviera real estate and many of the big hotels have rooftop spas and bars open to non-guests. Nice's **Hôtel Grand Aston** (www.hotel-aston.com) has a fabulous rooftop pool where you can spend the day lounging (admission even includes a sandwich and drink!).

4 GLAMOUR
For pure glamour it has to be Monaco's **Monte Carlo Bay Hôtel** (http://fr.montecarlobay.com). It is majestic, with huge colonnades everywhere, and the spa is out of this world: a great big greenhouse full of lush vegetation with a beautiful circular pool and a bridge that you swim under to get outside. There are sun loungers everywhere and poolside spas, and the Blue Gin Bar is perfect for an aperitif.

5 PRICELESS GEM
Cave Romagnan (http://caveromagnan.free.fr) in Nice is a tiny, unpretentious wine bar and cellar with an excellent selection of wine. On Saturdays, locals of all ages gather to dance until midnight to live jazz, blues and rock bands.

Three Corniches

This trio of clifftop roads (p340) between Nice and Menton provides one of France's most iconic drives. Hitchcock memorably used the *corniches* as a backdrop in *To Catch a Thief* (1956) starring Cary Grant and Grace Kelly (who, ironically, died in a car crash along the same road in 1982). Don your shades, roll down the windows and tackle the hairpin bends en route to the millionaires' playground, Monaco (p341). Èze (p340)

3

The Camargue

5

Famous for its candy-pink flamingos and its wild horses, the Camargue (p314) is a wonderful place to escape the hustle and bustle of Provence's busy cities. One of France's largest natural wetlands, it's home to over 500 species of rare birds, and makes a fantastic area for wildlife spotting – don't forget to bring binoculars, and a telephoto lens for your camera.

PETER THORNTON

Les Arènes de Nîmes

Long before the rich and famous arrived, the Romans recognised the seductive charms of southern France. The region is studded with many well-preserved Roman monuments, including this almost-intact amphitheatre in Nîmes (p321). Built to seat over 10,000 spectators, it served as the stage for gladiatorial contests and bloodthirsty shows, and is – controversially – still used for bullfights to this day.

MANFRED GOTTSCHALK

GLENN BEANLAND

Pont du Gard

The scale of this Unesco World Heritage Site near Nîmes (p323) is gargantuan: the 35 arches straddling the Roman aqueduct's 275m-long upper tier contain a watercourse designed to carry 20,000 cu metres of water per day. View it from afloat a canoe on the River Gard or pay extra to take a guided walk across its top tier.

Carcassonne

The first glimpse of La Cité's sturdy stone witch's-hat turrets above Carcassonne (p324) in the Languedoc is enough to make your hair stand on end. To savour this fairy-tale walled city in its true glory, linger at dusk after the crowds have left, when the old town belongs once again to its 100-odd inhabitants and the few visitors staying at the few lovely hotels within its ramparts.

Porte Narbonnaise (p324)

Provence & the French Riviera's Best…

Beaches

○ **Plage de Pampelonne** (p338) Play Brigitte Bardot on St-Tropez's finest golden sand.

○ **Promenade des Anglais** (p326) Beach-lounge on a sky-blue chair beside Nice's mythical seaside prom.

○ **St-Jean-Cap Ferrat** (p340) Dip into secluded coves between millionaires' mansions.

○ **Îles de Lérins** (p335) Trade Cannes madness for perfect castaway beaches.

Nature Spots

○ **Île de Port-Cros** (p346) Sail to France's only marine national park, part of the idyllic Îles d'Hyères.

○ **Marseille's Calanques** (p317) Hike through scented *maquis* and enjoy sweeping Mediterranean views.

○ **Gorges du Verdon** (p317) Pilot a kayak along Europe's longest canyon.

○ **Jardin Exotique** (p343) Discover exotic plants from across the globe in Monaco's clifftop botanical garden.

Artistic Addresses

○ **Chapelle du Rosaire** (p334) This bijou chapel was Matisse's pride and joy.

○ **Fondation Maeght** (p334) World-class art in St-Paul de Vence.

○ **Musée Picasso** (p332) View Picassos in Antibes' 12th-century château turned studio.

○ **Mamac** (p331) Nice's modern-art museum is as interesting for the architecture as the art.

○ **Aix-en-Provence** (p310) Check off the artistic sights around Cézanne's home town.

Gourmet Experiences

o **Mantel** (p337) Spot the celebs at this up-and-coming Cannes address.

o **Mandarine** (p346) Great views over Monte Carlo, and Michelin-starred food.

o **L'Oustau de Baumanière** (p320) Superb French food in an idyllic hilltop setting.

o **L'Epuisette** (p310) *The* place to savour Marseille's famous bouillabaisse.

o **Fenocchio** (p330) Savour unusual flavours such as rhubarb, avocado and liqorice at Nice's knock-out ice-cream maker.

Need to Know

ADVANCE PLANNING

o **As early as possible** Book accommodation, especially for July, August and during the Cannes Film Festival and Monaco Grand Prix (both in May). Reserve tickets for Avignon's theatre festival (p318) and *férias* (bullfighting festivals) in Arles and Nîmes.

o **Two weeks before** Book tables for big-name restaurants, especially in Marseille, Nice and St-Tropez.

o **Two days before** Order bouillabaisse at Marseille's bistros (p310).

RESOURCES

o **Provence-Alpes-Côte d'Azur** (www.decouverte-paca.fr) Pan-regional information, including advice on accommodation and green travel.

o **Nice Tourisme** (www.nicetourisme.com) Nice's main tourist office website.

o **PACA** (www.crt-paca.fr) Umbrella site for Provence and the Riviera.

o **Côte d'Azur Tourisme** (www.cotedazur-tourisme.com) Comprehensive online resource for the Riviera.

GETTING AROUND

o **Train** An ideal way to explore the Riviera coastline. Base yourself in Nice and take day trips to Monaco and Cannes, stopping off at lovely Riviera towns en route.

o **Car** Essential in Provence. On the coast July and August means hellish road traffic, especially on Saturdays and pretty much all summer around St-Tropez. Take extra care when driving along the Corniches.

o **Boats** Scenic cruises depart from Marseille, Cannes and St-Tropez; don't miss a trip to the Îles de Lérins (p335) or the Îles d'Hyères (p346).

BE FOREWARNED

o **Petty theft** From backpacks, pockets and bags is rife on the Riviera. Be extra vigilant at train stations and on the beach.

o **Cannes hotel prices** Soar to astronomical levels during May's film festival.

o **Monaco motorists** You can't drive into Monaco Ville unless you have a Monaco or local 06 number plate.

o **Mosquitos** Bring repellent for a buzz-free night.

Left: Gorges du Verdon (p317);
Above: St-Jean-Cap Ferrat (p340)

PHOTOGRAPHERS: (LEFT) GLENN BEANLAND; (ABOVE) JEAN-PIERRE LESCOURRET

Provence & the French Riviera Itineraries

No trip to France would be complete without a few days spent exploring the French Riviera. With its swaying palm trees, hilltop towns and sparkling beaches, this is the essence of southern France. Savour every moment.

3 DAYS

NÎMES TO VAISON-LA-ROMAINE
ROMAN PROVENCE

Gloriously intact amphitheatres, triumphal arches and other public buildings transport travellers back to Provence's heyday as a Gallo-Roman province.

Devote day one to **(1) Nîmes**, with its resplendent amphitheatre and theatre, still occasionally used for *férias*, concerts and bullfights. Just outside Nîmes is one of the great achievements of the Gallo-Roman world – the incredible **(2) Pont du Gard**, the world's highest aqueduct. It's particularly awe inspiring when seen up close – via either a guided walk across the top tier or a self-paddled canoe trip beneath its great arches.

Spend day two in **(3) Arles**, with its duo of impressive Roman theatres. If you've got some extra time, take a detour through the idyllic **(4) Camargue**, where you can spot wild horses and flamingos in the peaceful setting of one of France's largest natural wetlands.

On day three visit France's most-stunning Roman amphitheatre, at **(5) Orange** – built to stage bloodthirsty gladiatorial contests watched by over 10,000 baying spectators – or **(6) Vaison-la-Romaine**, with its ancient remains left over from the original Roman town, not to mention one of the region's liveliest outdoor markets.

NICE TO CANNES
RIVIERA HIGHLIGHTS

5 DAYS

This trip takes in the key sights of the Côte d'Azur. Begin in the millionaires' playground of **(1) Monaco**, where you can ogle the yachts, have a flutter at the casino and spoil yourself at the luxurious Ni Hôtel.

On day two, tackle **(2) the Corniches**, a trio of white-knuckle roads snaking across the clifftops west of Monaco. Stop for a wander around the clifftop gardens of **(3) Èze**. By late afternoon you'll reach the classic Riviera city, **(4) Nice**; check into the Hôtel Windsor and have an authentic Niçois meal in the atmospheric old town.

Day three's for more Nice exploration: don't miss the Cours Saleya street market, the Promenade des Anglais, the Musée Matisse and Musée d'Art Moderne et d'Art Contemporain (Mamac).

On day four, head inland to hilltop **(5) St-Paul de Vence**, where everyone from Matisse to Picasso once went to paint and party. View the art collection at the Fondation Maeght, and overnight at the legendary Colombe d'Or.

Your last day takes you to cinematic **(6) Cannes**, home of France's starriest film festival. If you can spare an extra day, catch a boat to the lovely **(7) Îles de Lérins**.

Les Arènes (p313), Arles

Discover Provence & the French Riviera

Calanque de Morgiou (p317)
PHOTOGRAPHER: JEAN-PIERRE LESCOURRET

PROVENCE

Marseille

POP 860,360

Marseillais will tell you that the city's rough-and-tumble edginess is part of its charm and that, for all its flaws, it is a very endearing place. They're right. Marseille grows on you, with its history, fusion of cultures, *souq*-like markets, millennia-old port and *corniches* (coastal roads) along rocky inlets and sun-baked beaches. The ultimate vindication came with Marseille's selection as European Capital of Culture for 2013.

 Sights

The **Marseille City Pass** (€22/29 for a 1-/2-day pass) gives you access to the city's museums, guided tours of the town and unlimited travel on all public transport (including the little train to Notre Dame).

VIEUX PORT
Historic Neighbourhood

Ships have been docking for more than 26 centuries at Marseille's colourful Vieux Port.

Guarding the harbour are **Bas Fort St-Nicolas** on the southern side and, across the water, **Fort St-Jean**, founded in the 13th century by the Knights Hospitaller of St John of Jerusalem.

Standing guard between the old and the 'new' port is the striking Byzantine **Cathédrale de la Major**. Its 'stripy' facade is made of local Cassis stone and green Florentine marble.

On the Vieux Port's southern side, late-night restaurants and cafés pack **place Thiars** and **cours Honoré d'Estienne d'Orves** pedestrian zone. See p308 for more information.

LE PANIER · Historic Neighbourhood

North of the Vieux Port is Marseille's old city, Le Panier quarter (2e). Its name translates to 'the basket', and it was the site of a Greek *agora* (marketplace). Today its winding, narrow streets are a jumble of artisans shops and washing lines strung outside candy-coloured houses.

CHÂTEAU D'IF · Island Château

(http://if.monuments-nationaux.fr/en/; adult/child €5/free; ☺9.30am-6.30pm, closed Mon winter) Immortalised in Alexandre Dumas' classic 1840s novel *Le Comte de Monte Cristo* (The Count of Monte Cristo), the 16th-century fortress-turned-prison Château d'If sits on a 3-hectare island 3.5km west of the Vieux Port.

Frioul If Express (☎04 91 46 54 65; www.frioul-if-express.com; 1 quai des Belges, 1er; 20-min return trip €10) boats leave for Château d'If from the Vieux Port at the corner of quai de la Fraternité and quai de Rive Neuve. There are more than 15 daily departures in summer, fewer in winter.

BASILIQUE NOTRE DAME DE LA GARDE · Church

(Montée de la Bonne Mère; ☺basilica & crypt 7am-7pm, longer in summer) The opulent, domed 19th-century Romano-Byzantine basilica occupies Marseille's highest point, lording it over the city skyline. Built between 1853 and 1864, it's ornamented with col-oured marble, murals depicting the safe passage of sailing vessels and intricate gold-laid mosaics, which were superbly restored in 2006.

By foot, allow 30 minutes (expect steep hills) each way from the Vieux Port.

 Tours

LE GRAND TOUR · Bus Tour

(☎04 91 91 05 82; www.marseillelegrandtour.com; adult/child €18/8; ☺10am-7pm) This hop-on,

hop-off, open-topped double-decker bus travels between the main sights, starting at Vieux Port and including the corniche and Basilique Notre Dame de la Garde.

Guided Tour · Walking Tour

(per person €6.50; ☺tours 10am Sat Jul & Aug, 2pm every other Sat Sep-Jun) From the tourist office.

Croisières Marseille Calanques · Boat Tour

(☎08 25 13 68 00; www.croisieres-marseille-calanques.com, in French; 74 quai du Port, 2e) Boat trips (narrated in French) from the Vieux Port to Cassis (€25), passing the Calanques.

 Sleeping

CASA HONORÉ · Boutique B&B €€€

(☎04 96 11 01 62, 06 09 50 38 52; www.casahonore.com; 123 rue Sainte, 7e; d €150-200; ❄☎☎M Vieux Port) Los Angeles meets Marseille at this four-room *maison d'hôte* built around a central courtyard with a lap pool shaded by banana trees. One complaint: bathrooms are partitioned by curtains, not doors.

HÔTEL RÉSIDENCE DU VIEUX PORT · View Hotel €€€

(☎04 91 91 91 22; www.hotelmarseille.com; 18 quai du Port, 2e; d €180-200, apt €260; ❄@☎M Vieux Port) Marseille's top view hotel got a makeover in 2010 in vaguely Jetsons-meets-Mondrian style, with swoop-backed furniture and bold pri-mary colours. Every room looks sharp, and has a balcony with knockout views of the old port and Notre Dame.

LE PETIT NICE-PASSÉDAT · Luxury Inn €€€

(☎04 91 59 25 92; www.passedat.fr; Anse de Maldormé, 7e; d from €370; ❄@☎☎) Marseille's very best small luxury hotel is home to virtuosic **Gerald Passédat** (menus €85-250; ☺Tue-Sat), Marseille's only three-Michelin-star restaurant.

HÔTEL SAINT-FERRÉOL · Small Hotel €€

(☎04 91 33 12 21; www.hotelsaintferreol.com; 19 rue Pisançon, 1er; d €99-120; ❄@☎M Vieux

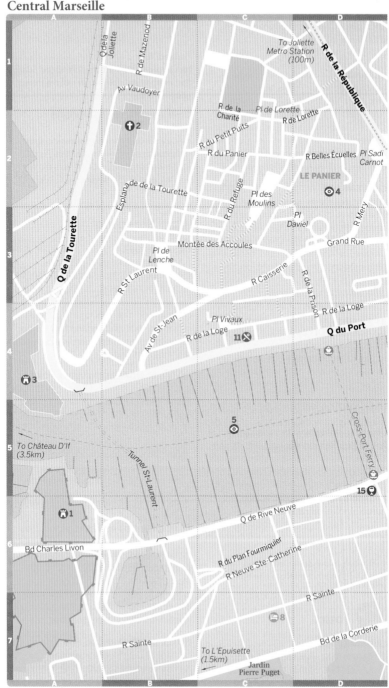

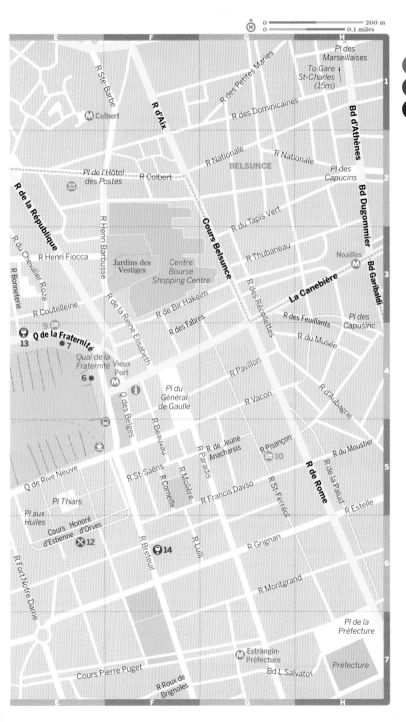

Central Marseille

Port) On the corner of the city's prettiest pedestrianised street, this plush hotel has individually decorated rooms, many inspired by artists like Van Gogh and Cézanne, with thick carpeting and spotless bathrooms. Exceptional service.

Eating

PÉRON Contemporary €€€

(☏ 04 91 52 15 22; www.restaurant-peron.com, in French; 56 corniche Président John F Kennedy, 7e; mains €35; ☉ lunch Tue-Sun, dinner Tue-Sat) Perched on the edge of the corniche, with magnificent views of the Château d'If, Péron is one of Marseille's top tables. The seafood-heavy menu (think marinated tuna, scallops with lemon polenta) is phenomenal; book before dark to watch the sunset.

CHEZ MADIE LES GALINETTES

Provençal €€

(☏ 04 91 90 40 87; 138 quai du Port, 2e; menus €25-35; ☉ Mon-Sat, closed Sat lunch in summer; 🚼 Ⓜ Vieux Port) The portside terrace is

perfect on long summer evenings, but if the weather isn't cooperating, the interior's modern art brings consolation. The Provençal-rooted menu features lots of fish and good bouillabaisse, which you'll need to order 48 hours ahead.

LA CANTINE French-Corsican €€

(☏ 04 91 33 37 09; 27 cours Honoré d'Estienne d'Orves, 1er; mains €15-18; ☉ Mon-Sat, dinner Sun; Ⓜ Vieux Port) Down-tempo beats, low lighting and wood-beamed ceilings set a sexy backdrop for Corsican specialities, including *figatelli* (coarse-ground robustly seasoned sausage), and earthy French dishes such as sautéed veal liver *en persillade* (parsley, garlic and herbs) and grilled fish. Reservations advised.

CHEZ JEANNOT Marseillais €€

(☏ 04 91 52 11 28; 129 rue du Vallon des Auffes; mains €12-25; ☉ Tue-Sat, lunch Sun) An institution among Marseillais, the jovial rooftop terrace overlooking the port of Vallon des Auffes books days ahead (but you can usually score an inside table).

Drinking

Cafés and bars surround the Vieux Port. Students and artists congregate near cours Julien and its surrounding streets. Sundays are dead.

LA CARAVELLE Café, Bar

(34 quai du Port, 2e; ☉ 7am-2am; Ⓜ Vieux Port) Look up or miss this standout, upstairs hideaway, styled with rich wood and leather, zinc bar and yellowing vintage murals.

La Part des Anges Wine Bar

(33 rue Sainte; mains €15, ☉ Mon-Sat, dinner Sun) The wine list at this happening wine bar and restaurant is an oenologist's dream.

Le Bar de la Marine Bar

(15 quai de Rive Neuve, 7e; ☉ 7am-1am; Ⓜ Vieux Port) Marcel Pagnol filmed the card-party scenes in *Marius* at this Marseille institution, which draws folks from every walk of life.

Shopping

Prado Market Market
(⊙8am-1pm; Ⓜ Castellane or Périer) This daily
market stretches from the Castellane metro
station along av du Prado to the Périer metro
station, with a staggering array of clothes, fruit
and speciality items. There's a flower market on
Friday morning.

Markets Markets
(cours Julien; ⊙8am-7pm; Ⓜ Notre Dame du
Mont-Cours Julien) Wednesday-morning organic
fruit and vegetable market and an Aladdin's
cave bric-a-brac market every second Sunday
of the month.

Information

Dangers & Annoyances

Marseille isn't a hotbed of violent crime, but petty
crimes and muggings are commonplace. Play it
cool. Don't get visibly drunk and stumble home
alone at 4am – you may as well wear a target.

Tourist office (☎ 04 91 13 89 00; www.
marseille-tourisme.com; 4 La Canebière, 1er;
⊙9am-7pm Mon-Sat, 10am-5pm Sun; Ⓜ Vieux
Port)

Basilique Notre Dame de la Garde (p303)

Getting There & Away

Air

Aéroport Marseille-Provence (MRS; ☎ 04 42
14 14 14; www.marseille.aeroport.fr) Twenty-five
kilometres northwest of town in Marignane.

Boat

The passenger-ferry terminal (www.marseille
-port.fr; Ⓜ ⛴ Joliette) is 250m south of place de
la Joliette (1er).

Train

Gare St-Charles (⊙information 9am-8pm Mon-
Sat, tickets 5.15am-10pm) is served by both metro
lines.

From Marseille trains, including TGVs, go all
over France and Europe.

Avignon €23, 35 minutes, 27 daily

Lyon €47, 1¾ hours, 16 daily

Nice €30, 2½ hours, 21 daily

Paris Gare de Lyon €84, three hours, 21 daily

Getting Around

Marseille has two metro lines (Métro 1 and
Métro 2), two tram lines (yellow and green) and

Vieux Port

An Itinerary

Bold and busy and open-armed to the sea, Marseille is France's oldest city. Standing on the quai des Belges it's hard to get a sense of the extent of the old port, a kilometre long on either side, running down to the great bastions of St-Jean and St-Nicolas, which once had their guns trained on the rebellious population rather than out to sea. Immerse yourself in the city's history with this full-day itinerary.

Go early to experience the fish market **1**, where you'll swap tall tales with the gregarious vendors. Hungry? Grab a balcony seat at La Caravelle, where views of the Basilique Notre Dame de la Garde accompany your morning coffee. Afterwards, take a boat trip **2** to Château d'If, made famous by the Dumas novel, *The Count of Monte Cristo*. Alternatively, stay landside and explore the apricot-coloured alleys of Le Panier **3**, browsing the exhibits at the Centre de la Vieille Charité **4**.

In the afternoon, hop on the free cross-port ferry to the port's south side and wander into the Abbaye St-Victor **5** to see the bones of martyrs enshrined in gold. You can then catch the sunset from the stone benches in the Jardin du Pharo **6**. As the warm southern evening sets in, join the throngs on cours Honoré d'Estienne d'Orves, where you can drink pastis beneath a giant statue of a lion devouring a man – the *Milo de Croton* **7**.

CAPITAL OF CULTURE 2013

The largest urban renewal project in Europe, the Euroméditerranée project aims to rehabilitate the commercial Joliette docks along the same lines as London's Docklands. The city's green-and-white striped Cathédrale de la Major, for years abandoned in an area of urban wasteland, will form its centrepiece.

GLENN BEANLAND

Le Panier
The site of the Greek town of Massilia, Le Panier woos walkers with its sloping streets. Grand Rue follows the ancient road and opens out into place de Lenche, the location of the Greek market. It is still the place to shop for artisan products.

Cathédrale de la Major

Fort St-Jean

Centre de la Vieille Charité
Before the 18th century, beggar hunters rounded up the poor for imprisonment. The Vieille Charité almshouse, which opened in 1749, improved their lot by acting as a workhouse. It's now an exhibition space and only the barred windows recall its original use.

Jardin & Palais du Pharo

Jardin du Pharo
Built by Napoléon for the Empress Eugénie, the Pharo Palace was designed with its 'feet in the water'. Today it is a private centre, but the gardens with their magnificent view are open all day.

Fish Market
Marseille's small fish market still sets up each morning to hawk the daily catch. Take a lesson in local seafood, spotting sea squirts, scorpion fish, sea urchins and conger eels. Get there before 9am if you're buying.

Milo de Croton
Subversive local artist Pierre Puget carved the savage *Milo de Croton* for Louis XIV. The statue, whose original is in the Louvre, is a meditation on man's pride and shows the Greek Olympian being devoured by a lion, his Olympic cup cast down.

Frioul If Express
Catch the Frioul If Express to Château d'If, France's equivalent to Alcatraz. Prisoners were housed according to class: the poorest at the bottom in windowless dungeons, the wealthiest in paid-for private cells, with windows and a fireplace.

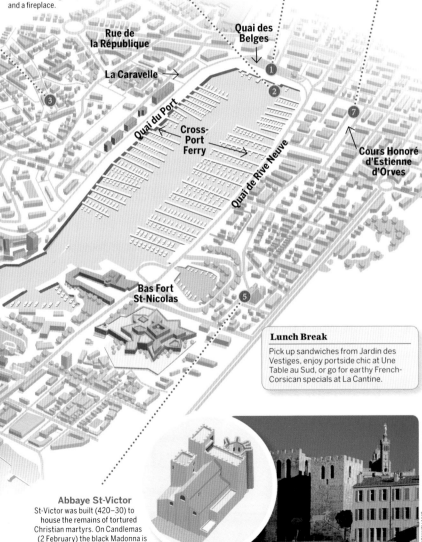

Rue de la République

Quai des Belges

La Caravelle →

Quai du Port

3

Cross-Port Ferry →

Quai de Rive Neuve

← Quai du Port

1

2

7

Cours Honoré d'Estienne d'Orves

Bas Fort St-Nicolas

5

Lunch Break
Pick up sandwiches from Jardin des Vestiges, enjoy portside chic at Une Table au Sud, or go for earthy French-Corsican specials at La Cantine.

Abbaye St-Victor
St-Victor was built (420–30) to house the remains of tortured Christian martyrs. On Candlemas (2 February) the black Madonna is brought up from the crypt and the archbishop blesses the city and the sea.

TOR EIGELAND/ALAMY

DAN HERRICK

Bouillabaisse

Originally cooked by fishermen from the scraps of their catch, bouillabaisse is Marseille's classic signature dish. True bouillabaisse includes at least four different kinds of fish, sometimes shellfish, which is why it's served to a minimum of two people. The real McCoy costs about €55 per person and should be reserved 48 hours ahead.

Le Rhul (☎ 04 91 52 01 77; www.lerhul.fr, in French; 269 corniche John F. Kennedy; €50) This long-standing classic has atmosphere (however kitschy): a 1940s seaside hotel with Mediterranean views.

L'Epuisette (☎ 04 91 52 17 82; www.l-epuisette.com; Vallon des Auffes; €55; ☻Tue-Sat) The swankest (by far) has a Michelin star and knockout water-level views from an elegantly austere dining room.

Restaurant Michel (Chez Michel; ☎ 04 91 52 30 63; http://restaurant-michel-13.fr, in French; 6 rue des Catalans; €60; ☻dinner) Tops since 1946.

an extensive bus network run by the Régie des Transports Marseillais (RTM).

Bus, metro or tram tickets (€1.50) can be used on all public transportation for one hour after they've been time-stamped.

Aix-en-Provence
POP 146,700

It's hard to believe Aix (pronounced ex) is just 25km from chaotic, exotic Marseille, and it's no surprise the two remain perennially at odds. Aix is rich in culture (two of its most famous sons are painter Paul Cézanne and novelist Émile Zola) and oh-so respectable, with plane-tree-shaded boulevards and fancy-pants boutiques.

◉ Sights & Activities

Brilliant savings come in the form of the **Aix City Pass**, which costs €15, lasts five days and includes admission to Atelier Paul Cézanne, Bastide du Jas de Bouffan and Musée Granet, as well as a trip on the minitram and one of the tourist office's guided walks.

MUSÉE GRANET Art Museum
(www.museegranet-aixenprovence.fr, in French; place St-Jean de Malte; adult/child €4/free;

☻11am-7pm Tue-Sun) Housed in a 17th-century Knights of Malta priory, this museum's pride and joy are its nine Cézanne paintings. The unique De Cézanne à Giacometti collection features works by Picasso, Léger, Matisse, Tal Coat and Giacometti, among others.

CATHÉDRALE ST-SAUVEUR Cathedral
(rue Laroque; ☻8am-noon & 2-6pm) Built between 1285 and 1350 in a potpourri of styles, the cathedral includes a Romanesque 12th-century nave in its southern aisle, chapels from the 14th and 15th centuries and a 5th-century sarcophagus in the apse. The acoustics make Gregorian chants (4.30pm Sunday) unforgettable.

CÉZANNE SIGHTS Art Appreciation
His star may have reached its greatest heights after his death, but the life of local lad Paul Cézanne (1839–1906) is treasured in Aix. To see where he ate, drank, studied and painted, follow the **Circuit de Cézanne** (Cézanne Trail), marked by footpath-embedded bronze plaques inscribed with the letter C. An informative English-language guide to the plaques is available free from the tourist office.

Though none of his works hang here, Cézanne's last studio, **Atelier Paul**

Cézanne (www.atelier-cezanne.com; 9 av Paul Cézanne; adult/student €5.50/2; ⊙10am-noon & 2-6pm, closed Sun winter), on a hilltop 1.5km north of the tourist office, is a must for any Cézanne fan. It's painstakingly preserved as it was at the time of his death, strewn with his tools and still-life models; his admirers claim this is where Cézanne is most present. Take bus 1 or 20 to the Atelier Cézanne stop, or walk (20 minutes) from the centre.

The other two main Cézanne sights in Aix are the **Bastide du Jas de Bouffan** (on the western fringes of the city), the former family home where Cézanne started painting as a young man, and the **Bibémus quarries**, where he did most of his Montagne Ste-Victoire paintings.

Tours

The tourist office has DIY **walking itineraries** and runs a packed schedule of **guided walking** (€8) and **bus tours** (from €28) in English, such as Retracing Cézanne's Steps.

🛏 Sleeping

HÔTEL CARDINAL   Small Hotel   €
(☎04 42 38 32 30; www.hotel-cardinal-aix.com; 24 rue Cardinale; s/d/ste €60/70/110) Beneath stratospheric ceilings, Hôtel Cardinal's 29 romantic rooms are beautifully furnished with antiques and tasselled curtains, and have recently tiled bathrooms.

HÔTEL CÉZANNE   Boutique Hotel   €€€
(☎04 42 91 11 11; http://cezanne.hotelaix.com; 40 av Victor Hugo; d €179-249; ❄ @ 🛜) Aix's hippest hotel is a study in clean

lines, with sharp-edged built-in desks and love seats that feel a touch Ikea. Best is breakfast (€19), which includes smoked salmon and Champagne. Free parking.

HÔTEL SAINT-CHRISTOPHE
Full-Service Hotel   €€
(☎04 42 26 01 24; www.hotel-saintchristophe.com; 2 av Victor Hugo; s €82-108, d €89-117, ste €128-152; ❄ 🛜 ♿) The Saint-Christophe is a proper hotel, with a big lobby and helpful staff. Rooms nod to art deco in their styling and have the standard midbudget amenities, including good bathrooms; some have terraces, some can sleep four. Parking (€12) by reservation.

Eating

LE POIVRE D'ANE   Contemporary €€
(☎04 42 21 32 66; www.restaurantlepoivredane.com; 40 place des Cardeurs; menus €28-45; ⊙dinner Thu-Tue) Poivre d'Ane isn't afraid to break ranks with culinary norms; fancy a haddock milkshake, duck sushi,

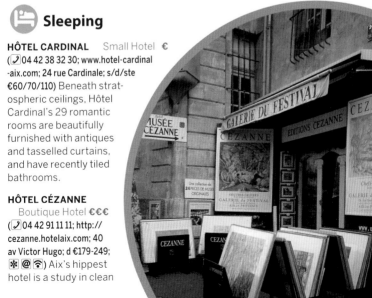

Cézanne gallery
PHOTOGRAPHER: CHRIS MELLOR

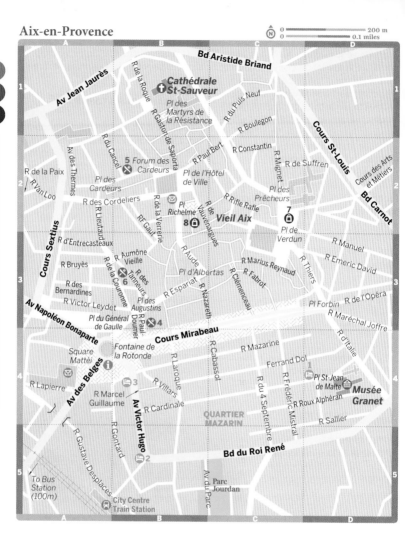

Aix-en-Provence

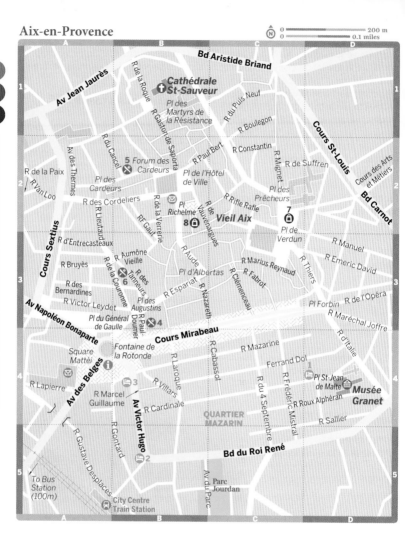

or thyme-and-cinnamon apple tart with Baileys whipped cream? Reservations essential.

AMPHITRYON   Provençal French €€
(📞04 42 26 54 10; www.restaurant-amphitryon.fr; 2-4 rue Paul Doumer; lunch menus €25, dinner menus €30-40; 🕑Tue-Sat) Run by fiery duo maître d' Patrice Lesné and chef Bruno Ungaro, Amphitryon enjoys a solid reputation among Aix's bourgeoisie, particularly in summer, for its market-driven cooking and alfresco dining

in the cloister-garden. The attached **Comptoir de l'Amphi** (mains €12-17) is a less-expensive alternative.

LA TOMATE VERTE
                Contemporary Provençal €€
(📞04 42 60 04 58; www.latomateverte.com, in French; 15 rue des Tanneurs; lunch/dinner menus €19/29; 🕑Tue-Sat) The house speciality at this apple-green bistro is green-tomato tart, a tangy, delicious lead to the Provençal comfort food, simple as roast lamb with rosemary and garlic.

DISCOVER PROVENCE & THE FRENCH RIVIERA **PROVENCE**

312

Shopping

Produce Market   Market
(place Richelme) Each morning, tables display olives, lavender, honey, melons and other sun-kissed products.

Food Market   Food Market
(place des Prêcheurs) Tuesday, Thursday and Saturday mornings.

Information

Tourist office (www.aixenprovencetourism.com; 2 place du Général de Gaulle; ◎8.30am-7pm Mon-Sat, 10am-1pm & 2-6pm Sun) Longer hours in summer.

Getting Around

Aix's bus station is linked to both the TGV station (15km outside town; €3.70) and the airport (€8) from 4.40am to 10.30pm by half-hourly Navette shuttles.

Arles
POP 52,400

Arles' poster boy is the celebrated Impressionist painter Vincent van Gogh. If you're familiar with his work, you'll be familiar with Arles: the light, the colours, the landmarks, the atmosphere, all faithfully captured.

After Caesar plundered Marseille, which had supported his rival Pompey the Great, Arles eclipsed Marseille as the region's major port. Within a century and a half, it boasted a 12,000-seat theatre and a 20,000-seat amphitheatre to entertain its citizens with gruesome gladiatorial spectacles and chariot races.

 Sights & Activities

If you're keen to dig into Arles' Roman past, the 'Circuit Romain' combined ticket (€9/7 per adult/child) gives access to Les Arènes, the Théâtre Antique and other Roman sites. The Pass Monument (€13.50/12) accesses all of Arles' museums and sites.

LES ARÈNES   Roman Amphitheatre
(adult/student, incl Théâtre Antique €6/4.50; ◎9am-7pm) Arles' remarkable Roman amphitheatre was built around the late 1st or early 2nd century.

Amphitheatre admission is also good for the **Thermes de Constantin** (rue du Grand Prieuré; without amphitheatre adult/student €3/2.20; ◎9am-noon & 2-7pm), partly preserved Roman baths near the river, built for Emperor Constantin's private use in the 4th century; and for the **Cryptoporticus du Forum** (entrance via Hôtel de Ville, place de la République; without amphitheatre adult/student €3.50/2.60; ◎9am-noon & 2-7pm May-Sep) 1st-century BC storerooms.

THÉÂTRE ANTIQUE   Roman Theatre
(enter on rue de la Calade; adult/student €3.50/2.60; ◎9am-7pm) Still regularly used for projections and plays, the Théâtre Antique dates from the end of the 1st century BC.

VAN GOGH SIGHTS
Although Van Gogh painted around 200 canvases in Arles, not a single one remains here today. Fitting tributes to Van Gogh's art include **Fondation Vincent Van Gogh** (24bis Rond Point des Arènes; adult/student €6/4; ◎10am-7pm), where important

JEAN-BERNARD CARILLET

Don't Miss **The Camargue**

Just south of Arles, Provence's rolling landscapes yield to the flat, marshy wilds of the Camargue, famous for its teeming birdlife (roughly 500 species). King of all is the pink flamingo, which enjoys the expansive wetlands' mild winters. Equally famous are the Camargue's small white horses; their mellow disposition makes horse riding the ideal way to explore the region's patchwork of salt pans, rice fields and meadows dotted with grazing bulls. Bring binoculars and mosquito repellent.

The Camargue's two largest towns are the seaside pilgrim's outpost **Les Stes-Maries-de-la-Mer** and, to the northwest, the walled town of **Aigues Mortes**.

Inside an 1812-built sheep shed, the **Musée Camarguais** gives a fantastic introduction to this unique area, covering history and ecosystems as well as the traditional lifestyle of the *gardian,* Camargue's cowboys. A 3.5km nature trail leads to an observation tower with bird's-eye views. Find it 10km southwest of Arles on the D570 to Les Stes-Maries-de-la-Mer.

Get up close and personal with some 2000 pink flamingos at **Le Parc Ornithologique du Pont de Gau**, a wonderful semiwild nature reserve 4km north of Les Stes-Maries on the D570.

Two buses leave Les Stes-Maries for Montpellier (€10.50, two hours) via Aigues Mortes daily in July and August.

NEED TO KNOW

Musée Camarguais (☎ 04 90 97 10 82; Mas du Pont de Rousty; adult/child €4.50/free; ☺ 9am-6pm Wed-Mon); Le Parc Ornithologique du Pont de Gau (☎ 04 90 97 82 62; adult/child €7/4; ☺ 9am-sunset); Réserve Nationale de Camargue Office (☎ 04 90 97 00 97; www.reserve-camargue.org; La Capelière; ☺ 9am-6pm, closed Tue Oct-Mar)

modern-day artists, including David Hockney, Francis Bacon and Fernando Botero, pay homage to the artist's distinctive style.

The best way to get a sense of Van Gogh's time in Arles is to take the excellent **Van Gogh Trail**, a walking circuit of the city marked by footpath-embedded plaques.

MUSÉE RÉATTU Museum, Gallery

(10 rue du Grand Prieuré; adult/child €7/5; ⏰10am-12.30pm & 2-6.30pm Tue-Sun) Housed in a former 15th-century priory, this splendid museum has two Picasso paintings and 57 sketches from the early 1970s. It also contains works by 18th- and 19th-century Provençal artists, but it's best known for its cutting-edge photographic displays.

 Tours

From July to September the tourist office runs guided tours (€6), with the Vieil Arles tour in English on Saturdays at 5pm, and the Van Gogh tour on Tuesdays at 5pm.

 **Sleeping**

L'HÔTEL PARTICULIER
Boutique Hotel €€€

(✆04 90 52 51 40; www.hotel-particulier.com; 4 rue de la Monnaie; d €239-259; ❄@ 📶 ⛱) A hidden spot, this exclusive boutique hotel with restaurant, spa and *hammam* oozes chic charm. From the big black door with heavy knocker to the crisp white linens and minimalist decor, everything about this 18th-century private mansion enchants.

HÔTEL DE L'AMPHITHÉÂTRE
Historic Hotel €€

(✆04 90 96 10 30; www.hotelamphitheatre.fr; 5-7 rue Diderot; d €55-95; ❄@ 📶) Crimson, chocolate, terracotta and other rich earthy colours dress the 17th-century stone of this stylish hotel, which steals hearts with its narrow staircases, roaring fire and alfresco courtyard breakfasts.

LE BÉLVEDÈRE HÔTEL
Boutique Hotel €€

(✆04 90 91 45 94; www.hotellebelvedere-arles. fr; 5 place Voltaire; d €70-90; ❄ 📶) This sleek 17-room hotel is one of the best Arlésian

Le Pont de Langlois aux Lavandieres (also known as Van Gogh's Bridge), Arles

ANDREW BAIN

pads. A red-glass chandelier adorns the lobby-lounge and the rooms are fitted out in stylish red, chocolate brown, grey and beige colour schemes.

Eating

L'ATELIER — Gastronomic €€€
(☎ 04 90 91 07 69; www.rabanel.com; 7 rue des Carmes; lunch/dinner menus from €45/85; ☷Wed-Sun) Opt for a series of seven or 13 edible works of art, then sit back and revel in Jean-Luc Rabanel's superbly crafted symphony of fresh organic tastes. No wonder this green-fingered urban chef with his own veggie patch has two Michelin stars.

LE CILANTRO — Provençal €€
(☎ 04 90 18 25 05; www.restaurantcilantro. com, in French; 31 rue Porte de Laure; mains €35; ☷Tue-Fri, dinner Sat) Chef Jêrome Laurant, a born-and-bred local lad, runs this hot spot and combines local ingredients with world spices to create accomplished dishes such as lamb in almond oil.

LA MULE BLANCHE — Bistro €€
(☎ 04 90 93 98 54; www.restaurant-mule-blanche. com, in French; 8 rue du Président Wilson; mains €12-20; ☷Wed-Sun, lunch Tue, closed Sun winter) Jazz piano tinkles in the White Mule's domed interior, but the hottest tables at this soulful bistro are aboard the pavement terrace, easily the town's prettiest, with its violet awning, Saturday-morning market view and lazy mood.

ℹ Information

Tourist office main office (☎ 04 90 18 41 20; www.tourisme.ville-arles.fr; esplanade Charles de Gaulle; ☷9am-6.45pm Apr-Sep, 9am-4.45pm Mon-Sat & 10am-12.45pm Sun Oct-Mar); train station (☎ 04 90 43 33 57; ☷9am-1.30pm & 2.30-4.45pm Mon-Fri Apr-Sep)

ℹ Getting There & Away

AIR Nîmes Airport (p323), 20km northwest of Arles, via the A54. No public transport between the airport and Arles.
TRAIN Trains go to the following:
Avignon €7, 20 minutes
Marseille €13, 55 minutes
Nîmes €7.50, 30 minutes

Avignon
POP 93,600

Ringed by 4.3km of superbly preserved stone ramparts, this graceful city is the belle of Provence's ball. Its turn as the papal seat of power has bestowed Avignon with a treasury of magnificent art and architecture, none grander than the massive medieval fortress and papal palace, the Palais des Papes. Avignon is also known for its fabled bridge, the Pont St-Bénézet, aka the Pont d'Avignon.

Le Verdon River
PHOTOGRAPHER: BILL BACHMANN

Sights

Wrapping around the city, Avignon's **ramparts**, built between 1359 and 1370, were restored during the 19th century, minus their original moats. One of the city's chief joys is to wander aimlessly, peeking into its hidden corners.

PALAIS DES PAPES Historic Palace
(Palace of the Popes; ☎ 04 90 27 50 00; www.palais-des-papes.com; place du Palais; adult/child incl audioguide €6/3; ☉9am-7pm)
This Unesco World Heritage Site, the world's largest Gothic palace, was built when Pope Clement V abandoned Rome in 1309 and settled in Avignon. The immense scale of the palace, with its cavernous stone halls and vast courtyards, testifies to the wealth of the popes; the 3m-thick walls, portcullises and watchtowers emphasise their need for defence.

PONT ST-BÉNÉZET
Landmark Bridge
(Pont d'Avignon; adult/child €4.50/3.50; ☉9am-8pm, 9.30am-5.45pm Nov-Mar)
According to legend, pastor Bénézet had three saintly visions urging him to build a bridge across the Rhône. Known to countless kids as the **Pont d'Avignon** from the chirpy French rhyme, it was completed in 1185 and linked Avignon with Villeneuve-lès-Avignon, controlling trade at this vital crossroads. It was rebuilt several times before all but four of its spans were washed away in the mid-1600s.

MUSÉE ANGLADON Art Museum
(☎ 04 90 82 29 03; www.angladon.com; 5 rue Laboureur; adult/child €6/4; ☉1-6pm Tue-Sun Apr-Nov, 1-6pm Wed-Sun Jan-Mar) Born out of the private collection of couturier Jacques Doucet (1853–1929), this charming museum harbours Impressionist treasures, including the only Van Gogh painting in Provence (Railway Wagons), and works by Cézanne, Manet, Degas and Picasso.

♥ If You Like… Wild Nature

It's hard not to be bewitched by the unspoiled beauty of the Camargue, but the south of France has plenty more wild corners to explore.

1 GORGES DU VERDON
Twenty-five kilometres long and between 250m to 700m deep, these plunging gorges form the largest canyon in Europe, and provide fantastic walking and canoeing. The two main bases for exploring are Moustiers Ste-Marie (☎ tourist office 04 92 74 67 84; www.moustiers.fr) and Castellane (www.castellane.org).

2 PARC NATIONAL DU MERCANTOUR
(www.mercantour.eu) Spread across six valleys, this isolated park is one of the last bastions of true wilderness in Provence. The valley's only town is Barcelonnette; public transport is pretty much non-existent.

3 MONT VENTOUX
Visible from miles around, Mont Ventoux (1909m) is nicknamed le géant de Provence (Provence's giant). From its summit, accessible by road between May and October, vistas extend to the Alps and, on a clear day, the Camargue. You can reach the mountain by car from Sault via the D164, or (summer only) from Malaucène or St-Estève via the D974.

4 THE CALANQUES
(www.gipcalanques.fr) These rocky promontories stretch for 20km around Marseille, and afford gorgeous views along the Mediterranean coastline. Scheduled to become France's newest national park in June 2011, the Calanques are criss-crossed by walking trails, although they are often closed from July to September due to fire risk. Marseille's tourist office (p307) leads guided walks.

Tours

The tourist office has an English map with four **walking tours** around the old town.

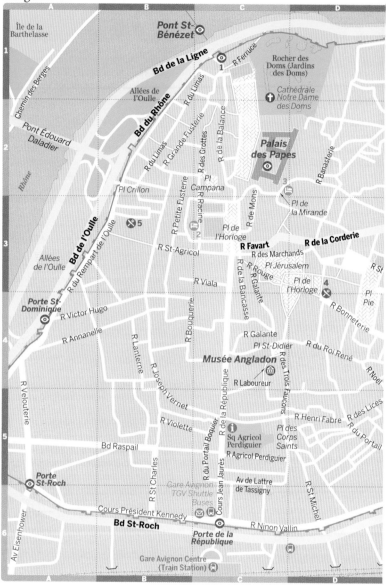

Île de la Barthelasse

Chemin des Berges

Pont Édouard Daladier

Rhône

Bd de la Ligne

Allées de l'Oulle

Bd du Rhône

R du Limas

R du Limas

R Grande Fusterie

R des Grottes

Pl Crillon

R Petite Fusterie

Pl Campana

R Racine

Pl de l'Horloge

Bd de l'Oulle

Allées de l'Oulle

R du Rempart de l'Oulle

Pont St-Bénézet

R Ferruce

Rocher des Doms (Jardins des Doms)

Cathédrale Notre Dame des Doms

R de la Balance

Palais des Papes

R Banasterie

Pl de la Mirande

R de Mons

R Favart

R des Marchands

R de la Corderie

Pl Jérusalem

R Rouge

R Galante

Pl de l'Horloge

Pl Pie

R Bonneterie

R St-Agricol

R Viala

R de la Balancasse

R Bouquerie

R Galante

Pl St-Didier

R du Roi René

R Noel

R des Lices

Porte St-Dominique

R Victor Hugo

R Annanelie

R Lanterne

R Joseph Vernet

Musée Angladon

R Laboureur

R des Trois Faucons

R Henri Fabre

R St

R Velouterie

R Violette

R du Portail Boquier

R de la République

Sq Agricol Perdiguier

Pl des Corps Saints

R du Portail

Porte St-Roch

Bd Raspail

R St-Charles

R Agricol Perdiguier

Gare Avignon TGV Shuttle Buses

Av de Lattre de Tassigny

R St-Michel

Av Eisenhower

Cours Président Kennedy

Bd St-Roch

Cours Jean Jaurès

Porte de la République

R Ninon Vallin

Gare Avignon Centre (Train Station)

Guided Tours Walking Tours
(adult/child €17/7; ⊙ 10am daily, Sat only Nov-Mar) Two-hour tours of Avignon in English and French depart from the tourist office.

Festivals & Events

Festival d'Avignon Performing Arts
(☎ Bureau du Festival 04 90 27 66 50; www.festival-avignon.com; Espace St-Louis, 20 rue

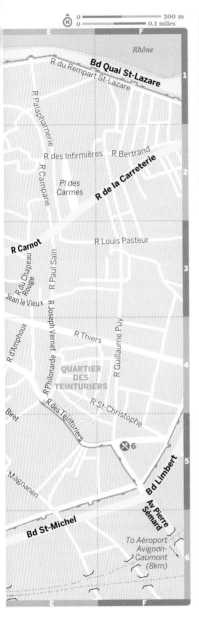

Sleeping

HÔTEL LA MIRANDE Luxury Hotel €€€
(☎ 04 90 14 20 20; www.la-mirande.fr; 4 place de
la Mirande; d €390-540; ❄ @ 🛜) Avignon's
top hotel (by far) occupies a converted
16th-century cardinal's palace with
dramatic high-ceilinged spaces decked
out in oriental rugs, gold-threaded tapestries, marble staircases and dizzying
over-the-top Gallic style.

HÔTEL DE L'HORLOGE Hotel €€
(☎ 04 90 16 42 00; www.hotels-ocre-azur.com;
place de l'Horloge; r €95-180; ❄ 🛜) Most
rooms at this supercentral hotel are
straightforward (comfortable, all mod
cons), but the five terrace rooms have
the edge, with sophisticated furnishings
and views: ask for 505 with its incredible
view of the Palais des Papes.

Eating

CUISINE DU DIMANCHE
Provincial French €€
(☎ 04 90 82 99 10; www.lacuisinedudimanche.
com, in French; 31 rue Bonneterie; mains €15-
25; ⏱ closed Sun & Mon Oct-May) Spitfire
chef Marie shops every morning at Les
Halles to find the freshest ingredients
for her earthy, flavour-packed cooking,
and takes no culinary short cuts. Make
reservations.

du Portail Boquier; tickets €16-50) Hundreds of
artists take to the stage and streets during this
world-famous performing arts festival, founded
in 1946 and held every year from early July to
early August.

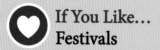

If You Like...
Festivals

If you've a penchant for the frolics of Nice Carnival and Festival d'Avignon, you'll have a ball at these festivals:

1 FÊTE DU CITRON
(www.feteducitron.com; Menton) Every February, the sunkissed town of Menton celebrates with this lemon-themed extravaganza. Lemon-adorned floats weave processions along the seafront and gargantuan wire-framed sculptures bearing zillions of lemons speckle the town.

2 COURSES CAMARGUAISES
(www.arenes-arles.com; Arles) Camargue bullfights (courses Camarguaises) do not end with a dead bull. Rather, amateur razeteurs remove rosettes and ribbons tied to the bull's horns using a hooked comb clasped between their fingers. Arles' bullfighting season begins at Easter with the Féria Pascale and charges through to September's rice harvest festival.

3 LES CHORÉGIES D'ORANGE
(www.choregies.asso.fr; Orange) Balmy summer nights in July and August usher in a series of operas, classical concerts and choral performances at Orange's Roman amphitheatre.

4 FÉRIA DE PENTECÔTE
(www.arenesdenimes.com; Nîmes) Nîmes becomes more Spanish than French during this five-day féria (bullfighting festival) in June; the three-day Féria des Vendanges celebrates the grape harvest in the third weekend in September.

LES 5 SENS Gastronomic €€
(☏04 90 85 26 51; www.restaurantles5sens.com; 18 rue Joseph Vernet; lunch menus €20, lunch mains €13-17, dinner mains €22-30; ⏰Tue-Sat) Chef Thierry Baucher, one of France's meilleurs ouvriers (top chefs), reveals his southwestern origins in specialities including cassoulet and foie gras, but goes contemporary-Mediterranean in his gastronomic dishes, such as butternut-squash ravioli with escargots.

NUMÉRO 75 Contemporary French €€
(☏04 90 27 16 00; 75 rue Guillaume Puy; menus €26-32; ⏰Mon-Sat) The stately dining room of absinthe inventor Jules Pernod's former mansion is a fitting backdrop for stylised Mediterranean cooking. On balmy nights, book outside in the lush courtyard garden.

ⓘ Information

Tourist office (www.avignon-tourisme.com; 41 cours Jean Jaurès; ⏰9am-5pm Mon-Sat, 9.45am-5pm Sun)

ⓘ Getting There & Away

Avignon has two train stations: Gare Avignon TGV, 4km southwest in Courtine; and central Gare Avignon Centre (42 bd St-Roch) with service to/from:

Arles €6.50, 20 minutes

Nîmes €8.50, 30 minutes

Orange €5.50, 20 minutes

Some TGVs to/from Paris stop at Gare Avignon Centre, but TGVs for Marseille (€23, 35 minutes) and Nice (€54, three hours) only use Gare Avignon TGV.

Les Baux de Provence
POP 380

At the heart of the Alpilles and spectacularly perched above picture-perfect rolling hills carpeted with vine-yards, olive groves and orchards is one of the most-visited villages in France: Les Baux de Provence, 30km south of Avignon towards Arles.

Château des Baux (☏04 90 54 55 56; www.chateau-baux-provence.com; adult/child €7.50/5.50; ⏰9am-6pm, to 8pm Jul & Aug) perches on a 245m-high grey limestone baou (Provençal for rocky spur) at the top of the village and dominates the surrounding countryside.

Legendary **L'Oustau de Baumanière** (☏04 90 54 33 07; www.oustaudebaumaniere.com; menus €95-150; ☏) serves rarefied cuisine, including a (trés gourmet) vegetarian menu, with ingredients plucked from its own organic garden. There is also fine accommodation (doubles from €290). Head chef and owner Jean-André Charial's kingdom also includes the Michelin-star restaurant and luxury rooms of **La Cabro d'Or** (☎ 04 90 54 33 21; www.lacabrodor.com; d from €245), also in Les Baux.

Fontaine de Vaucluse
POP 694

France's most-powerful spring surges out of nowhere above the pretty little village of Fontaine de Vaucluse. The miraculous appearance of this crystal-clear flood draws 1.5 million tourists each year; aim to arrive early in the morning before the trickle of visitors becomes a deluge.

Fontaine de Vaucluse is 21km southeast of Carpentras and 30km west of Apt.

LANGUEDOC

Languedoc takes its name from *langue d'oc* (Occitan), a language closely related to Catalan and distinct from *langue d'oïl*, the forerunner of modern French spoken to the north (the words *oc* and *oïl* meant

'yes' in their respective languages). The plains of Bas-Languedoc boast all Languedoc's towns of consequence, its beaches, rich Roman heritage and France's largest wine-producing area.

Nîmes
POP 146,500

Plough your way through the bleak, traffic-clogged outskirts of Nîmes to reach its true heart, still beating where the Romans established their town more than two millennia ago. Here you'll find some of France's best-preserved classical buildings, together with a few stunning modern constructions as the city continues its centuries-old rivalry with Montpellier, just along the autoroute.

 Sights

LES ARÈNES   Roman Arena
(adult/child incl audioguide €7.80/4.50; ☺9am-6.30pm) Nîmes' magnificent Roman amphitheatre is the best preserved in the whole of the Roman Empire. It was built around AD 100 to seat 24,000

Fontaine de Vaucluse

GLENN VAN DER KNIJFF

spectators. The arena hosted animal fights to the death, stag hunts, man against lion or bear confrontations and, of course, gladiatorial combats. In the contemporary arena it's only the bulls that get killed.

There's a mock-up of the gladiators' quarters and, if you time it right, you'll see a couple of actors in full combat gear slugging it out in the arena.

MAISON CARRÉE   Roman Temple
(Square House; place de la Maison Carrée; adult/child €4.50/3.70; ⊙10am-6.30pm) The Maison Carrée is a remarkably well preserved rectangular Roman temple, constructed around AD 5 to honour Emperor Augustus' two adopted sons. Within, a 22-minute 3D film, *Héros de Nîmes*, is screened every half-hour.

JARDINS DE LA FONTAINE
     Roman Remains
Nîmes' other major Roman monuments enrich the elegant Jardins de la Fontaine (Fountain Gardens). The **Source de la Fontaine** was the site of a spring, temple and baths in Roman times. The remains of the **Temple de Diane** are in the lower northwest corner.

A 10-minute uphill walk brings you to the crumbling shell of the 30m-high **Tour Magne** (adult/child €2.70/2.30; ⊙9.30am-6.30pm), raised around 15 BC. Built as a display of imperial power, it's the largest of a chain of towers that once punctuated the city's 7km-long Roman ramparts.

Sleeping

ROYAL HÔTEL   Hotel €€
(☎04 66 58 28 27; www.royalhotel-nimes.com, in French; 3 bd Alphonse Daudet; r €60-80; ❄ 🛜) You can't squeeze this 21-room hotel, popular with visiting artists and raffishly bohemian, into a standard mould. Rooms, some with ceiling fans, others with air-con and nearly all with bathtubs, are furnished with flair. Most overlook pedestrian place d'Assas, a work of modern art in its own right – though the noise might be intrusive on summer nights.

HÔTEL AMPHITHÉÂTRE   Hotel €
(☎04 66 67 28 51; http://perso.wanadoo.fr/hotel-amphitheatre; 4 rue des Arènes; s €41-45, d €53-70; ❄) The welcoming, family-run Amphithéâtre is just up the road from its namesake. Once a pair of 18th-century mansions, it has 15 rooms decorated in warm, woody colours, each named after a writer or painter.

Eating

CARRÉ D'ART
     Classic French €€
(☎04 66 67 52 40; www.restaurant-lecarredart.com, in French; 2 rue Gaston Boissier; 1-/2-/3-course menus €19/24/29; ⊙closed Sun) This is a place to enjoy exceptional cuisine in

Temple de Diane, Jardins de la Fontaine
PHOTOGRAPHER: BETHUNE CARMICHAEL

Detour:
The Luberon

The picture-perfect area that makes up the Luberon takes the shape of a rectangle on a map. But navigating its bucolic rolling hills, golden-hued perched villages and hidden valleys is a bit like fitting together a jigsaw puzzle. The Luberon is named after its main mountain range, which is split in the centre by the Combe de Lourmarin.

The region's capital, **Apt**, is a central hub for practicalities, but the heart of the Luberon is in the tiny stone villages fanning out across the countryside, which encompasses a 1200-sq-km regional park, the Abbaye de Sénanque and ancient stone *bories* (dry-walled huts).

Framed by fields of lavender in July, **Abbaye Notre-Dame de Sénanque** (☎04 90 72 05 72; guided tour in French adult/child €7/3; ⏱tours by reservation) is a picture-postcard Cistercian abbey 4km northwest of Gordes off the D177 in a magical valley. The abbey was founded in 1148 and is inhabited by a few monks who celebrate mass at noon Tuesday to Saturday, and 10am Sunday.

sublime surrounds. The classical decor, with its gilded mirrors and moulded ceilings, blends harmoniously with fresh flowers; bright, contemporary artwork; cascading, feather-light chandeliers; and *sotto voce* canned jazz.

LE MARCHÉ SUR LA TABLE
Modern French €€

(☎04 66 67 22 50; 10 rue Littré; mains €17-19; ⏱Wed-Sun) Up-and-coming young chef Éric Vidal buys fresh and organic from the nearby food market (his fish is never farmed) and his partner, Caroline, maintains a large selection of local wines. Eat in the attractively furnished interior or quiet, green rear courtyard.

ⓘ Information

Tourist office (☎04 66 58 38 00; www.ot -nimes.fr; 6 rue Auguste; ⏱8.30am-6.30pm Mon-Fri, 9am-6.30pm Sat, 10am-5pm Sun) Rents out audioguides to central Nîmes (one/two terminals €8/10).

ⓘ Getting There & Away

AIR Nîmes' **airport** (☎04 66 70 49 49), 10km southeast of the city on the A54, is served only by Ryanair, which flies to/from London (Luton) and Liverpool in the UK.

TRAIN More than 12 TGVs daily run to/from Paris Gare de Lyon (€52 to €99.70, three hours). Frequent trains serve the following:

Arles €7.50, 30 minutes

Avignon €8.50, 30 minutes

Marseille €19, 1¼ hours

ⓘ Getting Around

TO/FROM THE AIRPORT An **airport bus** (€5, 30 minutes) meets and greets Ryanair flights, leaving from the train station. To confirm times, call ☎04 66 29 27 29.

Pont du Gard

A Unesco World Heritage Site, this exceptionally well-preserved, three-tiered Roman aqueduct was once part of a 50km-long system of water channels built around 19 BC to bring water from nearby Uzès to Nîmes. The scale is huge: the 35 arches of its 275m-long upper tier, running 50m above the River Gard, contain a watercourse designed to carry 20,000 cu metres of water per day.

Its **visitors centre** (☎04 66 37 50 99; www.pontdugard.fr; ⏱9.30am-7pm May-Sep; to 5pm or 6pm Oct-Apr) on the left, northern bank, rents out multilingual **audioguides** (€6). During July and August for an extra thrill (and extra €2)

you can walk the bridge's topmost tier. A guide leads the group every half-hour between 10am and 11.30am and from 2pm to 5.30pm.

Entry to the site for a car and up to five passengers costs €15 from April to October, and €10 from November to March; cyclists and walkers get free entry to the site, but admission to the museum, film and Ludo costs €10. There is free parking and entry to the site after 7pm or 8pm May to September, and after 6pm October to April.

The Pont du Gard is 21km northeast of Nîmes and 26km west of Avignon. Parking in the extensive car parks on each bank of the river costs €5.

Carcassonne

POP 49,100

From afar, Carcassonne looks like some fairy-tale medieval city. Bathed in late-afternoon sunshine and highlighted by dark clouds, La Cité (as the old walled city is known), is truly breathtaking. Luring almost four million visitors annually,

it can be a tourist hell in high summer. That said, you'll have to be fairly stone-hearted not to be moved.

La Cité, dramatically illuminated at night, is enclosed by two rampart walls and punctuated by 52 stone towers. But only the lower sections of the walls are original; the rest, including the anachronistic witch's-hat roofs (the originals were altogether flatter and weren't covered with slate), were stuck on by Viollet-le-Duc in the 19th century.

If you enter via the main entrance, before you rears a massive bastion, the **Porte Narbonnaise**, and just inside is the tourist office annexe. Rue Cros Mayrevieille, suffocating in kitschy souvenir shops, leads up to place du Château, the heart of La Cité.

South of place du Château is **Basilique St-Nazaire** (☉9am-11.45am & 1.45-5pm). Highlights are the graceful Gothic transept arms with a pair of superb 13th- and 14th-century rose windows at each end.

Left: Carcassonne; **Below:** Vieux Nice as seen from Colline du Château (p326)
PHOTOGRAPHER: (LEFT) IZZET KERIBAR; (BELOW) GLENN VAN DER KNIJFF

ℹ️ Information

Main tourist office (☎ 04 68 10 24 30; www.carcassonne-tourisme.com; 28 rue de Verdun; ⊘ 9am-6pm or 7pm Mon-Sat, 9am-noon or 1pm Sun) Borrow an **audioguide** to the Ville Basse (lower city; €3 for two hours).

ℹ️ Getting There & Away

TRAIN Carcassonne is on the busy main line linking Toulouse (€14, 50 minutes) with Narbonne (€9.80, 30 minutes) and Montpellier (€22.70, 1½ hours).

THE FRENCH RIVIERA

With its glistening seas, idyllic beaches and fabulous weather, the Riviera encapsulates many people's idea of the good life. The beauty is that there is so much more to do than just going to the beach – although the Riviera does take beach-going *very* seriously: from nudist beach to secluded cove or exclusive club, there is something for everyone.

Nice
POP 352,400

This classic Riviera city offers exceptional quality of life: shimmering Mediterranean shores, the very best of Mediterranean food, a unique historical heritage and Alpine wilderness within an hour's drive.

Nice was founded around 350 BC by the Greek seafarers who had settled Marseille. They named the colony Nikaia, apparently to commemorate a nearby victory (*nike* in Greek).

◎ Sights

Nice has a number of world-class sights, but the star attraction is the city itself. Atmospheric, beautiful, photogenic, it's a wonderful place to stroll or watch the world go by, so make sure you leave yourself plenty of time to soak it all in.

325

Detour:
Arènes d'Orange

Orange's Roman theatre, **Théâtre Antique** (www.theatre-antique.com; adult/child €8/6, 2nd child free; ☺9am-6pm Mar-Oct, to 4.30pm Nov-Feb), 32km north of Avignon, is by far the most impressive Roman sight in France. Its sheer size and age are awe-inspiring. Designed to seat 10,000 spectators, it's thought to have been built during Augustus Caesar's rule (27 BC–AD 14). The 103m-wide, 37m-high stage wall is one of only three in the world still standing in its entirety (the others are in Syria and Turkey) minus a few mosaics and with a new roof. Admission includes a seven-language audioguide.

VIEUX NICE   Old Town
Leave your maps and books behind and embrace Nice's labyrinthine baroque old town. Cours Saleya, running parallel to the seafront at the southern end of Vieux Nice, is the venue for one of the most vibrant, vividly hued local **markets** in the south of France.

COLLINE DU CHÂTEAU   Park
The shaded hill and park at the eastern end of quai des États-Unis are named after a 12th-century château that was razed by Louis XIV in a fit of pique in 1706 and never rebuilt. To reach the park you can walk up montée Lesage, climb the steps at the eastern end of rue Rossetti or take the **ascenseur** (lift; per person €1.10; ☺9am-7pm) under Tour Bellanda.

MUSÉE MATISSE   Art Museum
(www.musee-matisse-nice.org; 164 av des Arènes de Cimiez; ☺10am-6pm Wed-Mon) Housed in a 17th-century Genoese mansion, this small museum reveals Matisse's evolution as an artist rather than wowing the crowds with masterpieces. There are some well-known works such as the blue paper cut-outs *Blue Nude IV* and *Woman with Amphora*, but you'll also see a number of lesser-known sculptures and experimental pieces using cloth, paper, oils, ink etc.

Take bus 17 from the bus station or bus 22 from place Masséna to the Arènes stop.

PROMENADE DES ANGLAIS   Promenade
Established by English expats in 1822, this wide, palm-lined promenade is a timelessly elegant place for a beachfront stroll. The Promenade des Anglais is lined with grand buildings, chief among them the 1912 pink-domed **Hôtel Negresco**. Another landmark is art deco **Palais de la Méditerranée**, saved from demolition in the 1980s and now part of a luxury hotel.

CATHÉDRALE ORTHODOXE RUSSE
ST-NICOLAS   Cathedral
(Russian Orthodox Cathedral of St-Nicolas; Av Nicolas II; admission €3; ☺9am-noon & 2.30-5pm Mon-Sat, 2.30-5pm Sun) Crowned by six multicoloured onion domes, St-Nicolas' is the largest Russian Orthodox cathedral outside Russia. Shorts, miniskirts and sleeveless shirts are forbidden.

Tours

Guided walking tours   Walking Tours
The tourist office runs 2½-hour **walking tours** (adult/child €12/6; ☺9.30am Sat) of Vieux Nice, in English, departing from the main office on the promenade des Anglais. The **Centre du Patrimoine** (☎04 92 00 41 90; www.nice.fr, in French; tours adult/child €5/2.50) also runs 11 thematic two-hour walking tours. English-language tours must be booked two days in advance. The tourist office has a full listing.

Trans Côte d'Azur   Boat Tours
(www.trans-cote-azur.com, in French; quai Lunel; ☺Apr-Oct) Scenic one-hour coastal cruises (adult/child €15/9) as well as day trips to the Îles de Lérins (adult/child €34/24), St-Tropez (adult/child €55/41) and Monaco (adult/child €32/23).

Festivals & Events

Carnaval de Nice   Carnival
(www.nicecarnaval.com) This two-week carnival,
held in February, is particularly famous for its
battles of flowers, where thousands of blooms
are tossed into the crowds from passing floats,
as well as its fantastic fireworks display.

Sleeping

VILLA RIVOLI   Boutique Hotel €€
(☎ 04 93 88 80 25; www.villa-rivoli.com; 10 rue
de Rivoli; s €85-155, d €99-175, q €210; ❄ 🛜)
This stately villa feels like your own pied-
à-terre in the heart of Nice. A marble
staircase leads to spotless, character-
rich rooms, some with fabric-covered
walls, gilt-edged mirrors and marble
mantelpieces.

HÔTEL WINDSOR   Boutique Hotel €€
(☎ 04 93 88 59 35; www.hotelwindsornice.
com; 11 rue Dalpozzo; d €120-175; ❄ @ 🛜 🛝)
Though owned by the same family since
1942, there's nothing traditional about
the Windsor. Graffiti artists have decorated several of the oversized rooms
with aggressive splashes of colour.
Other rooms are more soothing
yet still nod to the arts with hand-
painted wall murals.

HÔTEL LA PÉROUSE
            Luxury Hotel €€€
(☎ 04 93 62 34 63; www.
hotel-la-perouse.com; 11 quai
Rauba Capeu; d €260-510;
❄ @ 🛜 🛝) Built into
the cliff next to Tour
Bellanda, La Pérouse
captures the vibe
of a genteel villa.
Lower rooms face the
lemon-tree-shaded
courtyard and infinity
pool; upper rooms have
magnificent vistas of
the promenade and sea.

NICE GARDEN HÔTEL
            Boutique Hotel €€
(☎ 04 93 87 35 63; www.nicegardenhotel.com;
11 rue du Congrès; s/d €75/100; ❄ 🛜) Behind
heavy iron gates hides this little gem: nine
beautifully appointed rooms, the work of
the exquisite Marion, are a subtle blend
of old and new and overlook a delightful
garden with a glorious orange tree.

VILLA LA TOUR   Boutique Hotel €€
(☎ 04 93 80 08 15; www.villa-la-tour.com; 4
rue de la Tour; s/d €78/89; ❄ @) Small but
perfectly formed, the Villa la Tour is delightful, with warm, romantic Provençal
rooms, a location at the heart of Vieux
Nice, and a diminutive flower-decked
roof terrace with views of the Colline du
Château and surrounding rooftops.

Eating

LUC SALSEDO   Modern French €€€
(☎ 04 93 82 24 12; www.restaurant-salsedo.
com, in French; 14 rue Maccarani; lunch/dinner
menu €26/44, mains €26; ☙ Fri & Sun-Tue,

Cathedral of St-Nicolas
PHOTOGRAPHER: DAN HERRICK

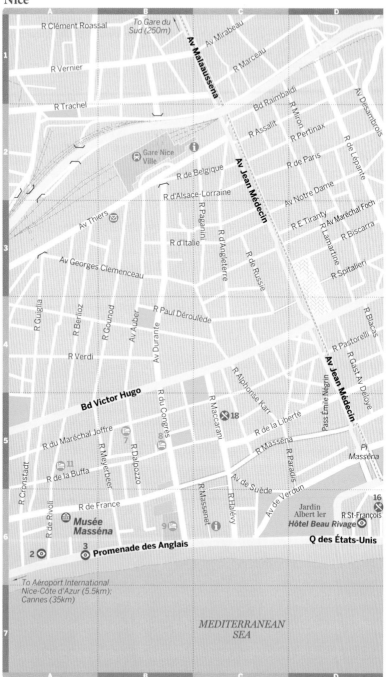

R Clément Roassal

To Gare du Sud (250m)

Av Mirabeau

Av Malaussena

R Vernier

R Marceau

R Trachel

Bd Raimbaldi

R Miron

R Assalit

R Pertinax

Av Desambrois

R de Lépante

Gare Nice Ville

R de Belgique

Av Jean Médecin

R de Paris

R d'Alsace-Lorraine

Av Notre Dame

R Paganini

R E Tiranty

Av Maréchal Foch

Av Thiers

R d'Italie

R d'Angleterre

R de Russie

R Biscarra

R Lamartine

R Spitalieri

Av Georges Clemenceau

R Paul Déroulède

R Blacas

R Guigla

R Berlioz

R Gounod

Av Auber

Av Durante

R Pastorelli

R Verdi

Bd Victor Hugo

R Alphonse Karr

R Maccarani

Av Jean Médecin

R Gast Av Deloye

18

R du Congrès

R de la Liberté

R du Maréchal Joffre

7

R Meyerbeer

R Dalpozzo

8

R Masséna

R Paradis

Pass Émile Négrin

Pl Masséna

R Cronstadt

11

R de la Buffa

R de France

R Masséna

R Masseret

R Halévy

Av de Suède

Av de Verdun

16

Musée Masséna

R de Rivoli

9

Jardin Albert Ier

R St-François

Hôtel Beau Rivage

2

3

Promenade des Anglais

Q des États-Unis

To Aéroport International Nice-Côte d'Azur (5.5km); Cannes (35km)

MEDITERRANEAN SEA

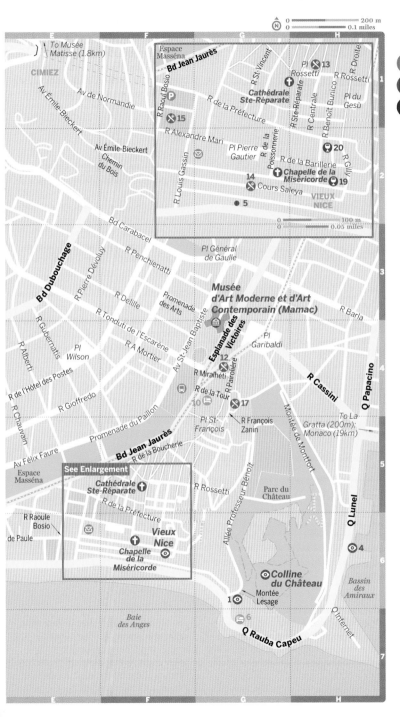

To Musée
Matisse (1.8km)

CIMIEZ

Av Émile-Bieckert

Av de Normandie

Av Émile-Bieckert
Chemin
du Bois

Bd Carabacel

Espace
Masséna

Bd Jean Jaurès

R Raoul Bosio

R de la Préfecture

R St-Vincent

Pl
Rossetti

R Rossetti

R Droite

Cathédrale
Ste-Réparate

R Ste-Réparate

R Centrale

R Benoît Bunico

Pl du
Gesù

R Gilly

R Alexandre Mari

R Louis Gassin

Pl Pierre
Gautier

R de la
Poissonnerie

R de la Barillerie

20

14

Chapelle de la
Miséricorde

19

Cours Saleya

VIEUX
NICE

5

0   100 m
0   0.05 miles

Bd Dubouchage

R Pierre Dévoluy

R Penchienatti

Pl Général
de Gaulle

R Delille

Promenade
des Arts

Musée
d'Art Moderne et d'Art
Contemporain (Mamac)

R Barla

R Tonduti de l'Escarène

Av St-Jean Baptiste

Esplanade des
Victoires

Pl
Garibaldi

R A Mortier

R Alberti

R Gubernatis

Pl
Wilson

12

R Miralhéti

R Paroirière

R Cassini

Q Papacino

R de l'Hôtel des Postes

R Gioffredo

R de la Tour

10

17

To La
Gratta (200m);
Monaco (19km)

R Chauvain

Promenade du Paillon

Pl St
François

R François
Zanin

Montée de Montfort

Av Félix Faure

Bd Jean Jaurès

R de la Boucherie

Espace
Masséna

See Enlargement

Cathédrale
Ste-Réparate

R Rossetti

Parc du
Château

Q Lunel

R Raoule
Bosio

de Paule

R de la Préfecture

Vieux
Nice

Chapelle
de la
Miséricorde

Allée Professeur Bénoit

4

Colline
du Château

Montée
Lesage

1

Bassin
des
Amiraux

Baie
des Anges

6

Q Rauba Capeu

Q Internet

329

Nice

dinner Thu & Sat, dinner only Jul-Aug; ✆) The cuisine of Salsedo, a young chef who's built a fine reputation, is local and seasonal. His menu (which, unusually, caters well for vegetarians) changes every 10 days to reflect the mood of the market stalls.

LA MERENDA   Niçois Cuisine   €€
(4 rue Raoul Bosio; mains €12-15; ⏱Mon-Fri) Closed at weekends, with no phone number or credit card machine, tiny La Merenda is one of a kind. It serves some of the most unusual fare in town: stockfish (dried cod soaked in running water for a few days and then simmered with onions, tomatoes, garlic, olives and potatoes) is a house speciality, as is tripe.

LA PETITE MAISON Niçois Cuisine €€€
(✆04 93 92 59 59; www.lapetitemaison-nice. com; 11 rue St-François de Paule; mains €20-40; ⏱Mon-Sat) Nice's hottest table draws celebs and politicians for its happening scene and elegantly executed Niçois specialities. Reservations essential.

FENOCCHIO   Ice Cream   €
(2 place Rossetti; ice cream from €2; ⏱9am-midnight, closed Nov-Jan) The best place to beat Nice's heat is this *glacier,* serving 50 flavours of ice cream – eschew predictable favourites and indulge in a new taste sensation: black olive, tomato-basil, rhubarb, avocado, rosemary, *calisson* (almond biscuit frosted with icing sugar), lavender, ginger or liquorice.

CHEZ RENÉ SOCCA   Bistro   €
(2 rue Miralhéti; dishes from €2; ⏱9am-9pm Tue-Sun, closed Nov) Forget about presentation and manners; here, it's all about taste. Grab a portion of *socca* (chickpea-flour pancake) or a plate of *petits farcis* (stuffed vegetables) and head across the street to the bar for a *grand pointu* (glass) of red, white or rosé.

LA TABLE ALZIARI   Niçois Cuisine   €€
(✆04 93 80 34 03; 4 rue François Zanin; mains €9-15; ⏱Tue-Sat) Run by the grandson of the famous Alziari olive-oil family, this citrus-coloured restaurant off the busy rue Pairolière is not here to brag about anything. The day's menu is chalked on a blackboard, with local specialities such as *morue à la niçoise* (cod served with potatoes, olives and a tomato sauce) or grilled goat's cheese, and regional wines.

Self-Catering

Pack the ultimate picnic hamper from cours Saleya's magnificent **fruit and vegetable market** (⏱6am-1.30pm Tue-Sun), where long trestle tables groan with shiny fruit and veg, pastries, *fruits confits* (glazed or candied fruits such as figs, ginger, pears etc) and more.

Don't Miss Musée d'Art Moderne et d'Art Contemporain (Mamac)

Designed by Yves Bayard and Henri Vidal, Mamac is worth a visit for its stunning architecture alone, but it also houses some fantastic avant-garde art from the 1960s to the present. Exhibits include iconic pop art from Roy Lichtenstein, and Andy Warhol's 1965 *Campbell's Soup Can*. An awesome panorama of Vieux Nice unfolds from the rooftop garden/gallery, which features works by Nice-born Yves Klein (1928–62).

NEED TO KNOW

Museum of Modern & Contemporary Art; www.mamac-nice.org; Promenade des Arts; ⊙10am-6pm Tue-Sun

 Drinking

Vieux Nice's little streets runneth over with local bars and cafés: from an espresso to a pastis (the tipple of choice in the south of France), a chilled evening beer or a midnight cocktail, the choice is yours.

LES DISTILLERIES IDÉALES Café
(24 rue de la Préfecture; ⊙9am-12.30am)
Whether you're after an espresso on your way to cours Saleya or a sundowner, the atmosphere here is infectious. You're bound to leave with a skip in your step.

La Civette du Cours Café
(1 cours Saleya; ⊙8am-1am) Nurse a hangover with a cappuccino in the morning sun, or join the locals for a prelunch pastis at this cheerful café.

 Shopping

Cours Saleya markets Markets
(⊙6am-5.30pm Tue-Sat, to 1.30pm Sun) Split between its beautiful **flower market** and rightly famous **food market**. On Mondays from 6am to 6pm, flowers and food make way for an **antiques market**.

ℹ Information

Tourist office Airport tourist information desk (Terminal 1; ⊘8am-9pm, closed Sun Oct-May); main tourist office (www.nicetourisme.com; 5 promenade des Anglais; ⊘8am-8pm Mon-Sat, 9am-7pm Sun); train station (av Thiers; ⊘8am-8pm Mon-Sat, 9am-7pm Sun)

ℹ Getting There & Away

Air

Aéroport International Nice-Côte d'Azur (www.nice.aeroport.fr) lies 6km west of the city centre. A free **shuttle** (⊘every 10min 4.30am-midnight) connects its two terminals.

Train

Gare Nice Ville (av Thiers) is 1.2km north of the beach. There are frequent services to coastal towns, including Antibes (€4, 30 minutes), Cannes (€6.50, 40 minutes), Menton (€4.50, 35 minutes), Monaco (€3.40, 20 minutes) and St-Raphaël (€11, 50 minutes). Direct TGV trains link Nice with Paris' Gare de Lyon (€115, 5½ hours).

ℹ Getting Around

To/From the Airport

Ligne d'Azur operates two airport buses; the €4 ticket is then valid on other buses for the entire day. Route 99 departs Gare Nice Ville and goes directly to the airport every half-hour from 8am to 9pm daily. Route 98 departs from the bus station every 20 minutes (every 30 minutes on Sunday), making stops en route along the Promenade des Anglais, from 6am to 9pm.

Taxis from the airport to the city centre cost €25 to €30, depending on the time of day.

Tram

Nice's sleek new trams are ideal for getting around. Line 1 runs a V-shaped northwest–south–northeast itinerary from 4.30am to 1.30am, serving convenient areas such as the train station, old town and the Acropolis in the centre.

Antibes-Juan-les-Pins
POP 76,800

Antibes is a concentrate of Mediterranean history: the town's sea walls bear witness to a defensive past (when neighbouring Nice had switched allegiance to rival Savoy); Golfe Juan staged Napoléon Bonaparte's triumphant return from exile in Elba; Picasso painted in the Château Grimaldi; and F Scott Fitzgerald wrote his seminal novel *Tender is the Night* based on life in Antibes.

Nowadays, Antibes sports the second-biggest marina in Europe and attracts throngs of 'yachties' in search of seafaring adventures.

◉ Sights & Activities

MUSÉE PICASSO
Art Museum
(www.antibes-juanlespins.com; Château Grimaldi, 4 rue des Cordiers; adult/child €6/3; ⊘10am-6pm Tue-Sun) Spectacularly positioned

Antibes-Juan-les-Pins

KRISTIN PILJAY

overlooking the sea, 14th-century **Château Grimaldi** served as Picasso's studio from July to December 1946. The museum houses an excellent collection of the master's paintings, lithographs, drawings and ceramics, as well as a photographic record of the artist at work.

VIEIL ANTIBES — Old Town

Vieil Antibes is a pleasant mix of food shops, boutiques and restaurants. Mornings are a good time to meander along the little alleyways, when the **marché (market; Cours Masséna)** is in full swing. Check out the views from the sea walls: from the urban sprawl of Nice to the snowy peaks of the Alps and nearby Cap d'Antibes.

CAP D'ANTIBES — Walking

Cap d'Antibes' 4.8km of wooded shores are the perfect setting for a walk–swim–walk–swim afternoon. The tourist office maps show itineraries.

 ## Sleeping

HÔTEL LA JABOTTE — B&B €€

(✆ 04 93 61 45 89; www.jabotte.com; 13 av Max Maurey, Cap d'Antibes; s/d incl breakfast from €108/118; ❄ 🤶) A hotel with *chambre d'hôte* (B&B) feel, La Jabotte is Antibes' hidden gem. Just 50m from the sea (and 20 minutes' walk from Vieil Antibes), its 10 Provençal rooms all look out onto an exquisite patio where breakfast is served from spring to autumn.

VILLA VAL DES ROSES — Boutique B&B €€€

(✆ 06 85 06 06 29; www.val-des-roses.com; 6 chemin des Lauriers; d incl breakfast low/high season from €140/250; ❄ @ 🤶 🏊) This beautiful 19th-century bourgeois villa with marble floors and a laptop and jacuzzi bath in each room is a 20-minute stroll from the old town.

 ## Eating

LE BROC EN BOUCHE — Modern French €€

(✆ 04 93 34 75 60; 8 rue des Palmiers, Antibes; mains €15-30; 🕑 closed Tue dinner & Wed) You'll melt for Flo and Fred's gourmet bistro, their *foie gras,* their *magret de canard* (duck breast) and whatever daily special they've come up with.

DAN HERRICK

Auberge Provençale
Seafood €€

(☎04 93 34 13 24; www.aubergeprovencale.com; 61 place Nationale, Antibes; menus €17.50-60; ⏰Tue-Sat) The auberge is famed for its fabulous seafood. In winter, make sure you get a table in the Vieux Couvent; in summer, opt for the courtyard.

 Getting There & Away

Antibes is an easy day trip by train from Nice (€4, 30 minutes) or Cannes (€2.60, 15 minutes).

St-Paul de Vence
POP 3400

What distinguishes the medieval hilltop village of St-Paul de Vence from every other medieval hilltop village around is its phenomenal art legacy. St-Paul attracted many seminal 20th-century artists, such as Russian painter Marc Chagall, who is now buried in St-Paul's interdenominational cemetery.

 Sights

FONDATION MAEGHT
Gallery

(www.fondation-maeght.com; 623 chemin des Gardettes, St-Paul de Vence; adult/child €14/9; ⏰10am-7pm) Browsing the gallery-lined village streets (64 galleries in total!) is a fine entrée for art lovers, but the pièce de résistance is this private gallery, about 500m from the old village. Its extraordinary permanent collection of 40,000 works is exhibited on a rotating basis.

CHAPELLE DU ROSAIRE
Chapel

(Rosary Chapel; www.vence.fr/the-rosaire-chapel. html; 466 av Henri Matisse, Vence; admission €3; ⏰2-5.30pm Mon, Wed & Sat, 10-11.30am & 2-5.30pm Tue & Thu, closed mid-Nov–mid-Dec) While living in Vence, Matisse's friendship with his former nurse, Dominican Sister Jacques-Marie, inspired him to design what he called his masterwork, completed when he was 81.

 Sleeping & Eating

LA COLOMBE D'OR
Boutique Hotel €€€

(☎04 93 32 80 02; www.la-colombe-dor.com; St-Paul de Vence; r from €250-430, lunch mains €20-60, dinner mains €60-70; ⏰closed Nov-Christmas; 🖥🏊) This world-famous inn could double as the Fondation Maeght annexe. Located outside the walls, at the entrance of the village, it was the party HQ of many 20th-century artists (Chagall, Braque, Matisse, Picasso etc), who often paid for their meals in kind, resulting in an incredible private art collection. Don't expect to get a table (or a room) unless you book well in advance.

ℹ Getting There & Away

From Nice, the frequent bus 400 stops in St-Paul de Vence (€1, 55 minutes) and Vence (€1, one hour).

Cannes
POP 71,800

Most people have heard of Cannes and its eponymous film festival. The latter only lasts for two weeks in May, but the buzz and glitz are there year-round – unlike neighbouring St-Tropez, which shuts down in winter – mostly thanks to regular visits from celebrities enjoying the creature comforts of bd de la Croisette's palaces.

However, what people may not know is that, for all its glamour, Cannes retains a genuine small-town feel.

guided tours (adult/child €3/free; ☺2.30pm) several times a month, except in May.

BEACHES   Beaches

The central, sandy beaches along bd de la Croisette are sectioned off for hotel patrons.

A microscopic strip of sand near the Palais des Festivals is free, but you'll find better free sand on **Plages du Midi** and **Plages de la Bocca**, west from the Vieux Port along bd Jean Hibert and bd du Midi.

ÎLES DE LÉRINS   Islands

Although just 20 minutes away by boat, the tranquil Îles de Lérins feel far from the madding crowd.

The closest of these two tiny islands is the 3.25km by 1km **Île Ste-Marguerite**, where the mysterious Man in the Iron Mask was incarcerated during the late 17th century.

Smaller still, at just 1.5km long by 400m wide, **Île St-Honorat** has been a monastery since the 5th century. **Riviera Lines** (www.riviera-lines.com) runs ferries to Île Ste-Marguerite (return adult/child

◉ Sights & Activities

LE SUQUET   Old Town

Predating the glitz and glam of the town's festival days, Cannes' historic quarter has retained a quaint village feel with its steep, meandering alleyways.

PALAIS DES FESTIVALS Landmark
(Festival Palace; bd de la Croisette) At the western end of La Croisette, this concrete bunker is the unlikely host of the world's most-glamorous film festival. The tourist office runs 1½-hour

A Côte d'Azur beach
PHOTOGRAPHER: MICHELLE LEWIS

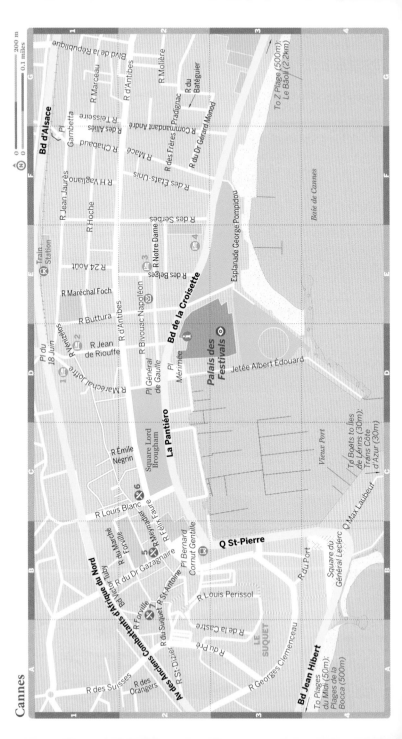

Cannes

Bd d'Alsace

Blvd de la République
R Marceau
R d'Antibes
R Molière
R du Bateguier

Pl Gambetta
R Teisseire
R des Alliés
R Commandant André
R des Frères Pradignac
R du Dr Gérard Monod
R Chabaud
R Macé

To Z Plage (500m);
Le Bâoli (2.2km)

R Jean Jaurès
R H Vagliano
R des États-Unis

R Hoche
R des Serbes

Esplanade George Pompidou

Train Station
R 24 Août
R Notre Dame

R Maréchal Foch
R des Belges

Baie de Cannes

R Buttura
R d'Antibes
R Bivouac Napoléon

Pl du 18 Juin
R Venizélos
R Jean de Riouffe
Pl Général de Gaulle
Pl Mérimée

Bd de la Croisette

R Maréchal Joffre

La Pantiéro

Palais des Festivals
Jetée Albert Édouard

R Émile Négrin

Square Lord Brougham

Victux Port

R Louis Blanc
R Meynadier
R Félix Faure

Q St-Pierre

To Boats to Îles de Lérins (30m);
Trans Côte d'Azur (30m)

Bd Victor Tuby
R du Marché Forville
R du Dr Gazagnaire
Pl Bernard Cornut Gentille

R du Port
Q Max Laubeuf

Bd d'Antique du Nord

Av des Anciens Combattants d'Afrique du Nord

R Forville
R du Suquet
R St-Antoine
R Louis Perissol

Square du Général Leclerc

R des Suisses
R des Orangers
R St-Dizier
R du Pre
R de la Castre

LE SUQUET

R Georges Clemenceau

Bd Jean Hibert

To Plages du Midi (50m);
Plages de la Bocca (500m)

200 m
0.1 miles

Cannes

€11.50/6), while **Compagnie Planaria** (www.cannes-ilesdelerins.com) operates boats to Île St-Honorat (return adult/ child €12/6).

 Tours

Trans Côte d'Azur   Boat Tour
(📞04 92 98 71 30; www.trans-cote-azur.com; quai Max Laubeuf) The most serene way to see the coast. There are day trips to the stunning red cliffs of the Massif de l'Estérel (adult/child €25/15), St-Tropez (adult/child €41/28) and Monaco (adult/child €46/28).

 Sleeping

Hotel prices in Cannes fluctuate wildly according to the season, and soar during the film festival – when you'll need to book months in advance.

HÔTEL 7E ART   Boutique Hotel   €
(📞04 93 68 66 66; www.7arthotel.com; 23 rue Maréchal Joffre; s €68, d €60-98; ✳🛜) Hôtel 7e Art opened in 2010, putting boutique style within reach of budgeters. The owners schooled in Switzerland and got the basics right, with great beds, sparkling-clean baths and excellent soundproofing.

HÔTEL LE MISTRAL Boutique Hotel   €€
(📞04 93 39 91 46; www.mistral-hotel.com; 13 rue des Belges; d from €89; ✳🛜) This small hotel wins the Palme d'Or for best value in

town: rooms are decked out in flattering red and plum tones, bathrooms feature lovely designer fittings, there are sea views from the top floor and the hotel is a mere 50m from La Croisette.

HÔTEL ALNÉA   Hotel   €€
(📞04 93 68 77 77; www.hotel-alnea.com; 20 rue Jean de Riouffe; s/d €68/88; ✳🛜) Noémi and Cédric have put their heart and soul into their hotel, with bright, colourful rooms, original paintings and numerous little details such as the afternoon coffee break, the self-service minibar and the bike or *boules* (to play *pétanque*) loans.

HÔTEL MAJESTIC BARRIÈRE
             Luxury Hotel   €€€
(📞04 92 98 77 00; www.lucienbarriere.com; 10 bd de la Croisette; r from €300; ✳@🛜🏊) Cannes' most magnificent luxury hotel reopened in 2010, following an €80 million renovation. This is where the stars stay during the film festival.

 Eating

MANTEL   Modern European   €€
(📞04 93 39 13 10; www.restaurantmantel.com; 22 rue St-Antoine; lunch/dinner menus €25/28; ⏰closed Wed & lunch Tue & Thu) The Italian maître d' will make you feel like a million dollars and you'll melt for Noël Mantel's divine cuisine and great-value prices.

COQUILLAGES BRUN   Seafood   €€
(📞04 93 39 21 87; www.astouxbrun.com; 27 rue Félix Faure; menus from €28; ⏰noon-1am) Cannes' most-famous seafood brasserie is *the* place to indulge in oysters, mussels, prawns, crayfish and other delightfully fresh shellfish with a glass of crisp white wine. The restaurant is full every night, so make sure you book.

AUX BONS ENFANTS
             Traditional French   €€
(80 rue Meynadier; menu €23; ⏰Tue-Sat) This familial little place doesn't have a phone, and there are no plans to get one any time soon: it's always full. The lucky ones who get a table (get there early or

late) can feast on regional dishes made from ingredients picked up at the adjacent market.

 Information

Tourist office (☎ 04 92 99 84 22; www.cannes.travel; bd de la Croisette; ☺9am-7pm Mon-Sat)

ⓘ Getting There & Away

TRAIN Destinations within easy reach include Nice (€6.50, 40 minutes), Grasse (€3.80, 30 minutes) and Marseille (€22, two hours), as well as St-Raphaël (€6.50, 25 minutes), from where you can get buses to St-Tropez and Toulon.

St-Tropez

POP 5700

In the soft autumn or winter light, it's hard to believe that the pretty terracotta fishing village of St-Tropez is another stop on the Riviera celebrity circuit. It seems far removed from its glitzy siblings further up the coast. But come spring or summer it's a different world: the town's population increases tenfold, prices triple, and fun-seekers come in droves to party till dawn, strut their stuff and enjoy the creature comforts of an exclusive beach.

If at all possible, visit outside of July and August.

◉ Sights

MUSÉE DE L'ANNONCIADE Art Museum
(place Grammont, Vieux Port; adult/child €6/4; ☺10am-noon & 3-7pm Wed-Mon, closed Nov)
Located in a disused chapel, the Musée de l'Annonciade displays an impressive collection of artworks by Matisse, Bonnard, Dufy and especially Signac, who set up his home and studio in St-Tropez.

Citadelle de St-Tropez Monument
(admission €2.50; ☺10am-6.30pm) The panoramas of St-Tropez' bay from the elevated 17th-century Citadelle de St-Tropez are worth the climb.

Activities

BEACHES Beaches
The glistening sandy **Plage de Tahiti**, 4km southeast of town, morphs into the celebrity-studded **Plage de Pampelonne**, which in summer incorporates a sequence of exclusive restaurant/clubs.

🛏 Sleeping

LOU CAGNARD Hotel €€
(☎ 04 94 97 04 24; www.hotel-lou-cagnard.com; 18 av Paul-Roussel; d €69-140, tr €160; ❄ ☎) Book well ahead for this great-value courtyard charmer, shaded by lemon and fig trees, and owned by schooled hoteliers.

St-Tropez harbour
PHOTOGRAPHER: TONY BURNS

PASTIS
Boutique Hotel €€€

(📞04 98 12 56 50; www.pastis-st-tropez.com; 61 av du Général Leclerc; d from €200-350; ❄️🏊) This stunning hotel is the brainchild of an English couple besotted with Provence and passionate about modern art. If it doesn't sound like an obvious combination, one look at Pastis will dispel any doubt; you'll die for the pop-art-inspired interior, and long for a swim in the emerald-green pool and snooze under the centenarian palm trees.

HÔTEL ERMITAGE
Boutique Hotel €€€

(📞04 94 27 52 33; www.ermitagehotel.fr; av Paul Signac; r €180-300; ❄️@🛜) Kate Moss and Lenny Kravitz favour St-Trop's latest rocker crash pad, which draws inspiration from St-Trop in the '50s through '70s – disco meets midcentury modern. Its residential, hillside location ups the exclusivity factor, and yields knockout views over town.

 Eating

AUBERGE DES MAURES
Provençal €€

(📞04 94 97 01 50; 4 rue du Docteur Boutin; menu €49, mains €31-39; 🕑dinner) The town's oldest restaurant remains the locals' choice for always-good, copious portions of earthy Provençal cooking, such as *daube* or tapenade-stuffed lamb shoulder. Book (essential) a table on the leafy courtyard.

BRASSERIE DES ARTS
Modern French €€

(📞04 94 40 27 37; www.brasseriedesarts.com; 5 place des Lices; mains/menu €20/29) Wedged in a line-up of eating and drinking terraces jockeying for attention on St-Tropez' people-watching square, BA (as it is known) is where the locals go.

Place des Lices market Market €
(🕑mornings Tue & Sat) A highlight of local life; people come for the gossip as much as the colourful stalls.

♥ If You Like...
French Markets

If you love the hubbub of the markets in Nice and St-Tropez, you mustn't miss the region's other atmospheric markets:

1 CARPENTRAS
(📞tourist office 04 90 63 00 78; www.carpentras-ventoux.com) Each Friday morning, Carpentras' central streets overflow with hundreds of stalls laden with breads, honeys, cheeses, olives, nuts, fruit and rainbow-coloured *berlingots* (stripy hard-boiled sweets).

2 NARBONNE
(📞tourist office 04 68 65 15 60; www.narbonne-tourisme.com) This Languedoc town was capital of the Roman region of Gallia Narbonensis. Its imposing art nouveau covered market, Les Halles, is an architectural gem and a colourful place to browse for fresh local produce.

3 VAISON-LA-ROMAINE
(📞tourist office 04 90 36 02 11; www.vaison-la-romaine.com) Nestled in a valley at the crossroads of seven hills, this quintessential Provençal village has some fascinating Roman remains, but the Tuesday-morning market has become an attraction in its own right.

ℹ Information

Tourist office (📞04 94 97 45 21; www.ot-saint-tropez.com; quai Jean Jaurès; 🕑9.30am-12.30pm & 2-7pm) Keeps a useful list of hotels and restaurants that are open in the low season.

ℹ Getting There & Away

BOAT Les Bateaux de St-Raphaël (www.bateauxsaintraphael.com, in French) runs boats between St-Raphaël and St-Tropez (single/return adult €14/23, child €9/13) from April to October.

Trans Côte d'Azur (www.trans-cote-azur.com) runs day trips from Nice (adult/child €55/41) and Cannes (adult/child €41/28) between April and September.

DISCOVER PROVENCE & THE FRENCH RIVIERA THE FRENCH RIVIERA

The Corniches

A trio of corniches (coastal roads) hugs the cliffs between Nice and Monaco, each higher up the hill than the last. The middle corniche ends in Monaco; the upper and lower continue to Menton.

Corniche Inférieure

Skimming the villa-lined waterfront, the Corniche Inférieure (also known as the Basse Corniche, the Lower Corniche or the N98) sticks pretty close to the train line, passing (west to east) through Villefranche-sur-Mer, St-Jean-Cap Ferrat, Beaulieu-sur-Mer, Èze-sur-Mer and Cap d'Ail.

VILLEFRANCHE-SUR-MER   Fishing Port

The picturesque pastel-coloured, terracotta-roofed fishing port Villefranche-sur-Mer overlooking the Cap Ferrat peninsula was a favourite with Jean Cocteau, who painted the frescos in the 17th-century **Chapelle St-Pierre**. Looking down on the township is the 16th-century citadel.

ST-JEAN-CAP FERRAT   Village

On the Cap Ferrat peninsula, this fishing-village-turned-playground-for-the-wealthy conceals an enclave of millionaires' villas, with illustrious residents both present and past. On the narrow isthmus of the town, the extravagant **Villa Ephrussi de Rothschild** (www.villa-ephrussi.com; adult/child €10/7.50; ⏲10am-6pm) gives you an appreciation of the area's wealth.

Moyenne Corniche

The Moyenne Corniche – the middle coastal road (N7) – clings to the hillside. From Nice, the Moyenne Corniche travels past Col de Villefranche, through Èze and to Beausoleil, the French town bordering Monte Carlo.

ÈZE   Walled Village

On the pinnacle of a 427m peak is the medieval stone village of Èze. Once occupied by Ligurians and Phoenicians, today it's home to one-off galleries and artisan boutiques within its enclosed

walls (there's only one doorway in or out of the village). The high point is the **Jardin Èze** (admission €5; ☼9am-sunset), a slanting cliff-side garden of exotic cacti, with views of the Med all the way to Corsica (on a good day).

On the seaside below is the village's coastal and very belle époque counterpart, **Èze-sur-Mer** (where U2's Bono has a villa).

Grande Corniche

The Grande Corniche, whose panoramas are the most dramatic of all, leaves Nice as the D2564. It passes **La Turbie**, which sits on a promontory directly above Monaco and offers vertigo-inducing views of the principality. The best views are from the town's **Trophée des Alps** (cours Albert 1; adult/child €5/3.50; ☼9.30am-1pm & 2.30-6.30pm Tue-Sun), one of only two Roman trophy monuments in the world (the other's in Romania), built by Augustus in 6 BC.

MONACO (PRINCIPAUTÉ DE MONACO)

POP 32,000 / ☎377

The world's second-smallest state (a smidgen bigger than the Vatican), is as famous for its tax haven status as it is for its glittering casino, thriving performing-arts and sports scene (Formula One, world-famous circus festival and tennis open), and royal family (its members regularly feature in gossip magazines).

In terms of practicalities, Monaco is a sovereign state but there is no border control. It has its own flag (red and white), national holiday (19 November), postal system (good for the card home to grandma) and telephone country code (☎377), but the official language is French and the country uses the euro even though it is not part of the European Union.

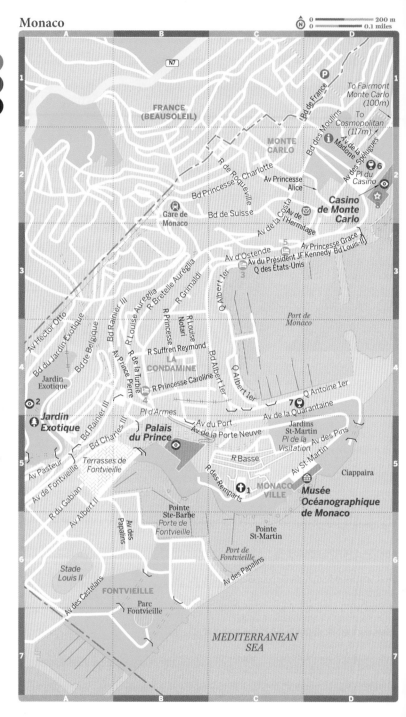

Monaco

◎ Sights & Activities

CASINO DE MONTE CARLO   Casino

(www.casinomontecarlo.com; place du Casino; admission to European/Private Rooms €10/20; ☺European Rooms from noon Sat & Sun, from 2pm Mon-Fri) Living out your James Bond fantasies just doesn't get any better than at Monte Carlo's monumental, richly decorated showpiece, the 1910-built casino. The European Rooms have poker/slot machines, French roulette and *trente et quarante* (a card game), while the Private Rooms offer baccarat, blackjack, craps and American roulette. The jacket-and-tie dress code kicks in after 10pm. See p344 for more information.

MUSÉE OCÉANOGRAPHIQUE DE MONACO   Aquarium

(www.oceano.org; Av St-Martin; adult/child €13/6.50; ☺9.30am-7pm) Propped on a sheer cliff-face, the graceful Musée Océanographique de Monaco, built in 1910, houses a fantastic aquarium. And don't miss the spectacular views from the rooftop terrace.

PALAIS DU PRINCE   Palace

(www.palais.mc; Monaco Ville; adult/child €8/3.50; ☺9.30am-6.30pm, closed Nov-Mar) For a glimpse into royal life, you can tour the state apartments with an 11-language audioguide. The palace is what you would expect of any aristocratic abode: lavish furnishings and expensive 18th- and 19th-century art. Guards are changed outside the palace at 11.55am every day.

CATHÉDRALE DE MONACO   Cathedral

(4 rue Colonel) An adoring crowd continually shuffles past Prince Rainier's and Princess Grace's graves, located inside the cathedral choir of the 1875 Romanesque-Byzantine Cathédrale de Monaco.

JARDIN EXOTIQUE   Garden

(www.jardin-exotique.mc; 62 bd du Jardin Exotique; adult/child €7/3.70; ☺9am-7pm) Flowering year-round, over 1000 species of cacti and succulents tumble down the slopes of the Jardin Exotique. Admission also includes a half-hour guided visit of the stalactites and stalagmites in the **Observatory Caves**.

Sleeping

NI HÔTEL   Boutique Hotel   €€

(☎97 97 51 51; www.nihotel.com; 1bis rue Grimaldi; s/d from €120/150; ✲ ☎) This uberhip and modern hotel is the new kid on the block in Monaco. Its distinctive design makes bold use of flashy primary colours (the shower walls, chairs and stairs are made of see-through coloured plastic).

HÔTEL MIRAMAR   Hotel   €€

(☎93 30 86 48; http://miramar.monaco-hotel.com; 1 av du Président JF Kennedy; d €145; ✲ ☎) This 1950s seaside hotel with rooftop terrace bar for those lazy breakfasts, lunches and evening drinks is a fabulous option right by the port.

PORT PALACE   Boutique Hotel   €€€

(☎97 97 90 00; www.portpalace.com; 7 av du Président JF Kennedy; r from €365; ✲ @ ☎) Built into the hillside overlooking the yacht

Monte Carlo Casino

A Timeline

1863 Charles III inaugurates the first Casino on the Plateau des Spélugues. The atrium **1** is a small room with a wooden platform from which an orchestra 'enlivens' the gambling.

1864 Hôtel de Paris opens and the area becomes known as the 'Golden Square'.

1865 Construction of Salon Europe **2**. Cathedral-like, it is lined with onyx columns and lit by eight Bohemian crystal chandeliers weighing 150kg each.

1868 The steam train arrives in Monaco and Café de Paris **3** is completed.

1878–79 Gambling moves to Hôtel de Paris while Charles Garnier is charged with building a new casino with a miniature replica of the Paris Opera House, Salle Garnier **4**.

1890 The advent of electricity casts a glow on architect Jules Touzet's newly added gaming rooms **5** for high rollers.

1903 Inspired by female gamblers, Henri Schmit decorates Salle Blanche **6** with caryatids and the painting *Les Grâces Florentines*.

1904 Smoking is banned in the gaming rooms and Salon Rose **7**, a new smoking room, is added.

1910 Salle Médecin **8**, immense and grand, hosts the high-spending Private Circle.

1966 Celebrations mark 100 years of uninterrupted gambling despite two World Wars.

TOP TIPS

Bring photo ID

Jackets are required in the private gaming rooms, and after 8pm

The cashier will exchange any currency

In the main room, the minimum bet is €10, the maximum €2000

In the Salons Privés, the minimum bet is €500, with no maximum

JOHN VLAHIDES

Salle Blanche

Look up, away from the jarring wall-to-wall slot machines, to admire Schmit's caryatids, wings spread for flight. They illustrate the emerging emancipation of women, modelled on fashionable courtesans like La Belle Otero, who placed her first bet here age 18.

Salon Rose

Smoking was banned in the gaming rooms after a fraud involving a croupier letting his ash fall on the floor. The gaze of Gallelli's famous cigarillo-smoking nudes are said to follow you around the room.

Hôtel de Paris

Notice the horse's shiny nose (and testicles) on the lobby's statue of Louis XIV on horseback. Legend has it, rubbing them brings good luck in the casino.

Hôtel de Paris

Salle Garnier

Taking eight months to build and two years to restore (2004–06), the opera's original statuary is rehabilitated using original moulds saved by the creator's grandson. Individual air-con and heating vents are installed beneath each of the 525 seats.

JOHN VLAHIDES

Atrium

The casino's 'lobby', so to speak, is paved in marble and lined with 28 Ionic columns, which support a balustraded gallery canopied with an engraved glass ceiling.

Salon Europe

The oldest part of the casino, where they continue to play *trente-et-quarante* and European roulette, which have been played here since 1863. Tip: the bull's-eye windows around the room originally served as security observation points.

Café de Paris

With the arrival of Diaghilev as director of the Monte Carlo Opera in 1911, Café de Paris becomes the go-to address for artists and gamblers. It retains the same high-glamour ambience today. Tip: snag a seat on the terrace and people-watch.

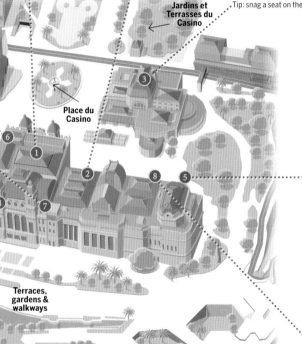

Jardins et Terrasses du Casino

Place du Casino

Salles Touzet

This vast partitioned hall, 21m by 24m, is decorated in the most lavish style: oak, Tonkin mahogany and oriental jasper panelling are offset by vast canvases, Marseille bronzes, Italian mosaics, sculptural reliefs and stained-glass windows.

Terraces, gardens & walkways

Hexagrace mosaic

Fairmont Monte Carlo

Best Views

Wander behind the casino through manicured gardens and gaze across Victor Vasarely's vibrant op-art mosaic, *Hexagrace*, to views of the harbour and the sea.

Salle Médecin

Also known as Salle Empire because of its extravagant Empire-style decor, Monégasque architect François Médecin's gaming room was originally intended for the casino's biggest gamblers. Nowadays, three adjoining Super Privés rooms keep them hidden from prying eyes.

Detour:
Îles d'Hyères

For some inexplicable reason, these paradisaical islands (also known as Îles d'Or – Golden Islands – for their shimmering mica rock) have remained mostly unknown to foreign crowds.

The easternmost and largest of this trio of islands is the little-visited **Île du Levant**, split into an odd combination of army land and nudist colony. **Île de Port-Cros**, the middle and smallest island, is the jewel in the islands' crown. France's first **marine national park** (www.portcrosparcnational.fr, in French), it boasts exceptional marine fauna and flora, which makes it a snorkelling paradise.

The largest and westernmost island is **Île de Porquerolles** (www.porquerolles.com). Run as a hacienda in the early 20th century, it has kept many of its sprawling plantation features.

ℹ Getting There & Away

Vedettes Îles d'Or (www.vedettesilesdor.fr) operates boats to all three islands from Le Lavandou, and between Port-Cros and Porquerolles in summer.

TLV-TVM (www.tlv-tvm.com) runs services to Porquerolles (return adult/child €17/15, 10 minutes) from the La Tour Fondue port at the bottom of the Giens Peninsula. It also runs services to Port-Cros (return adult/child €25/22, one hour) and Levant (adult/child €25/22, 1½ hours) from Hyères' port.

---

harbor, this discreetly sexy boutique hotel was styled by Hermès' artistic director, who used fine silks, Carrara marble and (of course) stitched buttery-soft leather, but eschewed the colour black.

Eating

MANDARINE   Gastronomic €€€
(📞 97 97 90 00; www.portpalace.com; 7 av du Président JF Kennedy; mains €32-37) The casually sophisticated, glass-walled dining room at the Port Palace hotel has mesmerising views over the yacht harbour, and gained a Michelin star in 2010 for its earthy cooking, artistic presentations and thoughtful service.

COSMOPOLITAN Modern European €€
(📞 93 25 78 68; www.cosmopolitan.mc; 7 rue du Portier; lunch menu €19.50, mains €16-31) Cosmopolitan serves timeless international classics with gusto: say hello to fish and chips, three-cheese gnocchi or veal

cutlets in Béarnaise sauce, all revisited by Cosmo's talented chefs. The result is refreshingly good and unpretentious, and tastes even better with one of the many wines on offer (including a dozen available by the glass)

Drinking

STARS 'N' BARS   Bar
(www.starsnbars.com; 6 quai Antoine 1er; ☺ noon-2.30am, closed Mon Oct-May; ) Any star worth his or her reputation has partied at this American western saloon. Check out the gazillion pictures of in-situ celebrities and admire the Grand Prix paraphernalia while you prop up the bar with a bottled beer or heavy-duty cocktail.

CAFÉ DE PARIS   Café
(www.montecarloresort.com; place du Casino; mains €17-53; ☺ 7am-2am) Adjacent to the opulent Monte Carlo Casino, this is a fabulous spot for a decadent – if grossly

Plage de Notre Dame, Île de Porquerolles

DAVID TOMLINSON

overpriced – coffee or aperitif while limo-spotting from the sprawling 300-seat terrace.

 Entertainment

Opera de Monte-Carlo Opera
(www.opera.mc) Adjacent to the casino, the magnificent Opera de Monte-Carlo generally stages productions from October to May.

 Information

Monaco's tourist office (www.visitmonaco.com; 2a bd des Moulins; ⊙9am-7pm Mon-Sat, 11am-1pm Sun) is across the public gardens from the casino.

Getting There & Away

There are frequent trains to Nice (€3.40, 20 minutes), and east to Menton (€1.90, 10 minutes) and the first town across the border in Italy, Ventimiglia (€3.80, 20 minutes).

In Focus

Hiker relaxing under a tree, Corsica
PHOTOGRAPHER: STEPHANE VICTOR

France Today

Paris (p51)

> **in 2010 a controversial law banning face-covering veils in public was approved**

belief systems
(% of population)

87 · 1 · 2 · 10

Roman Catholic · Protestant · Jewish · Muslim

if France were 100 people

77 would live in cities
23 would live in rural areas

population per sq km

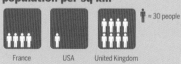

France · USA · United Kingdom

♟ ≈ 30 people

A New Breed of President

Presidential elections in 2007 ushered out old-school Jacques Chirac (in his 70s with two terms under his belt) and brought in Nicolas Sarkozy (b 1955). Dynamic, ambitious and far from media-shy, the former interior minister and chairman of centre-right party UMP *(Union pour un Mouvement Populaire)* wooed voters with big talk about job creation, lower taxes, crime crackdown and help for France's immigrant population – something that had particular pull coming from the son of a Hungarian immigrant father and Greek Jewish-French mother.

Yet rather than the work of knuckling down to implement his rigorous economic reform platform, it was Sarkozy's personal affairs that got the attention in his first months in office – falling out of love with wife Cecilia, divorcing, falling in love with Italian multimillionaire singer Carla Bruni and remarrying, all in a few hasty months. His popularity plummeted and dragged national morale down with it.

age, currently 60, should be extended to at least 62 (it is much higher in almost every other European country).

Helter-Skelter Downhill

If the results of the 2010 regional elections are anything to go by, Sarkozy could be out of a job after the next presidential elections in 2012.

By spring 2010 unemployment was hovering at 10% and government popularity was at an all-time low.

What was seen as a measurement of just how volatile the country had become came the same month – riots ripped through the Alpine town of Grenoble after a 27-year-old man was shot dead by police while allegedly trying to rob a casino. The burning cars and street clashes with riot police echoed the violence that had bloodied a Parisian suburb in 2005 – and spread like wildfire countrywide creating a state of emergency – following the death of two teenage boys of North African origin, electrocuted after hiding in an electrical substation while on the run from the police.

Banning the Burqa

The wearing of crucifixes, the Islamic headscarf and other overtly religious symbols in state schools has been banned in France since 2004, and in September 2010 a controversial law banning face-covering veils in public was approved by the Senate – by 246 votes to one. Intended to place school children on an equal footing in the classroom, the law is seen by many Muslims in particular as intolerant and evidence that the French State is not prepared to truly integrate them into French society. Women caught wearing a burqa will be fined €150 and be required to attend 'citizenship classes'.

BRUCE BI

Economic Woes

Sarkozy pledged to reduce unemployment and income tax (between 5.5% and 40%), create jobs and boost growth in a economy that nonetheless ranks as the world's eighth largest. Unemployment frog-leaped from 8.7% in 2007 to 7.6% during the global banking crisis in 2008 (when the government injected €10.5 billion into France's six major banks) to 9.1% in 2010 – all to the horror of the French, who traditionally have great expectations of their economy.

Hard-line attempts to reform a pension system, unchanged since 1982, which entitles 1.6 million workers in the rail, metro, energy-supply and fishing industries to draw a full state pension after 37.5 working years (and everyone else after 40), only provoked widespread dismay and a series of national strikes and protests. So too have suggestions that the retirement

Cathédrale de Notre Dame de Paris (p80)

Few nations have a history as rich and rewarding as France. With everything from ancient artworks to Gothic cathedrals and regal châteaux, France often feels like one long history textbook. Even the tiniest towns and villages are littered with reminders of the nation's often turbulent past. Encompassing everything from courtly intrigue to intellectual enlightenment, artistic endeavour and bloody revolution, one thing's for sure – French history certainly isn't dull.

Prehistory

The first people to settle in France in significant numbers were small tribes of hunter-gatherers, who arrived around 50,000 to 35,000 years ago. These nomadic tribes lived seasonally from the land while pursuing game such as mammoth, aurochs, bison and deer. They often used natural caves as temporary shelters, leaving behind many sophisticated artworks, such as those in the Vézère Valley.

c 30,000 BC
Cro-Magnon people arrive in the Vézère Valley and create many cave paintings.

The next great wave of settlers arrived after the end of the last Ice Age, from around 7500 BC to 2500 BC. These Neolithic people were responsible for the construction of France's many megalithic monuments, including dolmens, burial tombs, stone circles and the massive stone alignments of Carnac. During this era, warmer weather allowed the development of farming and animal domestication, and humans increasingly established themselves in settled communities, often protected by defensive forts.

Gauls & Romans

Many of these communities were further developed from around 1500 BC to 500 BC by the Gauls, a Celtic people who migrated westwards from present-day Germany and Eastern Europe. But the Gauls' reign was shortlived; over the next few centuries their territories were gradually conquered or subjugated by the Romans. After decades of sporadic warfare, the Gauls were finally defeated in 52 BC when Caesar's legions crushed a revolt led by the Celtic chief Vercingetorix.

France flourished under Roman rule. With typical industriousness, the Romans set about constructing roads, temples, forts and other civic infrastructure, laying the foundations for many modern French cities (including Paris) and (more importantly in the opinion of many) planting the country's first vineyards, notably around Burgundy and Bordeaux.

The Rise of the Kings

Following the collapse of the Roman Empire, control of France passed to the Frankish dynasties, who ruled from the 5th to the 10th century, and effectively founded France's first royal dynasty. Charlemagne (742–814) was crowned Holy Roman Emperor in 800, around the same time that Scandinavian Vikings (also called Norsemen, thus Normans) began to raid France's western and northern coasts. Having plundered and pillaged to their hearts' content, the Normans eventually formed the independent duchy of Normandy in the early 11th century.

In 1066, the Normans launched a successful invasion of England, making William the Conqueror both Duke of Normandy and King of England. The tale of the invasion is graphically recounted in the embroidered comic-strip known as the Bayeux Tapestry.

During this time, Normandy was one of several independent duchies or provinces (including Brittany, Aquitaine, Burgundy, Anjou and Savoy) within the wider French kingdom. While each province superficially paid allegiance to the French crown, they were effectively self-governing and ruled by their own courts.

1500–500 BC
The Celtic Parisii tribe settle on what is now the Île de la Cité, Paris.

c AD 100–300
The heyday of Gallo-Roman France results in the construction of many splendid Roman buildings.

987
The Capetian dynasty comes to power and remains the French royal family for 800 years.

The Best Roman Sites

Intrigue and infighting was widespread. Matters came to a head in 1122 when Eleanor, Queen of Aquitaine, wed Henry, Duke of Anjou (who was also Duke of Normandy and, as William the Conqueror's great-grandson, heir to the English crown). Henry's ascension to the English throne in 1124 effectively brought a third of France under England's control, and sowed the seeds for several centuries of conflict collectively known as the Hundred Years' War (1337–1453).

Following particularly heavy defeats for the French at Crécy and Agincourt, John Plantagenet was made regent of France on behalf of Henry VI in 1422, and less than a decade later he was crowned king of France. The tide of the war seemed to have taken a decisive turn, but luckily for the French, a 17-year-old warrior by the name of Jeanne d'Arc (Joan of Arc) rallied the French forces and inspired the French king Charles VII to a series of victories, culminating in the recapture of Paris in 1437.

Unfortunately things didn't turn out well for Joan – she was subsequently betrayed to the English, accused of heresy and witchcraft, and burnt at the stake in Rouen in 1431.

Renaissance to Revolution

During the reign of François I (r 1515–47), the Renaissance arrived from Italy, and prompted a great flowering of culture, art and architecture across France. Many lavish royal châteaux were built along the Loire Valley, showcasing the skills of French architects and artisans and projecting the might and majesty of the French monarchy. This great era of castle-building reached its zenith under the reign of Louis XIV (1643–1715), known as the Sun King, who emphasised the supposedly divine status of the French monarchy, and constructed the ultimate playground palace at Versailles.

The pomp and profligacy of the ruling elite didn't go down well with everyone, however. Following a series of social and economic crises that rocked the country during the 18th century, and incensed by the corruption and bourgeois extravagance of the aristocracy, a Parisian mob took to the streets in 1789, storming the prison at Bastille and kickstarting the French Revolution.

Inspired by the lofty ideals of *liberté, fraternité, égalité* (freedom, brotherhood, equality), the Revolutionaries initially found favour with the French people. France was declared a constitutional monarchy, but order broke down when the hard-line

1066

William the Conqueror invades England, making Normandy and England rivals of the kingdom of France.

1337–1453

The French and English battle for control of France during the Hundred Years' War.

King William's Tower of London

GLENN BEANLAND

Off with His Head

Prior to the Revolution, public executions in France depended on rank: the nobility were generally beheaded with a sword or axe (with predictably messy consequences), while commoners were usually hanged (particularly nasty prisoners were also drawn and quartered, which involved being eviscerated while still alive and then pulled to pieces by four oxen).

In an effort to provide a more civilised end for the condemned, in the early 1790s a group of French physicians, scientists and engineers set about designing a clinical new execution machine involving a razor-sharp weighted blade, guaranteed to behead people with a minimum of fuss or mess. Named after one of its inventors, the anatomy professor Ignace Guillotin, the machine was first used on 25 April 1792, when the highwayman Nicolas Jacques Pelletie went down in history as the first man to lose his head to the guillotine.

During the Reign of Terror, at least 17,000 met their death beneath the machine's plunging blade. By the time the last was given the chop in 1977 (behind closed doors – the last public execution was in 1939), the contraption could slice off a head in 2/100 of a second.

Jacobins seized power. The monarchy was abolished and the nation was declared a republic on 21 September 1792. Three months later Louis XVI was publicly guillotined, as an example to the people, on Paris' place de la Concorde. His ill-fated queen, Marie-Antoinette, suffered the same fate a few months later.

As the pillars of French society crumbled, chaos ensued. Violent retribution broke out across France. During the Reign of Terror (September 1793 to July 1794) churches were closed, religious monuments were desecrated, riots were suppressed and thousands of aristocrats were imprisoned or beheaded. The high ideals of the Revolution had turned to vicious bloodshed, and the nation was rapidly descending into anarchy. France desperately needed someone to re-establish order, give it new direction and rebuild its shattered sense of self. From amidst the smoke and thunder, a dashing (if diminutive) young Corsican general stepped from the shadows.

The Napoleonic Era

Napoléon's military prowess quickly turned him into a powerful political force. In 1804 he was crowned emperor at Notre Dame Cathedral, and subsequently led the French armies to conquer much of Europe. His ill-fated campaign to invade Russia ended in disaster, however; in 1812, his armies were stopped outside Moscow and

1530s	1643–1715	1789–94
The Reformation embraces France, leading to Protestant–Catholic conflict during the Wars of Religion (1562–98).	Louis XIV assumes the French throne and shifts his royal court from Paris to Versailles.	Revolutionaries storm the Bastille. Louis XVI and Marie-Antoinette are guillotined.

The Best Historic Sights

decimated by the brutal Russian winter. Two years later, Allied armies entered Paris and exiled Napoléon to Elba.

But that wasn't the last of the little general. In 1815 Napoléon escaped, re-entering Paris on 20 May. His glorious 'Hundred Days' ended with defeat by the English at the Battle of Waterloo. He was exiled again, this time to St Helena in the South Atlantic, where he died in 1821. His body was later reburied under the Hôtel des Invalides in Paris.

New Republics

Post-Napoléon, France was dogged by a string of ineffectual rulers until Napoléon's nephew, Louis Napoléon Bonaparte, came to power. He was initially elected president, but declared himself Emperor (Napoléon III) in 1851.

While the so-called Second Empire ran roughshod over many of the ideals set down during the Revolution, it actually proved to be a relatively prosperous time. France enjoyed significant economic growth and Paris was transformed by the urban planner Baron Haussmann, who created the famous twelve boulevards radiating from the Arc de Triomphe (including the celebrated Champs-Élysées).

But like his uncle, Napoléon III's ambition was his undoing. A series of costly conflicts, including the Crimean War (1854–56), culminated in humiliating defeat by the Prussian forces in 1870. France was once again declared a republic – for the third time in less than a century.

The Belle Époque

The Third Republic got off to a shaky start: another war with the Prussians resulted in a huge war bill and the surrender of Alsace and Lorraine. But the period also ushered in a new era of culture and creativity that left an enduring mark on France's national character.

The belle époque ('beautiful age'), as it came to be known, was an era of unprecedented innovation. Architects built a host of exciting new buildings and transformed the face of many French cities. Engineers laid the tracks of France's first railways and tunnelled out the metro system still used by millions of Parisians today. Designers experimented with new styles and materials, while young artists

1851
Louis Napoléon proclaims himself Emperor Napoléon III of the Second Empire (1851–70).

1914–18
WWI: millions of French soldiers are killed and many historic cities destroyed.

1939–44
WWII: Nazi Germany divides France into a German-occupied zone and a puppet Vichy state.

invented a host of new 'isms' (including Impressionism, which took its title from one of Claude Monet's seminal early paintings, *Impression, Soleil Levant*).

The era culminated in a lavish Exposition Universelle (World Fair) in Paris in 1889, an event that seems to sum up the excitement and dynamism of the age, and also inspired the construction of one of the nation's most iconic landmarks – the Eiffel Tower.

The Great War

Sadly, the *joie de vivre* of the belle époque wasn't to last. Within months of the outbreak of WWI in 1914, the fields of northern France had been transformed into a sea of trenches and shell craters; by the time the armistice had been signed in November 1918, some 1.3 million French soldiers had been killed and almost one million crippled. A trip to the battlefields of the Somme or Verdun provides a chilling reminder of the unimaginable human cost of WWI.

Desperate to forget the ravages of the war, Paris sparkled as the centre of the avant-garde in the 1920s and 1930s. The liberal atmosphere (not to mention the cheap booze and saucy nightlife) attracted a stream of foreign artists and writers

Trophée des Alps (p341)
PHOTOGRAPHER: GLENN VAN DER KNIJFF

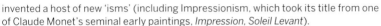

1949
France joins North America and Western Europe in a mutual defence alliance (NATO).

1981
The high-speed TGV smashes speed records. Journey time from Paris to Lyon falls to under two hours.

1994
The 50km-long Channel Tunnel links mainland France with Britain.

The French Resistance

Despite the myth of *'la France résistante'* (the French Resistance), the underground movement never actually included more than 5% of the population. The other 95% either collaborated or did nothing. Resistance members engaged in railway sabotage, collected intelligence for the Allies, helped Allied airmen who had been shot down and published anti-German leaflets, among other activities. Though the impact of their actions was relatively slight, the Resistance served as an enormous boost to French morale – not to mention the inspiration for numerous literary and cinematic endeavours.

to the city, and helped establish Paris' enduring reputation for creativity and experimentation.

WWII

Unfortunately, the inter-war party was short-lived. Two days after Germany invaded Poland in 1939, France joined Britain in declaring war on Germany. Within a year, Hitler's *blitzkrieg* had swept across Europe, and France was forced into humiliating capitulation in June the same year. Following the seaborne retreat of the British Expeditionary Force at Dunkirk, France – like much of Europe – found itself under Nazi occupation.

The Germans divided France into two zones: the west and north (including Paris), which was under direct German rule; and a puppet-state in the south based around the spa town of Vichy. The anti-semitic Vichy regime proved very helpful to the Nazis in rounding up Jews and other undesirables for deportation to the death camps.

After four years of occupation, on 6 June 1944 Allied forces returned to French soil during the D-Day Landings. Over 100,000 Allied troops stormed the Normandy coastline and, after several months of fighting, liberated Paris on 25 August. But the cost of the war had been devastating for France: half a million buildings had been destroyed, many cities had been razed to the ground and millions of French people had lost their lives.

Poverty to Prosperity

Broken and battered from the war, France was forced to turn to the USA for loans as part of the Marshall Plan to rebuild Europe. Slowly, under the government of the French war hero Charles de Gaulle, the economy began to recover and France began to rebuild its shattered infrastructure. The debilitating Algerian War of Independence (1954–62) and the subsequent loss of its colonies seriously weakened de Gaulle's government, however, and following widespread student protests in 1968 and a general strike by 10 million workers, De Gaulle was forced to resign from office in 1969. He died the following year.

2002

The French franc, first minted in 1360, is dumped when France adopts the euro.

2004

The National Assembly bans religious symbols such as the Islamic headscarf in state schools.

Euros

GREG ELMS

Subsequent French presidents Georges Pompidou (in power from 1969 to 1974) and Giscard d'Estaing (1974–81) were instrumental in the increasing political and economic integration of Europe, a process that had begun with the formation of the EEC (European Economic Community) in 1957, and continued under François Mitterand with the enlarged EU (European Union) in 1991. During Mitterand's time in office, France abolished the death penalty, legalised homosexuality, gave workers five weeks' holiday and guaranteed the right to retire at 60.

In 1995 Mitterand was succeeded by the maverick socialist Jacques Chirac, who was re-elected in 2002. Chirac's attempts at reform led to widespread strikes and social unrest, while his opposition to the Iraq war alienated the US administration (and famously lead to the rebranding of French fries as Freedom fries).

President Bling-Bling

Following Chirac's retirement, the media-savvy Nicolas Sarkozy was elected president in 2007, bringing a more personality-driven, American-style approach to French politics. His turbulent private life and celebrity lifestyle initially proved popular but have since backfired, and while Sarko's latest exploits are splashed across the tabloids, France continues to struggle with record levels of unemployment and a stubbornly stagnant economy. Whether he'll survive the next election remains to be seen, but regardless of President Bling-Bling's fate, there are sure to be a few more French fireworks on the horizon as the new decade unfolds.

The Best History Museums

2007
France's most significant presidential elections since WWII bring Nicolas Sarkozy to power.

2008
Sarkozy's popularity plummets following his showbiz-style marriage to Italian model and singer Carla Bruni.

2010
Widespread strikes oppose attempts to raise the state retirement age from 60 to 62.

The French

Parisian café

JOHN SC

Arrogant, bureaucratic, chau-
vinistic and stylish... France is a
country whose people has attracted
more myths and stereotypes than
any other in Europe, and over
the centuries dozens of tags have
been pinned on the garlic-eating,
beret-wearing, sacre-bleu-*swearing*
French. (The French, by the way,
hardly ever wear berets or use
old chestnuts such as 'sacre bleu'
anymore.)

Being French

Most people are extremely proud to be French and are staunchly nationalistic, a result of the country's republican stance – which places nationality (rather than religion, for example) at the top of the self-identity list. This has created an overwhelmingly self-confident nation, both culturally and intellectually, that often comes across as one with a superiority complex.

Contrary to popular belief, many French speak a foreign language fairly well, travel and are happy to use their language skills if necessary. French men, incidentally, deem an English gal's heavily accented French as sexy as she might find a Frenchman speaking English.

Lifestyle

The French are full of contradictions: they drink and smoke more than anyone else, yet live longer; they eat like kings, but have a lower rate of obesity than most European nations. But if there were such a thing as Monsieur et Madame Tout le Monde (Mr & Mrs Everyman), what might they be like?

Well, they'd most likely work in one of France's big cities, and rent their apartment from a private landlord (home ownership in France is low, with only 57% of households owning their own home). They'd dunk croissants in bowls of fresh coffee for breakfast, buy a baguette every day from the bakery and recycle nothing bar a few glass bottles.

Madame would buy stacks of weekly gossip magazines, while Monsieur would regularly pop out to meet his mates for a game of *boules* and a glass of *eau de vie*. They'd put everything on the *carte bleue* (credit or debit card) when shopping, and only ever holiday in August.

They'd eat out a couple of times a week, go to the flicks once a month, work precisely 35 hours a week, and have two kids who have both been through university (France's state-run universities are free to anyone who passes the *baccalauréat*).

Faux Pas

○ **Forget the school-textbook French** *'S'il vous plaît'* – never *'garçon'* (meaning 'boy') – is the *only* way to summon a waiter.

○ **Don't split the restaurant bill** The person who invites pays, although close friends often go Dutch.

○ **Don't fondle fruit, veg, flowers or clothing in shops** Ask if you want to touch.

○ **Get the name right** *'Monsieur'* for men, *'Madame'* for 'Mrs' and *'Mademoiselle'* for unmarried women.

French Kissing

Kissing is still the traditional way for French people to greet each other (although the expression 'French kissing', as in with tongues, actually doesn't exist in French).

In Paris it is definitely two kisses: anything more is deemed affected, although trendy 20-somethings and teenagers often swap three or four cheek-skimming kisses just to be different. Travel south and the *bisous* (kisses) multiply, three being the norm in Provence, and four in the Loire Valley.

To avoid any embarrassing moments, do as the French do and always start with the right cheek.

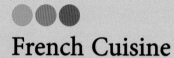

French Cuisine

OLIVER STR

If there's one thing the French are famous for, it's food. In many ways this is the nation that taught the rest of the world how to dine, and if you approach food and wine here with half the zest les français do, you'll be welcomed, encouraged and exceedingly well fed indeed.

Food

While chefs and critics often talk in sweeping terms about French cuisine, there's really no such thing. While there are certainly many classic national dishes, each region has its own distinctive flavours, ingredients and cooking styles. Discovering the differences is one of the great joys of travelling in France, but one thing's for sure – wherever you end up, you won't go hungry.

Meals in France

The classic French breakfast (*petit déjeuner*) consists of baguette, jam, coffee, and fruit juice (croissants and pastries are traditionally reserved as treats for the weekend, although they're normally always included in hotel breakfasts). Many hotels also offer a more generous buffet breakfast, which might feature cereals, cold meats, yoghurt, cheese, fruit and bread. Ask at the front desk when you check in to see what the hotel offers and whether it's likely to be worth the premium – you might well be better served by seeking out a local café instead.

Lunch (*déjeuner*) is served from noon to around 2pm, and is often the main meal of the day for French people. There is usually a good value 2- or 3-course *menu du jour* (daily menu) consisting of a *plat du jour* (daily special) with an entrée (starter) and/or a dessert. Most restaurants only offer the *menu du jour* at lunchtime, which is why it's often easier to find a free table for dinner than for lunch.

Dinner (*diner*) usually starts around 6.30pm and continues till around 10pm. Two or three courses are the norm; fixed menus generally offer better value than *à la carte*, but you'll have fewer dishes to choose from. Cheese and coffee is usually extra.

Cheese

Charles de Gaulle famously declared that it was impossible to govern a country with 246 types of cheese; the number of French *fromages* is over double that these days. The choice can be overwhelming to the uninitiated, but any decent *fromagerie* (cheese shop) will happily let you sample before you buy, and offer helpful advice on local varieties.

French cheeses are generally made using milk from cows (*fromage de vache*), ewes (*fromage de brébis*) or goats (*fromage de chèvre*). Contrary to the stereotype, the French don't eat cheese with every meal – it's usually reserved only for formal meals, when the cheese board customarily comes *before* dessert. Cheese is always served with baguette, never crackers, and no butter.

There are a few rules to observe when eating cheese at the table: round cheeses (such as Brie and Camembert) are cut into wedges like a pie – it's considered rude to cut the tip off a wedge, so cut from the tip to the rind instead; hard cheeses such as Comté are usually just cut horizontally in hunks; and when slicing blue or veined cheeses, where the middle is the best bit, take a fair share of the rind with your slice.

Bread

No French meal would be complete without a fresh baguette.

Buying bread is a daily ritual for French people, and it's usually served at breakfast, lunch and dinner. The French traditionally eat bread *sans beurre* (without butter) at meals, but will grudgingly supply a bit of butter if you ask nicely.

The classic French bread is the long, crusty stick known as the baguette. The *flûte* is similar but slightly fatter, while the *ficelle* is thinner and crispier. Baguettes are best eaten within four hours of baking. You can store them for longer in a plastic bag, but the crust becomes soft and chewy; if you leave them out, they'll be rock-hard within hours.

Most bakeries also offer a range of more expensive loaves, often made with grains, cereals, nuts or herbs. A common type is the *pain de campagne*, which is typically a round loaf made with white and wholemeal flour.

The Best Things to Try

1 Bouillabaisse in Marseille (p310)

2 Camembert in Normandy (p128)

3 Sausages in Lyon

4 Fondue in the French Alps

5 Oysters and shellfish in Brittany

6 Black truffles in the Dordogne

Meat & Charcuterie

Meat in France isn't simply a matter of steaks, chops and cutlets – French chefs make use of practically every part of the animal, including tongue, trotters and pretty much every type of offal you can imagine. Some of these might sound unsavoury, but don't dismiss them out of hand – once they've been marinaded, basted and slow-cooked, they can often be much tastier than more-traditional cuts. Some, however, are an acquired taste – *tête de veau* (calf's head) is probably best left to the nonsqueamish.

Charcuterie traditionally denotes meat products made from pork, but encompasses other things such as cold cuts, patés and terrines. The classic charcuterie is the *saucisson* (a cured sausage similar to salami), which you can buy whole or sliced. *Saucisse* denotes a fresh, uncooked sausage that's boiled, grilled or fried before eating.

Other things to look out for on the charcuterie counter are *jambon* (ham), *andouillette* (tripe sausage), *boudin* (blood sausage/black pudding) and *rillettes* (potted meat, usually spread cold over bread or toast). *Paté* in France tends to be smooth; *terrines* are coarser in texture and taste. *Cassoulet* is a casserole of beans and meat, traditionally eaten around Toulouse and the Languedoc.

If you're ordering steak, it helps to be able to say how you like it cooked: *bleu* (almost raw), *saignant* (rare), *à point* (medium rare), *bien cuit* (with just a hint of pinkness) or *très bien cuit* (very well done).

Fish & Seafood

Meat is a key feature of most French menus, but you'll nearly always be offered at least one type of *poisson* (fish), too. The choice obviously tends to be more varied along the coasts, especially in Brittany, Normandy and along the Mediterranean coastline.

You'll find classic dishes such as *moules-frites* (mussels and chips) nearly everywhere, but each region has its own seafood specialities. Brittany and the

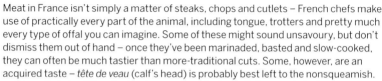

Types of French Cheese

○ **Goat's cheese** (*fromage de chèvre*) French goat's cheese is creamy, sweet and faintly salty when fresh, but hardens and gets saltier as it matures. Key varieties include Ste-Maure de Touraine, Crottin de Chavignol, Cabécou de Rocamadour, and St-Marcellin, a runny white cheese. A common French bistro dish is *salade au chèvre chaud*, in which discs of goat's cheese are melted over green salad leaves.

○ **Blue cheese** (*fromage à pâté persillée*) These veined, marbled, mature cheeses usually have the strongest flavour and fragrance. The most common varieties are powerful Roquefort and the more mild Fourme d'Ambert.

○ **Soft cheese** (*fromage à pâté molle*) Perhaps the classic variety of French cheese, served soft, smelly and runny. Common types include Camembert and Brie (both from Normandy) and Munster (from Alsace), but the most pungent by far is Époisses (from Burgundy) – proper smelly sock stuff.

○ **Semihard cheese** (*fromage à pâté demi-dure*) These cheeses have a squishy, semi-firm texture, a thick rind and a fairly mild flavour. They are especially common in the Alps and Pyrenees. Common types are Tomme de Savoie, Cantal, St-Nectaire and Ossau-Iraty.

○ **Hard cheese** (*fromage à pâté dure*) The hardest type of French cheese has a texture similar to cheddar. Common types include Beaufort, Comté, Emmental and Mimolette, an Edam-like bright-orange cheese from Lille.

Atlantic Coast are known for their shellfish and oysters; while Provence and the Riviera are the best places to try *bouillabaisse* (a rich seafood stew) and *soupe de poissons* (fish soup), both traditionally accompanied by *rouille* (a spicy mayonnaise of oil, chillis and garlic).

Les Diamants Noirs

The Dordogne's most celebrated delicacy is the *diamant noir* (black diamond or black truffle), a subterranean fungus that grows in chalky soils (often around the roots of oak and hazelnut trees) and is notoriously difficult to find; a good spot one year can be inexplicably bare the next, which has made farming them practically impossible. Serious truffle hunters use specially trained dogs (and sometimes pigs) to help them search. A vintage crop of truffles can fetch as much as €850 a kilo.

The height of truffle season is between December and March, when special truffle markets are held around the Dordogne.

Poultry

When it comes to birds, the French don't just limit themselves to chicken and turkey – they eat other types of poultry with equal gusto, including *canard* (duck), *oie* (goose), *perdrix* (partridge), *faisan* (pheasant), pigeon and *caille* (quail).

Pâté de foie gras (a rich, smooth paté of fattened duck or goose livers, sometimes flavoured with cognac and truffles) is a particular delicacy, especially in southwest France; while *confit de canard* and *confit d'oie* are duck or goose joints cooked very slowly in their own fat, making them very tender and packed with flavour.

Snails & Frogs' Legs

France suffers from its share of culinary clichés, but without any doubt, the most notorious French dishes are *escargots* (snails) and *cuisses de grenouille* (frogs' legs). Both are still a delicacy in France, but they're a lot less common than they

Cheese plate
PHOTOGRAPHER: OLIVER STREWE

French Cooking Styles

Here's a quick guide of some of the classic French sauces and cooking styles you're likely to encounter on restaurant menus:

- **à l'americaine** cooked in brandy, white wine and tomatoes
- **bourgignon** slow-cooked in red wine, often with onions and mushrooms
- **dijonaise** in a mustard sauce
- **dieppoise** a sauce of fish, shellfish, herbs and cider
- **florentine** in a creamy spinach sauce
- **normande** in a cream or butter sauce
- **provençale** in a tomato or herb sauce
- **lyonnais** a sauce of onions, wine, garlic and parsley
- **meunière** coated in flour, then pan-fried in butter, lemon juice and parsley

once were (ironically, you'll probably only find them in smarter restaurants nowadays).

Contrary to popular belief, the French don't simply eat any old snail they find on the garden path – the only one you'll find on menus is the *escargot de Bourgogne* (Burgundy snail, also known as the edible snail). They are most often eaten in a rich sauce of butter, parsley and garlic. This once-common snail has been all but obliterated as a wild species in France due to pesticides, and the vast majority of *escargots* now have to be imported from Turkey, Greece and Eastern Europe.

Similarly, *cuisses de grenouille* usually come from edible frogs (also known as the green frog or common water frog), which are specially reared on frog farms. The most common way to serve them is fried in breadcrumbs; the taste is said to be similar to chicken.

Cakes & Sweet Treats

Like many European nations, the French have a terrible sweet tooth. In any boulangerie or patisserie you'll be faced with an irresistible assortment of pastries, cakes and sweet treats, including the classics: the *croissant* (butter pastry), *pain au chocolat* (butter pastry with dark chocolate in the middle) and *éclair* (which comes in chocolate and coffee varieties). Other treats to look out for in bakeries are *macarons* (macaroons), *meringues* (meringues), *sablés* (shortbread biscuits) and *tartes aux fruits* (fruit tarts).

Dessert is equally indulgent. Common ones include *tarte tatin* (upside-down apple cake), *fine tarte aux pommes* (apple tart, usually served with cream) and various types of *gâteaux* (cakes) and *glaces* (ice creams, served by the *boule*, or scoop).

Another common dessert is the *crêpe*, a thin pancake served with a sweet filling of jam, chocolate or ice-cream. Crêpes can also be eaten with savoury fillings (especially in Brittany). *Galettes* are similar to *crêpes* but made with buckwheat flour.

Wine & Other Drinks

The French may no longer start the day with a shot of red wine to *tuer le ver* (kill the worm), but France still ranks in the world's top 10 boozing states. Wine, predictably, is the nation's favourite tipple, with seven key areas producing the vast majority of French wine: Alsace, Bordeaux, Burgundy, Champagne, Languedoc, the Loire and the Rhône.

The Art of Wine

The taste and quality of French wine is governed by four key factors: the type(s) of grape used, the climate, the soil and the skill of the *vigneron* (winemaker).

Quality wines in France are designated as *Appellation d'Origine Contrôlée* (AOC; literally, 'label of inspected origin'), indicating that they meet stringent regulations governing where, how and under what conditions they are grown and bottled. AOCs can cover a wide region (such as Bordeaux), a sub-region (such as Haut-Médoc), or a commune or village (such as Pomerol). Some regions only have a single AOC (such as Alsace), while Burgundy is chopped into scores of individual AOCs.

French wines are also divided by a complex grading system according to the quality of the wine; the very best are awarded the label of *grand cru* (literally 'great growth'), and command a premium price tag.

Key Winemaking Regions

Burgundy

Burgundy's vineyards are small (rarely more than 10 hectares) and produce small quantities of wine. Burgundy reds are produced with pinot noir grapes; the best vintages need 10 to 20 years to age. White wine is made from the chardonnay grape. The five main wine-growing areas are Chablis, Côte d'Or, Côte Chalonnaise, Mâcon and Beaujolais.

Bordeaux

Bordeaux has the perfect climate for producing wine; as a result its 1100 sq km of vineyards produce more fine wine than any other region in the world. Bordeaux reds are well balanced, a quality achieved by blending several grape varieties. The grapes predominantly used are merlot, cabernet sauvignon and cabernet franc. Bordeaux's foremost wine-growing areas are the Médoc, Pomerol, St-Émilion and Graves. The nectar-like sweet whites of the Sauternes area are the world's finest dessert wines.

Côtes du Rhône

The Rhône region is divided into northern and southern areas, the different soil, climate and grapes of which produce dramatically different wines.

Set on steep hills by the river, the northern vineyards produce red wines exclusively from the ruby-red syrah (shiraz) grape; the aromatic viognier grape is the most popular for white wines. The south is better known for quantity rather than quality. The grenache grape, which ages well when blended, is used in the reds, while the whites use the ugni blanc grape.

Champagne

Champagne has been the centre for bubbly production since the 17th century, when the monk Dom Pierre Pérignon perfected a technique for making sparkling wine.

Champagne is made from the red pinot noir, black pinot meunier or white chardonnay grape. To maintain exclusivity (and price), the designated areas where Champagne grapes can be grown and the amount of wine produced each year is limited. In 2008 the borders of the Champagne AOC label were extended to include an additional 40 villages, increasing the value of their vineyards and its produce by tens of millions of euros.

Champagne is labelled *brut* (extra dry with just 1.5% sugar content), *extra-sec* (dry, but not as dry as *brut*), *sec* (dry), *demi-sec* (slightly sweet) or *doux* (sweet). Famous Champagne houses include Dom Pérignon, Moët & Chandon, Veuve Clicquot, Mercier, Mumm, Krug, Laurent-Perrier, Piper-Heidsieck, Taittinger, De Castellane and Pommery.

The Best Places for Wine-Tasting

The Loire Valley

The Loire's 700 sq km of vineyards rank it as the third-largest area in France for the production of quality wines. Although sunny, the climate here is humid and not all grape varieties thrive. Still, the Loire produces the greatest variety of wines of any region in the country. A particular speciality of the region is rosé. The most common grapes are the Muscadet, cabernet franc and chenin blanc varieties, and wines tend to be light and delicate. The most celebrated areas are Pouilly-Fumé, Vouvray, Sancerre, Bourgueil, Chinon and Saumur.

Languedoc

Languedoc is the country's most-productive wine-growing region, producing up to 40% of France's wine (mainly cheap red table wine). In addition to the well-known Fitou label, the area's other quality wines are Coteaux du Languedoc, Faugères, Corbières and Minervois.

Alsace

Alsace produces unique white wines known for their clean taste and fresh finish. Unusually, some of the fruity Alsatian whites also go well with red meat. The vineyards closest to Strasbourg produce light red wines from pinot noir that are similar to rosé and are best served chilled.

Alsace's four most important varietal wines are riesling, known for its subtlety; the more pungent and highly regarded gewürztraminer; the robust pinot gris, which is high in alcohol content; and muscat d'Alsace, which is not as sweet as that made with muscat grapes grown further south.

Beer, Cider & Spirits

Though it's principally known for its wine, France also produces many excellent beers, especially in northern France and Alsace (thanks to its close cultural ties with nearby Germany). The main French breweries for Heineken and Kronenbourg can both be visited near Strasbourg, but there are many smaller breweries dotted across the region. Names to look out for include Bière de Scharrach, Schutzenberger Jubilator and Fischer d'Alsace, a hoppy brew from Schiltigheim.

The preferred tipples in Normandy and Brittany are *cidre* (apple cider) and pear-based *poiré* (perry). *Calvados* is a strong apple brandy that's often drunk as an aperitif or used to flavour desserts.

Common aperitifs include *kir* (white wine sweetened with cassis), *kir royale* (Champagne with cassis) or *pineau* (cognac and grape juice), while brandies such as Cognac and Armagnac often appear as after-dinner *digestifs*.

In many French bars (especially the further south you go), you'll often see people taking a shot of spirits with their coffee – *eaux de vie* (literally 'waters of life') and *pastis* (a 90% proof, aniseed-flavoured spirit) are the most popular (and potent).

Literature & the Arts

Galerie des Batailles, Château de Versailles (p105)

JOHN ELK III

In a country where style and panache count for so much, it comes as no surprise that culture still matters deeply to French people. France has a long and distinguished legacy in literature, painting, sculpture and cinema, and the arts continue to play a crucial role in the nation's collective culture.

Painting

From the dreamy landscapes of the Impressionists to the radical experiments of Cubism, France has been the crucible for a host of artistic movements.

Classical & Romantic

According to Voltaire, French painting began with Nicolas Poussin (1594–1665), whose dramatic paintings based on mythological and biblical scenes set the benchmark for classical French art. Later, Romantic painters such as David (1748–1825), Géricault (1791–1824) and Délacroix (1798–1863) drew their inspiration from French history and political events, creating lifelike canvases packed with power and emotion. Key works by all these artists can be seen in the Louvre in Paris.

The Best Art Trails

Other artists moved out of their studios in search of subjects from everyday life. Jean-François Millet (1814–75), the son of a Norman farmer, depicted peasant life in France's rural villages: his *L'Angélus* (The Angelus; 1857) is the best-known French painting after the *Mona Lisa* (the original *L'Angélus* is in Paris' Musée d'Orsay).

Impressionism & Post-Impressionism

During the late 19th century, artists experimented with capturing an 'impression' of a scene, emphasising colour, light and atmosphere above strictly realistic representation. This movement (dubbed 'Impressionism' after an early painting by Claude Monet, 1840–1926) included artists such as Claude Pissarro, Alfred Sisley, Eugène Boudin, Edgar Degas and Auguste Renoir, but it's Monet's work that encapsulates the spirit of Impressionism for many people – particularly his *Nymphéas* (Water Lily) paintings, painted in the grounds of his own garden in Giverny, near Paris.

During the Post-Impressionist period, artists continued to push the boundaries of acceptability, both in terms of subject and technique. The intense light and lush landscapes of Provence and the Riviera attracted many artists, including Paul Cézanne (1839–1906) and the Dutch artist Vincent van Gogh (1853–90), while the hustle and bustle of *fin-de-siècle* Paris attracted others, such as Henri de Toulouse-Lautrec (1864–1901), best known for his paintings of Parisian brothels. Other artists travelled further afield: Paul Gauguin (1848–1903) emigrated to Tahiti, where he produced rich, sensual paintings inspired by his adopted tropical home.

Meanwhile in St-Tropez, pointillist painters applied paint in small dots to produce a colourful mosaic-like effect: the works of Georges Seurat and his pupil Paul Signac (1863–1935) are on display at St-Tropez's Musée de l'Annonciade.

Fauvism, Cubism & Surrealism

The dawn of the 20th century inspired a bewildering diversity of artistic movements, many of which inspired considerable controversy. Fauvist artists such as Henri Matisse (1869–1954) and André Dérain (1880–1954) moved even further from the confines of representational art, often using bold, brash colours that bore little relation to reality; the movement famously got its name from a shocked art critic who compared the artists with *fauves* (wild animals) after an exhibition in 1905.

Fauvism marked the start of an experimental century. Cubism completely threw out the artistic rule book, breaking subjects into component shapes and ignoring long-established rules of perspective and composition: among its key figures were the Spanish-born artist Pablo Picasso (1881–1973) and the French artist Georges Braque (1882–1963).

Meanwhile, surrealist artists delved into their subconscious in search of hidden dreams and desires, inspired by the theories of the psychoanalyst Sigmund Freud. Dadaism, an offshoot of surrealism, was shot through with a rebellious spirit and an anarchic sense of humour – one of its most famous exponents, Marcel Duchamp (1887–1962), famously made a sculpture from a men's urinal and painted a goatee on the *Mona Lisa*.

Modern Art

After WWII, the focus shifted from Paris to southern France in the 1960s with new realists such as Arman (1928–2005) and Yves Klein (1928–62), both from Nice. In 1960 Klein famously produced *Anthropométrie de l'Époque Bleue,* a series of imprints made by naked women covered from head to toe in blue paint rolling around on a white canvas.

More-recent artists have increasingly moved towards conceptual art, using practically every medium other than paint to express their concerns. Among the best-known are Daniel Buren (b 1938), the *enfant terrible* of 1980s French art, and Sophie Calle (b 1953), who brazenly exposes her private life with her eye-catching installations.

Cinema

France is the nation that invented cinema, so it's hardly surprising that film continues to be one of its most enduring art forms. The *septième art*, as cinema is often known, is a passion for many French people, and a trip to the flicks still numbers as one of the nation's favourite pastimes. Every May, France celebrates its love affair with cinema at the annual Cannes Film Festival, which attracts big-name stars to the French Riviera and hands out one of the world's most coveted film prizes, the Palme d'Or.

Early Cinema

The Lumière Brothers (Auguste and Louis) shot the world's first-ever motion picture, *La Sortie des Usines Lumières* (Exit of the Lumières Factories) in one of their family factories on 19 March 1895. Today, the factory has been transformed into the Musée Lumière, which explores cinema's beginnings and screens classic films.

Despite several early classics, it wasn't until the 1930s that French cinema really hit its stride. The classic *La Grande Illusion* (The Great Illusion; 1937) is a devastating portrayal of the folly of war, based on the trench warfare experience of director Jean Renoir (1894–1979). Hot on its heels came Renoir's seminal *Les Règles du Jeu* (The Rules of the Game; 1939), a biting satire of the French upper classes, set in the years before WWII. Both films established French cinema's reputation for stylish photography, sharp dialogue and intellectual subject matter.

A decade later, the surrealist artist-writer-philosopher Jean Cocteau made two back-to-back masterpieces, *La Belle et la Bête* (Beauty and the Beast; 1945) and *Orphée* (Orpheus; 1950). But it was the directors of the *nouvelle vague* (new wave) who arguably made the greatest contribution to French cinema as an art form. With small budgets, no complex sets and no big stars, these young French directors made highly personal films, pioneering the use of fractured narratives, documentary-style camerawork and new editing techniques.

The Best Art Museums

1 Musée d'Orsay, Paris (p85)

2 Musée du Louvre, Paris (p75)

3 Monet's Garden & Musée des Impressionismes, Giverny (p120)

4 Musée des Beaux Arts, Lyon (p238)

5 Centre Pompidou-Metz (p174)

6 Mamac, Nice (p331)

IN FOCUS LITERATURE & THE ARTS

371

Key directors of the new wave include Claude Chabrol, Alain Resnais and François Truffaut, but the quintessential new wave director is Jean-Luc Godard (b 1930), who captured the essence of Parisian cool in *À Bout de Souffle* (Breathless; 1960) before later branching out into experimental films such as the apocalyptic black comedy *Le Weekend* (1969) and many more.

Almost forty years on, Godard continues to push the boundaries; his latest work, *Film Socialisme* (2010), is touted as a 'cinematic symphony in three movements', and is the director's first to be shot in high definition.

1970s to 1990s

After the fireworks of the new wave, French cinema lost its experimental edge. Lesser-known directors such as Éric Rohmer (b 1920) made beautiful but uneventful films in which the characters endlessly analyse their feelings. Other directors retreated into nostalgia, characterised by Jacques Demy's *Les Parapluies de Cherbourg* (The Umbrellas of Cherbourg; 1964), a bittersweet love story set in Normandy.

The trend continued into the 1970s and '80s, as filmmakers switched to costume dramas and commercial comedies in an attempt to compete with growing competition from the USA. Claude Berri's sentimental portraits of pre-war Provence in *Jean de Florette* (1986) and *Manon des Sources* (1986) found big audiences both at home and abroad, as did Jean-Paul Rappeneau's glossy version of the classic French fable *Cyrano de Bergerac* (1990); all three films starred France's best-known (and biggest-nosed) actor, Gérard Départdieu.

Other directors such as Luc Besson gave a Gallic spin to American genres, beginning with the thrillers *Subway* (1985) and *La Femme Nikita* (1990), followed by

Cannes Film Festival (p43)

TRAVEL AND PLACES/A

big-budget action in *Taxi* (1994), the hit-man movie in *Léon* (1995), sci-fi in *The Fifth Element* (1997) and historical epic in *Joan of Arc* (1999).

The 1990s also saw French cinema acquire a grittier edge, epitomised by Mathieu Kassovitz's hard-hitting *La Haine* (1995), which explored the bleak lives of French youth in Parisian housing estates.

Meanwhile, the filmmaking duo of Jean-Pierre Jeunet and Marc Caro showcased their fantastic imagination and unmistakeably French sense of humour in the cult films *Delicatessen* (1991) and *The City of Lost Children* (1995). Jeunet later enjoyed massive crossover success with *Le Fabuleux Destin d'Amélie Poulain* (Amélie; 2001), which explored the adventures of a Parisian do-gooder in typically quirky Gallic style.

Recent Cinema

French cinema has produced some significant hits over the last decade, most notably big-budget versions of the Astérix comics, and the knockabout spoofs of comic actor Jean Dujardin, such as the *OSS 117* spy films. However, relatively few filmmakers have been able to translate their domestic appeal to an international audience.

There have been some exceptions, though, including the quirky animation *Belleville Rendez-Vous* (The Triplets of Belleville; 2003) and *Les Choristes* (The Chorus; 2004), set in a school for troublesome boys in 1949. More recently, *La Môme* (known overseas as *La Vie en Rose*), a biopic of Édith Piaf, scooped the Best Actress Oscar for Marion Cotillard at the 2008 Academy Awards.

2008 also saw a French film win the Palme d'Or at Cannes for the first time since 1987. Laurent Cantet's *Entre Les Murs* (The Class) used real pupils and teachers to portray a year in the life of a school in a rough Parisian neighbourhood.

Other directors have found an audience by employing shock tactics. *Enfant terrible* Gaspar Noé ruffled feathers with his violent films *Irréversible* (2002) and *Into the Void* (2009), while Jacque Audiard's tough 2009 prison drama, *Un Prophète*, narrowly missed out on an Oscar for Best Foreign Film at the 2010 Academy Awards.

The major success of recent years, however, is undoubtedly *Bienvenue chez les Ch'tis* (Welcome to the Sticks; 2008), a warm-hearted comedy, directed by Dany Boon, that debunks grim stereotypes about the industrialised regions of northern France. Grossing an astonishing US$194 million in France and $245 million worldwide, it's the highest-grossing French film of all time.

French Cinema in 10 Films

- **1 La Règle du Jeu** (*The Rules of the Game,* 1939)
- **2 Les Enfants du Paradis** (*Children of Paradise,* 1945)
- **3 Les Vacances de M Hulôt** (*Mr Hulôt's Holiday;* 1953)
- **4 Les Quatre Cents Coups** (*The 400 Blows,* 1959)
- **5 À Bout de Souffle** (*Breathless,* 1960)
- **6 37.2°C du Matin** (*Betty Blue,* 1986)
- **7 La Femme Nikita** (*Nikita,* 1990)
- **8 Delicatessen** (1991)
- **9 Le Fabuleux Destin d'Amélie Poulain** (*Amélie,* 2001)
- **10 Belleville Rendez-Vous** (*The Triplets of Belleville,* 2003)

Literature

France has a long and distinguished literary tradition, and regularly features in the top ten of the world's best-read nations. With its illustrious roll-call of epic novelists, experimental poets and existential thinkers, it's also little wonder that France has been awarded more Nobel Prizes for Literature than any other country.

Early Literature

The earliest surviving examples of French literature are the epic lyrical poems written during the early medieval period, most of which were based around allegorical tales and mythological legends (courtly love and King Arthur were particularly popular subjects in early French literature). Chrétien de Troyes (12th century), Pierre de Ronsard (1524–85) and the mischievous François Rabelais (1494–1553) were among the most important writers of the period, while the influential prose writer Michel de Montaigne (1533–92) penned essays on topics ranging from cannibals to public drunkenness.

The 18th century was dominated by one of France's greatest writers and philosophers, Voltaire (1694–1778), a key figure of the European Enlightenment. Through a prodigious output of novels, plays, poems, essays and political pamphlets, Voltaire tirelessly championed the values of freedom, equality and civil liberties for everyone, not solely for the ruling elite. His writings subsequently played an important role in the development of the fundamental principles of the French Revolution a century later.

The Age of the Novel

The 19th century was the great era of the novel in France. French writers took to the form with gusto. Victor Hugo (1802–85) penned historical epics such as *Les Misérables* and *Notre-Dame de Paris* (The Hunchback of Notre Dame), while Alexandre Dumas (1802–70) wrote swashbuckling tales of derring-do such as *The Three*

Library, Musée d'Orsay (p85)
PHOTOGRAPHER: FELIX HUG

Musketeers and *The Count of Monte Cristo*, and Jules Verne (1828–1905) pioneered the sci-fi genre with his fanciful tales of moon rockets, submarines and round-the-world balloon flights.

Perhaps the greatest French novel writer of the period, however, was Gustave Flaubert (1821–80), whose 1857 tome *Madame Bovary* caused a storm of controversy due to its frank treatment of sex, adultery and the plight of women in French society.

The 19th century also witnessed the emergence of several important French poets, including Charles Baudelaire (known for his seminal collection *Les Fleurs du Mal*; 1857) and the symbolist poets Paul Verlaine (1844–96) and Arthur Rimbaud (1854–91).

Modern Literature

The early 20th century produced two great French writers. Nearly everyone in France has read at least one book by Colette (1873–1954), whose picaresque novels and short stories explored the amorous exploits of gutsy heroines such as Claudine and Gigi against the backdrop of bourgeois French society. By contrast, only the most dedicated readers make it through all of *À la recherche du temps perdu* (Remembrance of Things Past), published in seven volumes over 14 years by its author, Marcel Proust (1871–1922). At over 3200 pages, it's the longest novel ever written.

After WWII, Paris' Left Bank became the centre for existentialist writers who pondered cheery topics such as the meaninglessness of human existence: key figures include Jean-Paul Sartre (1905–80), Simone de Beauvoir (1908–86) and Albert Camus (1913–60), known for troubling novels including *The Outsider* and *The Plague*.

More recently, French writers have struggled to find much success beyond their own shores, although Françoise Sagan, Pascal Quignard, Léo Malet and the crime-writer Daniel Pennac have developed loyal non-French followings. One of the big successes of recent years was Martin Page's award-winning novel *Comment je suis devenu stupide* (How I Became Stupid), which documented a French student's attempts to become – well, an idiot.

The Best Books Set in France

1 *A Moveable Feast* (Ernest Hemingway)

2 *Birdsong* (Sebastian Faulks)

3 *Perfume* (Patrick Suskind)

4 *A Year in Provence* (Peter Mayle)

5 *Chocolat* (Joanne Harris)

6 *A Year in the Merde* (Stephen Clarke)

Architecture

RICHARD NEBE

Love it or hate it, French architecture nearly always makes a statement. From the illustrious châteaux of the Loire Valley to modern icons such as Paris' Centre Pompidou and Pyramide du Louvre, French architecture is always on a grand scale, and French leaders have long recognised the importance of an iconic building or two to their own political legacy.

Ancient & Roman Architecture

France's oldest architecture can be found in Brittany, where megalithic builders left behind many impressive stone monuments, including the 3000-odd menhirs of the Alignements de Carnac. In contrast, the nation's Gallo-Roman legacy is mainly concentrated in the south, including the impressive amphitheatres in Nîmes and Arles, Orange's Roman theatre and the huge Pont du Gard aqueduct near Nîmes.

Gothic Architecture

During the Gothic period France's architects really went in for scale, as demonstrated by monumental Gothic buildings such as Avignon's pontifical palace and the massive cathedrals of Chartres, Reims, Metz and Paris' Notre Dame. Tell-tale signs of French Gothic buildings include flying buttresses, ribbed vaults, pointed arches and plenty of luminous stained glass.

The Renaissance

During the 15th and 16th centuries architects developed a taste for extravagance, epitomised by the lavish châteaux of the Loire Valley. Embellished with sweeping staircases, gabled windows, lacy turrets and decorative motifs, these castles were built to impress rather than to defend against attack. The era of architectural showiness reached its peak with the royal palaces of Fontainebleu and Versailles, both near Paris.

Neoclassicism & the Belle Époque

The 18th and 19th centuries were about order and elegance. This was the era of the grand boulevard and the great public square, exemplified by Arras' Place des Héros, Nancy's Place Stanislas, Strasbourg's Place de la République, and Paris' most famous street, the Champs-Élysées. The era also inspired many of Paris' best-known buildings, including the Arc de Triomphe.

The late 19th century in France was a time of artistic experimentation and industrial innovation. Belle époque architects combined iron, brick, glass and ceramics in exciting new ways, and even the most mundane structures – from covered markets and town halls to swimming pools and metro stations – acquired a dash of class.

Modern Architecture

After the ravages of WWII, French architects were given free reign to reinvent the nation's shattered cities. Some favoured a brutally functional style of architecture, while others adopted a more playful approach. France's most celebrated architect, Le Corbusier (1887–1965), rewrote the architectural textbook during the 1950s with his sweeping lines and sinuous forms.

The French tendency for experimentation has continued throughout the modern era. The 1970s and 1980s witnessed the construction of many exciting buildings, including IM Pei's glass pyramid at the Louvre, the Grande Arche in the skyscraper district of La Défense and the world's first ever 'inside-out' building, Paris' Centre Pompidou.

France continues to be an exciting playground for modern architects: Frank Gehry, Norman Foster and Jean Nouvel are all currently working on new French buildings due for completion by 2015.

The Best Modern Buildings

1 Musée du Quai Branly (p74)

2 Centre Pompidou (p65)

3 Pyramide du Louvre (p75)

4 Centre Pompidou-Metz (p174)

IN FOCUS ARCHITECTURE

377

Outdoors

Cycling in the Célé Valley

ANDREW E

From the peaks, rivers and canyons of the French Alps to the sparkling beaches and craggy cliffs of the Riviera, France offers a wealth of exhilarating outdoor adventures.

Cycling

If there's one sport the French take seriously, it's cycling. Cycling is one of the country's most popular outdoor activities, and every year swaths of the country grind to a halt during the Tour de France. The country is criss-crossed by a network of *voies vertes* (literally, 'green ways') that have been developed specifically for cycling, often along the course of old bridleways or disused railway tracks.

Road-cycling is the most popular form in France, although VTT (*vélo tout-terrain*, or mountain biking) is rapidly catching up, especially in the Alps, Pyrenees and Massif Central. Bikes are a great (and green) way of exploring flat regions such as the Dordogne, Burgundy, the Loire Valley and the Lubéron in Provence. Local tourist offices can supply route suggestions and information on bike rental.

Skiing & Snowboarding

France has around 400 ski resorts, all of which offer a range of groomed runs suitable for both novice and experienced skiers; some also have dedicated snowparks that have been specifically designed for snowboarders. The ski season in France lasts from mid-December to late March or April. The slopes get very crowded during the February–March school holidays.

The biggest (and busiest) resorts are located in the Alps. Smaller resorts in the Pyrenees tend to be quieter and cheaper. The Jura is the centre for *ski de fond* (cross-country skiing). Usually, the cheapest way to ski is to travel on a package deal that includes flights, lift passes and accommodation.

Hiking

The French countryside has over 120,000km of *sentiers balisés* (walking paths). The best-known trails are the *sentiers de grande randonnée* (GR), long-distance paths marked by red-and-white-striped route markers. The trails wind through every conceivable type of terrain, from high mountain to coast, so there's something to suit all tastes and abilities.

Watersports

France's coastline is fantastic for all types of watersports. The best surfing is on France's west coast, especially around Biarritz. Windsurfing is especially popular in Brittany, Normandy and along the Atlantic Coast.

White-water rafting, canoeing and kayaking are practised on many French rivers, especially in the Alps, but also in the deep canyons of the Gorges de l'Allier, Gorges de l'Ardèche, Gorges du Tarn and Gorges du Verdon, and along the Dordogne and Lot Rivers.

The Best Natural Wonders

1 The Dune du Pilat (p275) near Arcachon is Europe's highest sand dune

2 Mont St-Michel (p129) in Normandy has Europe's highest tides

3 Mont Blanc near Chamonix (p245) is Europe's highest peak

4 The Gouffre de Padirac (p219) is France's deepest navigable underground river

5 The Gorges du Verdon (p317) is Europe's longest canyon system

Web Resources

○ **France Montagnes** (www.france-montagnes.com) Comprehensive information on skiing, snowboarding and other mountain pastimes.

○ **Fédération Française de la Randonnée Pédestre** (www.ffrp.asso.fr, in French) Hiking tips from the French Ramblers' Association.

○ **Rando Velo** (http://randovelo.fr) Multilingual site offering cycling routes across France.

○ **Voies Vertes** (www.voiesvertes.com, in French) Online guide for France's 'green ways'.

○ **Club Alpin Français** (www.ffcam.fr, in French) Mountain-activity advice from France's oldest alpine club.

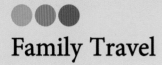

Family Travel

12th-century bridge, Lagrasse

GLENN BEANL

Be it dining, celebrating or travelling, the French are great believers in doing it en famille *(as a family), making France a great place to travel with kids. Big cities, especially Paris, present their own particular challenges, but still have plenty to see and do. Rural France is a family-travel dream.*

France for Kids

France has a wealth of things to experience and enjoy *en famille*, but the best way to avoid domestic strife is to plan, plan and then plan some more. Involving the kids in your pre-trip research will help them get interested in the adventure ahead and will ensure there are plenty of things for everyone to look forward to.

Museums and monuments can be fascinating, but roaming endless rooms of exhibits can be dull, so it's always worth trying to give a different spin to the experience to keep little minds interested. Everyone wants to visit Cathédrale Notre Dame de Paris, for example, but kids will especially love the climb to the top of the tower to see the gargoyles and Parisian views. Similarly, instead of the standard tour of Mont St-Michel, how about a barefoot guided walk across the sands? In Burgundy, vineyard tours can make a great family bike-ride, while at the Eiffel Tower, skip the daytime queues and dazzle the kids with a twinkly night-time tour instead.

History and art museums can be a particular challenge, so it's worth looking into the availability of *ateliers* (workshops) for children and/or families. They're offered by many Parisian museums, including the Louvre and the Orsay, but usually require booking.

Outside the capital, it's worth thinking about which area is likely to interest the kids most. They're bound to love the fairy-tale châteaux of the Loire Valley and the high-octane activities of the French Alps, for example, but might be less interested in the wine country around Bordeaux and Champagne. Coastal areas are always a good bet: the Atlantic Coast and the French Riviera offer plenty of seaside fun as well as brilliant beaches.

Eating Out

In general, eating out in France is likely to be one of the highlights of your trip. Most French restaurants are enormously accommodating of younger diners, and many offer a *menu enfant* (children's set menu, usually for under 12s).

Smarter restaurants tend to be a bit snootier when it comes to kids, so you'll find brasseries and cafés are usually a better idea for eating *en famille*. French chain restaurants, such as Hippopotamus and Bistro Romain, are useful fall backs if you're stuck.

Picnics are a super way of introducing kids to French cuisine. Choosing cheeses, fruits, cold meats, chocolates and pastries at French supermarkets, bakers and greengrocers is interesting as well as educational, not to mention a good way of practising the family French. It's also a useful way of keeping costs down while feeding the troops.

Travelling with Kids

Distances and travel times in France can be long, so it might be worth concentrating on a few areas rather than trying to pack all the sights into one marathon visit. Factor in day trips and detours to break up the journey, and take things to keep the kids entertained while en route. Car-rental firms have children's safety seats for hire; book in advance.

French towns and villages are frequently hilly and/or cobbled, so sturdy shoes are essential; pushchairs can often be more a hindrance than a help. Baby food, infant formula and nappies (diapers) are widely available, but remember that supermarkets and shops in smaller towns often close on Sundays.

IN FOCUS FAMILY TRAVEL

The Best Experiences for Kids

1 Get hands-on at Paris' Cité des Sciences et de l'Industrie (p84) or wander the spooky tunnels of the Catacombes (p71)

2 Take a day-trip to Disneyland (p105)

3 Dive the deep at Monaco's Musée Oceanographique (p343)

4 See a château under construction at Guédelon (p213)

5 Catch the gravity-defying cable-car from the Aiguille du Midi (p246)

6 Pilot a canoe along the Gorges du Verdon (p317)

7 Spot wild horses and pink flamingos in the Camargue (p314)

Need to Know

- **Changing facilities** Rare; bring a towel and improvise (no one minds)
- **Cots** Available in many midrange and top-end hotels
- **Health** Similar to most Western nations; no special inoculations required
- **Highchairs** Still fairly unusual in France
- **Kids' menus** Offered in many restaurants
- **Nappies (diapers)** Easily available in supermarkets and pharmacies
- **Strollers (pushchairs)** Steps and cobbles make pushchairs a challenge; bring a baby sling
- **Transport** Reduced fares for kids available on trains, buses and metros

Accommodation

Family-sized rooms in hotels can be hard to come by during busy periods and in rural areas. Fancier hotels have swimming pools and other facilities for kids.

Staying in a *chambre d'hôte* (B&B) can be great for families who want to immerse themselves in French culture. Camping is also very popular in France, but many campsites require booking well in advance, especially during high season.

If you're happy to stay in one area, the cheapest option is usually to book your own holiday home or apartment. **Tots2France** (www.tots2france.co.uk) and **Baby-friendly Boltholes** (www.babyfriendlyboltholes.co.uk) have lots of listings for family-friendly properties across France, and **Bienvenue à la Ferme** (www.bienvenue-a-la-ferme.com/en) has suggestions for arranging stays on French farms.

Survival Guide

Latin Quarter, Paris
PHOTOGRAPHER: KEVIN CLOGSTOUN

A-Z

Directory

●●●●

Accommodation

Be it a fairy-tale château, a boutique hideaway or a mountain refuge, France has accommodation to suit every taste and pocket.

CATEGORIES

As a rule of thumb, our budget category covers everything from bare-bones hostels to simple family-run places; midrange means a few extra creature comforts such as satellite TV and free wi-fi; while top-end places stretch from luxury five-star chains with air conditioning, swimming pools and restaurants to boutique-chic chalets in the Alps.

PRICE ICONS

The price indicators in this book refer to the cost of a double room, including private bathroom (any combination of toilet, bathtub, shower and washbasin) and excluding breakfast unless otherwise noted.

CATEGORY	COST
€ budget	< €70 (< €80 in Paris)
€€ midrange	€70–175 (€80–180)
€€€ top end	> €175 (> €180)

RESERVATIONS

Some tourist offices can make room reservations for you, often for a fee of €5, but many only do so if you stop by in person.

B&BS

For charm, a heartfelt *bienvenue* (welcome) and solid home cooking, it's hard to beat France's privately run *chambres d'hôtes* (B&Bs), which are urban rarities but are plentiful in rural areas. Many hosts prepare an evening meal (*table d'hôte*) for an extra charge of around €20 to €30. Pick up lists of *chambres d'hôte* at local tourist offices, or find one to suit your style on the following websites:

Bienvenue à la Ferme (www.bienvenue-a-la-ferme. com) Escape to the country at a *chambre d'hôte* on a farm. You can search online or order a catalogue.

Chambres d'Hôtes France (www.chambresdhotesfrance. com) Great selection of B&Bs, all searchable by region.

en France (www.bbfrance. com) A hand-picked selection of B&Bs and *gîtes* from Bordeaux to Brittany.

Fleurs de Soleil (http:// fleursdesoleil.fr, in French) Has a click-happy map of France showing *chambres d'hôte* by region.

Gîtes de France (www. gites-de-france.fr) Acts as an umbrella organisation for B&Bs. Check out their catalogue *Gîtes de Charme* (www.gites-de-france -charme.com), or ask at local tourist offices about Gîtes de France brochures.

HOTELS

Hotels in France are rated with one to five stars, although the ratings are based on highly objective criteria (eg the size of the entry hall), not the quality of the service, the decor or cleanliness.

❍ French hotels almost never include breakfast in their rates. Unless specified otherwise, prices quoted in this guide don't include breakfast, which costs around €7/10/20 in a budget/midrange/top-end hotel.

❍ A double room generally has one double bed (often two pushed-together singles!); a room with twin beds (*deux lits*) is usually more expensive, as is a room with a bathtub instead of a shower.

❍ Feather pillows are practically nonexistent in France, even in top-end hotels.

Book Your Stay Online

For more accommodation reviews by Lonely Planet authors, check out hotels.lonelyplanet .com/France. You'll find independent reviews, as well as recommendations on the best places to stay. Best of all, you can book online..

Business Hours

French business hours are regulated by a maze of government regulations, including the 35-hour working week.

o The midday break is uncommon in Paris but, in general, gets longer the further south you go.

o French law requires that most businesses close on Sunday; exceptions include grocers, *boulangeries*, florists and businesses associated with tourism.

o In some places shops close on Monday.

o Restaurants generally close one or two days of the week, chosen according to the owner's whim.

o Most (but not all) national museums are closed on Tuesday, while most local museums are closed on Monday, though in summer some open daily. Many museums close at lunchtime.

We've only listed business hours where they differ from the following standards.

BUSINESS	STANDARD HOURS
Bank	9 or 9.30am-1pm & 2-5pm Mon-Fri or Tue-Sat
Bar	7pm-1am Mon-Sat
Café	7 or 8am-10 or 11pm Mon-Sat
Nightclub	10pm-3, 4 or 5am Thu-Sat
Post office	8.30am or 9am-5pm or 6pm Mon-Fri, 8am-noon Sat
Restaurant	lunch noon-2.30 or 3pm, dinner 7-10 or 11pm
Shop	9 or 10am-noon & 2-6 or 7pm Mon-Sat
Supermarket	9am-7pm or 8pm Mon-Sat

Customs Regulations

Goods brought in and out of EU countries incur no additional taxes provided duty has been paid somewhere in the EU and the goods are for personal consumption. Duty-free shopping is available only if you are leaving the EU.

Duty-free allowances (for adults) coming from non-EU countries:

o 200 cigarettes

o 50 cigars

o 1L spirits

o 2L wine

o 50ml perfume

o 250ml eau de toilette

o other goods up to the value of €175 (€90 for under 15s)

Anything over these limits must be declared. For further details, see www.douane. gouv.fr (partly in English).

Climate

Bordeaux

Monaco

Paris

The Art of Sleeping

A château, a country manor, five-star opulence at the foot of the Eiffel Tower – whether you want to live like a lord, sleep like a log or blow the budget, there's a room with your name on it.

Alistair Sawday's (www.sawdays.co.uk) Boutique retreats and *chambres d'hôtes*, placing the accent on originality and authentic hospitality.

Hôtels de Charme (www.hotelsdecharme.com, in French) Abbeys, manors, châteaux – this is a mixed bag of (as the name says) charming hotels.

Logis de France (www.logis-de-france.fr) Small, often family-run hotels with charm and a warm welcome.

Relais & Châteaux (www.relaischateaux.com) Seductive selection of villas, châteaux and historic hotels.

Relais du Silence (www.relaisdusilence.com) Fall asleep to complete silence in a gorgeous château, spa-clad auberge, vineyard hotel...

Small Luxury Hotels of the World (www.slh.com) Super-luxurious boutique hotels, chalets and resorts.

Electricity

European two-pin plugs are standard. France has 230V at 50Hz AC (you may need a transformer for 110V electrical appliances).

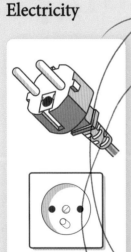

120V/60Hz

Gay & Lesbian Travellers

Laissez-faire perfectly sums up France's liberal attitude towards homosexuality, in part because of a long tradition of public tolerance towards unconventional lifestyles.

o Paris has been a thriving gay and lesbian centre since the late 1970s, and most major organisations are based there today.

o Bordeaux, Lille, Lyon, Montpellier, Toulouse and many other towns also have an active queer scene.

o Attitudes towards homosexuality tend to be more conservative in the countryside and villages.

o Introduced in 1999, PACS (civil solidarity pacts) afford same-sex couples most of the same rights, legal protections and responsibilities as their married counterparts.

o Gay Pride marches are held in major French cities from mid-May to early July.

Health

France is a healthy place so your main risks are likely to be sunburn, foot blisters, insect bites and mild stomach problems from eating and drinking with too much gusto.

BEFORE YOU GO

o Pack your medications in their original, clearly labelled, containers.

o A signed and dated letter from your physician describing your medical conditions and medications, including generic names (French medicine names are often completely different to those in other countries), is also a good idea.

o Dental care in France is usually good; however, it is sensible to have a dental check-up before a long trip.

o No vaccinations are required to travel to France but the World Health Organization (WHO) recommends that all travellers be covered for diphtheria, tetanus, measles, mumps, rubella and polio, regardless of their destination.

AVAILABILITY & COST OF HEALTH CARE

o Visitors to France can get excellent health care from hospital (*hôpital*) emergency rooms/casualty wards (*salles des urgences*) and at a doctors' office (*cabinet médical*).

o For minor illnesses, trained staff in pharmacies – which are found in every village and town, with a green-cross sign outside that flashes when open – give valuable advice, sell medications, can tell you when more specialised help is needed and will point you in the right direction.

o You will need to pay upfront for any health care you receive, be it at a doctor's surgery, pharmacy or hospital, unless your insurance plan makes payments directly to providers.

o The standard rate for a consultation with a GP/specialist is around €22 to €25.

o Emergency contraception is available with a doctor's prescription. Condoms (*les préservatifs*) are readily available.

Insurance

o Comprehensive travel insurance to cover theft, loss and medical problems is highly recommended.

o Some policies specifically exclude dangerous activities such as scuba diving, motorcycling, skiing and even trekking. Read the fine print.

o Check that your policy covers ambulances or an emergency flight home.

Practicalities

o **Newspapers & Magazines** Locals read their news in centre-left, highly intellectual *Le Monde* (www.lemonde.fr), right-leaning *Le Figaro* (www.lefigaro.fr) or left-leaning *Libération* (www.liberation.fr).

o **Radio** For news, tune in to the French-language France Info (105.5MHz), the multilanguage RFI (738kHz or 89MHz in Paris) or, in northern France, the BBC World Service (648kHz) and BBC Radio 4 (198kHz).

o **Smoking** Smoking is illegal in all indoor public spaces, including restaurants and pubs – and, to the surprise of some, the law is actually obeyed!

o **TV & Video** TV is Secam; videos work on the PAL system.

o **Weights & Measures** France uses the metric system.

o Find out in advance if your insurance plan will make payments directly to providers or reimburse you later for overseas health expenditures.

o If you have to claim later, make sure you keep all documentation.

o Paying for your airline ticket with a credit card often provides limited travel accident insurance – ask your credit-card company what it is prepared to cover.

o Worldwide travel insurance is available at www.lonelyplanet.com/travel_services. You can buy, extend and claim online anytime – even if you are already on the road.

Internet Access

o Wireless (wi-fi) access points can now be found at major airports, in many (if not most) hotels and at most cafés.

o To search for free wi-fi hot spots in France, visit www.hotspot-locations.co.uk or www.free-hotspot.com.

o Internet cafés can be found in towns and cities countrywide; some are listed under Information in this book's On the Road chapters. Prices range from €2 to €6 per hour.

o Public libraries (*bibliothèques* or *médiathèques*) often have free or inexpensive internet

What the icon means

Throughout this guide, only accommodation providers that have an actual computer that guests can use to access the internet are flagged with a computer icon (**@**). The 📶 icon indicates anywhere with wi-fi access.

European Health Insurance Card

Citizens of the EU, Switzerland, Iceland, Norway and Liechtenstein receive free or reduced-cost state-provided health-care cover with the European Health Insurance Card (EHIC) for medical treatment that becomes necessary while in France. (The EHIC replaced the E111 in 2006.) Each family member will need a separate card. UK residents can get application forms from post offices, or download them from the Department of Health website (www.dh.gov.uk), which has comprehensive information about the card's coverage.

The EHIC does not cover private health care, so make sure that you are treated by a state health-care provider (*conventionné*). You will need to pay directly and fill in a treatment form (*feuille de soins*); keep the form to claim any refunds. In general, you can claim back around 70% of the standard treatment cost.

Citizens of other countries need to check if there is a reciprocal arrangement for free medical care between their country and France.

access, though hours are limited and you may have to fill in some forms.

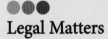

Legal Matters

POLICE

○ French police have wide powers of search and seizure and can ask you to prove your identity at any time – whether or not there is 'probable cause'.

○ Foreigners must be able to prove their legal status in France (eg passport, visa, residency permit) without delay.

○ If the police stop you for any reason, be polite and remain calm. Verbally (and of course physically) abusing a police officer can lead to a hefty fine, and even imprisonment.

○ You may refuse to sign a police statement, and have the right to ask for a copy.

○ People who are arrested are considered innocent until proven guilty, but can be held in custody until trial.

○ Because of the threat of terrorism, French police are

Legal Age

Age of majority 18

Buying alcohol 18

Driving 18

Minor under anti-pornography & prostitution laws under 18

Voting 18

very strict about security. Do not leave baggage unattended, especially at airports or train stations: suspicious objects may be summarily blown up.

Money

ATMS

Automated Teller Machines (ATMs) – known as *distributeurs automatiques de billets* (DAB) or *points d'argent* in French – are the cheapest and most convenient way to get money. ATMs connected to international networks are situated in all cities and towns and usually offer an excellent exchange rate.

CASH

You always get a better exchange rate in-country, but it is a good idea to arrive in France with enough euros to take a taxi to a hotel if you have to.

CREDIT & DEBIT CARDS

○ Credit and debit cards, accepted almost everywhere in France, are convenient, relatively secure and usually offer a better exchange rate than travellers cheques or cash exchanges.

○ Credit cards issued in France have embedded chips – you have to type in a PIN to make a purchase.

○ Visa, MasterCard and Amex can be used in shops and supermarkets and for train travel, car hire and motorway tolls, though some places (eg 24-hour petrol stations, some autoroute toll machines) only take French-style credit cards with chips and PINs.

- Don't assume that you can pay for a meal or a budget hotel with a credit card – enquire first.

LOST CARDS

For lost cards, these numbers operate 24 hours:

Amex (☏ 01 47 77 72 00)

Diners Club (☏ 08 10 31 41 59)

MasterCard (☏ 08 00 90 13 87)

Visa (Carte Bleue; ☏ 08 00 90 11 79)

MONEYCHANGERS

- Commercial banks usually charge a stiff €3 to €5 fee per foreign-currency transaction – if they even bother to offer exchange services any more.

- In Paris and major cities, *bureaux de change* (exchange bureaux) are faster and easier, are open longer hours and often give better rates than banks.

- Some post-office branches exchange travellers cheques and banknotes in a variety of currencies but charge €5 commission for cash; most won't take US$100 bills.

TIPPING

By law, restaurant and bar prices are *service compris* (include a 15% service charge), so there is no need to leave a *pourboire* (tip). If you were extremely satisfied with the service, however, you can – as many locals do – show your appreciation by leaving a small 'extra' tip for your waiter or waitress.

Drugs & Alcohol

- French law does not distinguish between 'hard' and 'soft' drugs.

- The penalty for any personal use of *stupéfiants* (including cannabis, amphetamines, ecstasy and heroin) can be a one-year jail sentence and a €3750 fine but, depending on the circumstances, it might be anything from a stern word to a compulsory rehab program.

- Importing, possessing, selling or buying drugs can get you up to 10 years' prison and a fine of up to €500,000.

- *Ivresse* (drunkeness) in public is punishable by a €150 fine.

WHERE/ WHO	CUSTOMARY TIP
bar	round to nearest euro
hotel cleaning staff	€1-1.50 per day
hotel porter	€1-1.50 per bag
restaurant	5-10%
taxi	10-15%
toilet attendant	€0.20-0.50
tour guide	€ 1-2 per person

TRAVELLERS CHEQUES

Travellers cheques, a relic of the 19th and 20th centuries, cannot be used to pay most French merchants directly and so have to be changed into euro banknotes at banks, exchange bureaux or post offices.

Public Holidays

The following *jours fériés* (public holidays) are observed in France:

New Year's Day (Jour de l'An) 1 January – parties in larger cities; fireworks are subdued by international standards

Easter Sunday & Monday (Pâques & Lundi de Pâques) Late March/April

May Day (Fête du Travail) 1 May – traditional parades

Victoire 1945 8 May – commemorates the Allied victory in Europe that ended WWII

Ascension Thursday May – celebrated on the 40th day after Easter

Pentecost/Whit Sunday & Whit Monday (Pentecôte & Lundi de Pentecôte) Mid-May to mid-June – celebrated on the seventh Sunday after Easter

Bastille Day/National Day (Fête Nationale) 14 July – *the* national holiday

Assumption Day (Assomption) 15 August

Strikes

France is the only European country in which public workers enjoy an unlimited right to strike, and they avail themselves of it with carefree abandon.

Getting caught in one of the 'social dialogues' that characterise labour relations in France can put a serious crimp in your travel plans. It is best to leave some wriggle room in your schedule, particularly around the departure times.

All Saints' Day (Toussaint) 1 November

Remembrance Day (L'Onze Novembre) 11 November – marks the WWI armistice

Christmas (Noël) 25 December

The following are *not* public holidays in France: Shrove Tuesday (Mardi Gras; the first day of Lent); Maundy (or Holy) Thursday and Good Friday, just before Easter; and Boxing Day (26 December).

Note: Good Friday and Boxing Day *are* public holidays in Alsace.

Safe Travel

France is generally a safe place in which to live and travel, but crime has risen dramatically in the last few years. While property crime is a major problem, it is extremely unlikely that you will be physically assaulted while walking down the street. Always check your government's travel advisory warnings.

NATURAL DANGERS

o There are powerful tides and strong undertows at many places along the Atlantic Coast, from the Spanish border north to Brittany and Normandy.

o Only swim in *zones de baignade surveillée* (beaches monitored by life guards).

o Be aware of tide times and the high-tide mark if walking or sleeping on a beach.

o Thunderstorms in the mountains and the hot southern plains can be extremely sudden and violent.

o Check the weather report before setting out on a long walk and be prepared for sudden storms and temperature drops if you are heading into the high country of the Alps or Pyrenees.

o Avalanches pose a significant danger in the French Alps.

THEFT

Pickpocketing and bag snatching (eg in dense crowds and public places) are prevalent in big cities, particularly Paris, Marseille and Nice. But there's no need whatsoever to travel in fear: a few simple precautions will minimise your chances of being ripped off.

o On trains, keep bags as close to you as possible: luggage racks at the ends of carriage are easy prey for thieves; in sleeping compartments, lock the door carefully at night.

o Be especially vigilant for bag-snatchers at train stations, airports, fast-food outlets, outdoor cafés, beaches and on public transport.

o Break-ins to parked cars are a widespread problem. Never, ever leave anything valuable – or not valuable – inside your car, even in the boot (trunk).

o Aggressive theft from cars stopped at red lights is occasionally a problem, especially in Marseille and Nice. As a precaution, lock your car doors and roll up the windows.

Telephone

IMPORTANT NUMBERS

France country code	☏33
International access code	☏00
Europe-wide emergency	☏112
Ambulance (SAMU)	☏15
Police	☏17

MOBILE PHONES

o French mobile phone numbers begin with ☏06 or ☏07.

o France uses GSM 900/1800, which is compatible with the rest of Europe and Australia but not with the North American GSM 1900 or the totally different system in Japan (though some North Americans have tri-band phones that work here).

o Check with your service provider about roaming charges – dialling a mobile phone from a fixed-line phone or another mobile can be incredibly expensive.

o It may be cheaper to buy your own French SIM card – and locals you meet are much more likely to ring you if your number is French.

o Recharge cards are sold at most *tabacs* and newsagents.

o SIMs are available at the ubiquitous outlets run by France's three mobile phone companies, **Bouygues** (www.bouyguestelecom.fr), France Telecom's **Orange** (www.orange.com) and **SFR** (www.sfr.com, in French).

PHONE CODES

Calling France from abroad Dial your country's international access code, then 🖉 33 (France's country code), then the 10-digit local number *without* the initial zero.

Calling internationally from France Dial 🖉 00 (the international access code), the *indicatif* (country code), the area code (without the initial zero if there is one) and the local number. Some country codes are posted in public telephones.

Directory inquiries For France Telecom's *service des renseignements* (directory inquiries) dial 🖉 11 87 12. Not all operators speak English. For help in English with all France Telecom's services, see www.francetelecom.com or call 🖉 09 69 36 39 00.

Emergency numbers Can be dialled from public phones without a phonecard.

Shopping Tips

Shopping in France isn't just a pastime – it's practically a way of life. Whether you're in the market for some haute couture or savoury souvenirs, you'll find shopping in France a pleasure – as long as you can get your head around the opening hours, that is...

Shops are generally open 10am to 6pm Monday to Saturday, although in bigger cities some stay open till 7pm. Sunday shopping is something of a no-go in France, except in Paris. Smaller shops often shut all day Monday, and generally close from noon to around 2pm on other days. Many larger stores hold *nocturnes* (late nights) on Thursdays, remaining open until around 10pm.

Food markets *(marchés alimentaires)* – both open-air street ones *(marchés découverts)* and covered markets *(marchés couverts)* – are an integral part of daily life. Practically every town and village hosts a weekly market one or two mornings a week, usually from around 7am to noon. Haggling isn't the norm in either shops or food markets, although it's always worth a try. Remember to take along your own bag or basket.

Some specialist shops to look out for on French high streets include:

o **Boulangerie** Fresh bread, fruit tarts and mouth-watering pastries

o **Pâtisserie** Mainly cakes, tarts and pastries

o **Fromagerie** Cheese shop

o **Traiteur** Delicatessen selling *charcuterie* (sliced meats), pâtés and other great picnic food

o **Épicerie** General greengrocer, selling a bit of everything

o **Boucherie** Butcher

o **Poissonnerie** Fresh fish and seafood

Hotel calls Hotels, *gîtes*, hostels and *chambres d'hôte* are free to meter their calls as they like. The surcharge is usually around €0.30 per minute but can be higher.

International directory inquiries For numbers outside France, dial 📞11 87 00.

PHONECARDS

○ For both international and domestic calling, most public phones use either a credit card or two kinds of *télécartes* (phonecards): *cartes à puce* (with a magnetic chip) issued by France Télécom and sold at post offices; and *cartes à code* (where you dial a free access number and then the card's scratch-off code), sold at *tabacs*, newsagents and post offices.

○ Phonecards with codes offer much better international rates than France Télécom chip cards or Country Direct services (for which you are billed at home by your long-distance carrier).

TARIFFS

NUMBER	PER-MINUTE
📞08 00	free
📞08 05	free
📞08 10	same as a local call
📞08 20	€0.12
📞08 21	€0.12
📞08 25	€0.15
📞08 26	€0.15
📞08 92	€0.34
📞11 87 12 (directory inquiries)	€1 per call, then €0.23 per minute
📞11 87 00 (international directory inquiries)	€2-3

Time

France uses the 24-hour clock and is on Central European Time, which is one hour ahead of GMT/UTC. During daylight-saving time, which runs from the last Sunday in March to the last Sunday in October, France is two hours ahead of GMT/UTC.

The following times do not take daylight saving into account.

CITY	NOON IN PARIS
Auckland	11pm
Berlin	noon
Cape Town	noon
London	11am
New York	6am
San Francisco	3am
Sydney	9pm
Tokyo	8pm

Toilets

Public toilets, signposted WC or *toilettes*, are not always plentiful in France, especially outside of the big cities.

Love them (as a sci-fi geek) or loathe them (as a claustrophobe), France's 24-hour self-cleaning toilets are here to stay. Outside of Paris – where they are free – these mechanical WCs cost around €0.50 a go. There is no time for dawdling either: you have precisely 15 minutes before being (ooh-la-la!) exposed to passers-by. Green means *libre* (vacant) and red means *occupé* (occupied).

Some older establishments and motorway stops still have the hole-in-the-floor *toilettes á la turque* (squat toilets). Provided you hover, these are actually very hygienic, but take care not to get soaked by the flush.

Keep some loose change handy for tipping toilet attendants, who keep a hawk-like eye on many of France's public toilets.

The French are more blasé about unisex toilets than elsewhere, so save your blushes when tiptoeing past the urinals to reach the ladies' cubicle.

Tourist Information

Almost every city, town, village and hamlet has an *office de tourisme* (a tourist office run by some unit of local government) or *syndicat d'initiative* (a tourist office run by an organisation of local merchants).

○ Many tourist offices make local hotel and B&B reservations, sometimes for a nominal fee. Some have limited currency-exchange services.

○ *Comités régionaux de tourisme* (CRTs; regional tourist boards), their *départemental* analogues (CDTs), and their websites are a superb source of information and hyperlinks.

Useful websites:

French Government Tourist Office (www.franceguide.com) The low-down on sights, activities, transport and special interest holidays in all of France's regions. Brochures can be downloaded online. There are links to country-specific websites.

Réseau National des Destinations Départementales (www.fncdt.net, in French) Find CRT (regional tourist board) websites here.

Travellers with Disabilities

While France presents evident challenges for *handicapés* (people with disabilities) – namely cobblestone, café-lined streets that are a nightmare to navigate in a wheelchair, a lack of kerb ramps, older public facilities and many budget hotels without lifts – don't let that stop you from visiting. With a little careful planning, you can enjoy a hassle-free accessible stay.

The Paris metro, most of it decades old, is hopeless, but taxi drivers are obliged by law to accept and assist passengers with disabilities (and their guide dogs, where relevant). Choose central accommodation to avoid spending a small fortune on taxi fares.

Accès Plus Transilien (☎ 08 10 64 64 64; www.infomobi.com, in French) Has comprehensive information on accessible travel in Paris.

Association des Paralysés de France (APF; www.apf.asso.fr, in French) National organisation for people with disabilities, with offices in every region in France.

Centre du Service Accès Plus (☎ 08 90 64 06 50; www.accessibilite.sncf.fr, in French) Can advise on station

accessibility and arrange a *fauteuil roulant* (wheelchair) or help getting on or off a train.

Mobile en Ville (www.mobile-en-ville.asso.fr, in French) Works to make Paris wheelchair accessible and publishes *Paris Comme sur les Roulettes*, which showcases 20 tours of the city.

Tourisme et Handicaps (www.tourisme-handicaps.org, in French) Issues the 'Tourisme et Handicap' label to tourist sites, restaurants and hotels that comply with strict accessibility and usability standards. Different symbols indicate the sort of access afforded to people with physical, mental, hearing and/or visual disabilities.

Tourism for All (☎ in UK 0845-124 9971; www.tourismforall.info) A UK-based group that provides tips and information for travellers with disabilities.

Visas

For up-to-date details on visa requirements, see the website of the **French Foreign Affairs Ministry** (www.diplomatie.gouv.fr) and click 'Going to France'. Tourist visas *cannot* be extended except in emergencies (such as medical problems). When your visa expires you'll need to leave and reapply from outside France.

VISA REQUIREMENTS

- EU nationals and citizens of Iceland, Norway and Switzerland need only a passport or a national identity card in order to enter France

and stay in the country, even for stays of over 90 days.

- Citizens of Australia, the USA, Canada, Israel, Hong Kong, Japan, Malaysia, New Zealand, Singapore, South Korea and many Latin American countries do not need visas to visit France as tourists for up to 90 days.

- Other people wishing to come to France as tourists have to apply for a **Schengen Visa**, named after the agreements that abolished passport controls between 15 European countries. It allows unlimited travel throughout the entire zone for a 90-day period.

Transport

Getting There & Away

 AIR

INTERNATIONAL AIRPORTS

Charles de Gaulle (Roissy) (www.aeroportsdeparis.fr)

Orly (www.aeroportsdeparis.fr)

Bordeaux (www.bordeaux.aeroport.fr)

Climate Change & Travel

Every form of transport that relies on carbon-based fuel generates CO2, the main cause of human-induced climate change. Modern travel is dependent on aeroplanes, which might use less fuel per per person than most cars but travel much greater distances. The altitude at which aircraft emit gases (including CO2) and particles also contributes to their climate-change impact. Many websites offer 'carbon calculators' that allow people to estimate the carbon emissions generated by their journey and, for those who wish to do so, to offset the impact of the greenhouse gases emitted with contributions to portfolios of climate-friendly initiatives throughout the world. Lonely Planet offsets the carbon footprint of all staff and author travel.

Lille (www.lille.aeroport.fr)

Lyon (www.lyon.aeroport.fr)

Marseille (www.mrsairport.com)

Mulhouse-Basel-Freiburg (EuroAirport) (www.euroairport.com, www.fly-euroairport.com)

Nantes (www.nantes.aeroport.fr)

Nice (www.nice.aeroport.fr)

Strasbourg (www.strasbourg.aeroport.fr)

Toulouse (www.toulouse.aeroport.fr)

Smaller provincial airports with international flights, mainly to/from the UK, continental Europe and North Africa, include Angoulême, Paris-Beauvais (Beauvais-Tillé), Bergerac, Béziers, Biarritz, Brest, Brive-Vallée de la Dordogne, Caen, Carcassonne, Deauville, Dinard, Grenoble, La Rochelle, Le Touquet, Limoges, Montpellier, Nîmes, Pau, Perpignan, Poitiers, Rennes, Rodez, St-Étienne, Toulon and Tours.

🚗 CAR & MOTORCYCLE

A right-hand-drive vehicle brought to France from the UK or Ireland must have deflectors affixed to the headlights to avoid dazzling oncoming traffic.

Police searches are not uncommon for vehicles entering France, particularly from Spain and Belgium (via which drugs from Morocco or the Netherlands can enter France).

A foreign motor vehicle entering France must display a sticker or licence plate identifying its country of registration.

EUROTUNNEL

High-speed **Eurotunnel shuttle trains** (🔲 in UK 08443-35 35 35, in France 08 10 63 03 04; www.eurotunnel.com) whisk bicycles, motorcycles, cars and coaches from Folkestone through the Channel Tunnel to Coquelles, 5km southwest of Calais, in air-conditioned and soundproofed comfort in just 35 minutes. Shuttles run 24 hours a day, every day of the year, with up to three departures an hour during peak periods.

Eurotunnel sets its fares the way budget airlines do: the further in advance you book and the lower the demand for a particular crossing, the less you pay; same-day fares can cost a small fortune. Standard fares for a car, including up to nine passengers, start at UK£53.

🚆 TRAIN

Rail services – including a dwindling number of overnight services to and from

Sample Train Fares

ROUTE	FULL FARE (€)	DURATION (HR)
Amsterdam-Paris	79	3¼
Barcelona-Montpellier	57	4½
Berlin-Paris	238	8
Brussels-Paris	44-64	1½
Frankfurt-Paris	106	4
Geneva-Lyon	25	2
Geneva-Marseille	65	3½
Vienna-Strasbourg	149	9

Spain, Italy and Germany – link France with virtually every country in Europe.

You can book tickets and get train information from **Rail Europe** (www.raileurope.com). In France, ticketing is handled by **SNCF** (☏ in France 36 35, from abroad +33-8 92 35 35 35; www.sncf.com); telephone and internet bookings are possible but they won't post tickets outside France.

EUROSTAR

The highly civilised **Eurostar** (☏ in UK 08432-186 186, in France 08 92 35 35 39; www.eurostar.com) whisks you from London to Paris in an incredible 2¼ hours, with easy onward connections to destinations all over France.

You'll get the best deals if you buy a return ticket, stay over a Saturday night, book well (ie up to 120 days) in advance – the cheapest fares sell out early – and don't mind nonexchangeability and nonrefundability. Discount fares are available if you're under 26 or over 60 on your departure date.

 SEA

For a map of ferry routes across the English Channel and the Mediterranean, see the Trains & Ferries map, p401.

To get the best fares, you might want to check out the booking service offered by **Ferry Savers** (☏ in UK 0844-371 8021; www.ferrysavers.com); booking by phone incurs a fee.

Foot passengers are not allowed on any Dover–Boulogne, Dover–Dunkirk or Dover–Calais car ferries except for daytime (and, from

International Ferry Companies

COMPANY	CONNECTION	WEBSITE
Brittany Ferries	England-Normandy, England-Brittany, Ireland-Brittany	www.brittany-ferries.co.uk; www.brittanyferries.ie
Celtic Link Ferries	Ireland-Normandy	www.celticlinkferries.com
Condor Ferries	England-Normandy, England-Brittany, Channel Islands-Brittany	www.condorferries.com
Irish Ferries	Ireland-Normandy, Ireland-Brittany	www.irishferries.ie; www.shamrock-irlande.com, in French
LD Lines	England-Channel Ports, England-Normandy	www.ldlines.co.uk
Manche Îles Express	Channel Islands-Normandy	www.manche-iles-express.com
Norfolk Line	England-Channel Ports	www.norfolkline.com
P&O Ferries	England-Channel Ports	www.poferries.com
SeaFrance	England-Channel Ports	www.seafrance.com
Transmanche Ferries	England-Normandy	www.transmancheferries.com

Calais to Dover, evening) crossings run by P&O Ferries. On ferries that do allow foot passengers, taking along a bicycle is often (but not always) free.

Getting Around

Driving is the simplest way to get around France but a car is a liability in traffic-plagued, parking-starved city centres, and those petrol bills and *autoroute* (dual carriageway/divided highway) tolls can really add up.

France is famous for its truly excellent public-transport network, which serves every corner of the land except some rural areas.

The state-owned Société Nationale des Chemins de Fer Français (SNCF) takes care of almost all land transport between *départements* (administrative divisions of France). Transport within *départements* is handled by a combination of short-haul trains, SNCF buses and local bus companies that are either government owned or government contracted.

🚲 BICYCLE

French law requires that bicycles must have two functioning brakes, a bell, a red reflector on the back and yellow reflectors on the pedals. After sunset and when visibility is poor, cyclists must turn on a white headlamp and a red tail lamp. When being overtaken by a vehicle, cyclists are required to ride in single file. Towing children in a bike trailer is permitted.

Never leave your bicycle locked up outside overnight if you want to see it – or at least most of its parts – again. Some hotels offer enclosed bicycle parking.

TRANSPORTATION

The SNCF does its best to make travelling with a bicycle easy and even has a special website for cyclists, www.velo.sncf.com (in French).

Bicycles (not disassembled) can be taken along on virtually all intraregional TER trains and most long-distance intercity trains, subject to space availability. Bike reservations can be made by phone (📞36 35) or at an SNCF ticket office but not via the internet.

With precious few exceptions, bicycles are not allowed on metros, trams and local, intra-*département* and SNCF buses (the latter replace trains on some runs).

BIKE RENTAL

Most French cities and towns have at least one bike shop or municipal sports complex that rents out *vélos tout terrains* (mountain bikes; generally €10 to €20 a day), popularly known as VTTs, as well as more road-oriented *vélos tout chemin* (VTCs), or cheaper city bikes. You usually have to leave ID and/or a deposit (often a credit-card slip) that you forfeit if the bike is damaged or stolen.

A growing number of cities – most famously Paris and Lyon, but also Aix-en-Provence, Amiens, Besançon, Caen, Dijon, La Rochelle, Marseille, Montpellier, Mulhouse, Nancy, Nantes, Orléans, Perpignan, Rennes, Rouen and Toulouse – have automatic bike-rental systems, intended to encourage cycling as a form of urban transport, with computerised pick-up and drop-off sites all over town. For details on Paris' Vélib' system, see p101.

🚌 BUS

Buses are widely used for short-distance travel within *départements,* especially in rural areas with relatively few train lines (eg Brittany and Normandy). Unfortunately, services in some regions are infrequent and slow, in part because they were designed to get children to their schools in the towns rather than transport visitors around the countryside.

Over the years, certain uneconomical train lines have been replaced by SNCF buses, which, unlike regional buses, are free if you've got a rail pass.

CAR & MOTORCYCLE

Having your own wheels gives you exceptional freedom and makes it easy to visit more remote parts of France. Unfortunately driving can be expensive, and in the cities traffic and finding a place to park are frequently a major headache. During holiday periods and over long weekends, roads throughout France also get backed up with traffic jams *(bouchons)*.

There are four types of intercity roads:

Autoroutes (highway names beginning with A) Multilane divided highways, usually (except near Calais and Lille) with tolls *(péages)*. Generously outfitted with rest stops.

Routes Nationales (N, RN) National highways. Some sections have divider strips.

Routes Départementales (D) Local highways and roads.

Routes Communales (C, V) Minor rural roads. Information on autoroute tolls, rest areas, traffic and weather is available from www.autoroutes.fr. The websites www.viamichelin.com and www.mappy.fr (in French) plot itineraries between your departure and arrival points.

Note that theft from cars is a major problem in France, especially in the south – see p390.

CAR HIRE

To hire a car in France, you'll generally need to be over 21 years old, have had a driving licence for at least a year, and have an international credit card. Drivers under 25 usually have to pay a surcharge *(frais jeune conducteur)* of €25 to €35 per day.

Car-hire companies provide mandatory third-party liability insurance but things

Road Distances (Km)

	Bayonne	Bordeaux	Brest	Caen	Cahors	Calais	Chambéry	Cherbourg	Clermont-Ferrand	Dijon	Grenoble	Lille	Lyon	Marseille	Nantes	Nice	Paris	Perpignan	Strasbourg	Toulouse
Bordeaux	184																			
Brest	811	623																		
Caen	764	568	376																	
Cahors	307	218	788	661																
Calais	164	876	710	339	875															
Chambéry	860	651	120	800	523	834														
Cherbourg	835	647	399	124	743	461	923													
Clermont-Ferrand	564	358	805	566	269	717	295	689												
Dijon	807	619	867	548	378	572	273	671	279											
Grenoble	827	657	1126	806	501	863	56	929	300	302										
Lille	997	809	725	353	808	112	767	476	650	505	798									
Lyon	831	528	1018	698	439	755	103	820	171	194	110	687								
Marseille	700	651	1271	1010	521	1067	344	1132	477	506	273	999	314							
Nantes	513	326	298	292	491	593	780	317	462	656	787	609	618	975						
Nice	858	810	1429	1168	679	1225	410	1291	636	664	337	1157	473	190	1131					
Paris	771	583	596	232	582	289	565	355	424	313	571	222	462	775	384	932				
Perpignan	499	451	1070	998	320	1149	478	1094	441	640	445	1081	448	319	773	476	857			
Strasbourg	1254	1066	1079	730	847	621	496	853	584	335	551	522	488	803	867	804	490	935		
Toulouse	300	247	866	865	116	991	565	890	890	727	533	923	536	407	568	564	699	205	1022	
Tours	536	348	490	246	413	531	611	369	369	418	618	463	449	795	197	952	238	795	721	593

such as collision-damage waivers (CDW, or *assurance tous risques*) vary greatly from company to company. When comparing rates and conditions (ie the fine print), the most important thing to check is the *franchise* (deductible/excess), which for a small car is usually around €600 for damage and €800 for theft. With many companies, you can reduce the excess by half, and perhaps to zero, by paying a daily insurance supplement of €10 to €16. Your credit card may cover CDW if you use it to pay for the rental but the car-hire company won't know anything about this – verify conditions and details with your credit-card issuer to be sure.

Arranging your car hire or fly/drive package before you leave home is usually considerably cheaper than a walk-in rental, but beware of website offers that don't include a CDW or you may be liable for up to 100% of the car's value.

International car-hire companies:

Avis (☎08 21 23 07 60; www.avis.com)

Budget (☎08 25 00 35 64; www.budget.com or www.budget.fr, in French)

Easycar (☎in UK 08710 500 444; www.easycar.com)

Europcar (☎08 25 35 83 58; www.europcar.com or www.europcar.fr, in French)

Hertz (www.hertz.com or www.hertz.fr, in French)

National-Citer (www.nationalcar.com or www.citer.fr)

Sixt (☎08 20 00 74 98; www.sixt.fr, in French)
French car-hire companies:

ADA (www.ada.fr, in French)

DLM (www.dlm.fr, in French)

France Cars (www.francecars.fr, in French)

Locauto (www.locauto.fr)

Renault Rent (📞 08 25 10 11 12; www.renault-rent.com, in French)

Rent-a-Car Système (📞 08 91 70 02 00; www.rentacar.fr)

Deals can be found on the internet and through companies such as the following:

Auto Europe (📞 in USA 1-888-223-5555; www.autoeurope.com)

DriveAway Holidays (📞 in Australia 1300 723 972; www.driveaway.com.au)

Holiday Autos (📞 in UK 0871-472 5229; www.holidayautos.co.uk)

Note that rental cars with automatic transmission are very much the exception in France and will usually need to be ordered well in advance.

All rental cars registered in France have a distinctive number on the licence plate, making them easily identifiable – including to thieves, so *never* leave anything of value in a parked car, even in the boot.

DRIVING LICENCE & DOCUMENTS

An International Driving Permit (IDP), valid only if accompanied by your original licence, is good for a year and can be issued by your local automobile association before you leave home.

Drivers must carry the following at all times:

○ passport or EU national ID card

○ valid driving licence (*permis de conduire;* most foreign licences can be used in France for up to a year)

○ car-ownership papers, known as a *carte grise* (grey card)

○ proof of third-party liability *assurance* (insurance)

FUEL

Essence (petrol), also known as *carburant* (fuel), costs around €1.40/L (US$7 per US gallon) for 95 unleaded (Sans Plomb 95 or SP95, usually available from a green pump) and €1.30 for diesel (*diesel, gazole* or *gasoil,* usually available from a yellow pump). Filling up *(faire le plein)* is most expensive at autoroute rest stops and often cheapest at hypermarkets.

Many small petrol stations close on Sunday afternoons and, even in cities, it can be hard to find a staffed station open late at night. In general, after-hours purchases (eg at hypermarkets' fully automatic, 24-hour stations) can only be made with a credit card that has an embedded PIN chip, so if all you've got is cash or a magnetic-strip credit card, you could be stuck.

INSURANCE

Third-party liability insurance *(assurance au tiers)* is compulsory for all vehicles in France, including cars brought in from abroad.

If you get into a minor accident with no injuries, the easiest way for drivers to sort things out with their insurance companies is to fill out a Constat Aimable

d'Accident Automobile (European Accident Statement), a standardised way of recording important details about what happened. In rental cars it's usually in the packet of documents in the glove compartment. Make sure the report includes any information that will help you prove that the accident was not your fault. Remember, if it *was* your fault you may be liable for a hefty insurance deductible/excess. Don't sign anything you don't fully understand. If problems crop up, call the police (📞17).

PARKING

In city centres, most on-the-street parking places are *payant* (metered) from about 9am to 7pm (sometimes with a break from noon to 2pm) from Monday to Saturday, except bank holidays.

ROAD RULES

Speed limits outside built-up areas (except where signposted otherwise):

Undivided N and D highways 90km/h (80km/h when raining)

Non-autoroute divided highways 110km/h (100km/h when raining)

Autoroutes 130km/h (110km/h when raining, 60km/h in icy conditions) Unless otherwise signposted, a limit of 50km/h applies in *all* areas designated as built up, no matter how rural they may appear. You must slow to 50km/h the moment you come to a white sign with a red border and a place name written on it; the speed limit applies until

Priority to the Right

Under the *priorité à droite* ('priority to the right') rule, any car entering an intersection (including a T-junction) from a road (including a tiny village backstreet) on your right has the right-of-way. Locals assume every driver knows this, so don't be surprised if they courteously cede the right-of-way when you're about to turn from an alley onto a highway – and boldly assert their rights when you're the one zipping down a main road.

Priorité à droite is suspended (eg on arterial roads) when you pass a sign showing an upended yellow square with a black square in the middle. The same sign with a horizontal bar through the square lozenge reinstates the *priorité à droite* rule.

When you arrive at a roundabout at which you do not have the right-of-way (ie the cars already in the roundabout do), you'll often see signs reading *vous n'avez pas la priorité* (you do not have right of way) or *cédez le passage* (give way).

you pass an identical sign with a horizontal bar through it.

You can be fined for going as little as 10km over the speed limit.

Other important driving rules:

o Blood-alcohol limit is 0.05% (0.5g per litre of blood) – the equivalent of two glasses of wine for a 75kg adult. Police often conduct random breathalyser tests and penalties can be severe, including imprisonment.

o All passengers, including those in the back seat, must wear seat belts.

Child-seat rules

o Children under 10 are not permitted to ride in the front seat (unless the back is already occupied by other children under 10).

o A child under 13kg must travel in a backward-facing child seat (permitted in the front seat

only for babies under 9kg and if the airbag is deactivated).

o Up to age 10, children must use a size-appropriate type of front-facing child seat or booster.

All vehicles driven in France must carry a high-visibility reflective safety vest (stored inside the vehicle, not in the trunk/boot), and a reflective triangle. The fine for not carrying one/both is €90/135.

LOCAL TRANSPORT

France's cities and larger towns have world-class public-transport systems. There are *métros* (underground subway systems) in Paris, Lyon, Marseille, Lille and Toulouse and ultramodern light-rail lines *(tramways)* in cities such as Bordeaux, Grenoble, Lille, Lyon, Nancy, Nantes, Nice, Reims, Rouen and Strasbourg, as well as parts of greater Paris.

TAXI

All medium and large train stations – and many small ones – have a taxi stand out front. In small cities and towns, where taxi drivers are unlikely to find another fare anywhere near where they let you off, one-way and return trips often cost the same. Tariffs are about 30% higher at night and on Sundays and holidays. There may be a surcharge to get picked up at a train station or airport and a small additional fee for a fourth passenger and/or for suitcases.

🚆 TRAIN

The jewel in the crown of France's public-transport system – alongside the Paris *métro* – is its extensive rail network, almost all of it run by the state-owned **SNCF** (☏ 36 35; www.sncf.com). Since its inauguration in the 1980s, the pride and joy of SNCF – and the French – is the renowned **TGV** (Train à Grande Vitesse; www.tgv.com), pronounced 'teh zheh veh', which zips passengers along at speeds of up to 320km/h (198mph). In 2007, a specially modified TGV achieved a new speed record for non-maglev (magnetic levitation) trains: 574.8km/h.

A train that is not a TGV is often referred to as a *corail*, a *classique* or, for intraregional services, a **TER** (Train Express Régional; www.ter-sncf.com, in French). Certain non-TGV services have been given peculiar names:

Corail Intercités Medium-haul routes.

Téoz (www.corailteoz.
com, in French) Especially
comfortable trains that run
southward from Paris Gare
d'Austerlitz to Clermont-
Ferrand, Limoges, Cahors,
Toulouse, Montpellier,
Perpignan, Marseille and Nice.

Transilien (www.transilien.
com) SNCF services in the Île
de France (the Paris region).

Information on train accessibility for people with disabilities can be found at www.
accessibilite.sncf.fr (in French)
and, for greater Paris, www.
infomobi.com (in French).

Long-distance trains
sometimes split at a station –
that is, each half of the train
heads off for a different
destination. Check the
destination panel on your car
as you board or you could
wind up very, very far from
wherever it was you intended
to go.

ROUTES

TGV Nord, Thalys & Eurostar
Link Paris Gare du Nord with
Arras, Lille, Calais, Brussels
(Bruxelles-Midi), Amsterdam,
Cologne and, via the Channel
Tunnel, Ashford, Ebbsfleet
and London St Pancras.

TGV Est Européen Connects
Paris Gare de l'Est with Reims,
Nancy, Metz, Strasbourg,
Zurich and Germany,
including Frankfurt and
Stuttgart. At present, the
super-high-speed track
stretches only as far east as
Lorraine but it's supposed to
reach Strasbourg in 2016.

**TGV Sud-Est & TGV Midi-
Méditerranée** Link Paris
Gare de Lyon with the

southeast, including Dijon,
Lyon, Geneva, the Alps,
Avignon, Marseille, Nice and
Montpellier.

**TGV Atlantique Sud-Ouest
& TGV Atlantique Ouest** Link
Paris Gare Montparnasse with
western and southwestern
France, including Brittany
(Rennes, Brest, Quimper),
Tours, Nantes, Poitiers, La
Rochelle, Bordeaux, Biarritz
and Toulouse.
For details on especially
scenic train routes all around
France, see www.trainstourist
iques-ter.com.

TICKETS & RESERVATIONS

Large stations often have
separate ticket windows for
international, grandes lignes
(long-haul) and *banlieue*
(suburban) lines, and for
people whose train is about
to leave (*départ immédiat* or
départ dans l'heure). Nearly
every SNCF station has at
least one *borne libre-service*
(self-service terminal) or *bil-
leterie automatique* (automatic
ticket machine) that accepts
both cash and PIN-chip credit
cards.

Using a credit card, you
can buy a ticket by phone or
via the SNCF internet booking
site (www.voyages-sncf.com,
in French) and either have
it sent to you by post (if you
have an address in France) or
collect it from any SNCF ticket
office or from train-station
ticket machines.

Before boarding the train,
you must validate (*composter*)
your ticket by time-stamping
it in a *composteur*, one of
those yellow posts located on
the way to the platform. If you
forget (or don't have a ticket

for some other reason), find a
conductor on the train before
they find you – otherwise you
can be fined.

CHANGES & REIMBURSEMENTS

For trains that do not assign
reserved seats (eg TER and
Corail Intercités trains),
full-fare tickets are useable
whenever you like for 61
days from the date they were
purchased.

If you've got a full-fare
Loisir Week-End ticket, you
can change your reservation
by phone, internet or at train
stations for no charge until
the day before your departure;
changes made on the day
of your reserved trip incur a
charge of €10 (€3 for tickets
bought with a discount card).

Pro tickets (eg TGV
Pro, Téoz Pro) allow full
reimbursement up to 30
minutes *after* the time of
departure (eg by calling ☎36
35). If you turn up at your
departure station up to two
hours after your original travel
time, you can reschedule your
trip on a later train.

SNCF FARES & DISCOUNTS

Full-fare tickets can
be quite expensive.
Fortunately, a dizzying
array of discounts are
available and station
staff are very good about
helping travellers find the
very best fare. But first,
the basics:
○ 1st-class travel, where
available, costs 20% to
30% extra.

○ Ticket prices for some
trains, including most TGVs,
are pricier during peak
periods.

Trains & Ferries

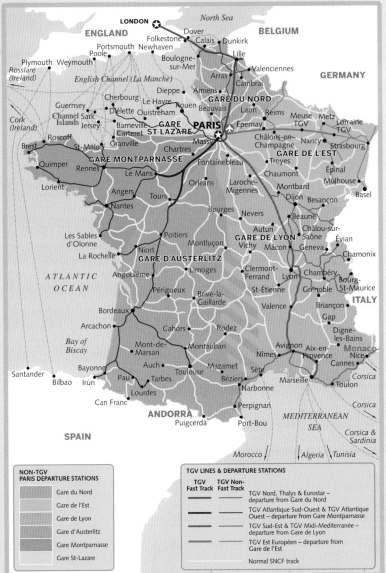

NON-TGV PARIS DEPARTURE STATIONS

- Gare du Nord
- Gare de l'Est
- Gare de Lyon
- Gare d'Austerlitz
- Gare Montparnasse
- Gare St-Lazare

TGV LINES & DEPARTURE STATIONS

TGV Fast Track	TGV Non-Fast Track	
		TGV Nord, Thalys & Eurostar – departure from Gare du Nord
		TGV Atlantique Sud-Ouest & TGV Atlantique Ouest – departure from Gare Montparnasse
		TGV Sud-Est & TGV Midi-Mediterranée – departure from Gare de Lyon
		TGV Est Européen – departure from Gare de l'Est
		Normal SNCF track

○ The further in advance you reserve, the lower the fares.

○ Children under four travel for free (€8.50 to any destination if they need a seat).

○ Children aged four to 11 travel for half price.

Discount Tickets

The SNCF's most heavily discounted tickets are known as **Prem's**. They

Left-Luggage Facilities

Because of security concerns, few French train stations still have *consignes automatiques* (left-luggage lockers), but in some larger stations you can leave your bags in a *consigne manuelle* (staffed left-luggage facility) – usually in an out-of-the-way corner of the station – where items are handed over in person and x-rayed before being stowed. Charges are €5 for up to 10 hours and €8 for 24 hours; payment must be made in cash.

can be booked on the internet, by phone, at ticket windows and from ticket machines a maximum of 90 days and a minimum of 14 days before your travel date. Once you buy a Prem's ticket, it's use it or lose it – getting your money back or changing the time is not allowed.

Bons Plans fares, a grab bag of really cheap options on a changing array of routes and dates, are advertised on www. voyages-sncf.com under the title 'Dernière Minute' (last minute).

In an effort to make train travel both affordable and hip for the iPod generation, the SNCF's youthful subsidiary **iDTGV** (www. idtgv.com) sells tickets (online only) for as little as €19 for advance-purchase TGV travel between about 30 cities.

On regional trains, discount fares requiring neither a discount card nor advance purchase:

Loisir Week-End rates Good for return travel that includes a Saturday night at your destination or involves travel on a Saturday or Sunday.

Découverte fares Available for low-demand 'blue-period' trains to people aged 12 to 25, seniors and the adult travel companions of children under 12.

Mini-Groupe tickets In some regions, these bring big savings for three to six people travelling together, provided you spend a Saturday night at your destination.

Certain French *régions* (eg Basse Normandie and Alsace) offer great deals on intraregional TER transport for day trips or weekend travel.

Discount Cards

Reductions of at least 25% (for last-minute bookings), and of 40%, 50% or even 60% (if you reserve well ahead or travel during low-volume 'blue' periods), are available with several discount cards (valid for one year):

Carte 12-25 (www.12-25-sncf. com in, French; €49) Available to travellers aged 12 to 25.

Carte Enfant Plus (www. enfantplus-sncf.com, in French; €70) For one to four adults travelling with a child aged four to 11.

Carte Escapades (www. escapades-sncf.com, in French; €85) For people aged 26 to 59. Gets you discounts on return journeys of at least 200km that either include a Saturday night away or only involve travel on a Saturday or Sunday.

Carte Sénior (www.senior -sncf.com, in French; €56) For travellers over 60.

Rail Passes

Residents of Europe who do not live in France can purchase an **InterRail One Country Pass** (www. interrailnet.com; 3/4/6/8 days €194/209/269/299, 12-25 yr €126/136/175/194), which entitles its bearer to unlimited travel on SNCF trains for three to eight days over the course of a month.

For non-European residents, **Rail Europe** (www.raileurope.com, www. raileurope.com.au) offers the **France Rail Pass** (www. francerailpass.com; 3/6/9 days over 1 month US$186/268/341).

A-Z

Language

The sounds used in spoken French can almost all be found in English. There are a couple of exceptions: nasal vowels (represented in our pronunciation guides by 'o' or 'u' followed by an almost inaudible nasal consonant sound 'm', 'n' or 'ng'), the 'funny' u sound ('ew' in our guides) and the deep-in-the-throat r. Bearing these few points in mind and reading our pronunciation guides below as if they were English, you'll be understood just fine.

To enhance your trip with a phrasebook, visit **lonelyplanet.com**. Lonely Planet iPhone phrasebooks are available through the Apple App store.

BASICS

Hello./Goodbye.
Bonjour./Au revoir.   bon·zhoor/o·rer·vwa
How are you?
Comment allez-vous?   ko·mon ta·lay·voo
I'm fine, thanks.
Bien, merci.   byun mair·see
Excuse me./Sorry.
Excusez-moi./Pardon.   ek·skew·zay·mwa/par·don
Yes./No.
Oui./Non.   wee/non
Please.
S'il vous plaît.   seel voo play
Thank you.
Merci.   mair·see
That's fine./You're welcome.
De rien.   der ree·en
Do you speak English?
Parlez-vous anglais?   par·lay·voo ong·glay
I don't understand.
Je ne comprends pas.   zher ner kom·pron pa
How much is this?
C'est combien?   say kom·byun

ACCOMMODATION

I'd like to book a room.
Je voudrais réserver   zher voo·dray ray·zair·vay
une chambre.   ewn shom·brer
How much is it per night?
Quel est le prix par nuit?   kel ay ler pree par nwee

EATING & DRINKING

I'd like ..., please.
Je voudrais ...,   zher voo·dray ...
s'il vous plaît.   seel voo play
That was delicious!
C'était délicieux!   say·tay day·lee·syer
Bring the bill/check, please.
Apportez-moi l'addition,   a·por·tay·mwa la·dee·syon
s'il vous plaît.   seel voo play

I'm allergic (to peanuts).
Je suis allergique   zher swee a·lair·zheek
(aux cacahuètes).   (o ka·ka·wet)
I don't eat ...
Je ne mange pas de ...   zher ner monzh pa de ...
   fish   *poisson*   pwa·son
   (red) meat   *viande (rouge)*   vyond (roozh)
   poultry   *volaille*   vo·lai

EMERGENCIES

I'm ill.
Je suis malade.   zher swee ma·lad
Help!
Au secours!   o skoor
Call a doctor!
Appelez un médecin!   a·play un mayd·sun
Call the police!
Appelez la police!   a·play la po·lees

DIRECTIONS

I'm looking for (a/the) ...
Je cherche ...   zher shairsh ...
   bank
   une banque   ewn bongk
   ... embassy
   l'ambassade de ...   lam·ba·sahd der ...
   market
   le marché   ler mar·shay
   museum
   le musée   ler mew·zay
   restaurant
   un restaurant   un res·to·ron
   toilet
   les toilettes   lay twa·let
   tourist office
   l'office de tourisme   lo·fees der too·rees·mer

Behind the Scenes

Author Thanks

OLIVER BERRY

Big thanks as always to everyone for keeping the home fires burning, but biggest thanks as always to Susie Berry and Molly Berry. Huge thanks also to the many helpful people I met along the way or who helped me during the research of this book, including Sandrine Cofflard, Emmanuelle Bouvet, Claire Thomas-Chenard and Jean-François Carille. Extra special thanks to Jo Potts for the gig, Nicola Williams for steering the France ship, and lastly to all my co-authors, whose hard work, tireless research and skilful prose made this book what it is. *Santé*, fellas.

Acknowledgments

Climate map data adapted from Peel MC, Finlayson BL & McMahon TA (2007) 'Updated World Map of the Köppen-Geiger Climate Classification', *Hydrology and Earth System Sciences*, 11, 163344.

Illustrations p76-7, p82-3, p102-3, p130-1, p308-9 and p344-5 by Javier Zarracina.

Cover photographs: Front: Parc du Château de Vaux-le-Vicomte, Tony Burns, Lonely Planet Images, Back: Arc de Triomphe and Avenue des Champs-Elysées, Richard l'Anson, Lonely Planet Images.

Many of the images in this guide are available for licensing from Lonely Planet Images: www.lonelyplanetimages.com.

This Book

This 2nd edition of *Discover France* was written and coordinated by Oliver Berry, and researched and written by Alexis Averbuck, Stuart Butler, Kerry Christiani, Steve Fallon, Emilie Filou, Catherine Le Nevez, Tom Masters, Daniel Robinson, Miles Roddis, John A Vlahides and Nicola Williams. This guidebook was commissioned in Lonely Planet's London office, and produced by the following:

Commissioning Editors Joanna Potts, Dora Whitaker

Coordinating Editor Angela Tinson

Coordinating Cartographer Valentina Kremenchutskaya

Coordinating Layout Designer Frank Deim

Managing Editors Sasha Baskett, Bruce Evans, Annelies Mertens

Managing Cartographer Amanda Sierp

Managing Layout Designer Celia Wood

Assisting Editors Cathryn Game, Jeanette Wall

Assisting Cartographers Diana Duggan, Jennifer Johnston

Cover Research Naomi Parker

Internal Image Research Aude Vauconsant

Language Content Branislava Vladisavljevic

Thanks to Shahara Ahmed, Judith Bamber, Melanie Dankel, Janine Eberle, Ryan Evans, Chris Girdler, Paul Iacono, Carol Jackson, Laura Jane, Yvonne Kirk Lisa Knights, Nic Lehman, John Mazzocchi, Wayne Murphy, Piers Pickard, Malisa Plesa, Mazzy Prinsep, Averil Robertson, Lachlan Ross, Mik Ruff, Carlos Solarte, Kerrianne Southway, Lyahna Spencer, Laura Stansfeld, Juan Winata

SEND US YOUR FEEDBACK

We love to hear from travellers – your comments keep us on our toes and help make our books better. Our well-travelled team reads every word on what you loved or loathed about this book. Although we canno reply individually to postal submissions, we always guarantee that your feedback goes straight to the ap propriate authors, in time for the next edition. Each person who sends us information is thanked in the next edition, and the most useful submissions are rewarded with a free book.

Visit **lonelyplanet.com/contact** to submit your updates and suggestions or to ask for help. Our award-winning website also features inspirational travel stories, news and discussions.

Index

000 Map pages

D

E

000 Map pages

000 Map pages

000 Map pages

How to Use This Book

These symbols will help you find the listings you want:

- ◉ Sights
- ➊ Activities
- ➋ Courses
- ➌ Tours
- ✪ Festivals & Events
- ☐ Sleeping
- ✖ Eating
- ☕ Drinking
- ★ Entertainment
- ➍ Shopping
- ➊ Information/Transport

Look out for these icons:

| FREE | No payment required |
| ⍉ | A green or sustainable option |

Our authors have nominated these places as demonstrating a strong commitment to sustainability – for example by supporting local communities and producers, operating in an environmentally friendly way, or supporting conservation projects.

These symbols give you the vital information for each listing:

- ☏ Telephone Numbers
- ⊙ Opening Hours
- Ⓟ Parking
- ⊜ Nonsmoking
- ✳ Air-Conditioning
- @ Internet Access
- 🛜 Wi-Fi Access
- 🏊 Swimming Pool
- ✔ Vegetarian Selection
- 📖 English-Language Menu
- 👪 Family-Friendly
- 🐾 Pet-Friendly
- ☐ Bus
- ⛴ Ferry
- Ⓜ Metro
- Ⓢ Subway
- ⊖ London Tube
- 🚋 Tram
- 🚆 Train

Reviews are organised by author preference.

Map Legend

Sights
- ◔ Beach
- ◔ Buddhist
- ◔ Castle
- ◔ Christian
- ◔ Hindu
- ◔ Islamic
- ◔ Jewish
- ◔ Monument
- ◉ Museum/Gallery
- ◔ Ruin
- ◔ Winery/Vineyard
- ◔ Zoo
- ◔ Other Sight

Activities, Courses & Tours
- ◔ Diving/Snorkelling
- ◔ Canoeing/Kayaking
- ◔ Skiing
- ◔ Surfing
- ◔ Swimming/Pool
- ◔ Walking
- ◔ Windsurfing
- • Other Activity/Course/Tour

Sleeping
- ▢ Sleeping
- △ Camping

Eating
- ✖ Eating

Drinking
- ⊖ Drinking
- ⊝ Cafe

Entertainment
- ✪ Entertainment

Shopping
- ➍ Shopping

Information
- ⊜ Post Office
- ➊ Tourist Information

Transport
- ◔ Airport
- ⊗ Border Crossing
- ⊜ Bus
- ⊶⊕⊷ Cable Car/Funicular
- ⊸⊛⊷ Cycling
- ◔ Ferry
- ◔ Metro
- ⊶⊕⊷ Monorail
- Ⓟ Parking
- Ⓢ S-Bahn
- ◔ Taxi
- ⊶⊕⊷ Train/Railway
- ⊶⊕⊷ Tram
- ⊖ Tube Station
- Ⓤ U-Bahn
- • Other Transport

Routes
- Tollway
- Freeway
- Primary
- Secondary
- Tertiary
- Lane
- Unsealed Road
- Plaza/Mall
- Steps
- ⫛⫛ Tunnel
- Pedestrian Overpass
- Walking Tour
- Walking Tour Detour
- Path

Boundaries
- — — International
- — — — State/Province
- — — Disputed
- Regional/Suburb
- Marine Park
- Cliff
- Wall

Population
- ⊛ Capital (National)
- ◉ Capital (State/Province)
- ● City/Large Town
- ● Town/Village

Geographic
- ◔ Hut/Shelter
- ◔ Lighthouse
- ◔ Lookout
- ▲ Mountain/Volcano
- ◔ Oasis
- ◔ Park
-)(Pass
- ◔ Picnic Area
- ◔ Waterfall

Hydrography
- River/Creek
- Intermittent River
- Swamp/Mangrove
- Reef
- Canal
- Water
- Dry/Salt/Intermittent Lake
- Glacier

Areas
- Beach/Desert
- Cemetery (Christian)
- Cemetery (Other)
- Park/Forest
- Sportsground
- Sight (Building)
- Top Sight (Building)

STEVE FALLON

Around Paris Steve, who has worked on every edition of Lonely Planet's *France* guide except the first, visited Paris for the first time at age 16 to drink *vin ordinaire* from plastic bottles and learn swear words, but returned *five* years later to complete a degree at the Sorbonne in proper French (and drink proper wine). Now based in East London, Steve gets over to the 'City of Light' frequently and will be just one Underground stop away when Eurostar trains finally start departing from Stratford.

EMILIE FILOU

The French Riviera & Monaco Emilie was born in Paris but spent most of her childhood holidays roaming the south of France and the Alps. She left France to travel when she was 18 and never quite made it back. She studied geography at Oxford and took a grand total of three gap years to see more of Africa, Asia and the Pacific. She is now settled in London, where she works as a journalist. She still goes to the Riviera every summer.

CATHERINE LE NEVEZ

Lyon & the Rhône Valley, The Dordogne & the Lot Catherine's wanderlust kicked in when she road-tripped throughout France from her Parisian base, aged four, and she's been road-tripping across the country at every opportunity since, completing her Doctorate of Creative Arts in Writing, Masters in Professional Writing, and qualifications in Editing and Publishing along the way. Catherine has authored or coauthored over two dozen guidebooks worldwide, including Lonely Planet's *France*, *Paris Encounter* and *Provence & the Côte d'Azur*, as well as newspaper and magazine articles.

TOM MASTERS

Normandy, Brittany Tom grew up in England and France to francophone parents who inculcated a love of all things French from childhood. With his parents now resident in Paris and rural Brittany, France's northwestern chunk seemed to be the natural place for Tom to research between obsessive-compulsive crêpe stops. His best experience while researching the 9th edition of Lonely Planet's *France* guide was getting caught up in a local wedding in Roscoff and partying with the locals until dawn. You can read more of his work at www.tommasters.net.

DANIEL ROBINSON

Flanders & the Somme, Champagne, Transport Over the past two decades, Daniel's articles and guidebooks – published in 10 languages – have covered every region of France, but he is particularly fond of the creativity and panache – and foresighted public-transport initiatives – of dynamic northern cities such as Lille and Reims. Brought up in the US and Israel, Daniel holds degrees from Princeton University and Tel Aviv University. His travel writing appears in the *New York Times* and various magazines.

MILES RODDIS

Languedoc-Roussillon Living over the Pyrenees in Valencia, Spain, Miles and his wife, Ingrid, visit France for work or simply for fun at least once a year. Among more than 50 Lonely Planet titles that he has written or contributed to are six editions of the France guide plus regional guidebooks to Languedoc-Roussillon, Corsica, Brittany and Normandy and – most satisfyingly of all – *Walking in France*.

JOHN A VLAHIDES

Provence, the French Riviera & Monaco John A Vlahides cohosts the TV series *Lonely Planet: Roads Less Travelled*, screening on National Geographic Channels International. John worked as a French–English interpreter in Paris, where he also studied cooking with the same chefs who trained Julia Child. He's a former luxury-hotel concierge and member of *Les Clefs d'Or*, the international union of the world's elite concierges. John lives in northern California, and looks forward to returning to Provence during tomato season. For more, see johnvlahides.com and twitter.com/johnvlahides.

NICOLA WILLIAMS

Paris, France Today Independent travel writer and editorial consultant Nicola Williams has lived in France and written about it for more than a decade. From her hillside house on the southern shore of Lake Geneva, it's a quick and easy hop to the French Alps (call her a ski fiend...), Paris (...art buff), southern France (...foodie). Paris this time around meant stylish apartment living in the heart of St-Germain des Prés. Nicola has worked on numerous Lonely Planet titles, including *France*, *Discover France*, *Paris*, *Provence & the Côte d'Azur* and *The Loire*. She blogs at tripalong. wordpress.com and tweets @Tripalong.

Our Story

A beat-up old car, a few dollars in the pocket and a sense of adventure. In 1972 that's all Tony and Maureen Wheeler needed for the trip of a lifetime – across Europe and Asia overland to Australia. It took several months, and at the end – broke but inspired – they sat at their kitchen table writing and stapling together their first travel guide, *Across Asia on the Cheap*. Within a week they'd sold 1500 copies. Lonely Planet was born.

Today, Lonely Planet has offices in Melbourne, London and Oakland, with more than 600 staff and writers. We share Tony's belief that 'a great guidebook should do three things: inform, educate and amuse'.

Our Writers

OLIVER BERRY

Coordinating author, The Pyrenees Oliver's French love affair began at the tender age of two, and he's since travelled practically every inch of the country while contributing to several editions of Lonely Planet's *France* guide, amongst many other books. Officially, he lives and works as a writer and photographer in Cornwall, but spends several months of the year on the road in search of new things to write about. France never fails to make it into his travel plans.

Read more about Oliver at:
lonelyplanet.com/members/oliverberry

ALEXIS AVERBUCK

Burgundy, Loire Valley, Provence Alexis Averbuck first came to France when she was four and now visits every chance she gets. Whether sipping wines in Burgundy, château-hopping in the Loire or careening through hilltop villages in Provence (she also contributes to Lonely Planet's *Provence & the Côte d'Azur*), she immerses herself in all things French. A travel writer for two decades, Alexis has lived in Antarctica for a year, crossed the Pacific by sailboat and is also a painter – see her work at www.alexisaverbuck.com.

Read more about Alexis at:
lonelyplanet.com/members/alexisaverbuck

STUART BUTLER

Atlantic Coast, French Basque Country Stuart's first encounters with southwest France came on family holidays. When he was older he spent every summer surfing off the beaches of the southwest until one day he found himself so hooked on the region that he was unable to leave – he has been there ever since. When not writing for Lonely Planet he hunts for uncharted surf on remote coastlines. The results of these trips appear frequently in international surf media. His website is www.oceansurfpublications.co.uk.

KERRY CHRISTIANI

Alsace & Lorraine, French Alps, Directory Kerry has been travelling to France since her school days to brush up her *français*, which she studied to MA level. On clear days she can just about spy the Vosges from her home in the Black Forest, an hour's drive from the French border. For the 9th edition of Lonely Planet's *France* guide, Kerry overindulged in Alsace, experienced whiteout in Chamonix and was among the first to step foot in the new Centre Pompidou-Metz. Kerry is also the author of Lonely Planet guides to Germany, Switzerland and Austria.

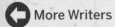 **More Writers**

Published by Lonely Planet Publications Pty Ltd
ABN 36 005 607 983
2nd edition – May 2011
ISBN 978 1 74220 112 2
© Lonely Planet 2011 Photographs © as indicated 2011
10 9 8 7 6 5 4 3 2 1
Printed in China

Although the authors and Lonely Planet have taken all reasonable care in preparing this book, we make no warranty about the accuracy or completeness of its content and, to the maximum extent permitted, disclaim all liability arising from its use.